Contents

THE POCKET
ENCYCLOPEDIA

Published 2001 by Geddes & Grosset,
an imprint of Children's Leisure Products Limited

© 1995 Children's Leisure Products Limited,
David Dale House, New Lanark, Scotland ML11 9DJ

First published 1997, reprinted 1998, 1999, 2001

ISBN 1 85534 738 5

Printed and bound in the UK

Space and Astronomy

From the ancient civilisations of Babylon and Egypt to the present day, man has been fascinated by the universe. Even with the high-tech developments of modern satellites, probes and telescopes, many questions about space remain a mystery. This section of *The Pocket Encyclopedia* explains the basic terms used in the study of astronomy and provides facts about the planets in our own solar system.

antimatter is MATTER that is made up of antiparticles, that is particles that have the same mass as ordinary matter but have opposite values for other properties (e.g. charge). So if matter is made up of electrons, neutrons and protons, antimatter is composed of *positrons*, anti-neutrons and anti-protons. The coming together of matter and antimatter results in the destruction of both particles and the production of energy.

asteroid alternatively called a *meteorite*, is actually a *planetoid*; a rocky or metallic body that is one of many orbiting the Sun between the orbits of Mars and Jupiter. Most of these tiny planets are very small, some reaching a few hundred kilometres across but the largest, *Ceres*, has a diameter of about 1000 kilometres. Collisions between asteroids sometimes produce smaller pieces that occasionally fall to Earth and these fragments are also called meteorites. The many craters seen on the surfaces of some planets are probably due to asteroid impact.

Meteors, or *shooting stars*, are the remnants of comet debris which, should they fall into the Earth's atmosphere, burn up as they are destroyed by friction (*see also* COMET).

astronaut is someone who has undergone very special and rigorous training to prepare for space travel. The first astronaut was Yuri Gagarin who orbited the Earth in 1961 and his spacecraft *Vostok I* took 98 minutes for one orbit. The first woman in space was Valentina Tereshkova; both astronauts were from the former Soviet Union.

In July 1969 an American team actually landing on the Moon and since then there have been numerous missions by the CIS (and recently joint missions with the USA) to an orbiting SPACE STATION, and the USA has launched several SPACE SHUTTLES, the first reusable vehicle capable of space flight.

When a rocket is launched from Earth there are tremendous forces pushing down on the astronaut, due to the enormously high acceleration required to reach orbit. An astronaut must therefore be very fit, and highly skilled in science and technology so that he or she can operate the equipment in the spacecraft and carry out numerous experiments in space. The early astronauts were test pilots from the armed forces but today more scientists and doctors are involved. Over 400 prople have now flown into space although only a small proportion are women. When actually in space it is necessary to wear a space suit which is specially designed to cater for the astronaut's safety. The suit is made up of layers of special material with tubular networks: it provides protection from radiation, the cold of space and supplies air from a portable pack. The helmet has a visor to cut out harmful rays from the Sun and a microphone with headphones to allow communication with other astronauts on the spacecraft.

astronomy is the scientific study of the various bodies in the 'heavens' and has been in existence for thousands of years. From the earliest times, people have plotted the positions of the stars and planets, devising a yearly calendar governed by the movements of the Earth and Moon relative to the Sun. When making a journey, people in former times always used the positions of the various heavenly bodies to guide the direction which they took. Hence some knowledge of astronomy was very important to early travellers and explorers. Early astronomers gained a great deal of knowledge from their studies and were able to predict the appearance of COMETS and ECLIPSES. It became possible to make many more discoveries in astronomy following the invention of the lens telescope, in 1608.

Up until the Middle Ages, it was thought that the Earth was at the centre of the universe and that other heavenly bodies revolved around it. Nicolaus Copernicus, during the 1540s, put forward the idea (which had first been taught, in 170 BC, by Aristarchus) that the Earth travelled around the Sun. The idea of the Sun being the centre of the SOLAR SYSTEM, gradually gained acceptance.

In the latter half of the 20th century, SATELLITES and space probes have given us much new and exciting information about the farthest regions of space. For example, modern astronomers have spent (and continue to spend) many years studying the wealth of data sent back to Earth by such space probes as *Viking* 1 and 2 and *Voyager* 1 and 2.

aurora this is the luminous and often highly coloured streaks or sheets of light in the sky, formed by high-speed, electrically charged solar particles entering the upper atmosphere of the Earth. Here, the particles give up electrons and molecules are created associated with the release of light. These effects are related to SUNSPOT activity and are called the *Northern Lights* (aurora borealis) in the northern hemisphere, and the *Southern Lights* (aurora australis) in the southern hemisphere.

big bang is a theory which has been put forward by some scientists to explain the origins of the universe. It proposes that about 15,000 million years ago there was a vast explosion which sent all the material spinning rapidly outwards as a mass of atoms. Physicists think that in a matter of minutes, a huge cloud of hydrogen atoms had formed and continued to spread outwards, dispersing into separate clouds as it did so. These hydrogen atoms make up about 90% of the universe, and the clouds formed GALAXIES of stars including the MILKY WAY. The outward expansion is still continuing but it is thought that this may one day cease. All the material may eventually collapse and collide together (the BIG CRUNCH) but it is thought that before this occurs, the Sun will burn hotter and the Earth will be consumed in about 5000 million years from the present.

big crunch gravity attracts the galaxies in the Universe together, and the force it exerts depends on their mass, but it is over-ridden by the expansion and moving apart which is still continuing, possibly as a result of the BIG BANG. The Big Crunch theory proposes that there may be hidden material (consisting of single atomic particles) between the galaxies which, if present in sufficient quantities, could add to the gravitational pull. This extra gravity might be enough to slow down and halt the expansion and indeed put it into reverse. If this occurred the galaxies would be pulled together, collide and be destroyed in the Big Crunch.

binary star a pair of stars held together by the force of gravity which orbit around each other. These double stars may be so close to one another that each goes round the other in a few hours. In this instance they are so close as to be almost touching and travel very fast. Others are vast distances apart and travel around each other in thousands or even millions of years. Many stars in the MILKY WAY are binary stars and each member of the pair may differ in shape, size and brightness.

black hole first put forward by the German astronomer Karl Schwarzschild , this is the proposal that there are black holes in space that are collapsed stars. It is believed that when a star (which may be many times larger than our Sun), comes to the end of its 'life,' it collapses (*implodes*) so quickly that no material, not even light, can be emitted. Because of the enormous gravitational force of the collapsed material, it is seen as a hole from which no light escapes. The space around the black hole is curved into a complete circle. It is thought that many apparent single stars are in fact BI-NARY STARS with a black hole as a partner.

calendar calendars were devised by Man to mark the passage of time, and were devised by early astronomers according to the phases of the Moon or on the orbit of the Earth around the Sun. The 365 day year was based on the *Julian* calendar introduced by the Roman Emperor, Julius Caesar, in 46BC. In fact, the Earth takes 365$\frac{1}{4}$ days to go once around the Sun (a solar year) so with this system, every fourth or *leap* year, an extra day has to be added. In fact, the calendar year is still inaccurate and several proposals have been put forward for its reform.

comet is composed of rock, ice, dust and frozen gases and usually cannot be seen. A comet becomes visible when it approaches closer to the Sun because it appears to flare up and look bright. It has a *head*, consisting of a solid core or nucleus of rock surrounded by a layer of gas, the *corona*. The nucleus is irregular in shape and just a few kilometres in diameter (In fact Halley's comet is elongated and is roughly 15 by 4 km). A comet moves in a long, eccentric orbit around the Sun and one complete cycle is called a *period*. The orbit may take the comet a long distance from the Sun when it cannot be seen. Near to the Sun, particles of dust and gas are knocked away from the head of the comet and trail out to form a brightly glowing *tail*. When the orbit takes the comet away from the Sun it leaves tail first. Comets are believed to be left over remnants of the BIG BANG explosion and each time they approach the Sun, some of the ice melts. Eventually, it is thought that a comet loses its ice, dust and gas and becomes a piece of orbiting rock. The shortest period belongs to Ericke's comet and is only 3$\frac{1}{2}$ years. Others have much longer periods lasting hundreds or even thousands of years (e.g. Ikeya-Seki, 880 years).

The most familiar comet, which has excited interest for a long time, is Halley's comet which appears every 76 years and is next due in 2062.

constellation a group of stars which are placed together and given a name, although there is no scientific basis for the grouping. Many were named by astronomers of the Babylonian empire some 2000 years before the birth of Christ and the most ancient form the twelve signs of the zodiac. Thirty nine constellations are visible in the northern hemisphere and forty six in the southern. Familiar examples in the northern hemisphere include the Great Bear (*Ursa Major*), the Bull (*Taurus*), the Hunter (*Orion*) and the Pole or North Star.

corona the coloured rings (seen through thin cloud) around the Sun or Moon, caused by DIFFRACTION of light by water droplets.

cosmic rays these are 'rays' composed of ionising radiation from space and consisting mainly of protons (*see* ATOM) and alpha particles (helium nuclei – *see* RADIOACTIVITY), and a small proportion of heavier atomic nuclei. When these particles interact with the Earth's atmosphere, secondary radiation is created, including mesons, neutrons (*see* ELEMENTARY PARTICLES), positrons (*see* ANTIMATTER) and electrons (*see* ATOM). Cosmic rays seem to come from three sources: galactic rays, possibly formed from SUPERNOVA explosions; solar cosmic rays and the SOLAR WIND.

daylength the length of daylight changes throughout the year except on the equator where there are approximately 12 hours of light and 12 hours of darkness. The changes occur because the Earth is tilted on its axis, and it alters on a daily basis as the Earth proceeds on its orbit around the Sun. At any point in the year, while countries in the northern hemisphere are tilted more towards the Sun, those in the south are further away and vice versa. This governs the onset of the four different seasons of the year. Latitude also affects daylength, and those countries at latitudes greater than 67° north or south experience the midnight sun during midsummer when it does not become dark at all. The lengths of day and night are the same throughout the world on the two equinoxes (21st March and 23rd September).

Earth the Earth is one of a group of nine planets which orbit a star that we call the SUN. It occurs in one small part of the GALAXY (also called the MILKY WAY) which is referred to as the SOLAR SYSTEM. The Earth is the fifth largest of the planets and the third nearest to the Sun. Most of the Earth's surface is covered by the oceans - about two-thirds compared to one third which is land. A layer of air, the ATMOSPHERE, surrounds the Earth which is sub-divided into a number of different regions according to height above the surface. The Earth, as viewed from space, is like a blue ball or sphere which is flattened at both the poles. At the equator, the radius of the Earth is 6378 km or 3963 miles.

The Earth itself is composed of four main layers; an outer *crust* overlying a *mantle*, followed by an *outer core* and *inner core*. The rocky crust varies in thickness, being about 40 km thick under the continents and 8 km under the oceans. It 'floats' on the mantle which is made up of extremely hot rock and is about 2900 km thick. The core is so hot that it is part liquid, with a temperature in the region of 6500 K. The outer core is believed to be about 2250 km thick and is thought to be more liquid than the inner core which is solid and composed mainly of iron and nickel. The Earth is the only one of the nine planets able to support life which exists entirely in a narrow band on or near the crust. The Earth's weight increases every day by about 25 tonnes because fine space dust finds its way down to the surface.

eclipse the name given to a total or partial disappearance of a planet or moon by passing into the shadow of another. A *solar eclipse* occurs when a new moon passes between the Earth and the Sun.

A *lunar eclipse* happens when the Sun, Earth and Moon are in a line and the Earth is situated between the Moon and the Sun and its shadow falls on the Moon. Different types of eclipse happen each year but a solar eclipse usually appears as partial when viewed from Earth. Even during a complete solar eclipse, the Moon is only just large enough to cover the Sun, and the shadow which it throws onto one part of the Earth is only a few kilometres wide so few people are able to see it. It is generally the case that the Moon is not completely in line and so the eclipse is only partial.

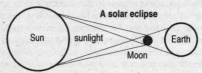

A solar eclipse

escape velocity this is the velocity necessary for a rocket or space probe to escape from the pull exerted by the gravity of a planet. The velocity varies according to the mass and diameter of the planet. For the Earth it is 25,000 mph and for the Moon, 5350 mph. No light escapes from a black hole because the escape velocity is greater than the speed of light.

expansion theory the theory that the galaxies of space are still rapidly moving apart which may have been caused by the BIG BANG explosion. The speed at which the galaxies are travelling is calculated by studying a property of light known as the *red shift*. For every extra million light years of distance (one light year is around 9.5 million million kilometres), the speed the galaxies are travelling increases by about 15 km per second. The relationship between speed and distance is called *Hubble's law*.

galaxy the name given to a huge group or band of stars. Our galaxy, which includes the Sun, is also called the MILKY WAY and it contains about 100,000 million stars. It is thought that there are many million more galaxies as well as the Milky Way, and the nearest large one to us is called *Andromeda*. Galaxies have different shapes, the Milky Way and Andromeda being spiral-shaped, others appearing as saucers. The Milky Way is approximately 10^5 light years across.

heat shield a spacecraft encounters extreme and intense heat especially when it re-enters the Earth's atmosphere from space.

The heat is caused by friction because the space ship is travelling so fast. A heat shield is a special heat resistant layer which prevents the spacecraft from burning up. In earlier space ships the shields were constructed from materials that could not be re-used, as they burned but only very slowly. The space shuttle has special heat-resistant tiles composed of silicon and carbon which can be used again.

infrared astronomy the study of infrared radiation (*see* ELECTROMAGNETIC WAVES) given off from heavenly bodies such as the stars and planets. Infrared radiation has a wavelength of 0.8 to 1000μm which is shorter than that of radio waves and longer than that of visible light. Infrared radiation passes through parts of the galaxy obscured by dust, highlighting otherwise invisible structures. More infrared radiation is emitted by hotter structures than by colder ones, and it penetrates the Earth's atmosphere more readily than visible light. The radiation tends to be obscured by water vapour in the Earth's atmosphere but this problem can be partially overcome by siting observatories at high altitudes. Hence infrared astronomers are able to gain valuable information about distant space bodies and have discovered 'young' stars which have not begun to glow brightly.

interstellar medium the matter found throughout space and comprising gas and dust – mainly hydrogen, helium and interstellar molecules. In all it amounts to about 10% of the mass of the galaxy.

Jupiter is the giant planet of our SOLAR SYSTEM, more than one thousand times larger than Earth. It is one of the 'gas giants' being composed mainly of hydrogen. Its atmosphere is made up of hydrogen with approximately 15% helium and traces of water, ammonia and methane. This forms a liquid 'shell' surrounding a zone of metallic hydrogen (that is the hydrogen is compressed so much that it behaves like metal), which itself surrounds a core made partly of rock and ice. This core has a mass ten times greater than that of the Earth. Violent storms and winds rage around Jupiter whipping up bands of frozen chemicals such as ammonia. One such storm is the *Great Red Spot,* visible on the surface as an enormous cyclone that has probably lasted for hundreds of years. Jupiter spins very rapidly so that one of its days lasts for only nine hours and fifty minutes. This rapid spin drags the whirling gases into bands which appear dark and light. A year on Jupiter lasts for nearly 12 Earth years because the planet is farther from the Sun and has a greater orbit. Jupiter is the fifth planet from the Sun and because of its rapid rate of spin, it bulges outwards at its equator. Hence the diameter at the equator is 142,800 km compared to 134,000 km at the poles. The outermost layers of Jupiter are very cold, in the region of -150°C, but the very centre of the planet is extremely hot probably exceeding the temperature of the Sun. Jupiter's great mass means that it exerts a strong gravitational pull and is able to hold down the molecules of gas which swirl around its bulk. A person on Jupiter would be twice as heavy compared to his or her weight on Earth.

Jupiter has its own satellites or moons orbiting around it and some of these are as large as Earth's moon. The *Voyager* spacecraft passed close to Jupiter in 1979 and sent fascinating information about the planet and its moons back to Earth. This revealed that two of the moons, called *Ganymede* and *Callisto*, have craters pitting their surface like Earth's moon. Another moon, *Europa*, was shown to be a ball of yellow ice. The closest moon to Jupiter, *Io*, has several erupting volcanoes and a surface of yellow sulphur. Enormous electrical energy exists between Io and Jupiter estimated to be equivalent, in any one second, to all the electrical power generated in the United States.

light year a measure of the distance travelled by light in one year, which is in the region of 9.467 by 10^{12} kilometres. Light travels at 299,792 kilometres per second and it takes 8 minutes for it to reach Earth from the Sun. The great distances between the various galaxies and heavenly bodies can be measured in light years. PROXIMA CENTAURI, the nearest star to Earth (after the Sun), is more than four light years distant (*see also* PARSEC).

Magellanic clouds are two separate GALAXIES, detached from the MILKY WAY which appear, when viewed from the southern hemisphere, as diffuse patches of light. The largest is approximately 180,000 LIGHT YEARS away and the smallest is 230,000 light years distant. Both contain several thousand million stars. They are the nearest galaxies and part of a larger group which includes the Milky Way. They were first discovered by a Portuguese sailor called Magellan in 1520 and can only be viewed from near the equator or in the southern hemisphere. NEBULAe are present in both clouds indicating the formation of new stars.

Mars is the fourth planet in the SOLAR SYSTEM and the one nearest to the Earth. Its orbit lies between that of the EARTH and JUPITER, and it is about half the size of Earth. It has a thin atmosphere, exerting a pressure less than one hundredth of that of the Earth. It also has a small mass about one tenth of that of the Earth so that a person on Mars would weigh about 60% less than Earth weight. Mars is often called the *Red Planet* as it has a dusty, reddish surface strewn with rocks. It is much colder than the Earth with an atmosphere mainly of carbon dioxide which is frozen at the two poles. The polar ice caps melt and re-form as the seasons change. Minimum surface temperatures are in the region of -100°C with the maximum only about -30°C. A year on Mars lasts for 687 Earth days and the length of one day is almost the same, 24 hours and 37 minutes. The diameter of Mars is 6794 km and the crust in the northern part of the planet is composed of basalt (volcanic rock, *see* IGNEOUS ROCKS). There are many extinct volcanoes, canyons and impact craters and evidence of water erosion at some stage in the planet's history. The mountains are much higher, and the valleys deeper than those which exist on Earth, hence there must have been violent movements of the crust during the past. The deepest valley called *Valles Marineris*, is 4000 km long, 75 km wide and up to 7 km deep. The highest mountain, *Olympus Mons*, rises 23 km from the surface of Mars, and is three times taller than Mount Everest.

There are two small, irregularly shaped SATELLITES or moons orbiting Mars, called *Phobos* and *Deimos*. Phobos, the larger, is only 27 km from one end to the other and just 6000 km above the planet's surface. Its orbit is a gradually descending spiral and it is estimated that in 40 million years' time it will collide with Mars. The *Viking* space probe landed on Mars in 1976 and many valuable photographs were taken and soil samples obtained. There had been speculation for many years about the possibility of the existence of life on Mars but the space probe failed to discover any evidence for this. Mars is currently being studied by menans of the *Surveyor* spacecraft.

matter any substance that occupies space and has mass, the material of which the UNIVERSE is made.*Compare* ANTIMATTER.

megaparsec a unit for defining distance of objects outside the galaxy, equal to 10^6 PARSECS (or 3.26 by 10^6 light years).

Mercury the first planet of the SOLAR SYSTEM and nearest to the SUN. It has no atmosphere, and so during the day the surface temperature reaches 425°C (enough to melt lead), but at night the heat all escapes and it becomes intensely cold, -170°C. A day on Mercury lasts for 59 Earth days but the planet travels its orbit so fast that a year is only 88 days. Mercury is a very dense planet for, although it is only slightly bigger than the Moon, it has an enormous mass which is almost the same as that of the Earth. It is thought that this is accounted for by Mercury having a huge metallic core. Very little was known about the surface of the planet until it was visited by the *Mariner 10* spacecraft which passed to within 800 km of it in 1974. It revealed that Mercury has a wrinkled surface with thousands of craters which have been caused by the impact of meteors and other larger space bodies. The largest crater, 1300 km across and known as the *Caloris Basin*, must have been caused by the collision of an enormous space body. Mercury has very little gravity and an elliptical orbit, which takes it to within 46 million kilometres of the Sun at its nearest point and 70 million kilometres when farthest away.

Milky Way the galaxy, which includes the SOLAR SYSTEM, and consists of millions of STARS and NEBULAE. It stretches for about 100,000 light years and our solar system is in the region of 30,000 light years from the centre. It has a spiral shape with trailing *arms* which slowly revolve around the centre. The solar system is one tiny part occurring a long way out on one of the trailing spiral arms. There are probably millions of galaxies, including others with the same spiral shape. The Milky Way appears as a glowing cloud of light thrown out by the many millions of stars it contains.

Moon the Earth's one SATELLITE, which orbits the Earth at an average distance of 384,000 kilometres (238,600 miles). It has no atmosphere, water or magnetic field, and surface temperatures reach extremes of 127°C and -173°C. It takes nearly 28 days to complete its orbit around the Earth, and always presents the same face towards Earth. As it orbits around the Earth each 28 days, the Moon passes through *phases* from new to first quarter to full to last quarter and back to new again. One half of the moon is always in sunlight and the phases depend upon the amount of the lit half which can be seen from Earth. A *new moon* occurs when the Earth, Moon and Sun are approximately in line with one another, and none of the lit half can be seen at all; it appears that there is no Moon. About a week later a small *sliver* of the lit half can be seen from Earth and this grows throughout the month until the whole of the lit half is visible at *full moon*. In the second half of the cycle, the amount of the lit half of the Moon which can be seen from Earth gradually declines once more. When the Moon is apparently growing in size, it is called *waxing* and when it is declining it is called *waning*.

The diameter of the Moon is 3476 kilometres and its mass is 0.0123 of that of the Earth. Its density is 0.61 of that of the Earth and it has a thick crust (up to 125 kilometres or 75 miles) made up of volcanic rocks. There is probably a small core of iron, with a radius of approximately 300 kilometres (186 miles).

The surface of the Moon is heavily cratered, probably due to meteorite impact, and the largest (viewed from Earth), is 300 kilometres (186 miles) across and surrounded by gigantic cliffs, (up to 4250 metres or 14,000 feet high). The dark side of the Moon was a mystery until 1959 when *Luna 3*, a Russian space rocket took photographs of it as it flew round. The surface is dry and rocky and in 1969, the American astronauts Neil Armstrong and Edwin Aldrin made the first human footprints on its dusty surface. Other spacecraft have since landed and brought back samples of lunar rock and soil, and analysis of these has revealed that the Moon must be at least 4000 million years old. A distinctive feature of the Moon is its *maria* (sing. *mare*) which were once thought to be seas. The name was coined before modern study found them to be dry, but their origin is not yet established although it is thought that they date from 3300 million years ago. The tendency now is to dispense with the Latin, e.g. *Sea of Showers* instead of *Mare Imbrium*.

Interest has recently been rekindled in the Moon with the rediscovery of ice. This makes it feasible to customise the Moon and use it as a base for further exploration into space.

nebula (pl. *nebulae*) a cloud of interstellar matter, consisting of gases and dust, in which stars originate and also die. When stars die, their gases and dust are poured back out into space forming *planetary nebulae*. Dark patches in the Milky Way galaxy are nebulae which obliterate the light from the stars behind them. Sometimes surrounding stars throw their light onto a nebula making it glow brightly. The *Orion Nebula* has a cluster of stars being formed within its cloud. It is 1300 LIGHT YEARS away and about 15 light years from one side to the other.

Neptune is normally the eighth planet of the SOLAR SYSTEM with its orbit between that of URANUS and PLUTO. However, for about twenty years in every 248 years, Pluto's orbit approaches closer to the Sun than Neptune's. At the time of writing, the two planets are within this period and Neptune will be the outermost one until 1999. Neptune is a vast planet, one of the *gas giants*, and is around 4497 million kilometres from the Sun. It is extremely cold with surface temperatures of approximately -200°C, and the atmosphere consists mainly of methane, hydrogen and helium. The diameter at the poles is 48,700 kilometres and at the equator it is 48,400 km which is about four times that of the Earth. The mass of the planet is 17 times greater than that of Earth and it takes 165 years to circle once around the Sun. Neptune is such a long way from the Earth that it can only be viewed using the most powerful telescopes, and even then it appears to be minute. Neptune spins once on its axis every 18 to 20 hours and probably has a core of frozen rock and ice.

Most information about Neptune has been obtained from the *Voyager 2* space probe in August, 1989. It took 9000 photographs which shows that Neptune is surrounded by a faint series of rings. There is a large dark cloud, the size of the Earth, called the *Dark Spot* which has a spinning oval shape. Winds whip through the atmosphere at velocities of 2000 kilometres per hour and there are white methane clouds which constantly change shape. Neptune has eight SATELLITES or moons, two of which are large and are called *Triton* and *Nereid*. Triton is the largest moon and is about the same size as MERCURY; its orbit is in the opposite direction to that of the other moons. It has a frozen surface with icy volcanic mountains and appears to have lakes of frozen gas and methane. The thin atmosphere of Neptune is composed mainly of nitrogen gas.

neutron star a small body with a seemingly impossibly high density. A star that has exhausted its fuel supply collapses under gravitational forces so intense that its electrons and protons are crushed together and form neutrons. This produces a star ten million times more dense than a WHITE DWARF – equivalent to a cupful of matter weighing many million tons on Earth. Although no neutron stars have definitely been identified, it is thought that PULSARS may belong to this group.

nova (plural *novae*) in the literal sense this is a new star, (nova being Latin for *new*), but it may also be a star that suddenly burns brighter by a factor of five to ten thousand. It seems that a nova is one partner in a BINARY STAR. The smaller star burns much hotter than the sun while the other partner is a vast expanse of hot red mist called a RED GIANT. An explosion results if cooler gas from the red cloud reaches the hot star, causing it to burn up more brightly – a nova. A red giant may eventually become a WHITE DWARF.

orbit the path of one heavenly body moving around another which results from the gravitational force attracting them together. The lighter body moves around the heavier one which is itself also in motion. The speed at which a heavenly body travels depends upon the size of its orbit. This is itself determined by the distance between the two heavenly bodies.

parallax the apparent movement in the position of a heavenly body due in fact to a change in the position of the observer. It is therefore caused, in reality, by the Earth moving through space on its orbit. The distance of a heavenly body from Earth can be calculated by astronomers using parallax. The direction of the body from Earth is measured at two six month intervals when the Earth is at either side of its orbit. From the apparent change in position, the distance of the body from Earth can be deduced.

parsec an astronomical unit of distance which is used for measurements beyond the SOLAR SYSTEM, and which corresponds to a PARALLAX of one sec-

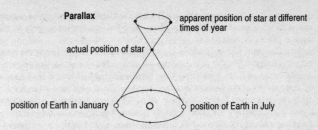

Parallax

apparent position of star at different times of year

actual position of star

position of Earth in January   position of Earth in July

ond of arc. (There are 3600 arc seconds in one degree). A parsec is 30,857,000,000,000 kilometres or 3.2616 LIGHT YEARS. The nearest star to Earth has been calculated as being 1.3 parsecs distant.

planet the name given originally to seven heavenly bodies that were thought to move among the stars, which were themselves thought to be stationary. It is derived from the Greek word for *wanderer*. The term is now used to describe those heavenly bodies moving in definite orbits around the SUN which, in order of distance are: MERCURY, VENUS, EARTH, MARS, JUPITER, SATURN, URANUS, NEPTUNE and PLUTO. Mercury and Venus are termed the *inferior planets* and Mars to Pluto the *superior planets*, the latter because they revolve outside the Earth's orbit. The planets travel their own particular orbit but are all moving in the same direction.

Pluto the ninth and smallest planet in the SOLAR SYSTEM and the one that lies farthest away from the SUN. The existence of Pluto was predicted by an American astronomer called Percival Lowell from the behaviour of the orbits of its closest neighbours, NEPTUNE and URANUS. Pluto was finally spotted in 1930, fourteen years after Lowell died. Pluto appears as a tiny speck when viewed from Earth and little is known about it, but it probably has an iron core and a rocky surface with a covering of methane ice. Since it is so far from the Sun (a maximum of 7,338 million kilometres), it must be extremely cold, in the region of -230°C. A day on Pluto lasts for almost seven Earth days and a year is 248.4 Earth years. At the equator, the planet has a diameter in the region of 3,500 kilometres. Pluto has a wide elliptical orbit which sometimes brings it closer to the Sun. In 1989, it was at its closest point to the Sun (called its *perihelion*), but this only occurs every 248 years. During this phase of its orbit, Pluto apparently has a thin atmosphere composed of methane gas. However, when it moves away from the Sun again it is possible that this becomes frozen once again. In 1979 it was discovered that Pluto has one small satellite (which was named *Charon*), and is about a quarter the size of Pluto. The two bodies effectively form a double planet system.

Proxima Centauri a small, faint red star which is the closest one to the SOLAR SYSTEM (some 4.3 light years away) yet to be discovered. It occurs in the constellation of *Centaurus* and is the third and smallest member of a series of three stars called *Alpha Centauri*. It takes about a million years for it to orbit the other two larger, brighter stars. Proxima Centauri occasionally burns more brightly for short periods of time but is usually quite dim.

pulsar pulsars are thought to be collapsed, rotating NEUTRON STARS which are left after a SUPERNOVA explosion. A pulsar is a source of radio frequency radiation which is given out in regular short bursts. The radiation is in the form of a beam which sweeps through space as the pulsar rotates, and is detected on Earth if Earth happens to lie in its path. The first pulsar was found to emanate from the *Crab Nebula* which is a supernova.

quasar any of the quasi-stellar objects (i.e. like stars) which are extremely compact, give out light and yet are enormously distant bodies – up to 10^{10} LIGHT YEARS away.

radio astronomy the detection of a large range of radio waves (especially radiation given off by hydrogen atoms in space) which are emitted by numerous sources. These include the SUN, PULSARS, remnants of SUPERNOVAe and QUASARS.

radiotelescope the instrument used to detect and analyse extra-terrestrial electromagnetic radiation (light and radio waves). There are two types - the *parabolic reflector*, which focuses the radiation on to an aerial, and the *interferometer*, where an interference pattern (*see* DIFFRACTION) of 'fringes' is formed and precise wave length measurements can be made. The latter is more accurate while the former is easier to move. The parabolic reflector is in the form of a large metal dish which can be pointed in different directions, used in conjunction with others and mounted on a rail so that it can be moved. The largest system in the world is built across a valley at Arecibo in Puerto Rico, and is 305 metres across.

red giant an ageing star that is extremely hot and has used up about 10% of its hydrogen. The outer layers are cooler than the intensely hot centre. As the name implies, these are very large stars. The red giant, *Aldebaran*, is 35 times larger than the SUN with a diameter of 50,100,000 kilometres. Some red giants go on to become WHITE DWARFS, using up their hydrogen at an increased rate. The Sun will eventually become a red giant in about 5000 million years time.

satellite any body, whether natural or manmade, that orbits a much larger body under the force of gravitation. Hence the MOON is a *natural satellite* of the Earth. All the planets, except for MERCURY and VENUS, have at least one natural satellite. *Artificial satellites* are manmade spacecraft launched into orbit from Earth. The first satellite to be launched was the Russian *Sputnik I* in 1957, but many hundreds have followed since then. Some satellites, especially those used for communications, are placed in a special *geostationary* orbit. This orbit is about 36,000 km above the Earth's surface. The satellite orbits the Earth in the same period of time as Earth rotates on its axis (24 hours). Hence the satellite maintains the same position relative to the Earth and appears to be stationary. Equipment on Earth therefore does not need to be adjusted to follow the satellite.

Many other satellites are used for other purposes such as meteorological recordings and weather forecasting. Each satellite has a dish aerial facing towards Earth and *thruster* motors to help maintain its position. When the fuel supply for the thrusters is exhausted, the satellite drifts out of its orbit and can no longer be used. The equipment on board a satellite or spaceship requires electricity which is usually derived from solar powered cells (*see* PHOTOELECTRIC CELL). (However, spacecraft travelling long distances away from the Sun have electricity generated by small nuclear reactors).

Saturn one of the four *gas giants*, the second largest planet and sixth in the SOLAR SYSTEM, with an orbit between that of JUPITER and URANUS. Saturn has a diameter at the equator of about 120,800 kilometres and is a maximum distance of 1,507,000,000 kilometres from the SUN. Saturn rotates very fast and this causes it to flatten at its poles and bulge at the equator. A day on Saturn lasts for $10\frac{1}{4}$ hours and a year, (or one complete orbit of the Sun), for 29.45 Earth years. Saturn is a cold planet of frozen gases and ice and has a surface temperature in the region of -170°C. It is mainly gaseous with an outer zone of hydrogen and helium over a metallic hydrogen layer and a core of ice silicate. The atmosphere is rich in methane and ethane. Saturn is well-known for its *rings* which are, in fact, ice particles and other debris thought to be the remains of a SATELLITE which broke up close to the planet. The rings are wide, in the region of 267,876 kilometres across, but they are extremely thin (only a few kilometres). The *Voyager* space probes approached close to Saturn in 1980 and 1981 and photographs taken revealed that there were many more rings than had previously been detected. They are brighter than those of any other planet.

Saturn has 24 satellites or moons, some of which were discovered by the *Voyager* spacecraft, including *Atlas, Prometheus* and *Calypso*. *Titan* is the largest moon and, at 5200 kilometres diameter, is larger than MERCURY. It is the only moon known to have a detectable atmosphere, a layer of gases above its surface.

Sirius also known as the *Dog Star* because it occurs in the constellation called the *Greater Dog, Canis Majoris*, this is the brightest star in the night sky. It is a BINARY STAR with a *white dwarf* as its partner and shines brightly because it lies quite close to Earth, only 0.5 light years distant.

solar energy is energy which reaches Earth from the sun in the form of heat and light. 85% of solar energy is reflected back into space and only 15% reaches the Earth's surface, but it is this energy which sustains all life.

solar system the system comprising the sun (a star of spectral type G), around which revolve the nine planets in elliptical orbits. Nearest the SUN is MERCURY, then VENUS, EARTH, MARS, JUPITER, SATURN, URANUS, NEPTUNE AND PLUTO. In addition, there are numerous SATELLITES, a few thousand AS-TEROIDS (so far discovered) and millions of COMETS. The age of the solar system is put at 4.5 to 4.6 billion years, a figure determined by the *radio-metric dating* (uranium-lead content) of iron meteorites (*see* DATING METH-ODS). They are thought to be fragments or cores from early planets and thus representative of the early stages of the solar system.

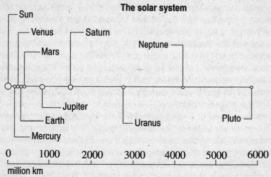

The solar system

solar wind the term for the stream of charged, high-energy particles (mainly electrons, protons and alpha particles) given out by the SUN. The particles travel at hundreds of kilometres per second, and the wind is greatest dur-ing flare and SUNSPOT activity. Around the Earth, the particles have velocities of 300-500 kilometres per second, and some become trapped in the magnetic field to form the VAN ALLAN RADIATION BELT. However, some reach the upper atmosphere and move to the poles, producing AURORA.

space probe is an unmanned spacecraft, such as *Voyager 1* and 2, launched to travel through the SOLAR SYSTEM and beyond and programmed to send back data and photographs. Space probes eventually move so far away that contact with them is lost forever but they continue to travel for thousands of years. Vehicles from space probes have landed on Venus and Mars, obtaining valuable information.

space station a manned space research centre, including living accommodation, in which astronauts live and work for several months at a time. The manned space station, *Mir*, of the former Soviet Union was launched in 1986. At the end of the 1990s a new space station designed for eight people will be launched. It is called *Freedom* and is a joint American, Canadian, European and Japanese venture and all the materials for its construction are being carried out by SPACE SHUTTLE and assembled in space. It will be 500km (310 miles) above the surface of the Earth.

space telescope is a telescope launched into orbit in order to obtain images of stars and other heavenly bodies which are much clearer than if viewed from Earth. Images viewed through Earth-based telescopes are subject to distortion due to atmospheric factors, but such problems do not affect telescopes that are sited in space. Space telescopes have a special mirror and the images are radioed back to Earth where they can be studied on a screen and photographs obtained. In April 1990, the SPACE SHUTTLE *Discovery* launched the *Hubble* space telescope to undertake observations of the stars. After the launch it was found that the telescope's huge mirror was not working properly and it was repaired during a later shuttle flight.

space time *see* RELATIVITY.

star a body of fiery gas, similar to the SUN, which is contained by its own gravitational field. Stars are glowing masses that produce energy by thermonuclear reactions (NUCLEAR FUSION). The core acts as a natural NUCLEAR REACTOR, where hydrogen is consumed and forms helium with the production of electromagnetic radiation. A classification system for stars, based upon the spectrum of light they emit, groups stars as various *spectral types*. The sequence is, in order of descending temperature: O – hottest blue stars; B – hot blue stars; A – blue-white stars; F – white stars; G – yellow stars; K – orange stars; M – coolest red stars. Stellar evolution is the various stages in the life of a star, beginning with its creation from the condensation of gas, primarily hydrogen. The growth of the gas cloud pulls in more gas, and the increase in gravity compresses the molecules together, attracting more material and creating a denser mass. The heat normally produced by molecules due to their vibratory motion is increased greatly and the temperature is raised to millions of degrees, which enables nuclear fusion to take place. The supply of hydrogen continues to be consumed (and the star occupies the main sequence of the Hertzsprung-Russell diagram) until about 10% has gone. (The Hertzsprung-Russell diagram is a graph of star types from hot to cooler, depending upon the stage each has reached in its evolution.) When 10% of the hydrogen has been consumed the rate of combustion increases. This is accompanied by collapses in the core and an expansion of the hydrogen-burning surface layers, forming a RED GIANT. Progressive gravitational collapses and burning of the helium (which is generated by the consumption of the hydrogen) results in a WHITE DWARF, which is a sphere of enormously dense gas. The white dwarf cools over many millions of years and forms a *black dwarf* – an invisible ball of gases in space. Other sequences of events may occur, depending upon the size of the star formed. BLACK HOLES and NEUTRON STARS may form red (super) giants via a SUPERNOVA stage.

Sun is the star nearest to Earth around which Earth and the other planets move in elliptical orbits. It is one of millions of stars in the MILKY WAY but is the centre of the SOLAR SYSTEM. It was formed around five thousand million years ago and is about half way through its life cycle. It has a diameter of 1,392,000 kilometres and a mass of 2 by 10^{30} kilograms. The interior reaches a temperature of 13 million degrees centigrade while the visible surface is about 6000°C. The internal temperature is such that thermonuclear reactions occur, converting hydrogen to helium with the release of vast quantities of energy. The Sun is approximately 90% hydrogen and 8% helium and will one day become a RED GIANT.

sunspots the appearance of dark areas on the surface of the SUN. The occurrence reaches a maximum approximately every eleven years in a phase known as the sunspot cycle. They are usually short-lived (less than one month) and are caused by magnetism drawing away heat to leave a cooler area which is the sunspot. The black appearance is due to a lowering of the temperature to about 4000K. Sunspots have intense magnetic fields and are associated with magnetic storms and effects such as the *aurora borealis* (*see* AURORA). They may send out solar flares which are explosions occurring in the vicinity of the sunspots.

supernova (*plural* **supernovae**) a large star that explodes, it is thought, because of the exhaustion of its hydrogen (*see* SUN), whereupon it collapses, generating high temperatures and triggering thermonuclear reactions. A large part of its matter is thrown out into space, leaving a residue that is termed a WHITE DWARF star. Such events are very rare, but at the time of the explosion the stars become one hundred million times brighter than the Sun. A supernova was sighted in 1987 in the large MAGELLANIC CLOUD, 170,000 light years distant.

telescope is an instrument for magnifying an image of a distant object, the main types of astronomical telescopes being *refractors* and *reflectors*. The refracting type have lenses to produce an enlarged, upside-down image. In the reflecting type there are large mirrors with a curved profile which collect the light and direct it onto a second mirror and into the eyepiece (*see also* RADIOTELESCOPE).

universe all matter, energy and space that exists which is continuing to expand since its formation (*see* BIG BANG).

Uranus is the seventh planet in the SOLAR SYSTEM and one of the four *gas giants* with an orbit between those of Saturn and Neptune. Uranus has a diameter at the equator of 50,080 kilometres and lies an average distance of 2,869,600,000 kilometres from the Sun. The surface temperatures are in the region of -240°C. It is composed mainly of gases with a thick atmosphere of methane, helium and hydrogen. Uranus was the first planet to be observed with a telescope and was discovered by William Herschel, a German astronomer in 1781. Uranus remained a mystery until quite recently but in 1986, *Voyager 2* approached close to the planet and obtained valuable information and photographs. The planet appeared blue, due to its thick atmosphere of gases and a faint ring system consisting of 13 main rings. Uranus was known to have five moons but a further ten, some less than 50 kilometres in diameter, were discovered by *Voyager 2*. A day on Uranus lasts for about 17½ hours and a year is equivalent to 84 Earth years. Its largest moon is *Titania* with a diameter of 1600 km. All five moons are very cold and icy with a surface covered in craters and cracks. *Ariel* has deep wide valleys and *Miranda*, the smallest moon, is a mass of canyons and cracks with cliffs reaching up to 20km. Uranus has a greatly tilted axis so that some parts of the planet's surface are exposed to the Sun for half of the planet's orbit (about 40 years) and are then in continuous darkness for the rest of the time. Due to the tilt of the axis, the Sun is sometimes shining almost directly onto each of Uranus' poles during parts of its orbit.

Van Allen belts are two belts of radiation consisting of charged particles (electrons and protons) trapped in the Earth's magnetic field. The result is the formation of two belts around the Earth. They were discovered in 1958 by an American physicist called James Van Allen. The lower belt occurs between 2000 and 5000km above the equator and its particles are derived from the Earth's atmosphere. The particles in the upper belt, at around 20,000km, are derived from the solar wind. The Van Allen belts are part of the Earth's magnetosphere, an area of space in which charged particles are affected by the Earth's magnetic field rather than that of the Sun.

Venus is the second planet in the solar system with its orbit between those of Mercury and Earth and it is also the brightest. It is known as the Morning or Evening star. Venus is about 108.2 million km (67 million miles) from the Sun and is extremely hot with a surface temperature in the region of 470°C. It has a thick atmosphere of mainly carbon dioxide, sulphuric acid and other poisonous substances which obscure its surface. The size of Venus is similar to Earth with a diameter at the equator of 12,300 km. The atmosphere of carbon dioxide traps heat from the Sun (the greenhouse effect) allowing none to escape. Hence the surface rocks are boiling hot and winds whip through the atmosphere at speeds in excess of 320 km/hr. Venus is unusual in being the only planet to spin on its axis in the opposite direction to the path of its orbit. Also it spins very slowly so that a 'day' on Venus is very long, equivalent to 243 Earth days. A year is 225 days. Venus has no satellites and because its surface is hidden, much of the known information about the planet has been obtained from SPACE PROBES. The *Magellan* space probe launched by the USA in 1989 visited Venus, sending back valuable photographs. *Venera 13*, a Russian probe landed on Venus in 1982, and obtained a rock sample and other information. The surface of the planet has been shown to be mountainous with peaks 12 kilometres high. It is covered with craters and also a rift vally. It is possible that there are active volcanoes.

white dwarf a type of star that is very dense with a low luminosity. White dwarfs result from the explosion of stars that have used up their available hydrogen (*see* STAR). Due to their small size, their surface temperatures are high, and they appear white (*see also* SUPERNOVA).

X-ray astronomy stars emit a variety of electromagnetic radiation including X-rays (*see* ELECTROMAGNETIC WAVES), but this is unable to penetrate the Earth's atmosphere to be detected. Very hot stars send out large amounts of X-rays which can be detected by equipment contained on space satellites. The satellite ROSAT launched in 1990 has equipment to undertake X-ray astronomy and obtain information about distant bodies in space (e.g. WHITE DWARFS and SUPERNOVAE) that are emitting X-rays.

Geography and Geology

This section of *The Pocket Encyclopedia* defines some of the theories, ideas and terms involved in the important study of the Earth – its natural physical features, natural resources and climate. The cross references, given in SMALL CAPITALS, will enable you to relate the terms to one another and so gain an overall perspective of the subject.

alluvium deposits produced as a result of the action of streams or RIVERS. Moving water carries sediment, particles of sand, mud and silt, and the faster it moves the greater the load it can carry. When the velocity of the water is checked due to it meeting a stationary or slower moving body of water, then much or all of the sediment is dropped forming alluvium. In mountainous regions where streams descend to lowlands, a fan or cone of sediment may build up. Rivers in areas of less extreme geography deposit alluvium on the flood plain where the water changes velocity along the curving course of the river, or when rivers overflow their banks during floods.

aquifer a layer of rock, sand or gravel that is porous and therefore allows the passage and collection of water. If the layer has sufficient porosity and permeability it may provide enough GROUNDWATER to produce springs or wells. If the layers above and below the aquifer are impermeable, the water is under pressure (*hydrostatic pressure*) and can be extracted in an *Artesian Well* whilst the level of the well is lower than that of the WATER TABLE. A significant proportion of London's water supply comes from the London Basin (an Artesian basin), although the supply is diminishing because the water table and pressure have fallen due to prolonged extraction of water. In many cases pumps may be required to raise the water to the surface.

An Artesian basin

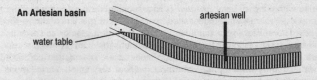

artesian well

water table

> *porosity*– the spaces within a rock or sediment referring to the pores that are able to release their contained water.
> *permeability*– the ability of a material to allow the passage of water, air, etc.
> *impermeable* – any material that does not allow passage of fluids.

atmosphere the layer of gases and dust surrounding the Earth which can be divided into shells, the lowermost being the TROPOSPHERE which is overlain by the STRATOSPHERE. The density falls with height and because it is thinner, breathing is more difficult at high altitudes. Almost 75% of the total mass is contained within the troposphere. The main gases found in the atmosphere are nitrogen (78%), oxygen (21%), the inert gas argon (0.9%), carbon dioxide (0.03%) and then very small amounts of other inert gases, with methane, hydrogen, water vapour and ozone. The ozone exists mainly in a layer (*see* OZONE LAYER) at a height of about 25 to 30 km although it is found elsewhere within the stratosphere.

Atmospheric pressure is the downward force of the atmosphere on the surface of the Earth and is roughly equivalent to a force of $1kg/cm^2$ and originally defined as the pressure that will support a column of mercury 760mm high at 0°C, sea level and a latitude of 45° (*see* ST: BAROMETER).

Beaufort scale a system for indicating wind strength, developed in 1805 by Admiral F.B. Beaufort. Measurements are taken 10m above the ground and each of 12 levels is characterised by particular features on the landscape or certain effects upon people or objects. Wind speed is measured in metres per second.

boulder clay a deposit that is glacial in origin and made up of boulders of varying sizes in finer-grained material, mainly clay. It is laid down beneath a glacier or ice sheet and shows little or no structure. Large blocks plucked from the terrain over which the ice has moved may be found in a matrix of finer material which has been ground down by the glacier. An alternative and more frequently used term is *till*, of which several types have been defined depending upon their specific mode of formation and position within the ice body. *Moraine* is an associated term referring to ridges of rock debris carried and deposited by ice sheets or glaciers of the various types; lateral moraine accumulates at the edge of a glacier and terminal moraine at the leading edge. Ground moraine is the same as boulder clay.

chalk a soft, fine-grained SEDIMENTARY ROCK made of calcium carbonate formed mainly from the skeletons and shells of very small marine organisms. It is formed primarily as deposits of calcareous mud in shallow seas, but it can also be formed by chemical precipitation. Chalk deposited in the Upper Cretaceous approximately 100 million years ago now covers much of northwest Europe, and can be seen in the White Cliffs of Dover and the cliffs near Calais. Chalk produces a particular scenery, with low rolling hills, dry valleys and steep scarps (an escarpment or steep slope which ends a flat or gently sloping area). Chalk is an important AQUIFER and is used in the manufacture of CEMENT and FERTILIZERS.

climate characteristic weather conditions produced by a combination of factors, such as rainfall and temperature. Whether taken singly or jointly these factors, together with influencing features such as altitude and latitude, produce a distinctive arrangement of zones around the Earth each with a generally consistent climate when studied over a period of time. The major climatic zones are, from the equator:

---

humid tropical – hot and wet
subtropical, arid and semi-arid – desert conditions, extremes
of daily temperature
humid temperate – warm and moist with mild winters
boreal (N. hemisphere) – long, cold, winters and short summers
sub-arctic (or sub-antarctic) – generally cold with low rainfall
polar – always cold

Climatic patterns are very dependent upon heat received from the Sun and at the poles the rays have had to travel further and in so doing have lost much of their heat, producing the coldest regions on the Earth. Conversely, air near the equator is very warm and can therefore hold a great deal of water vapour resulting in hot and wet conditions – humid tropical. There are more complex systems of climate classification, e.g. Köppen and Thornthwaite, which are based upon precipitation and evaporation, characteristic vegetation and temperature. In each system, the Earth can be split into numerous provinces and smaller areas producing quite a detailed overall picture.

cloud clouds are droplets of water or ice formed by the condensation of moisture in a mass of rising air. Water vapour formed by evaporation from seas, lakes and rivers is ordinarily contained in air and only becomes visible when it condenses to form water droplets. Warm air can hold more water vapour than cold air thus when air rises, becoming cooler, it becomes saturated ('full') of water and eventually droplets form, as cloud, each droplet forming around a central nucleus such as dust, pollen or a smoke particle. Clouds are classified firstly upon their shape, and also by their height.

There are three major groups: *cumulus* ('heap' clouds), *stratus* (sheetlike) and *cirrus* (resembling fibres) which are divided further as cloud forms show a mix of shape, e.g. *cirrocumulus*.

coal a mineral deposit that contains a very high carbon content and occurs in banded layers (seams) resembling rock. It is formed from ancient forest vegetation that has accumulated and been transformed into PEAT. With time, increasing pressure from sediments above and some heating, the peat becomes coal of various types, each type (or *rank*) being marked by the carbon content which increases with pressure and temperature, and the volatiles content, which decreases at the same time. Volatiles are substances that readily become gas, specifically in this case, a mixture of hydrogen, methane and carbon dioxide which are released when coal is heated.

The coal of highest rank is anthracite which is 95% carbon with a little moisture and volatile matter. Bituminous coals contain from about 45% to 75% carbon while lignite has 70% moisture and volatiles.

Coal beds occur in sequences of sandstone and shale called, collectively, *coal measures*. Most of the world's anthracite and bituminous coals accumulated in the Carboniferous period (*see* GEOLOGICAL TIMETABLE) and the coal measures reach thousands of metres in thickness in many countries. The countries with the greatest reserves of coal include USA, CIS, China, Australia and Germany.

Although coal is used less than it was as a primary energy source, its byproducts are still used in the chemicals industry, for the manufacture of dyes, drugs, pesticides and other compounds.

continent one of several large landmasses covering 29% of the Earth's surface of which 65% is in the northern hemisphere. Where the continent edge meets the sea is a continental shelf and slope which is often cut by submarine canyons. Further ocean-ward lies the deepest parts of the ocean, the abyssal plain. There are seven continents making up the Earth:

	highest point (metres)	area (sq km)
Asia	8848	43,608,000
Africa	5895	30,335,000
North and Central America	6194	25,349,000
South America	6960	17,611,000
Antarctica	5140	14,000,000
Europe	5642	10,498,000
Oceania	4205	8,900,000

crystal a solid that has a particular, ordered, structure and shape with usually flat faces and a chemical composition that varies little. The arrangement of the atoms in the crystal in a specific framework give it a characteristic shape and if conditions permit when the crystal is growing, the crystal faces are arranged in a constant geometric relationship. Many solids have a crystalline structure, from household items such as sugar and salt to chemicals, metals and the minerals within rocks. If a solution of a chemical or a magma (molten rock) is allowed to cool slowly, crystals will develop. Similarly, if a crystal is placed in a saturated solution of the same compound *crystallization* will occur. If, however, the solution or magma is cooled suddenly, either the crystals formed are microscopic or the resulting solid exhibits no crystalline form (is *amorphous*).

The regular formation of crystal faces is part of a crystal's *symmetry* which is described for each crystal system, by three properties: planes, axes and a centre of symmetry. These properties together create six crystal systems. These are:

Cubic	common salt
Tetragonal	zircon
Hexagonal	calcite; quartz
Orthorhombic	topaz; barytes; sulphur
Monoclinic	gypsum
Triclinic	feldspars

Crystallography is the scientific study of crystals, their form and structure.

cyclone an area of low atmospheric pressure with closely packed isobars producing a steep pressure gradient and therefore very strong winds. Due to the Earth's rotation, the winds circulate clockwise in the southern hemisphere and anticlockwise in the northern hemisphere. In tropical regions, cyclones (tropical hurricanes) combine very high rainfall with destructive winds which results in widespread damage and possible loss of life.

Outside the tropics, in more temperate climates, the term cyclone is being replaced by *depression* (or *low*) in which the pressure may fall to 940 or 950 mb (millibars). Compare this with the average pressure at sea-level which is 1013 mb.

An *anticyclone* is a high pressure area (around 1030–1050 mb) and usually results in stable weather.

dating methods are used in a number of scientific subjects, whether geography, geology or archaeology, where it is often necessary to date a sample and there are several ways in which this can be achieved. In many instances, a relative age can be determined quite readily, for example in geology one rock cutting across another can provide clues as to the order of formation of rock sequences, or the order in which rocks were folded or deformed (*see* FOLDS AND FAULTS). However, to obtain an *absolute* or true age (bearing in mind any experimental errors), the radioactive decay of ISOTOPES can be employed – *radiometric dating*.

Radiocarbon dating is one such method. This relies upon the uptake by plants and animals of small quantities of naturally-occurring radioactive ^{14}C (carbon-14) in the atmosphere. When the organism dies, the uptake stops and the ^{14}C decays with a half-life (*see* **ST**: RADIOACTIVITY) of 5730 years, and the age of a sample can be calculated from the remaining radioactivity. This method is useful for dating organic material within the last 70,000 years but the accuracy of the methods falls between 40,000 and 70,000 years.

Rocks can be dated by one of several methods each of which relies upon the radioactive decay of one element to another. In these cases the half-life is very long enabling the dating of very old rocks. Uranium-lead was an early method in which uranium-238 (^{238}U) decays to lead-206 with a half-life of 4.5 billion years.

The long half-lives make these systems useful in dating Lower Palaeozoic and Precambrian rocks (*see* GEOLOGICAL TIMESCALE). Sm/Nd is resistant to metamorphism and can be used on extraterrestrial materials: Th/Pb is often used with other methods because it is not an accurate method alone; Rb/Sr is useful for dating metamorphic rocks and in general the best results for dating are obtained from igneous or metamorphic rocks.

desert an arid or semi-arid (that is, dry and parched with under 25cm (10 in.) of rainfall annually) region in which there is little or no vegetation. The term was always applied to hot tropical and subtropical deserts, but is equally applicable to areas within continents where there is low rainfall and perennial ice-cold deserts.

The vegetation is controlled by the rainfall and varies from sparse, drought-resistant shrubs and cacti to sudden blooms of annual plants in response to a short period of torrential rain. If the groundwater conditions permit, e.g. if the water table is near to the surface creating a spring, or the geology is such that an artesian well (*see* AQUIFER) is created, then an oasis may develop within a hot desert, providing an island of green.

Hot deserts are found in Africa, Australia, United States, Chile and cold deserts in the Arctic, eastern Argentina and mountainous regions.

The process whereby desert conditions and processes extend to new areas adjacent to existing deserts is called *desertification*.

drainage is the movement of water derived from rain, snowfall and melting of ice and snow, over the land (and through it in subterranean waterways) which results eventually in its discharge into the sea. The flow of streams and rivers is influenced by the underlying rocks, how they are arranged and whether there are any structural features that the water may follow. Further factors affecting drainage include soil type, climate and the influence of man.

There are a number of recognizable patterns which can be related to the geology:

1 Dendritic   a random branching unaffected by surface rocks
2 Trellis   streams aligned with the trend of underlying rocks.
3 Parallel   streams running parallel to each other due to folded rocks, or steep slopes with little vegetation.
4 Rectangular   controlled by faults and joints, the latter often in igneous rocks.
5 Annular   formation of streams in circular patterns around a structure of the same shape (e.g. an igneous intrusion).
6 Barbed   a drainage pattern where the tributaries imply a direction of flow contrary to what actually happens.
7 Radial   streams flowing outwards from a higher area.
8 Centripetal   the flow of streams into a central depression where there may be a lake or river.

When a drainage pattern is a direct result of the underlying geology, it is said to be *accordant* (the opposite case being *discordant*).

earthquake movement of the earth, which is often violent, and caused by the sudden release of stress that may have accumulated over a long period. Waves of disturbance – *seismic* waves – spread out from the origin or *focus*, of the earthquake which is most likely to be movement along a FAULT, although some are associated with volcanic activity.

Earthquakes are classified by their depth of focus: shallow (less than 70km); intermediate (70 to 300km); deep (more than 300km).

Over three quarters of earthquake energy is concentrated in a belt around the Pacific and this is because most seismic activity occurs at the margins of tectonic plates (*see* PLATE TECTONICS). This means that certain regions of the world are more likely to suffer earthquakes, for example the west coast of N. & S. America, Japan, the Philippines, S.E. Asia and New Zealand.

The effects of earthquakes are naturally very alarming and can be quite catastrophic. Near the focus, ground waves actually throw about the land surface. Surface effects may include opening of fissures (large cracks), the breaking of roads and pipes, buckling and twisting of railway lines and the collapse of bridges and buildings. Secondary effects can be equally destructive if the ground vibrations initiate landslides, avalanches and TSUNAMI or cause fires.

Areas of earthquake activity

There are several systems of measuring the intensity of earthquakes, the one in common use being that devised by Richter, an American seismologist. The Richter Scale is:

	Rating	Identifying features
1	Instrumental	detected only by seismographs
2	Feeble	noticed by sensitive people
3	Slight	similar to a passing lorry
4	Moderate	loose objects are rocked
5	Rather strong	felt generally
6	Strong	trees sway; loose objects fall
7	Very strong	walls crack
8	Destructive	chimneys fall; masonry cracks
9	Ruinous	houses collapse where ground starts to crack
10	Disastrous	ground badly cracked; buildings destroyed
11	Very disastrous	bridges and most buildings destroyed; landslides
12	Catastrophic	ground moves in waves; total destruction

Because this is a logarithmic scale, the magnitude of one level is very much more than the previous level. Over the last ninety years not many earthquakes have registered over 8 on the Richter scale. Earlier ones include San Francisco (1906), Kansu in China (1920), Japanese trench (1933), Chile (1960) and offshore Japan (1968). *See also* SEISMOGRAPH.

erosion the destructive breakdown of rock and soil by a variety of *agents* that, together with weathering, forms *denudation*, or a wearing away of the land surface. Erosion occurs because of the mechanical action of material carried by agents: water (rivers, currents, waves), ice (glaciers) and wind. Wind laden with sand can scour rock, rocks embedded in glaciers grind down the rocks over which they pass and gravel and pebbles in streams and rivers excavate their own course and may create pot holes, undercut banks, etc. Water can also carry material in solution. There are six different kinds of erosion processes, each with a different effect:

process	effect
abrasion	wearing away through grinding, rubbing and polishing.
attrition	the reduction in size of particles by friction and impact.
cavitation	characteristic of high energy river waters (e.g. waterfalls, cataracts) where air bubbles collapse sending out shock waves that impact on the walls of the river bed (a very localised occurrence).
corrasion	the use of boulders, pebbles, sand etc. carried by a river, to wear away the floor and sides of river bed.
corrosion	all erosion achieved through solution and chemical reaction with materials encountered in the water.
deflation	the removal of loose sand and silt by the wind.

The effect of these processes can be very marked, with time, and can combine to deepen gorges, create and enlarge waterfalls and result in the movement of a waterfall upstream. The latter occurs through undercutting of lower, softer rocks which then cause the collapse of overhanging ledges.

Waterfall erosion

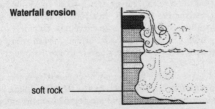

soft rock

evaporite a sedimentary rock formed by the evaporation of water containing various salts, resulting in their deposition. The particular sediment created depends upon the concentration of ions (*see* **ST**: ION) in solution, and the solubility (*see* SOLUTIONS) of each salt formed. The least soluble – calcium carbonate and magnesium carbonate – precipitate first, followed by sodium sulphate, then sodium chloride, potassium chloride and magnesium sulphate. A typical sequence of evaporite deposits could show calcite, possibly dolomite, gypsum (or anhydrite), rock salt, and finally potassium and magnesium salts (e.g. carnallite, $KCl.MgCl.6H_2O$).

There are several major deposits of evaporites in the world, e.g. the Stassfurt deposits in Germany, the Wieliczka salt mines in Poland, Texas and New Mexico, Chile and Cheshire in Britain. Some of these deposits are over 3500m thick, and since about 5m of evaporites would require the evaporation of 300m of seawater, it is clear that very special conditions existed in the past. To accumulate such vast thicknesses, there must be a shallow area of water from which evaporation and precipitation proceeds; which is periodically refilled with salt water, *and* there must be a gradual subsidence of the land to permit continued build up of the salts.

Modern evaporites are being formed in places such as the Caspian Sea, the Arabian Gulf and deposits have been formed recently in Eritrea.

faults *see* FOLDS.

floods a flood is where land not normally covered by water is temporarily underwater and can occur for several reasons and the scale of the flood may vary enormously. An increase in rainfall, particularly if prolonged may lead to flooding as may a sudden thaw of lying snow. Flooding of coastal areas by the sea may be caused by the combination of a very high tide and stormy conditions generating high waves. Perhaps most devastating of all are the TSUNAMI caused by earthquakes. Large areas of, for example, South East Asia, continually face the threat of floods.

When a river is in flood it carries a far greater load of rocks, boulders, sand and silt and its destructive power is therefore increased. In some cases, flood waters have been so powerful as to carve new channels for the river and in so doing demolish houses, roads, bridges, wash away trees and soil and transport vast piles of boulders and masonry seemingly impossible distances.

floodplain is the area in a river valley which may be covered by water when a river is in flood, and which is built up of ALLUVIUM. The floodplain is developed by a river's movement with time and the deposition and transport of sediment. Whether it is due to existing features along a river's course, or simply due to turbulence of flow and subsequent deposition of material where a river slows, the course of a river will include numerous bends. Subsequent erosion and deposition of sediment results in a meandering (*see* RIVERS) of the river with deposition of alluvium and a progressive movement along of the river bends, forming a floodplain.

Development of a floodplain

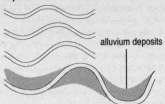

alluvium deposits

folds and *faults* are both geological features developed through tectonic activity. Folds are produced when rock layers undergo compression resulting in a buckling and folding of the rocks – a *ductile* or flowing deformation. There is an almost infinite variety in the shape, size and orientation of folds and an earlier generation of folds may be refolded by subsequent periods of deformation. Their size may range from microscopic to folds occupying hillsides or even whole mountains.

The way folds are formed will depend upon the amount of compression, the rock types involved and the thicknesses of the layers, because different rocks respond in different ways, but each fold possesses certain common features. The zone of greatest curvature is the *hinge* and the *limbs* lie between hinges or on either side of the hinge. The *axial plane* is an imaginary feature bisecting the angle between limbs and the *fold axis* is where the axial plane meets the hinge zone.

Faults are generally planar features, and are caused by *brittle* deformation. Rocks are moved, or *displaced*, across faults by as little as a few millimetres or as much as several kilometres (although possibly not all in the same event). There are several types of faults, depending upon the movement across the fault, and the orientation of the fault plane. The measurement of movement uses a horizontal and vertical component, the heave and throw respectively. If the movement is up or down the fault plane it is a dip-slip fault; if it is sideways, the term is strike-slip.

Two examples of vertical dip-slip fault movement viewed from the side

Two examples of horizontal strike-slip movement viewed from above

Many faults produce associated features such as zones of crushed rock, or striations (grooves) known as *slickensides*, on adjacent rock surfaces, where minerals such as quartz or calcite may grow.

Major faults today account for many surface features and are an important part of the *plate tectonic* structure and development of the Earth.

fossils are the remains of once-living plants and animals, or evidence of their existence, that have been preserved (usually) in the rock layers of the Earth. The term may include the preservation in ice of woolly mammoths that lived 20,000 years, although anything younger than about 10,000 years is not generally considered a fossil.

Fossils may be bones, shells, borings, trails, casts and the fossilised remains of something associated with or caused by an organism, e.g. tracks or a worm burrow, are called *trace fossils*. Although many rock sequences contain a large number of fossils, conditions prevailing at the time have to be just right to ensure preservation. Vital to the process is that the organism be covered quickly with sediment, something that will happen more readily in marine rather than terrestrial conditions. Even then, significant changes may occur – soft parts usually decay and shells may be replaced chemically, or dissolved away leaving a mould to be filled by a different material. Occasionally, a whole insect may be preserved in amber.

The scientific study of fossils is called *palaeontology*.

fossil fuels include PETROLEUM (oil), COAL and NATURAL GAS – fuels created by the fossilisation of plant and animal remains. Oil and gas are often found together with the gas lying over the oil and beneath the impermeable layer which seals the reservoir.

geochemistry a part of GEOLOGY that deals with the chemical make-up of the Earth, including the distribution of elements (and isotopes – *see* ST: ISOTOPE) and their movement within the various natural systems (ATMOSPHERE, LITHOSPHERE, etc.). Recently, it has also been taken to include other planets and moons within the solar system. The geochemical cycle, in broad terms, illustrates the way in which elements from MAGMA (the 'starting point') move through different processes and geochemical environments.

geochronology the study of time on a geological scale using *absolute* or *relative* dating methods. Absolute methods (*see* DATING METHODS) provide an age for a rock and involve the use of radioactive elements with known rates of decay. Relative ages are determined by putting rock sequences in order through study of their sequence of deposition or folding. Fossils can also be used in relative age dating.

geography the study of the Earth's surface, including all the land forms (*see*

GEOMORPHOLOGY), their formation and associated processes, which comprise *physical* geography. Such aspects as climate, topography and oceanography are covered. *Human* geography deals with the social and political perspectives of the subject including populations and their distribution. In addition, geography may cover the distribution and exploitation of natural resources, map-making and REMOTE SENSING.

geological timescale a division of time since the formation of the Earth (4600 million years ago) into units, during which rock sequences were deposited, deformed and eroded and life of diverse types emerged, flourished and, often, ceased.

The following table shows the various subdivisions, and many of the names owe their derivation to particular locations, rock sequences and so on.

Cenozoic (70 million years ago)	Recent Pleistocene Pliocene Oligocene Eocene Palaeocene	Modern Man Stone Age Man many mammals, elephants pig and ape ancestors horse and cattle ancestors
Mesozoic (245 million years ago)	Cretateous Jurassic Triassic	end of the dinosaurs and the ammonites appearance of birds and mammals dinosaurs appear; corals of modern type
Palaeozoic (600 million years ago)	Permian Carboniferous Devonian Silurian Ordovician Cambrian	amphibians and reptiles more common; conifer trees appear coal forests; reptiles appear, winged insects amphibians appear; fishes more common; ammonites appear; early trees; spiders first coral reefs; appearance of spore-bearing land plants first fish-like vertebrates: trilobites and graptolites common first fossils period; trilobites, grapolites, molluscs, crinoids, radiolaria, etc.
	Precambrian	sponges, worms, algae, bacteria; all primitive forms

Derivation of some geological names:

Cenozoic—recent life   *Palaeonzoic*—ancient life
Mesozoic—mediaeval life   *Archaean*—primaeval

The Roman name for Wales (*Cambria*) led to Cambrian, while the names of two Celtic tribes, the *Silures* and *Ordovices* provided the remaining lower Palaeonzoic names. Carboniferous is related to the proliferation of coal (i.e. carbon) and Cretaceous comes from *creta*, meaning chalk. The Triassic is a threefold division in Germany, while the *Jura* mountains lent their name to the Jurassic

geology the scientific study of the Earth, including its origins, structure, processes and composition. It includes a number of topics which have developed into subjects in their own right: GEOCHEMISTRY, MINERALOGY, petrology (study of rocks), structural geology, GEOPHYSICS, PALAEONTOLOGY, STRATIGRAPHY, economic and physical geology. Charles Lyell (1797–1875) was an influential figure in the early years of geological study and wrote *Principles of Geology*.

geomagnetism the study of the Earth's magnetic (*geomagnetic*) field which has varied with time. At mid-oceanic ridges (*see* PLATE TECTONICS) where new crust is created, measurement of the geomagnetic field shows stripes relating to reversals of the Earth's magnetic field which is taken up in the newly-formed rocks. This provides a tool in determining the age of much of the oceanic crust and is a vital piece of evidence in supporting the theory of plate tectonics.

Geomagnetic fields of the mid-Atlantic ridge

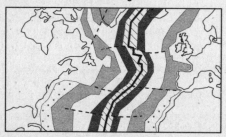

geomorphology a subject that grew out of geology around the middle of last century, and is the study of *landforms*, their origin and change, i.e. the study of the Earth's surface. Landforms are composed of various rock types and formed from the surface materials of the Earth by geomorphological processes which originate from tectonic movements and the climate. Landforms can be arranged into certain categories based upon factors such as the underlying structural geology, the nature of the topography, i.e. the surface features, and the terrain (soil, vegetation, etc), and the type of geomorphological processes dominant.

geophysics is the study of all processes *within* the Earth (i.e. the crust and the interior) and is concerned with the physical properties of the Earth. Included are seismology (*see* SEISMOGRAPH), GEOMAGNETISM, gravity, HYDROLOGY, oceanography (the study of the oceans, currents, tides, sea-floor and so on), heat flow within the Earth and related topics. As with many other subject areas, the component topics often develop to the point of becoming a subject in their own right, and boundaries between subjects merge.

geothermal energy the temperature within the Earth increases with depth (this is called the *geothermal gradient*), although not uniformly, and the average gradient is in the range 20 to 40°C per kilometre. At the edges of some tectonic plates (*see* PLATE TECTONICS) the gradient increases dramatically and it is sometimes possible to harness this heat as geothermal energy.

The high heat flow may be caused by magmatic activity (*see* MAGMA) or by the radioactive decay of certain elements. When water or brine (water containing dissolved salts) circulates through these rocks, it becomes heated and may appear at the surface as a warm spring, or if it is temporarily contained and heated further, it may force out a body of steam and water as a *geyser* (derived from geysir, the Icelandic for gusher or roarer).

Geothermal energy is 'tapped' all over the world, including Iceland, New Zealand, California and Italy. Iceland, New Zealand and Kenya have geothermal power stations.

glacier an enormous mass of ice, on land, that moves very slowly. About 10% of the Earth's land is covered by glaciers although during the last glaciation this was nearer 30%. Glaciers that cover vast areas of land, e.g. Greenland, Antarctic are called ice sheets (or ice caps if smaller) and these hide the underlying land features. The more typical glaciers are either those that flow in valleys or those filling hollows in mountains. Glaciers can be classified further into polar (e.g. Greenland), sub-polar (e.g. Spitzbergen) and temperate (e.g. the Alps) depending upon the temperature of the ice.

Although glaciers move slowly, they act as powerful agents of erosion on the underlying rocks. Large blocks may be dragged off the underlying rock, become embedded in the ice and then scratch and scour the surface as the glacier moves. This produces smaller particles of rock debris and the blocks themselves may be broken. Debris is also gathered from valley sides and carried along. Ridges or piles of this rock debris are called moraine and depending upon position relative to the glacier, may mark present or former edges of the ice. In addition to the formation of moraine and associated, characteristic formations, glaciers produce some typical large scale features such as U-shaped valleys and *truncated spurs*.

Glaciation is the term meaning an ice age or a part of an ice age when glaciers and ice sheets are enlarged significantly.

grasslands form one of the four major types of vegetation, the others being forest, savanna and DESERT. Grasslands are characterised by seasonal drought, limited precipitation and occasional fires and these all, with grazing by animals, restrict the growth of trees and shrubs. Typical grasslands include the pampas of Argentina, the veldts of South Africa, the Steppes in the Kazakhstan and the Ukraine and the prairies of central North America.

The coverage of grasslands expanded after the last glaciation when climates became generally hotter and drier and there was an increase in the number of large grazing mammals.

Savanna is similar to grassland, but with scattered trees and is found extensively in S. America, southern Africa and parts of Australia. There are usually well-defined seasons: cool and dry, hot and dry followed by warm and wet and during the latter there is a rich growth of grasses and small plants. Although savanna soils may be fertile they are highly porous and water therefore drains away rapidly.

groundwater water that is contained in the voids within rocks, i.e. in pores, cracks and other cavities and spaces. It often excludes *vadose* water which occurs between the water-table and the surface. Most groundwater originates from the surface, percolating through the soil (*meteoric* water). Other sources are *juvenile* water, generated during and coming from deep magmatic processes, and *connate* water which is water trapped in a sedimentary rock since its formation.

Groundwater is a necessary component of most weathering processes and of course its relationship to the geology, water-table and surface may lead to the occurrence of AQUIFERs and artesian wells.

hardness of minerals minerals differ in their physical hardness and a test introduced in 1822 is still in use today to aid mineral classification. Moh's scale lists 10 minerals ranked by hardness and each mineral will scratch

those lower on the scale where talc is the softest and diamond the hardest.
In addition it is common to use the finger nail (equivalent to 2.5) or a pen-
knife (5.5) to assist in the determination.

Moh's scale of hardness:

1	talc	6	orthoclase (feldspar)
2	gypsum	7	quartz
3	calcite	8	topaz
4	fluorite	9	corundum
5	apatite	10	diamond

humidity the amount of moisture in the Earth's atmosphere. *Absolute* humidity is the actual mass of water vapour in each cubic metre of air while
relative humidity is

$$\frac{\text{water vapour content of air at a given temperature}}{\text{water vapour content required for saturation at that temperature}} \times 100\%$$

The relative humidity of air therefore varies with temperature, cold air
holds little moisture, warm air much more. A *hygrometer* is the instrument
used to measure relative humidity.

hurricane a wind which on the BEAUFORT SCALE exceeds 75 mph (121 km/h).
Also an intense, tropical cyclonic storm that has a central calm area – the
eye – around which move winds of very high velocity (over 160 km/h).
There is usually very heavy rain, with thunderstorms and the whole system may be several hundred kilometres across.

Such storms occur mainly in the Caribbean and the Gulf of Mexico and
often affect the southern states of the USA, creating considerable destruction.

hydrology the study of water and its cycle, which covers bodies of water
and how they change. All physical forms of water – rain, snow, surface
water – are included as are such aspects as distribution and use. The way
in which water circulates between bodies of water such as seas, the atmosphere and the Earth forms the *hydrological cycle*.

The cycle consists of various stages: water falls as rain or snow of which
some runs off into streams and then into lakes or rivers, while some perco-
lates into the ground. Plants and trees take up water and lose it by transpiration to the atmosphere, while evaporation occurs from bodies of water.
The water vapour in the air then condenses to cloud which eventually repeats the cycle.

Of the 1.5 billion cubic kilometres of water on earth, the oceans hold

93.9%, groundwater 4.4%, polar ice 1.0%, with rivers, lakes, the atmosphere and soil holding the remainder.

The hydrological cycle

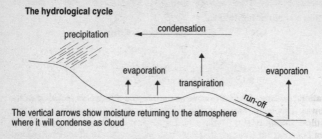

The vertical arrows show moisture returning to the atmosphere where it will condense as cloud

ice age a period in the history of the Earth when ice sheets expanded over areas that were normally ice-free. The term is usually applied to the most recent episode in the Pleistocene (*see* GEOLOGICAL TIMESCALE), but the rock record indicates that there have been ice ages as far back as the Precambrian. Within ice ages there are fluctuations in temperature producing interglacial stages when the temperatures increase.

igneous rocks one of the three main rock types. Igneous rocks crystallise from MAGMA and are formed at the surface as LAVA flows (*extrusive*) or beneath the surface as *intrusions*, pushing their way into existing rocks. There are numerous ways of classifying igneous rocks, from mineral content to crystal size and mode of origin and emplacement. Typical rocks are basalt, granite and dolerite.

Rocks erupted at the surface as lava are called *volcanic*, while *plutonic* rocks are those large bodies solidifying at some depth; *hypabyssal* rocks are smaller and form at shallow depths. When a body of magma has time to crystallise slowly, large mineral crystals can develop while extrusion at the surface leads to a rapid cooling and formation of very small crystals (or none, if molten rock contacts water, as in a glass). A further division into acid, intermediate, basic and ultrabasic rocks is based upon silica (SiO_2) content, this being greatest in acid rocks.

Igneous intrusions may occur in several forms either parallel to or cutting through the existing rocks, and the commonest are *sills* (concordant) and *dykes* (discordant). *Plugs* commonly represent the neck of a former volcano, while *batholiths* are massive, elongate bodies that may be hundreds of kilometres long.

Examples of igneous intrusions

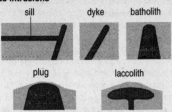

sill   dyke   batholith

plug   laccolith

irrigation is when water is taken to dry land to encourage or facilitate plant growth. The water may be applied by means of canals, ditches, sprinklers or the flooding of the whole area. Flood irrigation is not always a good idea because the water evaporates from the flooded field leaving behind any salts that were dissolved in the water. If this is done repeatedly, the build up of salts may harm the soil and make it infertile. Water may be conserved and used more effectively by means of a pipe with small holes being laid around a plant, and the water drips from the holes onto the soil. Irrigation can transform arid regions but rivers from which water is diverted will inevitably be much reduced.

isobar a line on a weather map that joins points of equal pressure corrected for the varying heights of recording. Over a large area, isobars produce a map of pressure lines, similar to contours on a topographic map, which identify the high and low centres, i.e. the anticyclones and depressions.

jet stream westerly winds at high altitudes (above 12 km) found mainly between the poles and the TROPICS, that form narrow jet-like streams. The air streams move north and south of their general trend, in surges, which are probably the cause of depressions and anticyclones. There are a number of separate jet streams but the most constant is that of the subtropics. Jet stream speed and location is of importance to high-flying aircraft.

latitude and **longitude** latitude is the angular distance, north or south from the equator, of a point on the Earth's surface. The equator is 0° and points can therefore be measured in degrees south or north of this line. The imaginary lines drawn on a map or globe are the lines of latitude.

Longitude is a similar concept. It is the angular distance of a point measured on the Earth's surface to the east or west of a 'central' reference point. The referent point in this case is the plane created by a *meridian* (an imaginary circle that cuts the poles and goes over the Earth's surface and the point in question) going through Greenwich in England. A point may be 0° longitude if it sits on this line or a number of degrees east or west. The Greenwich Meridian, based upon the Greenwich Observatory, was established by an international agreement in 1884. There is a time difference of one hour when travelling 15° of longitude at the equator (*see also* TROPICS).

lava molten rock at about 1100 or 1200°C erupted from a VOLCANO or a similar fissure. It may flow onto the ground (subaerial) or onto the sea floor (submarine). Due to rapid cooling in air or water, most lavas show a fine-grained or glassy structure. The way lava is erupted, flows, and its shape as a flow is determined by its viscosity. *Pahoehoe* lava is a fluid basaltic type which forms rope-like flows due to molten lava in the centre of the flow dragging the solidifying crust into folds. A more viscous lava, *Aa* (both terms are Hawaiian words) flows more slowly and forms jagged, pointed blocks. Often a stream of lava will be contained by craggy sides of partly solidified lava. *Pillow lavas* are formed on the sea floor and as their name suggests, consist of pillow-like shapes built up and out from the source with one pillow rupturing at some point to allow more lava out to form another pillow. *Pumice* is lava filled with small air bubbles, creating a light, rough stone.

There are roughly 10,000 active volcanoes occurring in belts coinciding with the margins between tectonic plates. Lavas may cover vast areas, e.g. 250,000 square kilometres of the Deccan Plain of India, and 130,000 square kilometres in the Columbia River plateau region of the western USA. Such eruptions have occurred throughout geological time.

lightning and **thunder** lightning is the discharge of high voltage electricity between a CLOUD and its base, and between the base of the cloud and the Earth. (It has been shown that in a cumulonimbus cloud, positive charge collects at the top and negative at the base). Lightning occurs when the increasing charge (of electricity) in the cloud overcomes the resistance of the air, leading to a *discharge*, seen as a flash. The discharge to ground is actually followed by a return discharge up to the cloud, and this is the visible sign of lightning. There are various forms of lightning, including sheet, fork and ball, and it may carry a charge of around 10,000 amps.

Thunder is the rumbling noise that accompanies lightning, and it is caused by the sudden heating and expansion of the air by the discharge, causing sound waves. The sound often continues for some time because sound is generated at various points along the discharge - the latter can be several kilometres long. The thunder comes after the lightning because sound travels more slowly than light, and this allows an approximate measure of distance from the flash to be made. For every 5 seconds between the flash and the thunder, the lightning will be roughly one mile away.

limestone a sedimentary rock that is made up mainly of calcite (calcium carbonate, $CaCO_3$) with dolomite ($CaMg(CO_3)_2$). There are essentially three groups of limestone: chemical, organic and detrital. These groups reflect the enormous variety of limestones, which may contain the broken remains of marine organisms – shells, coral, etc (detrital); minute organic remains of, for example, algae, foraminifera as in chalk, make an *organic* limestone; and grains formed as concentrically layered pellets (ooliths and pisoliths) in shallow marine waters, which with EVAPORITES are examples of chemical limestones.

Limestones are important economically and have many uses. They form AQUIFERS and reservoirs for oil and gas and are used in the manufacture of cement, in agriculture and as roadstone, and when cut and finished slabs of it are used to face buildings. Where limestone outcrops appears at the surface, the process of water flow and dissolution of the rock may lead to a *karst* topography, where there is a virtual absence of surface drainage and groundwater moves along joints into holes, enlarging them over time to form potholes and caves that, in well-developed and extensive cases, may result in collapses of rock over caves and voids to produce towering rock pinnacles (as in China).

magma the fluid, molten rock beneath the surface of the Earth. Magma may undergo many stages of change and movement before being extruded at the surface as *lava*, or intruded at some depth as an intrusion (*see* IGNEOUS ROCKS). The composition varies because in moving upwards through the crust, volatiles (gases and liquids) may be lost and some minerals may crystallise out, thus changing the nature of the remaining melt. Magma reaches the surface through pipes into volcanoes, or through fissures, but at depth it may form bodies many kilometres across.

Magmas are formed by the partial melting of mantle (the layer between the Earth's crust and core) in areas of *subduction*, where tectonic plates are destroyed (*see* PLATE TECTONICS) as one plate descends beneath another. Magmas usually undergo many changes in composition as they move towards the surface.

maps are flat, two-dimensional representations of three-dimensional subjects, e.g. an area of land, which contain a variety of data that will differ depending upon the type of map. Differing scales, that is the ratio of a distance on the map to the actual distance on the ground, enable smaller or larger areas of land to be represented.

A standard topographical map indicates the shape of the land by means of *contours* (lines joining points of equal height), and on it the road, rivers, railway lines, towns, forests and parkland may be marked. Maps can be drawn up to illustrate land usage, relief (i.e. the shape of the land surface), superficial deposits (river and glacial deposits on top of the underlying rocks) or solid geology (the rocks shown with all things above stripped away).

A *map projection* is the representation of the complete surface of the Earth on a plane. There is a large number of such projections and each presents the globe in a different way and thus finds different uses.

Projection	Types	Used for
Mercator	cylindrical	navigation
Conical	conic	maps of a small continent
Gnomonic	azimuthal	seismic survey; navigational
Peter's	modified cylindrical	depicts the Earth's densely populated areas in proportion
Stereographic	azimuthal	used widely in structural geology and crystallography

One of the commonest is the Mercator projection, named after the Flemish geographer who used it for his world map of 1569.

Projections are often used in the analysis of directional data. A grid, without the world map, can be used in the study of geological data, e.g. the orientation of folds.

metamorphic rocks are rocks formed by the alteration or recrystallisation of existing rocks by the application of heat, pressure, change in volatiles (gases and liquids), or a combination of these. There are several categories of *metamorphism* based upon the conditions of origin: *regional* – high pressure and temperature as found in *orogenic* (mountain-building) areas; *contact* – where the rocks are adjacent to an igneous body and have been altered by the heat (with little or no pressure); *dynamic* – very high, confined pressure with some heat, as generated in an area of faulting or thrusting, i.e. where rock masses slide against each other; *burial* – which involves high pressure and low temperature, e.g. as found at great depth in sequences of sedimentary rocks.

The key feature of all metamorphic rocks is that the existing *assemblage* (group) of minerals is changed by the pressure and/or heat and the presence of volatiles. New minerals grow that are characteristic of the new conditions. Typical metamorphic rocks are schist, slate, gneiss, marble, quartzite and hornfels. Depending on the type of metamorphism, there are systems of classification into *zones* or *grades* where specific minerals appear in response to increasing pressure and/or temperature.

meteorology is the scientific study of the conditions and processes within the Earth's atmosphere. This includes the pressure, temperature, wind speed, cloud formations, etc. which, over a period of time, enable meteorologists to predict likely future WEATHER patterns. Information is generated by weather stations, and also by satellites in orbit around the Earth.

mineralogy the scientific study of MINERALS, i.e. any chemical element or compound extracted from the Earth. It involves the following properties: colour, CRYSTAL form and cleavage, HARDNESS, specific gravity, lustre (how the mineral reflects light) and streak (the colour created by scratching the mineral on a special porcelain plate). Together, these properties help identify and classify minerals and one of the most important features is the *cleavage*.

Cleavage is the tendency for minerals to split along particular, characteristic planes which reflect and are controlled by the internal structure of the crystal. The plane of splitting is that which is weakest, due to the atomic structure of the crystal.

minerals are naturally-occurring inorganic substances that have definite and characteristic chemical compositions and CRYSTAL structures. Minerals have particular features and properties (*see, for example* HARDNESS *and also* MINERALOGY). Some elements occur as minerals, such as gold, diamond and copper but most minerals are made up of several elements (*see* **ST**: ELEMENT). Rocks are composed of minerals. There are about 2000 minerals, although the commonest rocks contain combinations from about 30 minerals, which in addition to quartz and calcite come from five or six main groups, all silicates. Silicate minerals are the most abundant rock-forming minerals and comprise about 95% of the Earth's crust, reflecting the fact that oxygen and silicon are the two commonest elements in rocks. The average make up of rocks in the crust is as follows:

silicia	SiO_2	59.3%	oxides	Fe_2O_3	3.1%
alumina	Al_2O_3	15.3%	potash	K_2O	3.1%
lime	CaO	5.1%	water	H_2O	1.3%
soda	Na_2O	3.8%	titania	TiO_2	0.7%
iron	FeO	3.7%	phosporus pentoxide	P_2O_5	0.3%
magnesia	MgO	3.5%			

Silicate minerals are based upon a tetrahedral arrangement of four oxygen ions with one silicon ion, and these tetrahedral units are joined in various ways to each other and differing metal ions.

Some of the mineral groups:

group	example	structure
Feldspars	orthoclase	framework (tectosilicate)
Pyroxenes	augite	single-chain (inosilicate)
Amphiboles	hornblende	double-chain (inosilicate)
Micas	biotite	flat sheets (phyllosilicate)
Clays	kaolinite	flat sheets (phyllosilicate)
Garnet	pyrope	linked tetrahedra (neosilicate)

Minerals are mined and extracted for diverse purposes, e.g. ornamental stone (in the form of rocks), to generate metals for further use (gold, copper, iron, etc.) or as valuable items in their own right, e.g. diamonds.

monsoon generally refers to winds that blow in opposite directions during different seasons. Monsoons are related to temperature changes in the subtropics and pressure alterations associated with changing JET STREAMS. The word is derived from the Arabic *mausim* which means season, and its meaning has been extended to include the rains that accompany the wind. The Indian subcontinent has a rainy season in its southwesterly monsoon and other areas where monsoons are seen to strongest effect are South East Asia, China and Pakistan. However, monsoons also occur in North Australia, and East and West Africa.

mountains the formation of mountain chains clearly involves phenomenal movements of the Earth's crust and unimaginable forces, even though the process takes place over many millions of years. The process of mountain building (OROGENY or orogenesis) involves the accumulation of enormous thicknesses of sediments which are subsequently folded, faulted and thrusted, with igneous intrusions at depth (plutons of granite), producing rock complexes involving sedimentary, igneous and metamorphic rocks.

A massive linear area that has been compressed in this way is called an orogenic belt and the formation of such belts is interpreted by the means of PLATE TECTONICS. Different mechanisms are postulated for the formation of mountain chains, e.g. the Andes by subduction of oceanic lithosphere; the collision of continents for the Himalayas and the addition of enormous basins of sedimentary rocks and *island arcs* onto an existing plate in the case of the North American Cordillera (*see* PLATE TECTONICS *for definition of terms*).

The result of these global crustal movements is the mountain ranges as we see them today where the higher peaks belong to the younger ranges.

The highest points on the seven continents are as follows:

peak	height	continent	country
Everest	8848m	Asia	Nepal/China
Acongagura	6960m	South America	Argentina
McKinley	6194m	North America	Alaska
Kilimanjaro	5895m	Africa	Tanzania
Elbrus	5642m	Europe	Georgia
Vinson Massif	5140m	Antarctica	Antarctica
Mauna Kea	4205m	Oceania	Hawaii

Mountains have a considerable effect on local weather conditions and south-facing slopes in the northern hemisphere are warmer and drier than north-facing slopes because they receive more sun. When warm, moist air reaches a mountain, it cools as it rises, releasing moisture so on the lee-ward side the air descends and absorbs moisture. In many instances, deserts occur on the leeward side of a mountain range, e.g. the Gobi Desert (Asia), and the Mojave Desert of western North America. It is well-known that the temperature falls with height on a mountain – approximately 6°C for each 100m. Mountains thus show a variety of plants that vary with altitude.

natural gas hydrocarbons in a gaseous state which when found are often associated with liquid petroleum. The gas is a mixture of methane and ethane, with propane and small quantities of butane, nitrogen, carbon dioxide and sulphur compounds.

As with petroleum, gas owes its origin to the deposition of sediments that contain a lot of organic matter. After deposition and burial and through the action of heat, with time, oil and gas are produced. These migrate to a suitable reservoir rock where they reside until extracted by drilling. World gas reserves:

oceans technically, those bodies of water that occupy the ocean basins, the latter beginning at the edge of the continental shelf. Marginal seas such as the Mediterranean, Caribbean and Baltic are not classed as oceans. A more general definition is all the water on the Earth's surface, excluding lakes and inland seas. The oceans are the North and South Atlantic; North and South Pacific; Indian and Arctic. Together with all the seas the salt water covers almost 71% of the Earth's surface.

From the shore the land dips away gently in most cases – the continental shelf – after which the gradient increases on the continental slope leading to the deep sea platform (at about 4 km depth). There are many areas of shallow seas on the continental shelf (*epicontinental seas*) e.g. North Sea, Baltic and Hudson Bay. In the ice age, much of the shelf would have been land and conversely should much ice melt, the continents would be submerged further. The floors of the oceans display both mountains, in the form of the mid-oceanic ridges, and deep trenches. The ridges rise 2-3 km from the floor and extend for thousands of kilometres while the trenches reach over 11 km below sea level, at their deepest (Mariana Trench, southeast of Japan).

The six ocean zones are:

littoral zone		between low and high water spring tides
pelagic zone	0–180m	floating *plankton* and swimming *nekton*
nerietic zone	low tide –180m	*benthic* organisms
bathyal zone	180–1800m	beyond light penetration, but much benthic life (crawling, burrowing or fixed plants and animals)
abyssal zone	>1800m	
abyssal plain	<4000 m	ooze of calcareous and siliceous skeletal remains; red clay only below 5000 m

The oceans contain *currents*, i.e. faster-moving large-scale flows (the slower movements are called *drifts*). Several factors contribute to the formation of currents, namely the rotation of the Earth, prevailing winds, differences in temperature and sea water densities. Major currents move clockwise in the northern hemisphere and anticlockwise in the southern hemisphere. Well-known currents include the Gulf Stream and the Humboldt current.

The major currents

Oceanography is the study of all aspects of the oceans from their structure and composition to the life within and the movements of the water.

ore a naturally-occurring substance that contains metals or other compounds that are commercially useful and which it is economically feasible to mine for profit. *Native ores*, such as gold and copper, occur as the metallic element itself and not in a compound but most metals have to be extracted from compounds, commonly the oxide or sulphide. Minerals containing metallic elements are called ore minerals and ore deposits are aggregates of these minerals.

Extraction of an ore commonly involves removal from a pit (open cast mine) or shaft (in a deep mine). The ore rock is then crushed and possibly washed and sorted before being treated with heat or mixed with chemicals. A furnace may then be used to smelt the ore to produce the metal which separates off from the waste or slag.

Ores are produced geologically in several ways. Some mineral concentrations are associated with magmas, e.g. nickel, cobalt, chromium, platinum or tungsten compounds. Ore minerals are usually found in veins with no obvious connection to igneous activity and in this case may be formed by percolation of hot water laden with metals. Weathering and erosion can also lead to the concentration of certain ore minerals (bauxite or gold and zircon respectively).

orogeny *see* MOUNTAINS.

ozone layer a part of the Earth's atmosphere, at approximately 15-30 km height, that contains ozone. Ozone is present in very small amounts (one to ten parts per million) but it fulfils a very important role by absorbing much of the Sun's ultraviolet radiation, which has harmful effects in excess, causing skin cancer and cataracts and unpredictable consequences to crops, and plankton.

Recent scientific studies have shown a thinning of the ozone layer over the last 20 years, with the appearance of a hole over Antarctica in 1985. This depletion has been caused mainly by the build-up of CFCs (chlorofluorocarbons) from aerosol can propellants, refrigerants and chemicals used in some manufacturing processes. The chlorine in CFCs reacts with ozone to form ordinary oxygen, lessening the effectiveness of the layer. CFCs are now being phased out but the effects of their past use will affect the ozone layer for some time to come.

peat an organic deposit formed from plant debris which is laid down with little or no alteration or decomposition (break down) in a water-logged environment. Bogs, fens, swamps, moors and wetlands are all sites of peat production with some variation in peat structure depending upon the acidity of the conditions.

The conditions are vital so that oxygen is not available for the decay of plant material. As peat accumulates over the years, water is squeezed out and the lower peat layers shrink. However, air drying is essential when peat is cut for fuel. Acid conditions are commonest and *sphagnum moss* is the dominant peat vegetation. However, peat may form in shallow lakes through the gradual takeover by marsh vegetation, or it may develop in shallow lagoons, flood plains or deltas. Conditions for peat formation are currently found all over the world, and in addition to Ireland and Scotland, also on the coastal plains of Virginia and North Carolina, in the Everglades of Florida, Indonesia, India and Malaysia. After the last ice age there were lengthy periods of peat formation. The preserving properties of peat bogs have been seen to great effect over recent years when whole baby woolly mammoths and humans have been found.

permafrost is ground that is permanently frozen, save for surface melting in the summer. It is technically defined as being when the temperature is below 0°C for two consecutive years, and it can extend to depths of several hundred metres. The top layer that thaws in the summer is called the *active layer* and there may be unfrozen ground between this and the permafrost, a zone which is called *talik*. Depths of 1500 metres in Siberia and 650 metres in North America have been recorded and today permafrost underlies 20–25% of the Earth's land area – a figure that was much greater during parts of the Pleistocene (*see* GENEOLOGICAL TIMESCALE).

The ground in areas of permafrost shows distinctive features including patterns of circles, polygonal cracks; mounds and pingos. Polygonal cracks are due to the contraction caused by cooling in winter and in Spitzbergen the polygons may reach 200 metres across. Mounds are caused simply by the increase in volume that accompanies freezing of water which pushes up surface layers of soil. Large mounds, up to 40 to 50 metres high are called *pingos*.

petroleum (or *crude oil*) is a mixture of naturally-occurring hydrocarbons formed by the decay of organic matter which, under pressure and increased temperatures, form oil. The often mentioned '*reservoir*' is the rock in which oil (and gas) is found and common types of reservoir rock are sandstone, limestone or dolomite. The oil migrates, after formation from the source rocks to the reservoir (because such vast quantities could not have been formed in place) where it must be contained by a *trap*. A trap is a particular geological configuration where the oil is confined by impermeable rocks.

Most of the world's petroleum reserves are in the Middle East although the USA currently produces a significant proportion of the world's oil.

The modern oil industry began over a century ago when a well was bored for water in Pennsylvania, and oil appeared. Petroleum also occurs in the form of *asphalt* or *bitumen*, syrupy liquids or near solid in form, and there are significant deposits today. The Pitch Lake of Trinidad, over 500 metres across and about 40 metres deep, is fed from beneath as the asphalt is removed. There are similar occurrences in Venezuela and California and in Alberta, Canada are the famous Athabasca Oil Sands, where the sandstone is full of tar, an oil of asphalt.

Petroleum consists of many hydrocarbons (*see* **ST**: HYDROCARBONS) of differing composition with small amounts of sulphur, oxygen and nitrogen. The components are separated and treated chemically to provide the basic building blocks and products for the vast petrochemicals industry (*see* **ST**: PETROCHEMICALS).

plate tectonics a concept that brings together the variety of features and processes of the Earth's crust and accounts for continental drift, sea-floor spreading, volcanic and earthquake activity, and crustal structure.

It has long been noticed how coastlines on opposite sides of oceans, e.g. the Atlantic, seemed to fit together. Other geological features led to the theory that continents were joined together millions of years ago. This theory was supported by a reconstruction of fossil magnetic poles and in 1962 by the idea of sea-floor spreading where ocean ridges were the site of new crust formation, with slabs of crust moving away from these central sites. All this was brought together with the idea that the *lithosphere* (the crust and uppermost part of the mantle) is made up of seven large and twelve smaller plates composed of oceanic or continental crust. The plates move relative to each other with linear regions of creation and destruction of the lithosphere.

There are three types of plate boundary; *ocean ridges* where plates are moving apart (constructive); *ocean trenches* where plates are moving together (also for young mountain ranges) (destructive); *transform faults* where plates move sideways past each other (conservative). At destructive plate boundaries one tectonic plate dips beneath the other at an oceanic trench in a process called *subduction* and in so doing old lithosphere is returned to the mantle. *Island arcs* are an example of volcanic activity associated with subduction at an ocean trench, where there is very often also earthquakes. Where two continental plates converge, the continents collide to produce mountains as seen in the Alps and Himalayas today. The transform faults of conservative plate boundaries are generated by the relative motion of two plates alongside each other and the best known example is the San Andreas fault in California, a region which suffers earthquakes along this major fracture.

Two types of plate boundary

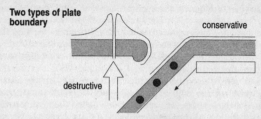

rain one form of precipitation in which drops of water condense from the water vapour in the atmosphere to form rain drops. Other types of precipitation, all water in some liquid or solid form, include snow, hail, sleet, drizzle and also dew. Snow forms below 0°C and depending upon the temperature, occurs in different shapes. When the temperature is well below freezing, it forms ice *spicules* which are small and needle-like. Nearer to 0°C, the characteristic snowflakes grow, but at extremely low temperatures snow becomes powdery. Because snow can vary in its form and accumulation, accurate measurement of falls is difficult, but 25mm of water will be produced by about 300 mm of newly-fallen snow.

Hail is a small pellet of frozen water that forms by rain drops being taken higher into colder parts of the atmosphere. As it then falls, the hailstone grows by adding layers of ice, due to condensation of moisture upon the cold nucleus. *Dew* is the condensation of water vapour in the air caused by a cooling of the air.

remote sensing is the collection of a variety of information without contact with the object of study. This includes aerial photography from both aircraft and satellites and the use of infrared, ultraviolet and microwave radiation emitted from the object, e.g. an individual site, part of a town, crop and forest patterns. Another type of remote sensing involves the production of an impulse of light, or radar, which is reflected by the object and the image is then captured on film or tape.

Using these various techniques, large areas of the ground can be studied and surprisingly sharp pictures obtained which can be used in many ways. Remote sensing is used in agriculture and forestry, civil engineering, geol-

ogy, geography and archaeology, amongst others. In addition, it is possible
to create pictures with a remarkable amount of detail which would otherwise take a very long time to collect.

rivers streams of water that flow into the sea or in some cases into lakes or
swamps. Rivers form part of the cyclical nature of water, comprising water falling from the atmosphere as some form of precipitation (*see* RAIN)
and being partly fed by groundwaters or run-off from the melting of glaciers (both of which in any case are derived from atmospheric water).

Rivers develop their own immediate scenery and a river valley will owe
its form to the original slope of the land, the underlying rocks and the climate. A river with its tributaries is called a *river system*, and the area from
which its water is derived is the *drainage basin* (*see also* DRAINAGE). As
rivers grow in size and velocity, rock and soil debris washed into them is
carried downstream, eroding the river bed and sides as it goes. As a river
continues to flow and carry debris, depositing much material in times of
FLOOD, it widens its valley floor, forming a FLOODPLAIN. As it does so, the
river swings from side to side forming wide loops, called *meanders*. Eventually as meanders develop into ever more contorted loops, a narrow neck
of land may be left which is eventually breached. Thus the river alters and
shortens its course, leaving a horseshoe-shaped remnant, or *ox-bow* lake.

rocks are aggregates of MINERALS or organic matter, and can be divided into
three types, based upon the way they are formed: IGNEOUS, SEDIMENTARY
and METAMORPHIC.

sedimentary rocks are rocks formed from existing rock sources through the
processes of erosion, weathering and include rocks of organic or chemical
origin. They can be divided into *clastic* rocks, that is made of fragments,
organic or *chemical*.

The clastic rocks are further divided on grain size into coarse (or
rudaceous, grains of 1-2 mm), medium (or *arenaceous*, e.g. sandstone)
and fine (or *argillaceous* up to 0.06 mm). When the grains comprising
clastic rocks are deposited (usually in water) compaction of the soft
sediment and subsequent *lithification* (that is, turning into rock) produces
the layered effect, or *bedding*, that is often visible in cliffs and outcrops in
rivers. It is also common for original features to be preserved, for example
ripples, small or large dune structures, which in an exposed rock face
appear as inclined beds called *current bedding*. *Graded bedding* shows a
gradual change in grain size from the base, where it is coarse, to the top of
a bed, where it is fine and this is due to the settling of material onto the sea
floor from a current caused by some earth movement.

Many sedimentary rocks, particularly shale, limestone and finer sandstone contain FOSSILS of animals and plants from millions of years ago, and with the original features mentioned above, these are useful in working out the sequence of events in an area where the rocks have been strongly folded.

seismograph in the study of earthquakes (*seismology),* seismographs are used to record the shock waves (*seismic* waves) as they spread out from the source. The seismograph has some means of conducting the ground vibrations through a device that turns movement into a signal that can be recorded. There are numerous seismic stations around the world that record ground movements, each containing several seismographs with numerous *seismometers* (the actual detector linked to a seismograph).

soil is the thin layer of uncompacted material comprising organic matter and minute mineral grains that overlies rock and provides the means by which plants can grow. Soil is formed by the breakdown of rock, in a number of ways. Rock is initially fractured and broken up by weathering: the action of water, ice and wind, and any acids dissolved in water moving over, or percolating through the rock. This allows in various organisms that speed up the breakdown process and mosses, lichens, fungi then take hold and after a while there forms a mixture of organisms including bacteria, decayed organic material, weathered rock and *humus* which is called *topsoil*. Humus is decomposing (breaking down) organic material produced from dead organisms, leaves and other organic material by the action of bacteria and fungi.

The texture of the soil affects its ability to support plants and the most fertile soils are *loams* which contain mixtures of sand, silt and clay with organic material. This ensures there is sufficient water and minerals (which 'stick' to the finer particles) while the coarser sand grains provide air spaces, vital to roots. In addition to plant roots, soil contains an enormous number of organisms including fungi, algae, insects, earthworms, nematodes and several billion bacteria. Earthworms are useful in that they aerate the soil, and the bacteria alter the mineral composition of the soil.

The parent rock is the primary factor in determining the nature of a soil. While sand, silt and clay produce a loam, sand alone is too porous and clay too compacted and impervious (doesn't allow water through). A clay soil can be improved by adding lime, hence a *marl* (a lime rich clay) forms a good soil. Limestone itself does not produce a soil. The rate of breakdown of the rock is also important. Granites decompose slowly but basaltic rocks are the opposite and therefore yield their soil components quickly. This is seen particularly in volcanic areas where lava flows and volcanic ash quickly lead to very productive soils.It can take hundreds of years for soils to become fertile, but to be productive agriculturally, the soil has to be cared for with irrigation, fertilisation and prevention of erosion all being important factors. This is apparent when you consider that the soil provides approximately 18 kg of nitrogen, 4 kg of potassium and 3 kg of phosphorus to grow one ton of wheat grain.

stalactites and stalagmites in areas of LIMESTONE where caves form and streams trickle through the rocks and caves, calcium-rich waters tend to drop from cave roofs. As there is a little evaporation from these drops of water, some of the dissolved calcium is deposited, as calcite (calcium carbonate, $CaCO_3$). This deposit builds up very slowly into a stalactite projecting down from the roof. If water continues to drop to the floor, a complementary upward growth develops into a stalagmite – and often the two meet to form a column, or pillar.

Many limestone caves exhibit spectacular developments e.g. White Scar at Ingleton in Yorkshire; La Cave in the Dordogne; Wookey Hole in the Mendips and many other places.

stratigraphy is the branch of geology concerned with the study of stratified rocks, i.e. rocks that were originally laid down in layers. It deals with the position of rocks in geological time and space, their classification and correlation between different areas. Rock units can be identified and differentiated by several means.

Stratigraphy began about two hundred years ago when it was first realised that in a normal sequence of rocks, relatively unaffected by any tectonic movements, younger rocks will lie above older rocks. This was known as the 'law' of superposition, but it soon became apparent that all sorts of geological events could upset this simplistic theory.

stratosphere one of the layers of the atmosphere, lying above the TROPO-SPHERE. It lies at a height of between 10 and 50 km and shows an increase in temperature from bottom to top where it is 0ºC. (The average temperature above is -60ºC). A very large part of the ozone (*see* OZONE LAYER) in the atmosphere is found in the stratosphere and the absorption of ultraviolet radiation contributes to the higher temperature in the upper reaches. This inversion of temperature creates a stability which limits the vertical extent of cloud and produces the sideways extension of a cumulonimbus cloud into the characteristic shape.

thunder *see* LIGHTNING.

tides the regular rise and fall of the water levels in the world's oceans and seas which is due to the gravitational effect of the Moon and Sun. The

Moon exerts a stronger pull than the Sun (roughly twice the effect) and variation in tides is caused by the relative positions of the three bodies and the distribution of water on the Earth. When the Sun, Moon and Earth are aligned, the effects are combined and result in a maximum, the high *spring tide* (when the Moon is new or full), conversely when the Sun is at right angles to the Moon, the effect is minimised resulting in a low *Neap tide*.

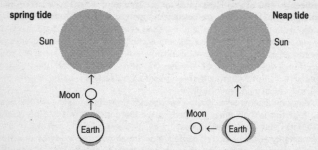

The effect of tides in the open oceans is negligible, perhaps one metre, and enclosed areas of water such as the Black Sea exhibit differences in the order of centimetres. However, in shallow seas where the tide may be channelled by the shores, tides of six to nine metres may be created.

The tides around Britain's coasts vary markedly due in part to the effect of the *Coriolis force*. This is when air or water is pushed to the side because of the Earth's rotation. Hence in the northern hemisphere, water moving across the surface is pushed to the right (and conversely in the southern hemisphere). Hence the tidal wave which passes northwards up the Irish Sea creates higher tides on the Welsh and English coasts than on the Irish side, and as the tidal wave moves into the North Sea, the Coriolis force pushes the water to the right giving higher tides on the British coastline than on the coasts of Norway and Denmark. The potential for generating energy from tides has long been realised and the first tidal power station was built in France and made operational in 1966.

time zones zones which run north-south, with some variations across the Earth, and which represent different times. Each zone is one hour earlier or later than the adjacent zone, and is 15° of *longitude*. The zones were devised for convenience, but to compensate for the accumulated time change, the *International Date-Line* was introduced. The line runs roughly on the 180° meridian, although it does detour around land areas in the Pacific Ocean, and to cross it going east means repeating a day, while in the opposite direction losing a day.

tornado a narrow column of air that rotates rapidly and leaves total devastation in its path. It develops around a centre of very low pressure with high velocity winds (well over 300 km/hour) blowing anticlockwise and with a violent downdraught. The typical appearance is of a funnel or snake-like column filled with cloud and usually no more than 150 metres across.

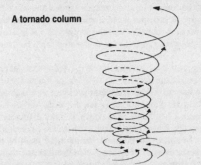

A tornado column

The precise way in which tornadoes form is not known although it involves the interface of warm moist air with dry cooler air and an inversion of temperatures with some event acting as a trigger, possibly an intense cold front. These conditions are found in many countries at mid to low latitudes but particularly so in the mid-west of the USA. The destruction created by tornadoes is due partly to the violent winds and partly to the very low pressure. This has the effect of causing buildings to explode outwards because the pressure outside exceeds that inside and although a tornado may affect an area only 100-150 metres across, the destruction is total. Tornadoes are often unpredictable in their behaviour and can lose contact with the ground or retrace their routes. When a tornado moves out over the sea, and once the tunnel has joined with the waves, a *waterspout* is formed.

tropics are two lines of LATITUDE that lie 23.5° north and south of the equator. The northern line is the *Tropic of Cancer* and the southern one the *Tropic of Capricorn*, and the region between them is called the tropics.

The term 'tropical' is often used to describe climate, vegetation, etc, but it is not an accurate usage of the word. In general a tropical climate does not have a cool season, and the mean temperature never falls below 20°C. Rainfall can be very high indeed, and in many countries these conditions produce a dense, lush vegetation, e.g. tropical rain forests.

troposphere the part of the Earth's atmosphere between the surface and the *tropopause* (the boundary with the STRATOSPHERE). The tropopause is the point at which the change in temperature with height (the lapse-rate) stops, and the temperature remains constant for several kilometres. Within the troposphere itself, the temperature decreases approximately 6.5°C for each kilometre of height. The troposphere is also the layer that contains most of the water vapour and about 75% of the weight of gas in the atmosphere, and it is the zone where turbulence is greatest and most weather features occur.

The level of the tropopause, and therefore the top of the troposphere, varies from about 17 km at the equator, falling to 9 km or lower at the poles. The height variation relates to temperature and pressure at sea-level.

tsunami (plural is also tsunami) an enormous sea wave caused by the sudden large-scale movement of the sea floor resulting in the displacement of large volumes of water. The cause may be an EARTHQUAKE, volcanic eruption, a submarine slide or slump of sediment, which may itself have been started by an earthquake or tremor. The slipping of thousands of tonnes of rock from the sides of fjords may also cause tsunami.

The effect of this sea floor movement in the open ocean may not be seen at all, as the resulting wave may only be one metre or less in height. However, because the whole depth of water is affected, there is a vast amount of energy involved, so when the waves reach shallow water or small bays, the effects can be catastrophic. The waves may travel at several hundred kilometres per hour (600-900) and reach heights of 15-30 metres. The devastation caused is clearly going to be terrible and there are many such instances in the record.

The word originates from the Japanese (*tsu*: harbour and *nami*: waves) where there have been many instances of destructive tsunami. In 1933, an earthquake triggered tsunami with waves up to 27 metres high and thousands of people were drowned along the Japanese coast. The waves were actually recorded about 10 hours later in San Francisco, having crossed the Pacific. It seems that tsunami are generated by submarine earthquakes registering 8 or over on the Richter scale.

tundra is the treeless region between the snow and ice of the arctic and the northern extent of tree growth. Large treeless plains can be found in northern Canada, Alaska, northern Siberia and northern Scandinavia. The ground is subject to PERMAFROST but the surface layer melts in the summer, so soil conditions are very poor, being waterlogged and marshy. The surface therefore can support little plant life. Cold temperatures and high winds also limit the diversity of plants, restricting the *flora* to grasses, mosses, lichens, sedges and dwarf shrubs. Some areas of tundra receive the same low level of precipitation as deserts yet the soil remains saturated due to the partial thaw of the permafrost. Most growth occurs in rapid bursts during the almost continuous daylight of the very short summers.

Due to the inhospitable conditions, animal life is also limited, although more numerous in summer. In addition to insects (midges, mosquitoes, etc.) and migratory birds, there are wolves, arctic foxes, lemmings, hares, snowy owls and the herbivorous reindeer in Europe and caribou in northern America. Polar bears occur at the coast.

In addition to this arctic tundra, there is also *alpine tundra* which is found on the highest mountain tops and is therefore widely spread. However, conditions differ because of daylight throughout the year and plant growth in the tropical alpine tundra also occurs all year round.

unconformity is a break in the deposition of SEDIMENTARY ROCKS representing a gap in the geological record. The unconformity is the junction between younger rocks (above) and older and is formed by a succession of rocks being pushed and possibly folded, eroded and then submerged again so that new sediment is deposited on the older rocks. Usually the rocks above and beneath the unconformity lie at different angles.

It is possible, however, for an unconformity to be represented by differing beds with the same orientation (*disconformity*), or simply by a surface that indicates non-deposition but shows no other apparent breaks, or by sediments being deposited on an igneous intrusion that has been eroded.

volcano a natural vent or opening in the Earth's crust that is connected by a pipe, or *conduit*, to a chamber at a depth that contains MAGMA. Through this pipe (usually called a *vent*) may be ejected LAVA, volcanic gases, steam and ash, and it is the amount of gas held in the lava, and the way in which it is released on reaching the surface, that determines the type of *eruption*.

Volcanoes may be *active*, i.e. actually erupting whether just clouds of ash and steam or lava; *extinct*, i.e. the activity ceased a long time ago; or *dormant*. Dormant volcanoes have often in the past been thought to be extinct, only to erupt again with startling ferocity.

Volcanoes can be described by the type of eruption that is named after a particular volcano that exhibits a specific eruption pattern. These are:

Hawaiian	violent eruptions with viscous lava and *nuées ardentes**
Peléean	moderate eruptions, small explosions and lava of average viscosity
Strombolian	very explosive after a dormant period with ash/gas clouds and gas filled lava
Vesuvian	very explosive with *pyroclastics*** ejected in a column up to 50 kg high producing thick airfall deposits
Plinian	outpouring of fluid lava and little explosive activity

* **nuées ardentes**: an old term meaning an incandescent ash flow that moves
rapidly.
** **pyroclastic**: volcanic rocks formed from broken fragments, e.g. bombs,
pumice, ash and cinders

Volcanoes of the Hawaiian type are also called *shield* volcanoes. The sides of the volcanoes are almost flat because of the rapid flow of the lava. *Composite* volcanoes show greater angles of slope because of a build-up of lava and pyroclastic material. Both shield and composite types are also called *central type* because the supply comes from a central vent, as opposed to *fissure* volcanoes, which erupt through splits where the crust is under tension.

Active volcanoes occur in belts associated with the tectonic plates (*see* PLATE TECTONICS) with about 80% of the active sub-aerial volcanoes at destructive plate margins, 15% at constructive plate margins and the remainder within plates. Most submarine volcanism is at constructive plate margins.

The environmental effect of volcanoes can be very significant, whether it be the enormous amounts of ash ejected into the atmosphere or the consequences of lava flows consuming the countryside. At the time of eruption, volcanic materials are often over 1000°C, hence flows either burn, push over or cover whatever they meet.

Over 500 volcanoes have been active in historic times but only about 50 erupt each year, often on a very small scale.

water table the level below which water saturates the spaces in the ground; the top of the zone where groundwater saturates permeable rocks. It is where atmospheric pressure is equalled by the pressure in the groundwater. The position (*elevation*) of the water table varies with the amount of rainfall, etc, loss through evaporation and transpiration from vegetation, and percolations through the soil. A spring or seepage occurs when, because of geological conditions, the water table rises above ground level (*see also* AQUIFER).

weather the combined effect of atmospheric pressure, temperature, sunshine, cloud, humidity, wind and the amount of precipitation which together make up the weather for a certain place over a particular (usually short) time period. The weather varies enormously around the Earth but some countries have a stable weather pattern while Britain has a changeable one because it is at a location where many different air masses meet. The surface at which two air masses with different meteorological properties meet is called a *front*.

A *warm front* occurs in a depression, between warm air moving over cold air, and it heralds drizzle followed by heavy rain that then gives way to rising temperatures. A *cold front* is the leading edge of a cold air mass, which moves under warm air, forcing the latter to rise. The result is a fall in temperature, with rainfall passing behind the front.

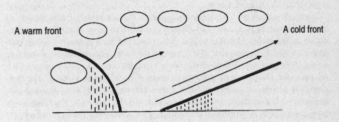

A warm front   A cold front

weathering is a combination of chemical and physical processes on the surface of the Earth, or very near to it, that breaks down rocks and minerals. Weathering takes various forms and can be divided into mechanical, chemical and organic:

mechanical
freeze-thaw action   alternate freezing and thawing of water in cracks, producing widening or break-up
exfoliation   peeling off in thin rock layers (like onion skin)
disintegration   into grains

chemical
carbonation   the reaction of weak carbonic acid (H_2CO_3) with the rock.
hydrolysis   combination of water with minerals to form insoluble residues (e.g. clay, minerals).
oxidation and *reduction*.

organic

breakdown by flora and fauna, e.g. burrowing animals, tree roots, and the release of *organic acids* from decomposed plants that react with minerals.

These weathering processes together produce a layer of material that may then be moved by processes of EROSION.

wind a generally horizontal or near-horizontal movement of air caused by changes in atmospheric pressure in which air normally moves from areas of high to low pressure. Wind speed is greater when the ISOBARS (lines joining points at the same pressure) are closely packed on weather maps, and the *Beaufort scale* provides a systematic guide to windspeed. Because of the Earth's rotation and the effect of the Coriolis force (*see* TIDES), air in the northern hemisphere flows clockwise around a high pressure area and anticlockwise around a low.

The *trade winds* play an important part in the atmospheric circulation of the Earth, and they are mainly easterly winds that blow from the subtropics to the equator. The *westerlies* flow from the high pressure of the subtropics to the low pressure of the temperate zone. The westerlies form one of the strongest wind flows, and their strength increases with height (*see* JET STREAM). Depressions are most common in this wind system. The *doldrums* is a zone of calms or light winds around the equator, applied particularly to the oceans, with obvious links to the time when sailing ships were becalmed. Also linked to sailing are the *Roaring Forties*, which are westerlies in the southern hemisphere where they tend to be stronger. However, the supposed link of trade winds with early travel on the sea is incorrect – their origin is from the Latin word meaning 'constant'.

In addition to its destructive power, wind provides an additional hazard when combined with cold. *Wind chill* is the effect wind has in lowering apparent temperatures through increasing heat loss from the body. For example, in calm conditions at 10°F there is little danger for someone properly clothed, but if the wind speed is 25 mph, then the wind chill creates an equivalent temperature of -29°F, which is potentially harmful.

Natural History

This section of *The Pocket Encyclopedia* details the different classes and groups of the animal and plant kingdom, describing the common characteristics by which they are classified. The general terms that are used to describe the natural world are also defined and the cross-references, in SMALL CAPITALS, will enable you to relate these terms to the classes and groups of species.

acid rain contains a high concentration of dissolved chemical pollutants such as sulphur and nitrogen oxides. The pollutants arise as gases, given off mainly by the burning of fossil fuels (coal and oil) by industries, vehicles and power stations. The wind may carry the acid gases a long way from their source, but eventually they dissolve in water and fall elsewhere as acid rain. Both the gases and the acid rain cause damage to plant and animal life and lead to an increase in the acidity of water sources such as lakes and rivers. This may cause long-term deterioration in the natural environment affecting numerous plants, animals and micro-organisms.

Actinozoa or **Anthozoa** includes the sea pens, sea pansies, sea feathers, sea fans, sea anemones and corals. It is a class of small marine animals belonging to the Phylum *Coelenterata* (CNIDARIA) which also includes jellyfish and hydras. They are very simple animals with a circular body plan (known as *radial symmetry*) in the form of a structure called a *polyp*. A polyp is a small cylinder attached to an underlying surface such as a rock, the free end usually having a ring of tentacles for feeding. The polyps may exist alone or in colonies, as with many of the corals. Corals have hard external skeletons (exoskeletons) made of calcium carbonate, which are often delicately shaped and coloured. Other animals in this group have structures forming a simple internal skeleton.

A sea anenome

adaptation a feature or characteristic of an organism that has evolved under the processes of natural selection. It enables the organism to exploit a particular aspect of its environment more efficiently. All organisms have adaptations enabling them to survive in their habitat.

Familiar adaptations include the shape and size of birds' beaks and animals' teeth (according to what they eat); the powerful, digging front legs and claws in such burrowing animals as moles and flippers in swimming animals such as seals. However, if they become too specialised, they may not be able to survive a sudden change (e.g. in climate) and may become extinct. There are fears for the survival of the panda, which is highly specialised and adapted in terms of its habitat and diet (because this consists solely of bamboo shoots).

The illustration below shows how the human foot has adapted for an upright stance whereas the chimpanzee foot has adapted for gripping and climbing.

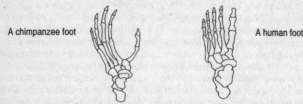

A chimpanzee foot   A human foot

adaptive radiation the separation of species through evolutionary process and natural selection (*see* **ST**: DARWIN and NATURAL SELECTION) into many descendant species which are able to exploit a variety of different habitats. An example is the vast numbers of different amphibians which have evolved since their early ancestors moved on to land.

Agnatha lampreys and hagfishes (order Cyclostomata) belong to the vertebrate class called Agnatha. These are aquatic, eel-like animals belonging to a very ancient group. Their characteristic feature is a lack of jaws and they have a sucking mouth with horny teeth. They are scavengers or parasites on larger fish.

alga the common name for a simple water plant which lacks roots, stems and leaves but is able to PHOTOSYNTHESIZE. *Algae* range in size from single cells to plants many metres in length.

amoeba *see* PROTOZOAN.

Amphibia salamanders, newts, frogs and toads, are members of this vertebrate class. Amphibians were the first vertebrates to colonise the land about 370 million years ago. The modern ones tend to be highly specialised and not typical of their fossil ancestors, and many of their characteristics are adaptations for life on land. However, most have to return to water to breed and the young (larvae – *see* ST: LARVA and METAMORPHOSIS) are aquatic and breathe through gills. In order to become adults they undergo METAMORPHOSIS. Adult amphibians respire through nostrils that are linked by a passage to the roof of the mouth, and also through their skin which is kept moist.

A common frog

anaconda *see* SQUAMATA.

Angiospermae a class of flowering plants. These are the most complex and highly developed plants and this enables them to live in a great many different habitats as they have evolved various specialisations. The female reproductive cell or gamete is formed within a structure called an *ovule*, itself protected by a closed sheath known as the *carpel*. After fertilisation, the ovule develops into a seed and seeds may be contained by fruits, (*see* also FLOWERS and PLANTS).

Annelida ragworms (class Polychaeta), earthworms (class Oligochaeta) and leeches (class Hirudinea) belong to the invertebrate phylum Annelida. These familiar animals have an outer layer or cuticle usually composed of *collagen*-like proteins. The body is cylindrical in shape and divided into segments each bearing stiff bristles (*chaetae*) made of chitin (a hydrocarbon with nitrogen). The body cavity is called the *coelom* and is fluid filled. It provides a firm base (*hydrostatic skeleton*), against which muscles present in the body wall can contract to cause movement. A simple nervous system (*see* ST: NERVOUS SYSTEM) consisting of a pair of *nerve cords* with *ganglia* (swellings) is present. Some worms live in the soil and leaf litter whereas others inhabit marine or freshwater habitats. Earthworms are a vital part of the cycle of decay, eating soil which passes through the gut, food substances being absorbed along the way. Waste material passes out of the body as *castings*. The activity of earthworms helps to till and aerate the soil and the castings improve the texture. Hence they are of great value to farmers, gardeners and horticulturists.

apes *see* **primates**

Arachnida spiders, scorpions, mites, ticks, king crabs, harvestmen, etc. all belong to this class of INVERTEBRATES called Arachnida.

Some animals in this group, especially the spiders, are very familiar to, and hold a special fascination for man. Most arachnids are terrestrial animals and, unlike insects, they have a head and thorax (middle region of the body) which are not divided from one another. These are formed from eight segments and make up a structure called the *prosoma*. The rest of the body is made up of 13 segments and is called the *opithosoma*. In the head region there are two pairs of projections or *appendages*. The first are called *chelicerae* and are adapted for piercing and grasping prey as most arachnids are carnivorous. The second pair are called the *pedipalps* and these can be specialised to perform a variety of different functions as sense organs, for copulation or noise production. Behind these are four pairs of walking legs and on the *opithosoma*, there may be other specialised appendages, e.g. for silk spinning (spinnerets in spiders) or for injecting poison (as with scorpions). Ticks and mites are parasites on other animals but most arachnids are free-living.

A spider

pedipalps

opithosoma

Arthropoda the largest phylum of INVERTEBRATE animals containing over one million known species which occupy many different habitats. They are often highly specialised and include such classes as the Crustacea (lobsters, crabs, shrimps), Insecta (insects), Arachnida (spiders, mites, scorpions) and Myriapoda (millipedes and centipedes).

Artiodactyla is a mammalian order that includes cattle, camels, hippopotamuses, pigs, deer, antelope, goats, sheep and llamas. These animals are even-toed with the third and fourth toes equally developed to support the whole weight of the body. They are one order of mammals which make up the group commonly called the Ungulates, the other being the Perissodactyla (horses, tapirs, rhinoceros and zebra).

Aves (birds) a *class* of VERTEBRATES which evolved from flying reptiles and still show some features of their ancestry. The most notable of these is the production of reptilian-like eggs and the presence of scales on the legs. Typically, the body of a bird is highly modified for flight with a lighter skeleton than that of other vertebrates. Some organs may even be absent to reduce weight, e.g. females possess only one ovary. The front limbs are developed as wings which are aerodynamically specialised for flight. Birds are covered with feathers and those of the wings are modified for flight while others provide insulation. The breastbone of the skeleton is well developed and has a structure called a *keel* to which the large flight muscles are attached. Birds lack teeth but grind up food in a special part of the gut called the *gizzard*. The jaws are developed to form a beak or bill and a great many different sizes and shapes occur enabling birds to exploit numerous different habitats and types of food.

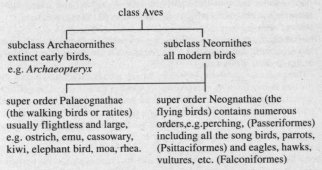

class Aves

subclass Archaeornithes
extinct early birds,
e.g. *Archaeopteryx*

subclass Neornithes
all modern birds

super order Palaeognathae
(the walking birds or ratites)
usually flightless and large,
e.g. ostrich, emu, cassowary,
kiwi, elephant bird, moa, rhea.

super order Neognathae (the
flying birds) contains numerous
orders,e.g.perching, (Passeriformes)
including all the song birds, parrots,
(Psittaciformes) and eagles, hawks,
vultures, etc. (Falconiformes)

Bacillariophyta is the division to which *diatoms*, a type of ALGAE, belong. They are simple, single-celled plants, which sometimes form chains or colonies, and live in both marine and fresh water environments. They are vital ORGANISMS in the PLANKTON and, since they PHOTOSYNTHESIZE, form the basis of FOOD CHAINS. They have beautiful and unique glassy cell walls made of silica and are important fossils. Enormous accumulations of their cell walls are mined as *diatomaceous earth* (or kieselguhr) which has various uses in industry. Planktonic diatoms store food as oil and this has contributed to the petroleum reserves that are extracted and used today.

barrier reef a reef of coral built up in a line running parallel to the shore but at some distance from it, so as to create a lagoon. A good example is the Great Barrier Reef, Australia which is almost 2000 km (1250 miles) long. A barrier reef usually provides a rich and varied habitat and is home to many different kinds of plants and animals.

beaver *see* RODENTIA.

benthos the benthos consists of all the plants and animals living in or on the bottom of the sea, lake or a river. The organisms are described as *benthic* and they may burrow, crawl or remain attached.

biome a geographical area that is characterised by particular ECOSYSTEMS of plants, animals and micro-organisms. It is created by and related to climate and is usually mainly distinguished by the form of vegetation it supports. Examples of biomes are desert, savanna, tropical forest, chaparral (scrubland), temperate grassland, temperate deciduous forest, taiga (coniferous or boreal forest) and tundra.

biosphere the region of the Earth's surface (both land and water) and its immediate atmosphere, which can support any living organism.

birds *see* AVES.

Bivalvia many species of shellfish, e.g. mussels, oysters, scallops, clams and razorshells belong to this class and are called bivalves (class Bivalvia) of the phylum Mollusca.

These animals are characterised by having a body enclosed within a shell divided into two halves (bivalve shell) which is flattened and hinged along the mid-line. They have a smaller head than that of most other molluscs and usually do not move around, living on the bottom of lakes or the sea. However, more mobile kinds such as scallops occur and also burrowing ones such as the shipworm and razorshell.

boa *see* SQUAMATA.

bony fishes most fish have a bony skeleton containing calcium phosphate and a body covered with overlapping scales. These are the bony fishes or class Osteichthyes and include many familiar freshwater and marine species. They have jaws (compare AGNATHA), gills covered by a protective flap called the *operculum* and often possess an air sac called a *swim bladder* for buoyancy. They usually lay large numbers of eggs which are fertilised externally and examples include cod, haddock, salmon, trout and sticklebacks.

Brachiopoda lampshells are an ancient group of marine animals belonging to the phylum Brachiopoda. Along with two other phyla, they possess a special structure called a lophophore which is used for feeding and RESPIRATION. They have a bivalve shell and a stalk, known as a peduncle, which attaches the animal to the surface on which it lives. Brachiopods are very important INDEX FOSSILS and one kind, *Lingula* has survived to the present day little changed from the Ordovician geological period, 500–440 million years ago.

Lingula

brackish water occurs in estuaries (*see* ESTUARY) and is intermediate in saltiness between sea and fresh water.

Bryophyta is the division of the plant kingdom to which mosses belong. These simple plants commonly thrive in shady, wet conditions and have a waxy, outer layer (*cuticle*) which helps to prevent them from drying out. Mosses lack true roots but may be attached to a surface by hairs (*rhizoids*) or use other plants for support. The hornworts and liverworts are other simple plants which are commonly included in the Bryophyta, although this is now considered to be scientifically incorrect. The three types, although sharing several common features, are probably not closely related.

butterflies *see* LEPIDOPTERA.

camels *see* ARTIODACTYLA.

camouflage a kind of colour pattern or body shape which helps to disguise an animal and enable it to blend into its background. This is useful for both predators and prey animals and can be seen in many different species from invertebrates to large MAMMALS. Patterns of camouflage have evolved through the processes of natural selection (*see* DARWIN) and may be quite intricate and complex.

Examples include moths patterned to look like bark or possessing false eye spots, preying mantis, many fishes and animals such as tiger and zebra.

capybara *see* RODENT.

Carnivora an order of mammals which are largely flesh-eaters, including both predators and carrion eaters and those which combine the two. Many of these animals show adaptations of the jaws and teeth. They possess a powerful bite and large piercing and shearing teeth. They often have retractile claws and two sub-orders are recognised, the toe-footed carnivores (*Fissipedia*) such as wolves, dogs, cats, raccoons, weasels and badgers, and the fin-footed carnivores (*Pinnepedia*), e.g. walruses, sea lions and seals.

carnivorous plants there are about 400 different species of carnivorous plants that are usually insectivorous. They often grow in poor conditions which would not normally supply enough minerals and nourishment.

Hence they are specially adapted to attract, trap and digest mainly insect prey in ingenious and highly effective ways. For example, *Sundews* secrete a sticky substance on the leaves which holds insects fast. *Pitcher plants* have modified leaves forming a water-filled trap with smooth sides into which an insect falls and drowns. *Venus fly traps* have hinged leaves with spines at the edges which snap shut over an insect. Once an insect (or other small prey) is caught, these carnivorous plants release digestive EN-ZYMES and eventually dissolved food substances are absorbed.

The pitcher plant

cartilaginous fishes a class of fishes called the Chondrichthyes which are highly specialised, having a skeleton composed entirely of CARTILAGE. The most familiar examples are the *rays*, *sharks* and *skates* (of the sub-class Elasmobranchii) and also the ratfish, sub-class Holocephali (Chimeras).

cats *see* CARNIVORA.

caterpillars *see* LEPIDOPTERA.

cattle *see* ARTIODACTYLA.

centipede *see* MYRIAPODA.

Cephalopoda nautilus, squids, cuttlefish, octopuses and the (extinct) fossil ammonites belong to this class. The most advanced group in the phylum Mollusca.

The ammonites had well-developed spiral shells with the animal living inside the last chamber, but *Nautilus* is the only living species that has this structure. In the modern species the shell is much reduced as in the squids, or is inside the body as in cuttlefish or absent altogether as in octopuses. Cephalopods are mainly marine predators, with a well-developed head surrounded by a ring of tentacles used to seize their prey. They swim by jet propulsion – expelling water from the body using muscular action. They have complicated eyes and excellent vision and a well-developed nervous system which makes them the most intelligent invertebrate animals. Cuttlefish are able to show remarkable colour changes possibly as a means of communication.

Cestoda a class of the phylum Platyhelminthes. These are the parasitic tapeworms which live inside the gut of a vertebrate. They have a head with suckers and hooks which attache the animal to the intestinal lining of its host. Behind the head there is a series of sacs (called *proglottids*) which give the appearance of segments. Each of these has male and female sex organs and these animals are *hermaphrodite*. The outer surface is protected from the digestive juices of the host's gut by a tough, outer CUTICLE. Tapeworms do not have a gut but dissolved food substances are absorbed over the whole body surface. The life cycle requires both a primary and secondary host. In one tapeworm that affects humans *Taenia saginata*, the beef tapeworm, the primary host containing the adult animal is man and the secondary hosts are cattle. Human beings are infected by eating poorly cooked meat containing cysts (immature worms with a protective shell) which develop into adults once they have been eaten.

The sucker head of the tapeworm   Cross-section of the body

Cetacea an order of marine mammals comprising the dolphins and whales. They are characterised by having forelimbs developed as *flippers*, and a powerful, flattened tail with two *flukes*, and a dorsal fin. These animals are excellent swimmers and have a thick layer of blubber (fat) beneath a nearly hairless skin serving as insulation and a food store. Air is drawn into the lungs through a blowhole on the upper surface and can be shut off when the animal dives. Dolphins, killer whales and toothed whales are predators belonging to the sub-order *Odontocetti*. Many of the great whales, e.g. the blue whale, are plankton-feeders belonging to the sub-order *Mysticetti*. They filter vast quantities of sea water through whalebone plates in order to extract their food. The blue whale is the largest known living animal, in excess of 150 tonnes in weight and 30 metres (100 feet) in length.

chameleon *see* SQUAMATA.

Chelonia an order of the class Reptilia (see REPTILE) comprising the turtles, terrapins and tortoises. The body of these animals is encased in a bony shell covered by horny plates. Both marine and land-dwelling species occur and they have jaws developed as horny beaks without teeth. These are a very ancient group of reptiles apparently little changed throughout their evolutionary history.

chimera *see* CARTILAGINOUS FISHES.

Chiroptera bats belong to the mammalian order Chiroptera, the main characteristic of which is flight. They have membrane-like wings spread between elongated forelimbs and fingers and the hind limbs and, occasionally, the tail. Most bats are nocturnal insect-eaters, catching their prey on the wing. They have large ears adapted for ECHO LOCATION by means of which they locate prey and sense their surroundings. Some are nectar-feeders, others eat fruit and *vampire* bats suck blood.

Chlorophyta green algae, belonging to the division Chlorophyta are the largest and most varied group of algae, possessing chlorophyll and able to photosynthesise. They are mainly aquatic in both marine and freshwater but are able to live on land in damp conditions. A well-known type is *Spirogyra*.

Cnidaria hydras, jellyfish and sea anemones and corals belong to the phylum Cnidaria (or *Coelenterata*). These simple aquatic invertebrates have two body forms, an attached stalk called a *polyp* and a free-swimming bell called a *medusa*. Depending upon the species, one or other body form may predominate or one may succeed another in what is known as an 'alternation of generations'. These animals are carnivorous, with stinging cells which immobilise their prey, and tentacles around the 'mouth.' (*see* ACTINOZOA and HYDROZOA).

cobra *see* SQUAMATA.

cockroach *see* ORTHOPTERA.

coelacanth a type of bony fish, belonging to the order Coelacanthiformes, sub-order Crossypterygii, the flesh-finned fishes. All were thought to be extinct but a living representative was discovered in 1938. Living coelacanths are members of the genus *Latimeria* and have a characteristic three-lobed tail fin. They are large fish living at great depths on the floor of the Indian Ocean and 'walk' on their crutch-like pectoral fins. Coelacanths give birth to live young and do not possess lungs. They are a remnant of numerous kinds of lobe-finned fishes that were present in the *Devonian* geological period (408–360 million years ago). However, these extinct forms were freshwater animals with lungs and some were the ancestors of the amphibians.

Coleoptera beetles and weevils belong to this vast order (the largest in the animal kingdom) of the class Insecta, and there are about 500,000 known species. They are found in a great number of different habitats, some feeding on vegetation, others on decaying material and the rest are predatory and carnivorous. They have two pairs of wings but the first are protective sheaths (called *elytra*) which are hard and, when folded, meet precisely in a line along the middle of the back. They protect the delicate, membranous hindwings which are used for flying (but are reduced or not present in other species). The mouth parts are often enlarged for biting, and both young (larvae) and adult beetles of certain species can be serious economic pests of crops, timber and stored food. Many beetles are beautifully coloured and patterned.

colony a group of individuals of the same species, living together and to some extent dependent on one another. In some cases the individuals may actually be joined, as in corals, and function as one unit. In others, e.g. social insets such as bees and ants, they are separate individuals but have a complex organisation with specialised functions.

commensalism *see* SYMBIOSIS.

conservation means managing the environment in such a way as to preserve the natural resources of plants, animals and minerals etc. and to minimise the impact of man. The natural environment is in a constant state of change, and species become extinct and landscapes and climate alters, but this is usually over a long period of time. Man's activities are often devastating and whole ECOSYSTEMS can be lost very rapidly (e.g. clearance of the tropical rainforest). The environment which is left after such activities is usually significantly poorer and man's gains tend to be short-lived. Hence conservation involves planning ahead, preservation, restoration and reconstruction all the while minimising damage. This may be on a small scale or global, and conservation is now recognised to be of vital importance to the survival and quality of life of human beings as well as other plants and animals.

Copepoda tiny marine and freshwater invertebrate animals which belong to this large sub-class of the class Crustacea. They are all between 0.5–2mm long and do not have a shell (carapace) or compound eyes. They have five or six pairs of swimming legs and are very important species in the PLANKTON. Some may be free-living filter feeders while others (e.g. the fish louse) are parasitic. A well-known freshwater type has one simple eye (ocellus) in the mid-line and is called *Cyclops*.

corals *see* ACTINOZOA.

cricket *see* ORTHOPTERA.

Crustacea lobsters, crayfish, crabs, shrimps, pill bugs, prawns, barnacles, water fleas and COPEPODS belong to this class of the phylum Arthropoda. They have a well-defined head and the body (thorax and abdomen) is divided into segments although these may not be obvious. Various projections called appendages are used for a variety of different purposes, e.g. swimming, feeding and as gills for RESPIRATION.

A freshwater shrimp

cyanobacteria the commonly-named 'blue-green algae' which are now regarded as bacteria. They are *procaryotic* organisms and may be single-celled or occur in colonies or as filaments. They are found in all aquatic environments and are often very specialised, growing, for example in hot springs. They possess the ability to photosynthesise and some are able to trap nitrogen and are important in soil fertility. Some kinds occur in the PLANKTON, others form *symbiotic* (SYMBIOSIS) relationships with other organisms (e.g. lichens). Blooms of some species in freshwater lakes which have been enriched with agricultural fertilizers can be a problem, as toxins are produced that are lethal to fish and other animals.

cyclostomata *see* AGNATHA.

Decapoda prawns, shrimps, lobsters and crabs belong to this order of the class Crustacea (*see* CRUSTACEA). These animals possess five pairs of walking legs, the first pair of which (in the crawling varieties) are modified to form powerful pincers. The others are used for feeding or swimming.

decomposers are organisms that break down dead organic matter such as plants, animals and animal waste in order to obtain energy, leaving behind simple organic or inorganic waste. Carbon dioxide is produced and heat is released during decomposition and the main organisms involved are bacteria and fungi but also earthworms (*see* ANNELIDA) and other INVERTEBRATES.

deforestation the felling and removal of trees from an area of natural forest which usually has a devastating effect on the environment. It is carried out to provide wood for fuel (for local people) or for the timber trade, or to clear land for agriculture. Often the soil is very low in minerals and its fertility is soon exhausted. On slopes the soil can be washed away by water gushing down, leading to erosion and landslides. The end result of deforestation can be the creation of near-desert conditions.

deer *see* ARTIODACTYLA.

diatoms *see* BACILLARIOPHYTA.

dinosaurs were a large group of reptiles that flourished some 190 to 65 million years ago during the *Jurassic* and *Cretaceous* geological periods (*see*

GEOLOGICAL TIMESCALE). They showed a tremendous variety of body shape and size and included flying species. It was once thought that they were all slow, cold-blooded creatures but now scientists believe that many were fast-moving and able to keep their bodies warm by metabolic activities.

The climate in the Cretaceous period changed considerably. For reasons that are still not absolutely clear, the vast majority of the dinosaurs disappeared in a mass extinction occurring over 5 to 10 million years at the end of the Cretaceous.

Diptera flies belong to this large insect order which contains about 80,000 species. These are called the true or two-winged flies but the back pair are modified to form knobs (*halteres*) used for balance. The mouth of a fly is adapted to pierce, lap or suck and they feed on sap, nectar and rotting organic matter. Some, e.g. mosquitoes, feed on blood. The LARVA (maggot) eventually forms a pupa and becomes an adult through 'metamorphosis.

The common house fly

dog *see* CARNIVORA.

dolphin *see* CETACEA.

earthworms *see* ANNELIDA.

Echinodermata starfish, brittle stars, sea urchins, sea cucumbers, sea lilies and sea daisies belong to the phylum Echinodermata. These marine invertebrates have existed for a very long time as fossil forms have been found in rocks 500 million years old. They commonly have five arms radiating from a central disc which is the body. The arms bear many tiny tube feet which act like suction pads and are used for movement, feeding and respiration. They have an external shell of plates containing calcium often with bumps or spines and some are able to regenerate lost arms.

echo location the use by animals of high-pitched pulses of sound which bounce off surrounding objects allowing the location of these to be determined. Nocturnal animals such as bats, and aquatic mammals like dolphins produce these sounds and echo location enables them to make sense of their environment and to locate prey.

ecology this is the study of the relationship between plants and animals and their environment. Ecology (also known as *bionomics*) is concerned with, for example, predator-prey relationships, population changes (in the species present) and competition between species.

ecosystem all the biological life and non-biological components (e.g. minerals in the soil) within an area and the inter-reactions and relationships between them all. Thus an ecosystem includes all the organisms in a community and the geology, chemistry and climate and it may be a lake, forest, region of tundra, etc. Various cycles operate within an ecosystem. Energy, in the form of sunlight, is converted to chemical energy by green plants and is then consumed by animals and released as heat. Food substances, or nutrients, are returned to the cycle as wastes.

Ectoprocta *see* MOSS ANIMAL.

Elasmobranchii *see* CARTILAGINOUS FISHES.

elephant *see* PROBOSCIDEA.

environment the area which surrounds and supports an organism, including all the other living creatures which share the area as well as all the inorganic elements (e.g. minerals contained in the soil).

epiphyte a plant that grows up on another plant purely for support and which is not rooted in the ground. The commonest examples are *mosses*, *lichens* and some tropical orchids.

estuary a coastal inlet that is affected by marine tides and freshwater in the form of a river draining from the land. An estuary is usually a drowned valley created by a rise in sea level after the last ICE AGE. Estuaries usually contain a lot of sediment (sand, silt, etc.) washed from the land and the tidal currents may produce channels, sandbanks and sand waves. Organisms which inhabit an estuary are adapted to cope with the changes in the *salinity* (saltiness) of the water. They often provide rich feeding grounds especially for many birds, e.g. waders, ducks and geese.

eutherian mammals which have a placenta with which to nourish their embryos within the womb of the mother, belong to the sub-class Eutheria.

eutrophic a body of water, usually a lake or slow-moving river, which is over-rich in nitrogen and phosphorus due to contamination by agricultural fertilisers or sewage. This leads to rapid growth of algae (*algal blooms*) which uses up the oxygen available to other species due to bacteria decomposing dead algae. The final outcome is the death of fish and other organisms. The process is known as *eutrophication*.

fanworm *see* POLYCHAETA.

Foraminifera a phylum of very small marine animals (Protozoans) which have hard shells made of calcium carbonate or silica and are important in the fossil record. Sedimentary rocks such as chalk may contain many foraminiferan fossils and modern species are often found in large number on the ocean floor.

Examples of Formanifera chamber shapes

fossil *see* **GG.**

frog *see* AMPHIBIA.

fungus any one of a number of kinds of simple plants without the photosynthetic pigment CHLOROPHYLL. Fungi cause decay in fabrics, timber and food
and diseases in some plants and animals. They may be single-celled or
form strands called filaments and are used in BIOTECHNOLOGY in baking,
brewing and to make antibiotics.

Gastropoda invertebrate animals, typically (but not always) with a shell
such as the limpets, whelks, conches, snails and slugs belonging to this
class of the phylum Mollusca. They have a large muscular foot used for
movement (hence *gastropod*), a distinct head with eyes and a coiled or
twisted shell. Most are marine but some live in freshwater and others are
adapted for life on land.

Simplified and schematic structure of a gastropod

tentacles
anus
gill
mouth

shell
heart
stomach
operculum
(lid of shell)
foot

gila monster *see* SQUAMATA.

goats *see* ARTIODACTYLA.

grasshopper *see* ORTHOPTERA.

greenhouse effect and global warming normally the solar radiation from
the sun is absorbed by the Earth's surface and re-emitted as INFRARED radiation. However, this radiation can become trapped in the Earth's atmosphere by carbon dioxide, water vapour, clouds and ozone causing a heating up and consequent rise in the global temperature. Due to the activities
of man, the amount of CO_2 in the atmosphere is rising caused, for example, by the clearance of forests (trees trap CO_2) and the burning of fossil

fuels. It has been estimated that the global temperature could rise by between 1.5°C and 4.5°C over the next 50 years. This would cause significant melting of the polar ice caps and a consequent rise in sea level causing widespread flooding of coastal areas throughout the world.

growth rings the rings seen if you cut through the woody stem of a plant, for example, the trunk of a tree. Each ring represents one year's growth and by counting the number of rings, the age of the tree can be discovered. Also, each ring is different and comparison of dead and living trees provides a dating method (and information about past climates) for periods within the past eight thousand years. This is known as DENDROCHRONOLOGY.

Gymnospermae conifers, cycads and ginkgos are seed plants belonging to this class (or subdivision) of the division Spermatophyta. They have an ancient history as fossils and are found in rocks dating back to the Devonian geological period (408–360 million years ago). They produce *naked seeds* (hence *gymnosperm*) which are not enclosed by a protective sheath (*carpel*). *Compare* ANGIOSPERMAE.

habitat the place where a plant or animal normally lives, e.g. river, pond, seashore.

hagfish *see* AGNATHA.

halophyte a plant that can tolerate a high level of salt in the soil. Such conditions occur in salt marshes, tidal river estuaries (and on motorway verges and central reservations) and a typical species is rice grass (*Spartina*).

hedgehogs *see* INSECTIVORA.

Hemiptera bugs belong to this order of the class Insecta. This is a very large group and includes leaf hoppers, scale insects, bed bugs, aphids, cicadas and water boatmen. The typical body shape is a flattened oval with two pairs of wings folded flat down on the back of the resting insect. Their mouths are tubes adapted for piercing and sucking; some are herbivorous, others carnivorous and yet others parasitic. Some are serious agricultural pests transmitting plant diseases through feeding on sap.

herbaceous (*herb-like*) describing a plant with little or no woody stem in which all the green parts die back at the end of each season. Either the whole plant dies (having produced and dispersed seeds) as in *annuals*, or parts of the plant (roots) survive beneath the ground and grow up again the following year, as in *perennials*.

hibernation an adaptation seen in some animals in which a sleep-like state occurs that enables them to survive the cold winter months when food is scarce. Some marked changes occur, notably a drop in body temperature to about 1°C above the surrounding air, and a slowing of the pulse and metabolic rate to about 1% of normal. In this state the animal's energy requirements are reduced and it uses up stored body fat. Bears, bats, hedgehogs, some fish, amphibians and reptiles are examples of animals that hibernate.

hippopotamus *see* ARTIODACTYLA.

holocephali *see* CARTILAGINOUS FISHES.

homeothermy (homiothermy) means warm-bloodedness and is the ability of an animal to keep up a constant body temperature, independent of the heat or cold of its environment. It is a typical feature of birds and mammals and various metabolic processes are involved (*see also* POIKILOTHERMY).

homing the ability of animals to find their way home, especially referring to birds. Many bird species fly thousands of miles over land and sea during annual migrations to return to the same area year by year. It is thought that they navigate by means of the sun and stars and by using magnetic fields.

hominid a member of the primate family Hominidae, which includes modern man as well as fossil hominids that may have evolved around 3.5 million years ago. All belong to the genus Homo. Their main physical characteristic is the ability to walk upright (known as *bipedalism*), and there are also changes in the shape of the skull and teeth compared to those of other primates. They have (or had) complex social and cultural behaviour patterns.

horse *see* PERISSODACTYLA.

human *see* HOMINID.

humus material that makes up the organic part of soil being formed from decayed plant and animal remains. It has a characteristic dark colour and its composition varies according to the amount and type of material present. It holds water (and it forms a physical state known as a COLLOID), which can then be used by growing plants and helps to prevent the loss of minerals from the soil by leaching. Hence it is very important in determining soil fertility. Humus may be more ACIDIC (*mor*), as in the soil of coniferous forests, or ALKALINE (*mull*), as found in the soil of deciduous woodlands and grasslands. Humus contains numerous MICRO-ORGANISMS and INVERTEBRATE animals, and its presence is of obvious economic importance in the cultivation of food crops.

Hydrozoa corals known as millepore corals, hydras and such animals as the Portuguese man-of-war (*Physalia*) and *Vellela* belong to this class of the phylum Cnidaria. These are mostly marine invertebrates although freshwater types (e.g. *Hydra*) do occur. Many are colonial so that what appears to be a single animal is, in reality, made up of numerous small individuals as with *Physalia* and *Vellela*.

Physalia is a colony of dozens or perhaps hundreds of individuals. Some form the gas-filled float, others are for feeding having tentacles and a mouth, yet others are protective, possessing stinging cells and some are for reproduction.

Hymenoptera bees (*see below*), wasps, ants, sawflies and ichneumon flies belong to this order of the class Insecta.

worker bee    queen bee   drone

These insects have a narrow 'wasp waist' and usually possess wings. The mouthparts are adapted in a variety of ways, i.e. for biting, sucking or lapping. A structure called an *ovipositor* at the hind end of the body is used for egg laying. It may be adapted for piercing, sawing or stinging and is often long and looped forward.

Some are social insects living in colonies, notably the ants and some bees and wasps. Honey bees have always been an important species to man.

ichneumon fly *see* HYMENOPTERA.

iguana *see* SQUAMATA.

insecta a very important class of invertebrate animals belonging to the phylum Arthropoda, with over three quarters of a million species known to Man. They inhabit a wide variety of habitats, both on land and in water, and there are 26 orders including beetles (Coleoptera), flies (Diptera), bees and ants (Hymenoptera), butterflies (Lepidoptera), grasshoppers (Orthoptera) and dragonflies (Odonata). The body of an insect is divided into three regions known as the head, thorax and abdomen. The head often bears projections called *antennae* which are sense organs, and eyes and mouthparts adapted to feed on various food substances. The thorax bears three pairs of legs and also possibly wings and is composed of three segments. The abdomen or rear part of the body is made up of 11 segments.

insectivora moles, shrews and hedgehogs are small mammals belonging to the order Insectivora. They are mainly nocturnal, with long snouts bearing sensitive hairs which respond to touch, and tweezer-like (incisor) teeth. Their diet is mainly insects although other foods are taken and they are quite a primitive group which seem to have changed very little since their emergence in the Cretaceous geological period about 130 million years ago.

isopod woodlice, fishlice and pill bugs belong to this order Isopoda of the class Crustacea. These familiar invertebrates inhabit marine, freshwater and terrestrial environments and many are parasites. Woodlice are important DECOMPOSERS living in damp places under stones and near the soil surface.

kangaroo *see* METATHERIA.

killer whale *see* CETACEA.

king crab *see* ARACHNIDA.

koala bear *see* METATHERIA.

lamprey *see* AGNATHA.

leaf hopper *see* HEMIPTERA.

leech *see* ANNELIDA.

Lepidoptera moths and butterflies belong to the order Lepidoptera of the class Insecta. The body, wings and legs of the adult insects are covered with numerous, minute scales and the mouth parts are in the form of a long tube (called a *proboscis*) which is often held coiled beneath the head. This is uncoiled and extended to enable the insect to feed on nectar. Two large pairs of fine wings, often brightly coloured, are characteristic of this group and are held vertically in resting butterflies whereas moths hold their wings in various positions. The immature insects are called caterpillars and they have a well-defined head with chewing mouthparts and a seg-mented body, usually with each segment bearing a pair of legs. Many cat-erpillars are serious economic pests of food crops and trees and may trans-mit plant diseases. The caterpillar becomes an adult by undergoing META-MORPHOSIS via a *pupa* (or *chrysalis*). The pupa may be surrounded by a silk cocoon which the caterpillar produces from special silk glands. Others use leaves or similar material to construct a cocoon.

lichen a plant-like growth formed from two organisms which live together in a symbiotic relationship (*see* SYMBIOSIS). The two organisms involved are a FUNGUS and an ALGA. A lichen forms a distinct structure which is not similar to either partner on its own. Usually most of the plant body is made up of the fungus with the algal cells distributed within. The fungus pro-tects the algal cells and the alga provides the fungus with food through PHOTOSYNTHESIS. A lichen is typically very slow growing and varies in size from a few millimetres to several metres across. It may form a thin flat crust, be leaf-like or upright and branching. Often, lichens are found in conditions that are too cold or exposed for other plants such as in the Arc-tic and mountainous regions. Reindeer moss and Iceland moss are lichens that provide an important food source in Arctic regions. Other lichens con-tain substances that are used in dyes, perfumes, cosmetics and medicines, and poisons.

limpet *see* GASTROPODA.

littoral a term for the shallow water environment of a lake or the sea that lies close to the shore. In the sea, the littoral zone includes the tidal area between the high and low water marks. Sunlight is able to penetrate so that rooted aquatic plants can grow and usually there is a wide variety and abundance of organisms.

llama *see* ARTIODACTYLA.

lobster *see* DECAPODA.

locust *see* ORTHOPTERA.

lugworm *see* POLYCHAETA.

Malacostraca prawns, and other similar marine and freshwater animals belong to the subclass Malacostraca of the class Crustacea. They typically have compound eyes on stalks and numerous legs or appendages used for a number of different functions including swimming, and a hard shell or carapace.

mamba *see* SQUAMATA.

mammal belonging to the vertebrate class Mammalia which contains approximately 4500 species. Mammals have a number of distinguishing characteristics. They have hair; four different types of teeth (*heterodont*); small bones in the middle ear which conduct sound waves; they are warm-blooded and able to regulate their body temperature and produce sweat as a cooling mechanism. The heart is four-chambered and keeps oxygenated and deoxygenated blood separate and a layer of muscle called the diaphragm is used to fill the lungs with air. The young of mammals develop within the body of the mother and fertilisation of the egg is internal. Mammary glands produce milk with which to feed the young once they are born. Mammals possess very complex sense organs and larger brains than other vertebrates of a similar size. They are adaptable and are found in almost all habitats.

mammoth *see* PROBOSCIDEA.

Metatheria a marsupial mammal belonging to the subclass Metatheria of the class Mammalia. The distinctive feature is that the female has a pouch on the lower part of the body (abdomen) which is called the *marsupium*. Marsupials are born at a very early stage of development and crawl into the pouch and fix on to a teat. Here they complete their development until they are able to leave their mother's pouch. Familiar marsupials include kangaroos, koala bears and opossums, and these mammals are only found in Australia and America. The group evolved about 80 million years ago during the late *Cretaceous* geological period. The break up of early land masses meant that the spread of marsupials was restricted. As a result, and especially in Australia, the marsupials have adapted to occupy habits and lifestyles which might otherwise have been filled by placental mammals.

An opossum

mice *see* RODENT.

migration the seasonal movement of animals especially birds, fish and some mammals (e.g. porpoises). Climatic conditions usually trigger off migration where perhaps lower temperatures result in less food being available. Some animals, particularly birds, travel vast distances, e.g. golden plovers, fly 8000 miles from the Arctic to South America. Migrating animals seem to use three mechanisms for finding their way. Over short distances an animal moves to successive familiar landmarks (*piloting*). In *orientation*, a straight line path is taken, based upon the animal adopting a particular compass direction. *Navigation* is the most complex process because the animal must first determine its present position before taking a direction relative to that. It seems that some birds use the sun, stars (often the North star which moves very little), and an 'internal clock' which makes allowances for the relative positions of these heavenly bodies. Even when the sun is hidden by cloud, many birds are able to continue their migration quite accurately by plotting their direction with respect to the Earth's magnetic field.

millipede *see* MYRIAPODA.

millipore coral *see* HYDROZOA.

mimicry a resemblance in which one species has evolved to look like another species. Mimicry occurs in both the plant and animal kingdoms but is mainly found in insects. There are two main types of mimicry. The first is called *Batesian mimicry*, (named after the British naturalist H.W. Bates, 1825–1892). In this, one harmless species mimics the appearance of another, usually poisonous, species. A good example of this is the non-poisonous Viceroy butterfly mimicking the orange and black colour of the poisonous Monarch butterfly. Predators learn to avoid the harmful butterfly and leave the mimic alone as well because of the close resemblance. The second type is *Mullerian mimicry* (named after the German zoologist

J.F.T. Müller, 1821–1897). In this, different species which are either poisonous or just distasteful to the predator, have evolved to resemble each other. The resemblance ensures that the predator avoids all the similar looking species so all achieve protection.

mites *see* ARACHNIDA.

mole *see* INSECTIVORA.

Mollusca invertebrate animals, many with shells, such as slugs and snails (class Gastropoda), mussels and oysters (class Bivalvia) and cuttlefish, squids and octopuses (class Cephalopoda) all belong to the phylum Mollusca. Most molluscs are marine but there are freshwater and land-living varieties and it is a large group of animals including over 50,000 species.

monitor lizard *see* SQUAMATA.

monkey *see* PRIMATE.

mosquito *see* DIPTERA.

moss animals and sea mats (phylum Ectoprocta or Bryozoa). These are a group of marine invertebrate animals, many of which are important reef builders. Individual animals are tiny, (only about 1mm across) and resemble the polyps of the phylum Cnidaria. However, they form colonies which may extend for over half a metre. There are around 5000 species and many have a hard external skeleton containing calcium into which the body can be withdrawn. They have a mouth surrounded by tentacles which waft in the water and trap particles of food.

moths *see* LEPIDOPTERA.

Myriapoda centipedes (subclass Chilopoda) and millipedes (subclass Diplopoda) belong to this class of the phylum Arthropoda. These familiar invertebrate animals have a distinct head with antennae and a long segmented body. Centipedes have one pair of legs per segment and are carnivorous. Millipedes have two pairs of legs on each segment and are herbivorous.

nautilus *see* CEPHALOPODA.

nekton animals which swim in the PELAGIC (*see also* OCEANS) zone of the sea or a lake such as jellyfish, fish, turtles and whales.

nematoda roundworms are invertebrate animals belonging to the phylum Nematoda. They have a characteristically rounded body which tapers at either end and some are only about 1mm in length while others may reach 1 metre. There are numerous species and they may inhabit water, leaf litter and damp soil and also occur in plant tissues and as PARASITES in animals. They only have muscles running lengthways (longitudinally) down the body and this is unique to the roundworms. Some free living species are of vital importance as DECOMPOSERS in the soil but others are serious eco-

nomic pests attacking the roots of crop plants. Yet others are serious parasites of man and animals. Humans can be affected by over 50 nematode
species, e.g. threadworms.

neritic zone the shallow water marine zone near the shore, which extends
from low tide to a depth of approximately 200 metres. Most *benthic* organisms (*see* BENTHOS) live in this zone because sunlight can penetrate to these
depths. Sediments deposited here are sand and clays, and those laid down
in ancient seas (now sandstones and mudstones), preserve features such as
ripple marks and fossils of marine organisms.

newt *see* AMPHIBIA.

niche all the environmental factors that affect an organism within its community. These factors include living space, available food, climate and all
the conditions necessary for the survival and reproduction of the species.
Although many species co-exist side by side, each occupies a specific niche
within a community with circumstances which apply uniquely to them.

octopus *see* CEPHALOPODA.

Odonata dragonflies and damselflies belong to the order Odonata of the
class Insecta. These familiar large insects are carnivorous both as adults
and *nymphs* (LARVAE). Eggs are laid in or near water and the aquatic
nymphs which hatch out have gills for breathing. They are skilful and voracious hunters with biting mouthparts that are on a plate or *mask* held beneath the head. This is shot out suddenly to seize the prey, which includes
invertebrates and even small fish. The nymph crawls up a stalk of a reed,
or other plant, right out of the water just before its final moult. The adult
which emerges has a pair of large compound eyes and two pairs of large
wings with conspicuous veins. In dragonflies the wings are always held
out horizontally at right angles to the body in the resting insect. In
damselflies, the resting insect holds its wings folded over its back. These
insects have very good eyesight and are excellent hunters catching insect
prey in flight with their legs. They are often brightly and beautifully coloured and are a very ancient group. Some fossil species found in rocks
from the Carboniferous era had wingspans of over half a metre.

A damselfly

Oligochaeta earthworms and some other worm species belong to the class Oligochaeta of the phylum Annelida. They are distinguished by having very few bristles (chaetae) which are not borne on special structures called *parapodia* (*see* ANNELID).

opossum *see* METATHERIA.

Orthoptera grasshoppers, crickets, locusts, preying mantis and cockroaches belong to the order Orthoptera of the class Insecta. This is a large order of insects containing many familiar species. They are usually large and mainly herbivorous with biting mouthparts. Two pairs of wings may be present but some species are wingless. The hind pair of legs are often large and modified for jumping. Many produce sounds by rubbing one part of the body against another (often wings and hind legs), using special *stridulatory* organs to produce noise which is called *stridulation*. Some species, especially locusts and cockroaches are pests of crops or buildings.

A cricket

osteichthyes *see* BONY FISHES.

paramecium *see* PROTOZOA.

pelagic any organisms swimming and living in the sea between the surface and middle depths including many fish, marine mammals and plankton. Pelagic sediments (called *ooze*) are deep water deposits made up of the shells of minute organisms and small quantities of fine debris.

Perissodactyla herbivorous grazing mammals such as horses, zebra, rhinoceros and tapir belong to this order of the class Mammalia. These animals characteristically have hoofed feet and an odd number of toes. The teeth are specialised for grinding and the gut adapted for the digestion of cellulose. This was a distinct mammalian line 60 million years ago in the EOCENE geological period (see MAMMAL).

photic zone the uppermost, surface layer of a lake or sea where sufficient light penetrates to allow PHOTOSYNTHESIS to take place. The extent varies according to the quality of the water, (i.e. whether it is cloudy due to suspended particles), but it can extend to a depth of 200 metres.

physalia *see* HYDROZOA.

pig *see* ARTIODACTYLA.

pitcher plant *see* CARNIVOROUS PLANTS.

plankton *see* ST.

Plasmodium *see* SPOROZOA.

Platyhelminthes flatworms, of which there are about 20,000 species, belong to the phylum Platyhelminthes. There are four classes in this group; the Turbellaria (free-living worms), Cestoda (tapeworms), Trematoda (parasitic flukes) and Monogenea (flukes).

platypus *see* PROTOTHERIA.

poikilothermy means cold-bloodedness and is a feature of all animals except mammals and birds. The body temperature of these animals varies according to that of the surrounding environment, but they adjust by seeking sun or shade as required. Also, the blood flow to some body tissues is adjusted according to whether heat needs to be lost or conserved (*see also* HOMEOTHERMY).

pollution is contamination of the natural environment with harmful substances which have usually been released due to the activities of Man. The substances which cause the pollution are called *pollutants* and include chemicals from industry and agriculture, gases from the burning of fossil fuels, industrial and domestic waste in landfill sites and sewage. Pollution is regarded as a serious problem because of the threat it poses to the health, not just of humans, but of all animals and plants. Many countries have now introduced stringent regulations in order to control pollution levels.

Polychaeta worms such as the ragworm (*Nereis*), lugworm (*Arenicola*) and fan worm (*Sabella*) belong to the class Polychaeta of the phylum Annelida. These characteristically possess a protruding pair of bumps or lobes on each segment, each having numerous bristles or chaetae. Most of these worms are marine animals and live in tubes constructed from pieces of shell and sand. Lugworms and ragworms make burrows in the mud or sand. Most species have a distinct head often with jaws and eyes.

population a group of individuals which belong to the same species. Populations may be genetically isolated, rarely breeding with other members of the same species outwith their particular area. Or, one dense population may merge with another. Usually, a population is affected by such factors as birth and death rates, density (numbers) and immigration and emigration.

population dynamics the study of the changes that occur in population numbers, whether plant or animal, and the factors that control or influence these changes. Distinction is made between factors that are dependent or independent of population density. For example, a natural occurrence such as a flood is an independent factor while food supply is dependent.

Porifera sponges, of which there are about 9000 species, belong to this phylum of invertebrate animals. Most sponges are marine and live attached to rocks or other surfaces. They have a hollow, sac-like body punctured with holes and an internal skeleton made up of tiny spines (spicules) of calcium carbonate, silica or protein. Sponges are filter feeders taking particles of food from the water drawn in through surface pores and digesting them. They are very simdple animals with no muscle or nerves and are able to regenerate lost parts of their body structure.

The general structure of a sponge

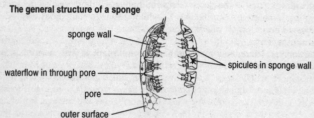

sponge wall

spicules in sponge wall

waterflow in through pore

pore

outer surface

Portuguese man-of-war *see* HYDROZOA.

prawn *see* MALACOSTRACA.

Praying mantis *see* ORTHOPTERA.

Primates the mammalian order which includes monkeys, lemurs, apes and humans. Evidence suggests that primates evolved from tree-dwelling INSECTIVORES late in the Cretaceous geological period. Characteristic features are manual dexterity (permitted by thumbs and big toes that can touch and grasp), good binocular vision and eye-to-hand co-ordination. The brain is large and the primates are highly intelligent. There are two suborders, the Prosimii (lemurs) and Anthropoidea (monkeys, apes and humans).

Proboscidea elephants belong to this order and are placental mammals characterised by having a trunk (proboscis) and tusks which are modified incisor teeth. The order evolved during the Eocene geological period and was much larger in numbers of species containing, for example, the extinct mammoths. There are just two modern species, the African and Indian elephant.

Prototheria two groups of mammals, the platypuses and spiny anteaters

(Echidnas) belong to the subclass Prototheria, the *monotremes*. These are the only living mammals that lay eggs and today they are only found in Australia and New Guinea. The monotremes resemble reptiles in the structure of their skeleton and in the laying of eggs. They are warm-blooded although the body temperature is variable and lower than that of most other mammals. It is thought that the monotremes originated about 150 million years ago early in the development of the mammals.

protozoa used to be the term for a phylum of small, single-celled (mainly) micro-organisms, but now a general word for the PROTISTA. Included are such organisms as *Amoeba* and *Paramecium* and they are very widely distributed in aquatic and damp terrestrial habitats. Some feed on decaying organic material (*saprophytes*) while others are parasites, e.g. *Trypsanosoma* which causes sleeping sickness.

pterophyta ferns belong to a division of the plant kingdom called the Pterophyta. There are about 12,000 species of ferns which emerged as far back as the Carboniferous geological period.

A fern

Ferns are just about all terrestrial and the majority are found in tropical regions. The leaves are usually called *fronds* and each is made up of numerous smaller leaflets. They are considered to be a fairly primitive group of plants and many of the extinct ferns grew to an enormous size and are well preserved as fossils.

quadrat a small sampling plot (usually one square metre), which is chosen at random and within which organisms found are counted and studied. This is like a 'window' into the area as a whole revealing the types of animals and plants to be found there. The sampling may be done in relation to a particular species or several different types of organisms.

race a group of individuals which is different in one or more ways from other members of the same species. They may be different because they occupy another geographical area, perhaps showing a variation in colour, or they may exhibit *behavioural, physiological* or even genetic differences. The term is sometimes used in the same way as sub-species. Usually, animals from different races are able to interbreed.

racoon *see* CARNIVORA.

Radiolaria tiny, marine protozoan animals, present in PLANKTON (*see* **ST**), belong to the order Radiolaria. These organisms have a spherical body shape and characteristically possess a beautiful intricate skeleton often composed of silica. This is perforated with holes to make a large variety of patterns, and may be in the form of a lattice of spheres, one inside the other. Often there are many spines or hooks projecting outwards. When Radiolarians die their skeletons, which are highly resistant to decay, settle on the ocean floor to accumulate as *Radiolarian ooze*. When compressed into rock it forms *flint* and *chert*. Radiolarian fossils are very important to geologists and are among the few found in the most ancient rocks from the Precambrian geological period (more than 590 million years old).

Various forms of radiolarian

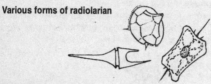

ragworm *see* POLYCHAETA.

rat *see* RODENTIA.

rattlesnake *see* SQUAMATA.

ray *see* CARTILAGINOUS FISHES.

reindeer moss *see* LICHEN.

Reptilia reptiles, a class of VERTEBRATES which were the first animals to truly colonise dry land and to exist entirely independently of water, often live in extremely hot conditions such as semi-desert. They have a dry skin covered with horny scales which protects them from drying out. Reptiles usually lay eggs in holes which they excavate in the sand or mud. The eggs are covered by a protective shell which is porous and allows for the passage of air. Some retain the eggs inside the body until they hatch. Reptiles are cold-blooded (*see* POIKILOTHERMY), but are able to maintain an even body temperature by behavioural means such as basking in the sun. There is evidence that some extinct reptiles (e.g. some of the DINOSAURS), were warm-blooded. Modern reptiles include snakes, lizards, turtles, tortoises and crocodiles.

rhinoceros *see* PERISSODACTYLA.

rice grass *see* HALOPHYTE.

Rodentia a widespread and successful order of mammals containing rats, mice, squirrels, capybaras and beavers. The upper and lower jaws contain a single pair of long incisor teeth which grow continuously throughout the animal's life. These are adapted for gnawing, and the absence of enamel on the back means that they wear to a chisel-like cutting edge. Rodents are herbivorous or omnivorous and tend to breed rapidly. Some, notably rats, are serious pests, spoiling food and are responsible for the spread of diseases.

roundworm *see* NEMATODA.

salamander *see* AMPHIBIA.

sawfly *see* HYMENOPTERA.

sea anemone *see* ACTINOZOA.

sea cucumber, sea daisy, sea lily, sea urchin *see* ECHINODERM.

sea lion and **seal** see CARNIVORA.

sea snake *see* SQUAMATA.

scale insect *see* HEMIPTERA.

scorpion *see* ARACHNIDA.

shark *see* CARTILAGINOUS FISHES.

sheep *see* ARTIODACTYLA.

shrimp *see* MALACOSTRACA.

skate *see* CARTILAGINOUS FISHES.

slug and **snail** see GASTROPODA.

snake *see* SQUAMATA.

spiny anteater *see* PROTOTHERIA.

spirogyra *see* CHLOROPHYTA.

Sporozoa a class of protozoan organisms which are parasites of higher animals and some cause serious diseases in Man. An example is *Plasmodium* which causes malaria and is transmitted by the mosquito.

Squamata lizards and snakes belong to the order Squamata of the class Reptilia. They are covered by horny scales and male animals are unique in possessing a paired penis. Lizards possess movable eyelids and most have four limbs, e.g. iguanas, monitor lizards, chameleons and gila monsters. Snakes lack movable eyelids and are able to dislocate their lower jaw in order to swallow large prey. Some are constrictor types, e.g. boas, pythons and anacondas, while others may be venomous, e.g. cobras, vipers, mambas, rattlesnakes and sea snakes.

squid *see* CEPHALOPODA.

squirrel *see* RODENTIA.

starfish *see* ECHINODERMATA.

sundew *see* CARNIVOROUS PLANTS.

tapeworm *see* CESTODA.

tapir *see* PERISSODACTYLA.

terrapin *see* CHELONIA.

territory a specific area that animals, whether singly or in groups, defend to exclude other members of their species. A territory may be used for feeding, mating and breeding, or all these activities, and the size varies greatly, from the small nesting territory of sea birds to the large areas used by red squirrels. Many mammals mark their territories with scent while birds use song. Territory differs from home range, the latter being the area in which an animal roams but which is not defended.

tick *see* ARACHNIDA.

toad *see* AMPHIBIA.

tortoise *see* CHELONIA.

trypanosome *see* PROTOZOA.

Turbellaria flatworms, such as *Planaria*, belong to the class Turbellaria of the phylum PLATYHELMINTHES. These are simple, small animals, mostly marine although Planarians are common in freshwater streams and ponds. They are carnivorous and move by undulating the body in a wave-like way or by means of small hairs, called *cilia*, on their underside.

turtle *see* CHELONIA.

ungulate *see* ARTIODACTYLA and PERISSODACTYLA.

variation the differences between individuals of the same population or species.

venus fly trap *see* CARNIVOROUS PLANTS.

Vertebrata a major subphylum, which includes all the animals with backbones: fishes, amphibians, reptiles, birds and mammals (*see* individual entries).

viper *see* SQUAMATA.

walrus *see* CARNIVORA.

water boatman *see* HEMIPTERA.

weevil *see* COLEOPTERA.

whelk *see* GASTROPODA.

zebra *see* PERISSODACTYLA.

Science and Technology

This section of *The Pocket Encyclopedia* defines the commonly used terms and basic concepts essential to the study of a range of subjects, including anatomy, chemistry, biology, maths, engineering and physics. The cross-references, given in SMALL CAPITALS, will enable you to gain an overall understanding the scientific world.

acceleration *see* VELOCITY.

acids and bases *acids* are chemical compounds in a liquid form which, depending upon their strength, may occur naturally in foods as very weak acids (e.g. citric acid in lemons) or may form corrosive liquids (e.g. sulphuric acid used in the manufacture of fertilisers and explosives) which has many industrial uses. Most acids have a sour taste, although it is not advisable to taste them as many are poisonous and can burn skin. Acids turn litmus paper from blue to red (*see* INDICATOR) and an acidic solution has a pH lower than 7. To aid digestion, our bodies produce acids to break down food.

A mixture of concentrated nitric and hydrochloric acids (in the ratio 1:4) is called *aqua regia* ('royal water') because it will dissolve the 'noble' metals such as gold.

Bases are the opposite to acids and if a base is reacted with an acid in the correct proportions, the two are cancelled out (*neutralised*), producing water and a salt. Nevertheless, bases can be highly reactive and corrosive. Bases turn red litmus paper blue. Examples of bases include caustic soda used in the manufacture of petrochemicals and magnesium oxide, used in antacid preparations.

If a compound (usually the oxide -O, or hydroxide -OH of a metallic element) can function as an acid *or* as an alkali (a soluble base) it is said to be *amphoteric*, that is it can combine with an acid or a base to form a salt.

acoustics *see* SOUND.

adhesives are materials that will bond (stick) solids together, through initially wetting the surfaces to be joined and then solidifying to form a joint. Some adhesives, or glues can be made from natural materials such as bones, horn and hides by boiling and simple chemical treatment. Glues made in this way are a mixture of proteins.

Adhesives made from chemicals are called synthetic, and these tend to be stronger than the natural forms.

aerodynamics the study of the movement and control of solid objects such as aircraft, rockets, etc. in air. As objects move through the air there is a resistance or *drag* which works against the direction of movement, and the drag increases with speed. All machines used in transport: aircraft, cars, trains, lorries, are designed with streamlined bodies to reduce drag to a minimum. This involves using smooth curved shapes rather than angular shapes.

Another important aspect of aerodynamics is *lift*, which is an upward force vital in the take off and flight of aircraft. All aircraft have wings with a curved top surface, and a flatter lower surface. This feature is based upon *Bernoulli's Theorem* (which applies to both liquid and air) which proves that when the flow of air speeds up, the air pressure is reduced. The characteristic *aerofoil* shape of a wing means that air travelling over the top, curved surface has to travel further than air beneath the wing. It therefore moves faster, causing a reduction in air pressure and the wing is lifted, or pushed upwards.

The aerofoil shape is not only used on aircraft – the same principle is applied to rudders, the vanes on a windmill, and even on racing cars, although in the latter case it is to keep the car on the racetrack.

aerosol a fine mist or fog consisting of liquid or solid particles in a gas. It also refers to a pressurised container with a spray mechanism for dispersal of a fine mist of fluid droplets. This system is used for deodorants, paints, insecticides and other chemicals. Within the can is the liquid to be sprayed, and a propellant gas which is under pressure. When the valve is opened by pressing the button, the gas forces (propels) the contents out through the nozzle. Until very recently, the propellants used were commonly CFCs or chlorofluorocarbons, but because it has been proven that these chemicals damage the ozone layer (*see* **GG**: OZONE LAYER), alternative compounds have been sought.

An *atomiser* is another way of creating an aerosol, but does not require a propellant gas.

ageing includes all the changes which take place as an animal grows older. Animals age at different rates, from some adult insects which only live for a day (mayflies), to elephants (up to 70 years) and tortoises and parrots which may have a life span of well over 100 years. Ageing is perhaps best understood and most studied in human beings. In people, the cells which make up the different parts of the body age at different rates, and while most are renewed some are not (e.g. brain cells), so the whole process is very complicated. As ageing occurs, noticeable physical changes take place which include wrinkling of the skin, greying hair, deterioration in sight, hearing, taste, smell, memory and stiffening of limbs and joints.

alcohols organic compounds containing carbon, oxygen and hydrogen and with a particular structure where a hydroxyl group, (oxygen and hydrogen, OH), is linked to a carbon. Alcohols are mainly liquids and are used in a variety of ways. For example, methanol (CH_3OH) is used in the manufacture of paints, solvents and varnishes, and ethanol (Ch_3CH_2OH) is used in the production of alcoholic beverages, perfumes and in the food industry.

The alcohols are produced by various chemical reactions, but ethanol occurs naturally by fermentation in which yeast converts sugar to alcohol with carbon dioxide being the side product.

aldehydes (also known as *alkanals*) another group of organic compounds containing carbon, hydrogen and oxygen which have a particular group, CHO, joined to another carbon atom. The oxygen is joined to the carbon by a double bond, the hydrogen by a single bond. Aldehydes are mainly colourless liquids or solids with typical odours and wide uses, including in the manufacture of chemicals, germicidals and sterilising fluids.

algebra is the use of symbols, usually letters, to help solve mathematical problems where the object is to find the value of an unknown quantity or to study complex theories. In its simplest form it may involve the determination of an unknown in an equation such as: $3x + 1 = 16$, where x is obviously equal to 5. Albert Einstein (1879–1955) used a very advanced form of algebra in deriving the equations for his general theory of relativity. The formal rules of algebra were developed by al Khuwārizmi, an Arab mathematician in the ninth century.

algorithm a set of rules that together form a mathematical procedure that allows a problem to be solved in a certain number of stages. Each rule is carefully defined so that, theoretically, a machine can undertake the process.

An algorithm is a way of reaching the right answer to a difficult problem by breaking the problem down into simple stages. The stages allow the action to be successfully achieved without necessarily understanding fully the whole process. To be an algorithm, a list of instructions must have an end and be short enough to allow each to be completed, and the process must end at some point. Computer programs contain algorithms, but simpler more everyday examples include making a telephone call and following a recipe. Long division is another example.

alimentary canal *see* DIGESTION.

alkali a base which when dissolved in water produces a solution with a pH over 7, e.g. Na_2CO_3, $Ca(OH)_2$. These are alkaline solutions. Hydroxides of the metallic elements sodium and potassium (NaOH and KOH respectively) produce strong alkalis, as does ammonia in solution (as ammonium hydroxide, NH_4OH).

alloys a mixture or compound containing two (or more) metals, or a metal with a non-metal, e.g. iron-carbon where the metal is the larger component. Alloys tend to have properties which are described as metallic, but alloying is a means of increasing a particularly useful property such as strength, resistance to corrosion or high temperatures.

aluminium is a silvery-white metallic element that in air forms a protective coating of aluminium oxide which prevents further corrosion. It is ductile and malleable (*see* DUCTILITY) and a good conductor of electricity and is used for the manufacture of a large number of things, from drinks cans and foil to pans, cars and aircraft. Aluminium is the commonest metallic element in the Earth's crust and the third most common overall (at about 8%). It is extracted from the mineral *bauxite* (aluminium hydroxides formed by weathering of aluminium-bearing rocks, in tropical conditions) by electrolysis (*see* ELECTROLYSIS). Salts of aluminium are important in the purification of waters and as catalysts (*see* CATALYSIS). The oxide is important in the production of cement, abrasives (*corundum*), refractories and ceramics.

ammonia is a colourless gas made up of nitrogen and hydrogen (NH_3) and it is a very useful chemical compound. It has a sharp, pungent smell, is lighter than air and very soluble in water. It is used in the manufacture of nitric acid, nylon, plastics, explosives and fertilisers. Ammonia is also used in refrigeration equipment as a coolant. Ammonia gas can be turned into a liquid by cooling to -33.5°C, and when it becomes gas again, it takes a lot of heat from the surroundings, thus producing the cooling effect.

ampere the unit used for measuring electric current, usually abbreviated to amps, which was named after the French physicist André Ampère (1775–1836) who did much important work in the early 19th century. Machines and appliances use differing currents and with a mains supply of 240 volts, an electric fire will use between 4 and 8 amps. The ampere has a very specific definition, created in 1948, relating to the force produced between two wires in a vacuum, when current is passed. Prior to that the unit related to the amount of silver deposited per second from a silver nitrate solution when one ampere was passed.

analogue *see* DIGITAL AND ANALOGUE.

analysis (in chemistry) involves the use of one, or a combination of several analytical techniques and pieces of equipment to identify a substance or a mixture of substances. *Qualitative* analysis is when the components are identified, and *quantitative* analysis involves the determination of the relative amount of constituents, usually elements, making up a sample.

anatomy is the scientific study of the structure of living things, which enables an understanding to be built up of how different parts of a plant or animal work. It often involves dissection of dead specimens.

animals – modern biologists usually group animals together in the biological kingdom called *Animalia* which contains many different *phyla* (*see* CLASSIFICATION). The simplest animals are the sponges (phylum *Porifera*) and the most complicated, including man and other mammals, belong to the phylum *Chordata*. These animals are constructed of many cells (multicellular) performing a variety of functions which, unlike those of plants, do not have outer cell walls. Animals cannot manufacture their own food but must take it in from the outside in some way. Also. animals possess nerves and muscles which vary greatly in complexity between the different groups. Most animals reproduce by means of sexual reproduction and store carbohydrates as an energy reserve in the form of glycogen (a compound made up of glucose units). In plants, carbohydrate is stored as starch.

anodising is a process for depositing a hard, very thin layer of oxide on a metal. The metal is usually aluminium or an alloy and the oxide layer provides a non-corrosive coating of aluminium oxide (Al_2O_3) which is resistant to scratches and which protects the underlying metal. Anodising is achieved by electrolysis and the metal made is the anode, often in a bath of sulphuric, chromic or oxalic acid. Such metals are used in many ways: for window frames, and in trains and aircraft, for example. The oxide coating may be rendered decorative by the use of a dye during electrolysis. Anodised items can be made to retain their natural brightness through the use of very high purity aluminium or an aluminium-magnesium alloy, because in these cases the oxide layer formed is transparent.

Archimedes' principle a law of physics, named after the Greek mathematician Archimedes (287–212 BC). It states that when a body is partly or totally immersed in a liquid, the apparent loss in weight equals the weight of the displaced liquid. Archimedes was a prolific inventor and investigator. He did much scientific work with levers and pulleys and invented the Archimedean screw which is essentially a hollow screw which, with its base in water, when turned, lifts water to a higher level. The device is still used for irrigation if pumps are not available.

arithmetic the science of numbers which includes addition, subtraction, division, multiplication, fractions, decimals, roots and so on. Arithmetic was first used by the Babylonians about 4000 years ago but the system currently used is that of Arabic numerals. The Romans used a different system in which letters represent quantities:

Roman	Arabic	Roman	Arabic
I	1	X	10
II	2	L	50
III	3	C	100
IV	4	D	500
V	5	M	1000

asexual reproduction any form of reproduction in which a new individual is produced from a single parent without the production or fusion of sex cells (gametes). It occurs in plants, micro-organisms and some of the simpler animals, often alternating with a sexual phase. Different types of asexual reproduction occur, one of which is by division of a single cell into two, known as *fission,* as seen in *Amoeba,* a member of the kingdom *Protista.* Another method is *fragmentation* in which parts of the plant or animal separate off, or the whole breaks up with new individuals being formed from the portions. This is seen in some invertebrate animals, particularly earthworms.

Budding is another form of asexual reproduction which occurs in such animals as hydras, sea anemones and corals. A small bud is produced from the parent which may break off and form a new animal or remain attached. Asexual reproduction is also seen in plants, e.g. in the production of bulbs, corms and tubers known as *vegetative propagation.* Such plants as ferns and mosses may have an asexual stage, producing spores, and this is known as the *sporophyte generation.*

atom the smallest particle that makes up all matter, and yet is still chemically representative of the element. Atoms are less than microscopic in size and yet they are made up of even smaller particles. At the centre of an atom is a relatively heavy *nucleus* containing *protons* and *neutrons.* The protons are positively charged and they are offset by an equal number of electrons with negative charge that occupy *orbitals* around the nucleus. The atom is overall electrically neutral and the various elements in the periodic table each have a unique number of protons in their nucleus. The electron weighs a little more than one two thousandth part of a proton.

Orbitals provide a means of simplifying and expressing *atomic structure* and related processes, such as bonding. The theory put forward by Niels Bohr (1885–1962), the famous Danish physicist, proposed that electrons encircled the nucleus in definite orbits. This was discovered to be too simple and the new theory visualised a charge cloud or orbital which represents the likely distribution of the electron in space. There are various types of orbital, each with a different cloud shape around the nucleus (dependent upon atomic structure) and these orbitals interact, merge and change when chemical bonds are formed. The precursor to this picture of atomic structure began with Democritus several hundred years BC. In the 19th century Dalton put forward theories to explain the structure of matter and was the first to calculate the weights of some atoms.

Elements that have more than 83 protons are unstable and decay radioactively, while those with over 92 protons occur only in the laboratory, as a result of high energy experiments (*see also* BONDS). Atoms of an element that have differing numbers of neutrons are called isotopes.

atomic number (*symbol* Z) is the number of protons in the nucleus of an atom. All atoms of the same element have the same number of protons but may have differing numbers of neutrons (producing isotopes). *Atomic weight* or *relative atomic mass* is the ratio of the average mass of an element (i.e. the average for the mixture of isotopes in a natural element) to one twelfth of the mass of carbon -12 atom. Chemical notation places the atomic number as a subscript before the symbol for the element, e.g. chlorine has 17 protons -$_{17}$Cl.

autotrophism means 'self-feeding' and describes the situation in which an organism manufactures the materials it requires for life from inorganic (*see* CHEMISTRY) substances. Plants are *photo-autotrophs*, using light as an energy source and carbon dioxide, minerals and water taken from the air and soil. Some bacteria are *chemoautotrophs* obtaining energy from chemical reactions using such substances as ammonia and sulphur.

averages in statistics, average is a general term for *mean, median* and *mode*. The arithmetic mean is the value obtained from a set of figures by adding all the values in the *data set* (collection of numbers) and dividing by the number of readings. The median is the middle reading in a set, so if there are nine readings for temperature, height, weight or a similar quantity, arranged in order, the median is the middle, or in this case, the fifth value. The mode is the value that occurs most frequently in a set of readings, hence in a range of temperatures such as 17°, 18°, 12°, 17°, 21°, 16°, 19°, 17°, the mode is 17°.

bacteria are single celled organisms belonging to the kingdom *Monera* and have a unique type of cell called procaryotic (procaryote). They were the first organisms to exist on Earth but their activities have always been extremely significant as they are important in all life processes. Bacteria may have a protective, slimy outer layer called a capsule and in some, 'hairs' known as filaments are present which cause movement. Two types of bacteria, which each have a different cell wall structure (Gram positive or Gram negative) are recognised by a test known as Gram's stain. Bacteria show a number of different shapes and forms which help to distinguish between the various types. These are *spiral* (spirilli, spirillus), *spherical* (cocci, coccus), *rod-like* (bacilli, bacillus), *comma-shaped* (vibrio) and *corkscrew-shaped* (spirochaetae). They may require an environment containing oxygen, in which case they are described as *aerobic*, or exist in conditions without oxygen, when they are known as *anaerobic*. Bacteria are vitally important in the decomposition of all organic (*see* CHEMISTRY) material and are the main agents in the chemical cycles of carbon, oxygen, nitrogen and sulphur. Most bacteria obtain their food from decaying or dead organic material (*saprotrophs*). Others are parasites and some are *autotrophs* (*see* AUTOTROPHISM), obtaining energy from chemical reactions using inorganic materials such as sulphur and ammonia. Bacteria usually reproduce asexually (*see* ASEXUAL REPRODUCTION) by simple fission but some have a form of sexual reproduction. Some are responsible for very serious diseases in animals, plants and man, e.g. typhoid, syphilis, tuberculosis, diphtheria and cholera.

ballistics is the study of the *flight path* of *projectiles* (i.e. an object that has been projected into the air) under the influence of gravity. The trajectory is the path taken by an object and is usually a particular length, distinguishing it from an orbit. A *ballistic missile* is a missile fired from the ground which follows a flight path shaped like a parabola and which is powered and guided only during the first phase of flight.

Ballistics is a term applied to bullets, rockets, missiles and similar objects.

bar code is a series of black bars printed on a white background that represent codes that can be scanned and interpreted by a reader and computer respectively. Bar codes are found on most products in supermarkets, on books and other items and they contain a product number and maker's identification number.

As the product is dragged past an optical scanner at the checkout, or a light pen is moved over the bar code, the computer matches the product with the price list in its memory. In addition to speeding up the process of adding up items, the use of bar codes helps an accurate analysis of stock to be made, allowing restocking to be undertaken before a product line is exhausted. It also facilitates the output of a detailed, itemised receipt.

barometer is an instrument used to measure atmospheric pressure, i.e. the pressure that the atmosphere exerts on the Earth. The principle of the barometer was discovered by Torricelli, a 17th-century Italian physicist. It is used to help predict forthcoming weather changes which result from changes in atmospheric pressure.

bases *see* ACIDS.

battery a device, usually portable, in which a chemical change is harnessed to produce electricity. Many batteries are to all intents and purposes non-rechargeable and these are called primary cells and the most important is the Leclanché type. One of the commonest arrangements is a positive electrode made up of a rod of carbon surrounded by a mixture of manganese dioxide and powdered carbon in a case and the whole thing stands in an *electrolyte* (*see* ELECTROLYSIS) of ammonium chloride in the form of a paste. The outer case of zinc acts as the negative electrode. When the battery is connected, a current flows due to reactions and the movement of ions between the various components, thus creating a voltage.

  The other important type of battery is the secondary cell, which can be recharged, e.g. the lead *accumulator*, or car battery. In this cell, plates of lead and lead oxide are suspended in sulphuric acid and on charging there are chemical changes (because of *electrolysis*) which are complete when it is charged. When the terminals are wired up, the chemical changes are reversed and current flows until the battery is discharged. The sulphuric acid used has to be of a certain relative density and discharge should not be continued beyond a certain point because insoluble salts build up on the plates. Other types of accumulator include nickel-iron, in which the nickel oxide plate is positive and the iron is negative, in a solution of potassium hydroxide; zinc-air, sodium/sulphur and lithium/chlorine. Although the last two are higher energy cells than most accumulators, they require high operating temperatures.

behaviour (in animals) this term includes all the activities that an animal (or person) carries out during its life and is a major area of scientific study. Those who study behaviour wish to find out why an animal acts in a particular way and what factors might affect this. Behaviour can be divided into three categories. These are known as *reflex*, *instinctive* and *learned*. Reflex behaviour is totally spontaneous and does not involve any conscious act of the will. For example, if you accidentally touch something hot, your hand is immediately and rapidly withdrawn from the source of heat. Instinctive behaviour is inborn and does not need to be learned, being present in all members of a species. The classic example is the male three-spined stickleback fish protecting his territory. Male sticklebacks have a red belly, and this acts as a trigger for the defensive behaviour. A male stickleback will attack models that only vaguely resemble a rival fish provided that the red coloration is present. More realistic stickleback models without a red underside are ignored. Much animal behaviour is *learned*, i.e. it is changed by experience, and this can be seen especially in the young of a species as they play and experiment in the environment that surrounds them. Various types of learned behaviour are recognised. It is generally agreed that all behaviour is a mix, instinct combined with learning and modification by environmental conditions.

benzene a hydrocarbon that is toxic and carcinogenic (may cause cancer). At room temperature it is a colourless liquid with a characteristic smell and it has the formula C_6H_6. The six atoms of carbon form a ring with bond angles of 120°. The ring structure is very stable because although the convention is to show benzene with three double bonds, the bonding electrons are not localised and are spread around the ring.

The ring structure for benzene

bimetal strip comprises a bar with strips of two different metals welded together. Because of the different rates of expansion, each expands (or contracts) by a different amount when subjected to heat (or cold), and the bar bends (the metal on the outside being the one that expands more). The two metals used are often brass and invar (an iron-nickel alloy), the brass expanding about twenty times more than invar. This property enables bimetallic strips to be used in thermostats, thermometers and thermal switches. Also the indicator bulbs in a car flash because of a small bimetal strip.

binary numbers is a system that uses a combination of two digits, 0 and 1, expressed to the base 2, thus beginning with the value 1 in the right-hand column, each move to the left sees an increase to the power of 2:

1×2^5	1×2^4	1×2^3	1×2^2	1×2^1	1×2^0	origin of binary numbers
32	16	8	4	2	1	binary numbers
1	0	1	1	1	0	example

Hence in the example, the figure is $32 + 8 + 4 + 2 = 46$.

The binary number system is the basis of code information in computers, as the digits 0 and 1 are used to represent the two states of on or off in an electronic switch in a circuit.

biochemistry the scientific study of the chemistry of biological processes occurring in the cells and tissues of living organisms. Chemical compounds are the building blocks of all plants and animals, and studying the ways in which these react with one another and how they contribute to life processes is the realm of biochemistry. Biochemists are involved in a wide variety of scientific studies including the search for cures of serious diseases such as cancer and Aids.

biological control a means of controlling pests by using their natural enemies rather than chemicals which might prove harmful to the environment. The control is artificially brought about in that large numbers of the 'predators' are introduced by human beings in order to control the pests. The method can be very successful, an example being the spread of the prickly pear cactus in Australia which was successfully controlled by the introduction of the cactus moth, whose caterpillars fed on and destroyed the young plant shoots. However, all the biological implications have to be thoroughly researched in advance as sometimes the attempted control has gone very wrong. An example of this was the introduction of large Hawaiian toads into Australian sugar cane plantations with the belief that these would eat the sugar cane beetles that damaged the crop. In fact, the toads did not eat the cane beetles but proved seriously damaging to other animals and are now a great problem in themselves. Another method of biological control used with insect pests (especially some which carry disease, such as the tsetse fly) is to use natural chemicals called pheromones which attract them so that they can be caught. Sometimes the males are caught and radiation is used to make them sterile and then they are released to mate with females. No offspring are produced from these matings and hence the number of insects decreases.

biology the scientific examination of all living things – plants, animals and micro-organisms etc. It is further subdivided into specialised areas of study.

bioluminescence the production of light by living organisms which is seen in many sea-dwelling animals, e.g. deep sea fish (angler fish), hydrozoans such as *Obelia*, molluscs, e.g. squids, and some crustaceans. It is also seen in some land-dwelling insects, e.g. fireflies and glow-worms and in some bacteria and fungi. Some animals have bacteria living with them (*see* SYMBIOSIS) and it is these which actually produce the light. The light may be given out continuously as in bacteria or 'switched' on and off as in fireflies. The light may be used to attract prey or a mate, or as a warning. A special protein (called a photoprotein) known as luciferin combines with oxygen and during this chemical reaction light is produced.

biophysics a combination of biology and physics in which the physical properties of biological mechanisms are the subject of study. The laws and techniques of physics can be used, for example, in the study of how the heart and muscles work, or in the mechanisms of respiration and blood circulation.

biotechnology the use by man of living organisms to manufacture useful products or to change materials. Examples include the fermentation of yeast to produce alcohol and in bread making, and the growth of special fungi to make antibiotics. Biotechnology mainly uses micro-organisms especially bacteria and fungi. In recent times, genetic engineering, which alters the genes (*see* CHROMOSOMES AND GENES), or 'building blocks', that determine the nature of an organism, is increasingly being used in the field of biotechnology.

biotic *see* ORGANISM.

blast furnace is a furnace comprising a large vertical tower used mainly for the smelting of iron from iron oxide ores. The tower is made of steel plates lined with refractory bricks (firebricks) to withstand the very high operating temperatures (in excess of 1600°C). After some time, about three years, the lining will wear out and the furnace is then shut down to allow the bricks to be replaced.

The furnace is fed from the top with ore, coke and limestone ($CaCO_3$). From near the base of the tower is introduced a high pressure blast of very hot air which ignites the coke, producing carbon monoxide (CO) which then reacts with the iron oxide to produce iron (molten) and at the same time the limestone breaks down to form lime (CaO) and carbon dioxide (CO_2). The lime subsequently combines with impurities from the ore to form a molten slag. As the iron is formed it collects at the base of the furnace, and the slag floats on top. Each is run off periodically, the iron to form bars of 'pig iron' (or cast iron) which contains about 4.5% carbon. The blast furnace can also be used for smelting copper.

The slag also finds a use as *ground granulated blast-furnace slag* (ggbfs) in which it is granulated, ground and then mixed with Portland cement for use in construction. Cements made with ggbfs improve workability and resistance to deleterious reactions and although it is slower to harden, it heats up less than most cements.

blood *see* CIRCULATION.

boiling point is the temperature at which a substance changes from the liquid to the gaseous state. This occurs when the vapour pressure of a liquid is equal to atmospheric pressure. This explains why at high altitudes, water boils at a lower temperature because air pressure decreases. Boiling points of liquids are therefore quoted as the value at standard atmospheric pressure (one atmosphere).

bonds are forces that hold atoms together to form a molecule; or molecules and IONS to form crystals or lattices. Bonds are created by the movement of electrons and the type of bond depends upon the atoms involved and their *electronegativity* (a measure of an atom's attraction for electrons, within a molecule). Three basic bond types are recognised: *ionic* (or electrovalent), where one atom loses an electron to another atom, as in NaCl which becomes Na^+ (positive ion or *cation*) and Cl^- (negative ion or *anion*). Such compounds dissociate (split) into ions in solution and therefore are able to conduct electricity; *covalent* bonds where electrons are shared, often one from each participating atom, although the sharing is equal only when the atoms are identical. Covalent bonding is common in organic compounds. *Metallic* bonding is where electrons are shared between many nuclei thus facilitating conduction of electricity.

bone the hard material that forms the skeleton of most vertebrate animals and contains living cells, called *oestoblasts* and *oestocysts*, responsible for the formation and repair of bones. Bone is made up of hard connective tissue, itself consisting of a tough protein called collagen and bone salts (crystals of calcium phosphate-hydroxyapatite) which both make it strong. The skeleton of an adult human being has 206 bones, some of which are fused together and others are very small.

bone marrow a soft and spongy tissue which is found in the centre of the long bones (e.g. those of the leg and arm) and also within the spaces of other bones. The bone marrow produces blood cells especially in young animals. In older animals only some bone marrow, known as red marrow and mainly found in the vertebrae, pelvis, ribs and breastbone produces blood cells. It contains special (*myeloid*) tissue in which are found cells known as erythroblasts which develop into red blood cells or *erythrocytes*. The cells of the myeloid tissue also develop into leucocytes or white blood cells which are an essential part of the body's immune system.

botany the scientific study of all aspects of the life of plants (*compare* ZOOL-OGY).

brain *see* NERVOUS SYSTEM.

breathing *see* RESPIRATION.

breeding and **hybrid** breeding is the production of offspring and usually refers to the interference by man to produce animals or plants with particular desirable characteristics. The results of breeding are particularly noticeable in domestic farm animals such as cattle or dogs, which look very different to their wild ancestors. Selective breeding has given us animals which provide more milk, wool or meat, and crops which produce more grain or larger, juicier fruits and succulent leaves.

A hybrid animal is the offspring of parents that are of two different species (*see* CLASSIFICATION), the most familiar example of which is the mule. A mule is the offspring of a female horse and a male donkey. Hybrid animals are usually sterile. N.B. hybrid has a different meaning in genetics where the differences in the parents are at the gene (*see* CHROMOSOMES AND GENES), rather than the species level.

bud (plant) a compact and immature plant shoot made up of many folded and unexpanded leaves or flower petals. These are tightly folded or wrapped around one another and may be enclosed in a protective, sometimes sticky sheath. When the bud opens, the petals or leaves grow and expand, a process which marks the onset of spring moving into summer. *See also* ASEXUAL REPRODUCTION.

bridges a structure used in civil engineering to cover a gap, whether over road, water or railway. For short *spans* (i.e. the distance between supports) of 300 to 600 metres, steel arches, suspension or cantilever bridges are suitable. Above 600 metres, steel suspension bridges are often used. In such bridges, the bridge deck (i.e. the floor that carries the load to the beams and supports) is hung from vertical rods or wire ropes connected to cables that go over the towers and are anchored in the ground. In the UK, the Severn bridge is such a case.

A *cantilever bridge* is usually symmetrical, comprising three spans. The two outer spans are anchored at each shore and then extend beyond the supporting pier to cover one third of the remaining span. This gap is then bridged by another element which rests on the arms of the two cantilevers.

There are other types of bridge, several with particular functions, e.g. swing bridges that rotate on a pivot to allow vessels to pass.

bromine is a typical member of the halogen group (*see also* PERIODIC TABLE). It is a dark red liquid with noxious vapours. It occurs naturally as bromide

compounds in sea water and salt deposits, and also in marine plants. When
sea water is evaporated, and after sodium chloride ('salt') crystals have pre-
cipitated out, the remaining fluid (*bittern*) contains magnesium bromide.

Bromine is very reactive and has numerous industrial uses including the
manufacture of disinfectants, fumigants, anti-knock agents for petrol and
in photography.

Brownian Movement is the erratic and random movement of microscopic
particles when suspended in a liquid or gas. The movement is due to the
continuous movement of molecules in the surrounding gas or liquid
which then impact with the particles. This phenomenon accounts for the
gradual dispersal of smells in the air and the mixing of fluids which will
happen with time, and which will be accelerated if the gas or fluid is hot.
As the particles become larger, there is a greater chance of impacts from
all sides cancelling each other out and so the movement can no longer be
observed. This occurs when the particles are 3–4μ (3–4 microns, or
micrometres μm; equal to 3-4 millionths of a metre).

Brownian movement is named after its discoverer, Robert Brown (1773–
1858), a Scot . He was a botanist and first observed this movement when
studying pollen. It is taken as evidence that kinetic energy applies to all
matter and exists even when it cannot be seen.

bubbles may be of a gas within a liquid, e.g. air in water, or air surrounded
by a thin soap film as with soap bubbles. Detergent or soap in water creates bubbles due to the detergent molecules forming a stable alignment.
The shape of a soap bubble is due to a balance between the pressure inside
trying to blow it apart and the surface tension of the liquid trying to contract it. The pressure inside a bubble decreases as the size of the bubble
increases, so smaller bubbles have greater pressure inside than larger ones.

building and construction is central to the development of countries and
their economies, and to the operation of almost all aspects of everyone's
daily life. There are many professional people; planners, surveyors, civil and
structural engineers, architects, builders etc, and the major parts of the construction process are: planning, design, construction for new projects, maintenance and refurbishment and restoration for existing buildings.

Bunsen burner *see* LABORATORY.

caffeine and tannin *caffeine* is an *alkaloid* (basic organic substance found
in plants) and *purine* that occurs in tea leaves, coffee beans and other
plants. It acts as a *diuretic* (a substance that increases urine formation) and
as a weak stimulant to the central nervous system. It is also found in cola
drinks-up to 10% in some cases.

Tannins are a large group of plant substances of use in the treatment of hides. However, the term is misused in connection with tea because tannic acid is not present and tannin is simply a general collective term. Tea does contain *polyphenols* which in some mixtures may resemble tannin in their chemical structure.

calculators are not a recent invention-only the development and inclusion of integrated circuits on silicon chips has been a recent and revolutionary step. Calculators began as mechanical devices in the 17th century and were, inevitably, laboriously slow. The first electronic calculator was produced in 1963, but its scope was very limited and calculators became generally available in the early 1970s. The first calculator that could be programmed to solve mathematical problems was made by Hewlett-Packard in 1974. Now there is an enormous variety of calculators available, some as small as credit cards.

calculus a large branch of mathematics that enables the manipulation of and working with quantities that vary continuously. The techniques of calculus were developed by two scientists at the same time, the German Gottfried Leibniz (1646–1716) and Isaac Newton in Britain. It had its origin in the study of falling objects. *Differential calculus* concerns the rate of change of a dependent variable and involves the gradient, maxima and minima of the curve of a given function. *Integral calculus* deals with areas and volumes, and methods of summation and many of its applications developed from the study of the gradients of tangents to curves.

calcium a soft silver-white metal at room temperature which tarnishes very quickly in air, and reacts violently with water. Calcium compounds are very widely distributed; as calcium carbonate ($CaCO_3$) in limestone and chalk; as calcium sulphate ($CaSO_4$) in gypsum; within silicates occurring in minerals and there are many other occurrences. In biological systems, Calcium ions (Ca^{2+}) are vital to life as constituents of bone and teeth.

Calcium is also important industrially as lime (CaO), as $CaCO_3$ in the production of iron from its ores, and in the preparation of certain transition element metals, (*see* PERIODIC TABLE).

camera *see* PHOTOGRAPHY.

camouflage *see* NH: CAMOUFLAGE.

cancer a disease of animal cells in which there is a rapid and uncontrolled rate of growth and reproduction. A collection of cancer cells is known as a *tumour* which is termed *benign* if it remains localised in one place. A *malignant* tumour spreads, invades and destroys surrounding healthy tissue. It spreads via the bloodstream and produces secondary cancers in other parts of the body by a process known as *metastasis*. These malignant cancers can often prove fatal as they disrupt the normal functioning of cells in the affected tissues. The search for the cure and causes of various kinds of cancer is a vast area of scientific and medical research. The treatment and life expectancy of people affected by most kinds of cancer has greatly improved in recent years. Some substances and environmental factors (known as *carcinogens*) are known to increase the risk of cancer developing and the best known of these is cigarette smoke. Cancer treatment involves surgery, radiotherapy (the use of radiation to destroy tumours), chemotherapy (the administration of drugs to destroy tumours) and the giving of more specialised drugs (cytotoxic) which attack the malignant cells in a special way.

capacitor a device for storing electric charge comprising two plates separated, in its simplest form, by air but usually by an insulating material called a *dielectric*. Commercial capacitors have foil plates separated by a dielectric such as Mylar, forming a sandwich which is rolled up into a cylindrical shape. This gives a large area of plate in a small device. Other dielectrics include mica, certain plastics and aluminium oxide. Capacitors are used a great deal in electrical circuits in televisions, radios and other electronic equipment. The capacitor works by a charge on one plate inducing an equal charge on the opposite plate and a change in the charge is mirrored between plates.

capillary *see* CIRCULATION.

capillary action a phenomenon related to surface tension in liquids in which there is an attraction between the sides of a glass tube and water molecules. The result is that water is pulled up a very thin glass tube (a *capillary tube*), and it will move further the thinner the tube. This action happens with other liquids including alcohol, but mercury moves in the opposite way. Many occurrences involving the movement of water involve capillary action, e.g. tissues soaking up water, walls taking in water producing damp.

capsule a widely used term in biology which describes a structure found in flowering plants, mosses and liverworts, bacteria and animals.

   1 In flowering plants, it is a dry fruit containing seeds which splits when ripe. The splitting and releasing of the seeds occurs in different ways, e.g. splitting into different parts, known as valves, in the iris, through holes or pores as in the snapdragon, or through a lid as in the scarlet pimpernel.

   2 In plants called bryophotes (*see* **NH**: BRYOPHOTES), which includes liverworts and mosses, a capsule contains spores and is produced on the end of a thick stalk (seta). It is known as a sporophyte.

3 Some bacteria produce an outer sheath of gelatinous material surrounding the cell wall which is protective and is called a capsule.

4 In vertebrate animals a connective tissue sheath known as a capsule surrounds some of the joints in the skeleton. Also, a membrane or fibrous connective tissue sheath called a capsule encloses and protects some vertebrate organs such as the kidney.

carbides are compounds of metals with carbon which in many instances result in hard, refractory materials with very high melting points. Tungsten or tantalum carbide are used for tools as are mixtures with cobalt and nickel. Titanium carbide is used in fast reactors , gas turbine blades and on coatings for rocket components. Chromium carbide is used for electrodes and for parts used with corrosive chemicals and Tantalum carbide is used for elements in eletric furnaces.

carbohydrates are chemical compounds made up of carbon, hydrogen and oxygen forming a very large and important group of substances. The most familiar ones are sugars, starch and cellulose and carbohydrates are manufactured by green plants during the process of photosynthesis. Carbohydrates are a vital food source for animals as they are broken down within the body to provide the energy required for all the various life processes.

carbon a non-metallic element that occurs as the element in two forms, graphite and diamond, and in numerous compounds. Carbon is unique in the enormous number of compounds it can form both in inorganic form, e.g. carbon dioxide, carbonates, and in being the basis of organic chemistry. Carbon is *allotropic*, i.e. it exists in several elemental forms-carbon black, in addition to graphite and diamonds, each differing in their crystalline structure and thus their properties.

Carbon is used extensively; in steelmaking, for motor brushes, cathode ray tubes and *active carbon* is used as a purifying agent in removal of air pollutants, water treatment and purification of chemicals, and as carbon fibres. Carbon is the standard for measuring atomic masses (*see* ATOMIC NUMBER) and the radioactive carbon 14 is used in radiocarbon dating (*see* **GG**: DATING METHODS).

carbon dioxide is a colourless gas at room temperature that *sublimes* at -78.5°C. It occurs naturally in the atmosphere and is the source of carbon for plants, playing a vital role in plant and animal respiration and metabolism (since it is exhaled by animals and absorbed by plants during photosynthesis). Carbon dioxide forms when coal, wood etc. are burned and it is a byproduct of fermentation. It is produced industrially from *synthesis gas* (a mixture of hydrogen and carbon monoxide) used in the production of ammonia. Its physical properties make it a useful refrigerant and it is dissolved in mineral waters and fizzy drinks, creating bubbles. Also, since it is heavier than air and does not support combustion it is used in fire extinguishers.

Sublimation is when a solid substance changes to the vapour phase *without* first becoming liquid.

carbon fibres fibres consisting of oriented carbon chains which produce a material that is very strong for its weight. Carbon (or graphite) fibres are manufactured by heating polyacrylonitrile $(CH_2.CHCN)_n$) fibres initially at low temperatures to stabilise the fibres and then at high temperatures (2500ºC) and under tension to orientate the graphite along the fibres. The resulting fibres are usually 8-11μm in diameter and are not generally totally crystalline, with graphite crystals in amorphous carbon. The fibres are used as a reinforcing material in resins and ceramics producing strong materials able to withstand high temperatures and with a higher strength to weight ratio than metals.

carbon monoxide a colourless gas with no smell that is formed when coke and similar fuels are burnt in a limited supply of air, i.e. incomplete combustion. It also occurs in the exhaust emissions of car engines. It is used industrially because of its reducing properties (*see* OXIDATION AND REDUCTION), for example in metallurgy.

One of its most important properties is its toxicity. It is poisonous when breathed in because it combines with haemoglobin in the blood, which reduces the capacity of the blood to carry oxygen (*see* CIRCULATION).

carnivore any animal that eats the flesh of other animals, often referring to mammals belonging to the order *Carnivora* (*see* **NH**). Some highly specialised plants are carnivorous, and these usually trap insects or small frogs, etc, and secrete enzymes that break them down, enabling the products of digestion to be absorbed.

cartilage a special type of connective tissue that, together with bone, forms the skeleton of vertebrate animals. It is composed of proteins and carbohydrates, especially collagen, which is a fibrous substance that makes cartilage tough and elastic. Cartilage is found in various parts of the skeleton, e.g. between the vertebrae of the backbone and around joints. It is also present in rings around the windpipe (trachea) and in the ears and nose.

cast iron or *pig iron* is the impure form of iron produced in a blast furnace. It contains 2–4.5% carbon in a form called *cementite* (Fe_3C) and other elements such as silicon, phosphorus, sulphur and manganese. Cast irons are often too brittle to use, but additions of other metals can improve its workability. Wrought iron is made by melting cast iron and scrap iron in a special furnace, removing most of the impurities. Cast iron melts at 1200°C, whereas wrought iron softens at 1000°C and melts at 1500°C (*see also* STEEL).

catalysis the use of a *catalyst* to alter the rate of a chemical reaction. A catalyst usually increases the speed at which a chemical reaction proceeds, but is itself unchanged at the end of the reaction. In practice the catalyst may be changed physically if not chemically. Catalysts are used a great deal in the chemical industry, iron and platinum being common examples. Metal oxides are also used (copper, zinc, aluminium, titanium), and *zeolites* have become more important over recent years. In biological systems, enzymes are the natural organic equivalent of catalysts.

A *catalytic converter* is fitted to new cars to reduce the volume of exhaust gases produced. The gases pass over a honeycomb structure (which greatly increases the surface area) that is coated with a catalyst such as platinum or palladium, and reactions produce water vapour and carbon dioxide.

Zeolites are natural or synthetic alumina silicates of sodium, potassium calcium and barium that contain cavities with water. The water can be removed by heating and then occupied by other molecules. With small amounts of platinum or palladium they are used in the catalytic cracking of hydrocarbons.

cathode ray tube is an evacuated tube in which *cathode rays* are produced and strike a fluorescent screen; it forms the basis of a television and a *cathode ray oscilloscope* which is used in laboratories and radar systems. At one end of the tube is an assembly (*electron gun*) that produces a beam of electrons which can be focused. The beam passes between two sets of plates, each of which can deflect the electron beam when a voltage is applied to the plates. The resulting beam then impinges upon the screen which is coated with zinc sulphide and fluoresces where the electrons strike.

Cathode ray tube

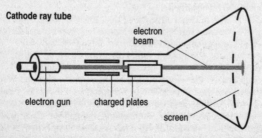

electron beam

electron gun   charged plates

screen

caustic soda chemically is sodium hydroxide (NaOH), a whitish substance that gives a strongly alkaline (*see* ALKALIS) solution in water and will burn skin. It is *deliquescent*, that is it picks up moisture from the air and may eventually liquefy. It is used a great deal in the laboratory and is a very important industrial chemical, being used in the manufacture of pulp and paper, soap and detergents, petrochemicals, textiles and other chemicals. Sodium hydroxide is itself manufactured by the electrolysis of sodium chloride solution, chlorine being the other product, or by the addition of hot sodium carbonate solution to quicklime (calcium oxide, CaO).

cell the smallest and most basic unit of all living organisms. A cell is able to perform the main functions of life which are metabolism, growth and reproduction and there are two main types, procaryote and eucaryote. Bacteria and blue-green algae are procaryotes and all other animals and plants are eucaryotes. The simple organisms consist of a single cell and are termed unicellular, e.g bacteria. However, most living creatures are formed of vast numbers of cells which congregate together to form highly specialised tissues and organs. A typical cell has an outer layer or membrane surrounding a jelly-like substance called *cytoplasm*. Various structures called organelles (*see* ORGAN) are contained within the cytoplasm which are responsible for a number of different activities. The largest structure present is the nucleus surrounded by a (nuclear) membrane which contains the chromosomes and genes. Plant cells differ from animal ones in having an outer wall composed of a carbohydrate substance called cellulose. These walls may be thick giving strength and shape to the structure of the plant. Substances pass into and out of cells across the cell membranes e.g. food materials and oxygen and carbon dioxide.

A typical cell

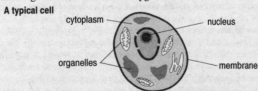

cytoplasm — nucleus

organelles — membrane

cell division the formation of two daughter cells from one parent cell, with the nucleus dividing first by a process known as *mitosis*. The end result is that the nucleus of each daughter cell contains the same number of chromosomes (carrying the genes) as the original parent cell. The chromosomes are in the form of strands of material which come together in pairs.

These eventually arrange themselves across the centre of the nucleus and the nuclear membrane disappears. Each member of a pair is now composed of two strands, known as *chromatids,* which are joined at a single point called a centromere. As mitosis progresses, the centromeres split and one chromatid from each of the pairs moves to opposite ends. A nuclear membrane forms around each group of chromatids, now the new chromosomes and then the cytoplasm itself divides to form two daughter cells each with its own nucleus. Another type of cell division occurs in the formation of sex cells (sperm and eggs), and this is known as *meiosis.* In meiosis, the stages of mitosis are repeated again after a resting phase. The end result is that four daughter cells are produced, each with half the number of chromosomes of the parent cell, a condition known as *haploid.* At fertilisation, two haploid cells (a sperm and an egg) fuse together so that the new individual has the full number of chromosomes, half from each parent, and this condition is known as *diploid.* Most cells are diploid with only the sex cells (gametes) being haploid. *See also* FERTILISATION, REPRODUCTION, CHROMOSOME AND GENE.

cellular communications are radios, but particularly telephones that can be used almost anywhere (car phones, portable telephone) and linked to exchanges and standard telephone lines by means of an almost countrywide network. The network is divided into cells and when a user with a portable or car phone makes a call, it is transmitted to a base station and then to a telephone exchange. From the exchange the signal is then directed to the recipient either via a landline or through a similar route of cells.

Each cell has a relay station to deal with all calls in that cell and when a user moves to another cell another station takes over.

cellulose a type of carbohydrate (known as a *polysaccharide*) which is composed of chains of glucose (sugar) units. It makes up the cells walls of many plants and has a fibrous structure which gives strength. Cellulose is not easily digested and some HERBIVORES have evolved a strategy for dealing with this in that they possess a four-chambered stomach containing bacteria which are able to break down cellulose. These are known as *ruminant* animals. In humans, cellulose is important as dietary fibre.

cement is any compound or mix that binds materials together, but generally refers to Portland cement used in building and construction. Cement is manufactured from chalk or limestone, with clay which provides the necessary lime, silica and alumina. The mix is crushed and heated in a KILN to form a *clinker* (a partly melted, dense ash) which contains calcium silicates and aluminates. The clinker is finely ground and gypsum (calcium sulphate, $CaSO_4$) added. The cement product then goes through complex *hydration* (combination with water) reactions which eventually result in a hard stone-like material.

There are now many different cements which have particular properties depending upon their composition. These include: ordinary Portland cement, rapid-hardening cement, Portland blast-furnace cement, sulphate-resistant cement and micro-silica cement.

centre of gravity of a body is the point through which the total effect of gravity acting upon all parts of the body are effectively concentrated. This usually coincides with the *centre of mass* and is the point at which the weight or downward force due to gravity acts. When applied to everyday objects, this means that some will fall over more easily than others. The stability of an object can be increased by lowering its centre of gravity, perhaps by enlarging its base. A good example is in transport where large tall loads are unstable (due to a high centre of gravity) whereas racing cars are designed to have a low centre of gravity to allow them to move at high speeds.

centrifuge a machine for separating out particles suspended in a liquid. It comprises two arms about a central pivot, each arm holding a tube. When the arms are rotated rapidly about the central point the suspended particles are forced outwards to the bottom of the tubes and different particles will separate at different speeds, depending upon their size and mass. An *ultracentrifuge* rotates at very high speeds (up to 60,000 rpm) and is used for determining the masses of polymers and proteins. In industry, centrifuges are used for separating mixtures and in the production of cream and sugar.

centripetal force is the force necessary to move an object in a circular path, such as a ball on the end of a rope. The ball follows a circular route because there is a force in towards the centre of the circle – the centripetal force. If the rope is released, the ball continues in the direction at the time and moves off at a tangent. The force can be felt easily when some weighty object is swung around and the person holding the rope stays in the same place, and an object will only move in a circle if the centripetal force is provided.

Centripetal force applies when a car corners, the friction between tyres and road providing the force and in some fairground rides. The same applies to a satellite orbiting the Earth where gravitational attraction between the bodies supplies the centripetal force.

ceramics is the term generally applied to items manufactured from clays and includes pottery and *porcelain* where a moist clay is moulded to shape and fired in a kiln until it hardens. Decorative glazes can be added and many domestic and commercial items are produced in this way. These are *traditional ceramics* made of 50-60% clay to which animal bone is added (to control the porosity) producing a non-porous *china*. The mineral *feldspar* can be added in place of bone, producing porcelain goods, e.g. insulators. Clay minerals with no additions are used to produce bricks, tiles, pipes and similar construction materials.

Considerable advances have been made in recent years in the field of materials technology and many ceramics or *composites* (a mix of materials, often as fibres of one material in a different matrix) have been developed.

Light ceramics	carbon fibres; carbides and nitrides; silicon dioxide; aluminium dioxide
Glasses (*see* GLASS)	there are three major commercial systems: a) soda-lime-silica (Na_2O-CaO-SiO_2) b) lead crystal (PbO-SiO_2) c) low expansion borosilicate (B_2O_3-SiO_2 -Na_2O-CaO)
Glass ceramics	glass containing very small crystals
Refractory oxides	able to withstand the action of corrosive solids, liquids and gases at high temperatures e.g. alumina (Al_2O_3) in lasers, zirconia (ZrO_2) in developing ceramic steels, magnesia (MgO) in pollution control, titania (TiO_2) in enamelling and catalysis
Refractory metals	metal carbides, nitrides, borides and silicides, for use in cutting tools, electrodes, heating elements and protective coatings

cereals are important food crops derived from wild grasses which have been grown by man for many thousands of years. Cereals are grown for their seeds, which are usually ground to produce flour and contain important nutrients such as carbohydrates, proteins, vitamins and calcium. Over the centuries farmers have selectively cultivated cereal crops sowing seeds from the best and biggest plants and those that produced the most grain. The end result of this plant breeding is that cultivated cereals now look very different from the wild grasses that are their 'ancestors.'

CFCs *see* CHLOROFLUOROCARBONS.

chemical reaction the interaction between substances (reactants) producing different or altered substances (products) in which the bond elements are broken and reformed. Reactions may proceed at normal pressure and temperature, or special conditions may be necessary, e.g. high pressure, or the presence of a catalyst (*see* CATALYSIS). Some terms refer to typical reactions; for example, *hydrolysis* is the breakdown of a substance by water. The *heat or reaction* is the heat given out or required when certain amounts of substances react under constant pressure. Other heat quantities of a similar nature include:

heat of combustion	the heat evolved when one mole (*see* MOLECULE) of a substance is burned in oxygen.
heat of dissociation	the heat required to dissociate (splitting a molecule into simpler fragments) one mole of a compound.
heat of formation	the heat given out or required when one molecule of a substance is formed from its constituent elements at standard pressure and temperature.

chemistry is the study of the composition of substances, their reactions and effects upon one another and the resulting changes. There are three main branches: physical, inorganic and organic. *Physical chemistry* deals with the link between chemical composition and physical properties and the physical changes due to reactions. *Inorganic chemistry* is the study of the elements and their compounds (excluding the organic compounds of carbon), and the group and period characteristics as arranged in the periodic table. *Organic chemistry* is the study of carbon compounds, of which there is an enormous number and many are compounds with hydrogen, the hydrocarbons. Organic chemistry also deals with compounds of significant benefit to man-drugs, vitamins, antibiotics, polymers and plastics, and many more.

chlorine the second element in the HALOGENS group which is a yellow-green choking gas which is harmful if inhaled. It occurs as the chloride, mainly sodium chloride (NaCl), but also magnesium chloride and others. It is manufactured by the ELECTROLYSIS of brine (which also produces sodium hydroxide, NaOH) and stored as a liquid. It is a very important material in the chemicals industry and its powerful oxidising properties are utilised in bleaches and disinfectants. It is also used in the production of hydrochloric acid and numerous organic chemicals. Compounds derived from chlorine are used in water sterilisation, paper manufacture, solvents, PVC and other polymers, refrigerants and more. Hydrocarbons containing chlorine account for a very large proportion of chlorine derivatives.

chlorofluorocarbons or CFCs are organic compounds that contain chlorine and fluorine (both halogens). Although CFCs have in the past had numerous industrial uses, as aerosol propellants, in refrigerants and are produced when manufacturing foam plastics, their use is now being curbed and much reduced because of their harmful environmental effect.

Although CFCs are stable for a long time, they do break down and release their chlorine which reacts with ozone in the atmospheric ozone layer (*see* **GG:** OZONE LAYER) producing oxygen and chlorine oxide. This reduction in ozone then has direct detrimental effects upon plants and animals on Earth.

chloroplast and chlorophyll chloroplasts are the organelles (*see* CELL) present within the cells of green plants and algae, e.g. *Spirogyra*, which are the site of photosynthesis. They contain chlorophyll which is the pigment that gives the plant its green colour. Chlorophyll is essential in photosynthesis as it traps energy from sunlight and helps the plant to manufacture its food from carbon dioxide and water. The chloroplasts (and chlorophyll) are mainly found in the leaves but also in the stems of green plants.

cholesterol a type of fatty substance which occurs naturally and is produced within animal bodies. In mammals such as man it is made mainly in the liver, carried in the bloodstream and stored within cell membranes. Cholesterol is used to make some hormones and also a substance known as bile which is important in digestion.

Cholesterol can cause a problem in some people when too much is present in the blood. It may build up on the inner walls of arteries (a condition known as *arteriosclerosis*), causing them to become narrow and more easily blocked by a blood clot which can lead to a heart attack (*see* CIRCULATION).

chromatography is a technique used in chemical and biological analysis in which the constituents of a mixture can be separated. There are numerous closely-related techniques but each depends upon one principle-the differing rate at which components of a mixture move through a stationary phase due to the presence of a mobile phase. The simplest case is that of a piece of blotting paper dipped into water. A drop of ink placed on the blotting paper will move up as the water ascends the paper, and in so doing will be separated into its component pigments. In this case the water is the mobile phase and the paper is the stationary phase, and this is essentially a form of paper chromatography.

Gas chromatography occurs where a gas is the mobile phase. It is used for complex mixtures of organic materials.

High performance liquid chromatography is the passage of the sample through a column by means of a liquid mobile phase under pressure.

Thin layer chromatography is the separation by solvent movement across a flat surface of special paper, powdered cellulose, silica gel, alumina (aluminium oxide) or other stationary phase.

Ion-exchange chromatography is the separation of ionic materials by a solution passing over the surface of a resin which contains ions that can be exchanged. It is used in inorganic chemistry to separate metal mixtures or to separate amino acids.

Gel permeation chromatography is where materials are separated by molecular size by a solution passing through a porous polymer gel, in which small molecules are trapped, while larger molecules move.

chromosomes and **genes** chromosomes are threads of material that are found within the nucleus of each living cell. They consist mainly of chains of DNA (composed of a substance called nucleic acid), and parts of these are called genes, which are the 'blueprints' or plans that determine everything about the organism. Each living organism has a particular number of chromosomes, which contain very many genes.

Human beings have 23 pairs of chromosomes, 22 of which look the same in both males and females. The 23rd pair are the sex chromosomes, which in males look like an XY and in females an XX. Although the chromosomes look similar in all individuals belonging to a particular species, the genes that they carry are all slightly different, hence each one is totally unique. *See also* HEREDITY and MUTATION.

circuit an electrically-conducting path that when complete allows a current to flow through it. A circuit may be very simple consisting merely of a battery connected by copper wire to a bulb and then back to the opposite terminal of the battery. When cells and batteries were first made (in the early 1800s by the Italian scientist Alessandro Volta [1745–1827]), how charge moved around a circuit remained a mystery. The convention became that current flowed as a positive charge from the positive terminal around to the negative terminal. This is contrary to what actually happens since electrons flow in the opposite direction, but the convention remains (*see also* ELECTRICITY).

A simple circuit diagram

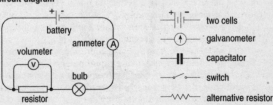

circulation (of the blood) is the process by which blood is moved around an animal's body by the pumping action of the heart.

The blood carries oxygen and food to all the cells of the body and also takes carbon dioxide from them to the lungs where it is eliminated. Blood which contains oxygen (oxygenated blood), is supplied to the left atrium, one of the four chambers of the heart, by the four pulmonary veins. It is passed into the left ventricle of the heart, a chamber that acts like a muscular pump, into a large blood vessel called the aorta and then on into the arteries. As the arteries reach the tissues and organs they become very tiny (arterioles and capillaries). Here blood releases its oxygen (becoming deoxygenated), and this is picked up and used by cells. Cells release carbon dioxide into the deoxygenated blood as it passes through more capillaries. The blood is now transported through tiny vessels (venules) which become larger veins. It then passes back to the right atrium of the heart via two large veins known as the inferior and superior vena cava. This is known as the systemic circuit. From here it passes to the lungs (via the right ventricle and pulmonary artery) where carbon dioxide is released and oxygen is picked up before it returns to the left side of the heart once again. This is known as the pulmonary circuit.

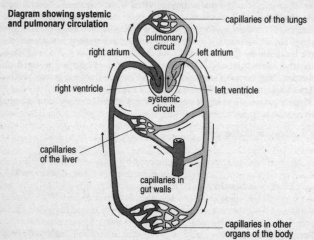

Diagram showing systemic and pulmonary circulation

capillaries of the lungs

pulmonary circuit

right atrium

left atrium

right ventricle

left ventricle

systemic circuit

capillaries of the liver

capillaries in gut walls

capillaries in other organs of the body

This type of blood circulation is described as 'double'. The heart is divided into two sides which each act as an independent pump with no communication between them. Each side is further divided into two chambers, the upper one is the *atrium* and collects incoming blood passing it to the lower *ventricle*. This strong, muscular pump contracts and pumps blood out either to the body or to the lungs. Arteries always carry oxygenated blood except for the pulmonary artery which takes blood from the heart to the lungs. Veins always transport deoxygenated blood except for the pulmonary vein which takes oxygenated blood from the lungs to the heart.

classification a means of grouping living organisms according to how similar they are to each other. For the early biologists, the physical similarities between organisms were the most important feature. However, increasingly in modern times the similarities between organisms at a genetic level have become more important in understanding their relationships.

One main method of classification is most commonly recognised and this was originally devised by a Swedish naturalist, Carolus Linnaeus (1707–88) and is known as the *Linnaean system*. In this, all living things belong to a particular species and very similar species are grouped together in a *genus* (*pl*. genera), (*see* CLASSIFICATION). Hence in biology, each living organism has a double-barrelled name, first its generic (genus) and then its specific (species) 'label' and these are given in Latin. Examples are *Lumbricus terrestris* (the earthworm), *Rana temporaria* (the common frog), *Homo sapiens* (human beings) and, among plants, *Quercus robur* (the common oak), *Primula vulgaris* (primrose) and *Taraxacum officinale* (the dandelion). Genera which show similar features are grouped into families and these in turn into orders. Numbers of orders are put into classes which are grouped into a phylum (*pl*. phyla).

Finally, phyla are placed together in a kingdom. In plants, the grouping division usually replaces phylum but otherwise the classification is the same.

clone a living organism which is an exact genetic copy of another individual and is produced from a single cell by an asexual process (*see* ASEXUAL REPRODUCTION).

cloning is an artificial process engineered by man and much used in the breeding of plants (e.g. cuttings). In February 1997, scientists in Scotland claimed they successfully produced a ewe, which they called Dolly, that had been cloned from another adult ewe. However, it was later conceded that there was a very remote possibility that Dolly might have been cloned from foetal cells that were circulating in the ewe's bloodstream.

colloids were defined originally as substances in solution that could not get through a dialysis (semi-permeable) membrane. The definition of a colloid now is one of particle size – when the size range is 10^{-4} to 10^{-6}mm, and it therefore falls between a coarse suspension and a true solution. Most substances can now be prepared to exist in this state, and many exist naturally as colloids. Common examples of colloidal solutions include starch and albumen, butter and cell cytoplasm.

An *emulsion* is a colloidal solution of one liquid in another; generally one is water or a solution in water and the other is an oil or a similar liquid that does not mix with water. Emulsions are used widely in industry in food and pharmaceuticals, cosmetics, paints and lubricants.

combustion or burning is actually a chemical reaction that occurs quickly and involves the high temperature oxidation of a substance, i.e. it combines with oxygen, to produce heat, light and flame, and of course ashes (oxides). Combustion of fossil fuels is the source of most energy used in homes, factories and offices. When coal or a similar fuel is burned, the carbon is converted to carbon dioxide or carbon monoxide and the hydrogen to water vapour. Combustion is a vital industrial process and although it generally refers to burning in oxygen, it is used on other occasions when, for example, a substance is burnt in hydrogen.

compact disc is a disc used to hold music, graphics or data for replaying. The disc has a layer of aluminium, and music is recorded as very small pits etched into the surface. The pits are tiny – about half a micrometre (μm) deep and one to three wide. Each track is about 1.5μm from the next. The music is replayed by focusing a laser beam on the disc as it turns at 250 revolutions per minute. The beam is partially reflected, depending upon whether or not it strikes a pit, and the reflected beam is detected as a series of pulses that are changed back into a copy of the original recording. Because there is no physical contact between the disc and the playing medium, compact discs are more resilient and should last much longer than their earlier counterparts: magnetic tapes and vinyl records.

compound is when two or more elements combine chemically in a substance and in definite proportions to produce molecules held together by chemical bonds. The formation of a compound necessitates a chemical reaction, and the elements cannot be separated physically. Also, the same compound is formed irrespective of its origin so one molecule of water is two atoms of hydrogen and one of oxygen no matter how it is made.

The above can be regarded as the specific definition of compound but there are instances when the boundaries are blurred. For example, many silicate minerals, e.g. the feldspars, have varying compositions, as do many polymers although all are chemically combined. Indeed materials such as glass and steel are not mixtures and yet they do not fall readily into the definition of compound.

concentration *see* SOLUTIONS.

concrete a building material comprising a mixture of sand, cement, stone and water, which after it is set becomes very hard. Concrete is used in vast quantities for all types of building and construction and often steel rods or meshes are set into the concrete to increase its strength-*reinforced* concrete. *Prestressed concrete* is when the concrete is under compression, achieved by stretching the reinforcing rods and keeping them in tension after the concrete has set. Prestressed concrete is useful for large spans or where beams have to be as light as possible.

condensation is the process by which a substance changes from the gaseous state to the liquid state. In so doing energy is lost, i.e. it is cooled. There are many everyday examples of condensation-water forming on a pan lid when vegetables are cooking; water droplets on a cold tap in the bathroom; the steam from a kettle which is actually the hot water vapour condensing as tiny water droplets in the cooler air. *Cloud* (*see* **GG**) is another example which is due to warm air saturated with water vapour being cooled.

   The physical process of condensation is used in the chemicals industry when substances are purified by distillation. In chemistry a *condensation reaction* is the reaction of one molecule with another and the elimination of a simple molecule such as water.

conduction and convection *conduction* of heat is a process of heat moving through a material and is due to molecular vibrations. When a material is heated, the molecules vibrate rapidly and knock into neighbouring molecules which transfers the heat (or thermal energy) along the material. Metals e.g. copper and aluminium are the best conductors of heat while liquids and gases are progressively poor conductors.

conductor and insulator electric conductors are materials that allow a flow of electrons, producing an electric current. As with conduction of heat, metals form the best electrical conductors because electrons around the outside of the atoms are loosely held and can move freely. Poor conductors include water, glass and air, indeed most non-metals.

   A material that does not conduct electric charge is called an *insulator*. Plastics, rubber, glass and air form insulators because their electrons are not usually free to move.

connective tissue a type of tissue which is commonly found in the bodies of animals. It is further divided into a variety of different sorts depending upon the materials from which it is composed. It is usually composed of a non-living core containing various fibres in which are spread a number of cells.

construction *see* BUILDING AND CONSTRUCTION.

contraction and expansion when a solid is heated and its molecules vibrate more due to the input of thermal energy, the result is that the molecules move apart a little and the solid *expands*, almost imperceptibly. When the reverse happens, the solid *contracts*. Although the expansion in a solid may be negligible, the resulting force can be very large. In construction particularly, account has to be taken for the expansion of steel and concrete and all bridges have expansion joints to avoid damage which would otherwise be caused. Railways lines have a similar feature but in this case, line ends have overlapping joints.

The property of expansion also has its useful aspects and it can be applied to numerous devices which contain a bimetal strip.

Liquids generally expand more than solids, producing an increase in volume. Water is a notable exception to this statement and its behaviour is quite complex. As water cools from boiling it contracts a very small amount until it reaches 4°C at which point it expands a little. As we all know, at 0°C it forms ice and expands a great deal but on further cooling it contracts more. At 4°C water has its least volume and therefore its greatest density and it will sink beneath colder or warmer water. This is the reason for ponds freezing on the surface while fish can survive in the slightly warmer water at depth.

convection *see* CONDUCTION AND CONVECTION.

copper is a red-brown metal which is very malleable and ductile (*see* DUCTILITY) and has numerous uses. It occurs as native copper (as the metal itself, often with silver, lead and other metals) and in a variety of mineral forms, for example, malachite ($CuCO_3.Cu(OH)_2$), bornite ($CuFeS_3$) and chalco-pyrite ($CuFeS_2$). The ores are concentrated and copper is extracted by smelting and refining by electrolysis. Copper has been an important metal for thousands of years in its alloys, brass and bronze, and it is now used in coins as an alloy (with nickel).

Pure copper is an excellent electrical conductor and is used in wiring and a significant proportion of copper production is taken in electrical applications. It is also used for pipes in plumbing although plastics are being used increasingly in this context. Copper is also employed in fungicides, paints, pigments and printing.

corrosion is the process of metals and alloys being attacked chemically by moisture, air, acids or alkalis. If left to continue, the metal will be gradually worn away. Corrosion may occur uniformly or it may be concentrated at weak points or joints. It may also produce an oxide layer, as on aluminium which protects against further attack. The more serious effects are seen with corrosion where some moisture is present because this sets up an electrolytic process and with underground corrosion the soil acts as the electrolyte (*see* ELECTROLYSIS).

coulomb is the unit of electrical charge defined as the charge passing a point in a circuit when a current of one ampère flows for one second. Thus a charge of 8 coulombs passes if a current of 2 ampères flows for 4 seconds. One coulomb is equal to the charge on approximately 6.25×10^{18} electrons.

cracking *see* PETROCHEMICALS.

cytology the branch of biology devoted to the scientific study of cells, including both their structure and function, that depends very much on the use of the light and electron microscope.

Darwin and natural selection. Charles Darwin (1809–1882) was one of the most famous naturalists ever to have lived and he devised the theory of evolution (known as *Darwinism*) to explain the great variety of plants and animals which he saw around him. He arrived at his theories during a five year voyage around the world (the voyage of HMS *Beagle*) and when he returned to England in 1859 he published a scientific paper (with the title *Origin of Species*). He proposed that some individuals in a species are more successful than others (they have a greater degree of 'fitness'). In the competition for food or for a mate they are more likely to be successful and these characteristics are inherited by their offspring which means that eventually these features become more widespread. He called this 'survival of the fittest.' Following from this, plants and animals were gradually able to change and adapt to new conditions and environments. Hence new species eventually evolved from an original, ancestral stock. Darwin's theories were not accepted at the time and caused outrage because they questioned the Biblical version of God's Creation as a one-off event. However, now they are largely accepted and have been expanded by the modern study of genes and inheritance. Darwin's theory can be summarised as follows: from organisms which have the ability to change, new species can emerge that will adapt to new environments. Old species which are no longer suited to the surrounding environment will eventually die out.

decibel *see* SOUND.

deciduous and evergreen deciduous plants shed their leaves at the end of the growing season, which is Autumn in temperate regions such as Britain. Examples include familiar trees such as the oak and sycamore. Evergreen plants on the other hand, keep their leaves all through the year and these include the cone-bearing coniferous trees (conifers) such as Sitka spruce.

decimal numbers is the most commonly used number system based on powers of ten. The *decimal point* is the dot that divides the number's whole part from the fractional part (i.e. that which is less than one). However, numbers need not contain a decimal point: 789 is also a decimal number. A decimal is itself less than one and is written after the decimal point e.g. 0.789 and 0.00987. Decimal numbers are written within the place value system, that is, the value given to a digit depends upon its position in the number and with the decimal system each column has ten times the value of the column to the right thus:

The number 7891 is really:

seven 1000s	eight 100s	nine 10s and one 1
(10^3)	(10^2)	(10^1) (10^0)
7	8	9 1

A common fraction such as $1/4$ can be changed into decimal form by dividing the 1 by 4 to give 0.25.

dehydration in a chemical reaction or process is the removal by heat of water held in a molecule or compound. Sometimes a catalyst is used, or a dehydrating agent such as sulphuric acid $(H2SO4)$. Dehydration is used a great deal in the food industry in the production of coffee, soups, sauces, mashed potato, milk and so on. It arrests the processes of natural decay because there is no moisture available for micro-organisms to survive and chemical reactions are slowed or stopped. Dehydration produces a reduction in volume and particularly weight which is useful for storage and transport.

In medicine, dehydration is the excessive, often dangerous, loss of water from body tissues, accompanied by loss of vital salts. The average daily intake of water is about 2 litres but lack of water for just a few days can be dangerous because the heart can be affected.

dendrochronology a technique of dating past events using the growth rings of trees. Each year a new ring of wood is added to the trunk just beneath the bark and this is called an annual ring. It is possible to date the rings in living trees by working back year by year. Then this pattern of rings can be used to date fossil trees or specimens of wood found at archaeological, or other sites. The longest living trees are the most useful and the standard one is the bristle cone pine, which can live for up to 5000 years and be used to date specimens older than this.

density is the mass of a substance, per unit volume, given by the following equation:

$$\text{density (d)} = \frac{\text{mass (M)}}{\text{volume (V)}}$$

It is measured in kilograms per cubic metre (kg/m^3), although it may be more convenient on occasion to use grams per cubic centimetre (g/cm^3). Density varies with temperature; only a little in the case of solids and liquids which usually expand and therefore become less dense, with gases the density varies a great deal depending upon its container and the surrounding pressure.

Relative density is the density of a material compared to that of water, given by the following equation:

$$\text{relative density} = \frac{\text{density of a substance}}{\text{density of water}}$$

Relative density used to be called *specific gravity*. It has no units, but is the same value as the density when measured in g/cm^3. Some typical densities:

	kg/m^3	g/cm^3		kg/m^3	g/cm^3
air	1.3	0.0013	aluminium	2700	2.7
soft wood	450	0.45	diamond	3500	3.5
hard wood	800	0.80	steel	7700	7.7
petrol	800	0.80	lead	11400	11.4
water	1000	1.00	mercury	13600	13.6
hardened cement	2200	2.2	gold	19300	19.3
granite	2600	2.6			

detergents and soaps are both cleaning agents that remove grease and dirt and hold it in suspension for washing away. Soap acts as a detergent but there are now many synthetic detergents derived from petroleum. The detergent molecules contain two distinct groups; one which gives the molecule solubility in water, e.g. a sulphate, and long hydrocarbon chains which enable it to dissolve oily materials. When detergent molecules come into contact with grease, the hydrocarbon chains which are *hydrophobic* (water-hating) attach to the grease, and the other end of the molecule which is *hydrophilic* (water-loving) is in the water. The grease is then enclosed and can be removed from the garment. Detergents are made in many forms: washing-up liquids, powders, shampoo, etc.

Soaps are sodium and potassium salts of *fatty acids* (an organic acid of animal or vegetable origin) which are heated in large vats with dilute sodium hydroxide (caustic soda) to effect *hydrolysis* (*see* CHEMICAL REACTION). Sodium chloride is then added to precipitate the soap from the solution.

Soap may be treated with perfumes before being made into bars or flakes.

Metallic soaps are a very different group of compounds, being insoluble in water. They are metal salts (metals such as lithium, aluminium, calcium, and zinc) of long carboxylic acid chains (organic acids with one or more carboxyl, -COOH, groups) and are used in cosmetics, pharmaceuticals, fungicides and lubricating oils.

differentiation a mathematical operation used in calculus for finding the derivative of a function. Depending upon the complexity of the function there are different methods of differentiation. The simplest relates to the common function;

$$f(x) \text{ or } y = x^n$$

This has the derivative (or differential coefficient);

$$f^1(x) \text{ or } \frac{dy}{dx} = nx^{n-1}$$

Thus, for example, if $y = 4x^3$, $\frac{dy}{dx} = 12x^2$

and for $y = 3x^3 + 4x^2$, $\frac{dy}{dx} = 9x^2 + 8x$

diffraction is the bending of waves around an obstacle and as they pass through a narrow gap. This applies to all waves; water, sound, light and electromagnetic, and can be detected by a change in the shape of the wavefront and by *interference* patterns. When a beam of light passes through a narrow slit it is diffracted but the slit has to be very narrow indeed (less than 0.01mm) to have any effect. If *monochromatic* (one wavelength) light is used, and the diffracted light is passed through two further slits, then an interference pattern of light and dark fringes is created. In 1801, Thomas Young the physicist used an experimental procedure such as this to measure the wavelength of light. The fact that sound can be diffracted is easily shown because it is possible to hear round corners.

diffusion is the process that occurs in gases and liquids whereby one liquid is spread throughout the body of another, e.g. an ink drop in water, due to the molecular motion of the water (*see* BROWNIAN MOTION), producing a more uniform concentration. The same process occurs with gases and accounts, for example, for the smell of a gas leak filling a room. The molecular movement of gases is more vigorous than liquids and the molecules distribute themselves equally within the volume in which they are enclosed.

Diffusion also occurs across cell membranes and a similar mechanism is used in dialysis as a means of separating certain molecules.

digestion the process by which organisms break down solid food into small particles which can be used by the body.

In human beings, the digestive process starts in the mouth where food is cut up into smaller particles by the teeth. The food is mixed with saliva containing an enzyme which breaks down starch into sugar. The food is then swallowed and passes via a tube called the *oesophagus* into the stomach. In the stomach a fluid, the gastric juice, is released which contains hydrochloric acid and enzymes. The stomach has muscular walls and is able to expand and contract and further manipulate the food. Proteins are broken down and eventually a semi-solid acidic mass (known as *chyme*), is passed into the small intestine. Alkaline fluid from an organ called the *pancreas* (pancreatic juice) is added here and this contains more enzymes which further break down the food. Also, *bile*, a thick fluid produced by the liver and stored in the *gall bladder* located nearby, is added to the food in the intestine. This contains bile salts, bile pigments and cholesterol and aids in the digestion of fatty substances. As the food passes along the highly coiled length of the small intestine it continues to be broken down into minute particles (molecules) which can be absorbed into fine blood vessels present in the intestinal wall. The blood circulation carries the food to all parts of the body where it is used by cells to perform all the functions of life and to provide energy.

Any food substances that cannot be digested, such as fibre, are passed to the large intestine which is the final part of the alimentary canal or digestive system. Here water is removed and reabsorbed into the body, and the final waste (*faeces*) is passed to the outside through the anus.

The human digestive system

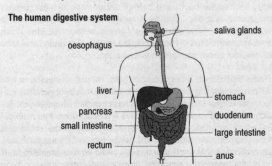

digital and analogue are two different ways of measuring a value - a digital system uses distinct units, e.g. electrical pulses, while analogue is a quantity that is similar to another quantity (e.g. a thermometer where the column of liquid represents a temperature).

The digital system uses binary numbers, which renders it admirably suited to use in computers. Numbers and letters are coded by groups of the digits 1 and 0, and each digit is represented in an electronic circuit by a component being on or off, e.g. passing or not passing current. In a magnetic system it could be magnetised or not magnetised, and that produces the on/off effect.

diode a device with two terminals that allows current to flow in only one direction. Modern varieties are *solid state* (electronic devices made up of solids, with no moving parts, filaments, etc.) and usually are made up of a special *silicon chip*. Silicon is a semiconductor used to make diodes. A crystal of silicon with phosphorus and boron added to opposite halves (a process called *doping*) has a poorly-conducting junction called the *depletion layer* between the two halves. The phosphorus increases the number of electrons available to move through the material and the boron makes holes into which electrons can move. Depending upon the current flow in the circuit, the diode passes current easily when the depletion layer is thin but when the current is reversed, the depletion layer thickens and no current is passed.

This property of diodes means they can be used to turn alternating current into a direct current, a process called rectification. Then the diode is called a *rectifier*. The diode may be used for *half-wave rectification* in which it simply blocks the backward half of the current, or with a more complex arrangement of diodes, *full-wave rectification* can be achieved in which the blocked half of the alternating current is reversed and flows through as direct current. This is the principle employed in radios and tape recorders that can use a mains adaptor, or batteries.

diploid *see* CELL DIVISION.

disease any illness that affects an organism which, in man, is caused in two main ways. Often diseases are caused by infectious micro-organisms e.g. bacteria, viruses and fungi (*see* FUNGUS). Bacteria can be killed with antibiotic drugs such as penicillin and examples of bacterial diseases are cholera, tuberculosis and typhoid. Viruses are not susceptible to antibiotics and the illnesses they cause have to be fought off by the body's immune system, although protection can be given against some of these by means of vaccination. The common cold is a viral disease, and those which can be prevented by vaccination include mumps and measles. The second group of diseases are caused by the failure of a body system to work properly. This may be an inherited disorder, e.g. cystic fibrosis, or occur at some stage in a person's life for an unknown reason. A common example is *Diabetes mellitus* which occurs when an organ called the pancreas fails to produce enough of the hormone insulin, itself responsible for the breakdown of sugars in food.

distillation is the separation of a liquid mixture into its components. The liquid is first heated to vapour which is then cooled so that it condenses and can be collected as a liquid. The mixture can then be separated if the components liquids have different boiling points, each one vaporising at a different temperature.

DNA stands for deoxyribonucleic acid and this is the material of which the chromosomes and genes are composed. It occurs as strands in the nucleus of each cell and contains all the instructions which determine the structure and function of that cell.

One of the most exciting discoveries of this century occurred in 1953 when two scientists, James Watson (1928–) and Francis Crick (1916–), worked out and demonstrated the structure of DNA. They found that it occurs as two spiral threads coiling round each other (a double helix) with 'bridges' across at intervals connecting the two, as in a ladder. Four types of molecules (known as bases) occur on the 'rungs' of the ladder and these pair up in particular ways (*base pairing*). These four molecules store all the genetic information by being built up in different combinations. In cell division, the two DNA threads split apart and each reproduces the missing half to rebuild the double helix. Sometimes the copying does not occur properly and can result in a mutation. Many mutations are lethal but minute changes can occur in this way and this is the genetic basis for evolution and species change.

DNA structure

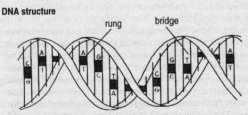

rung   bridge

Doppler effect is the change in the observed frequency or wavelength of a wave when the source producing the wave is moving. If the source, e.g. a vehicle, is moving towards the listener, the frequency increases (and the wavelength decreases) and the opposite happens as it moves away. The result is the pitch of the sound changes as the vehicle approaches, passes and moves away. The principle applies to all electromagnetic radiation including light. The light from a moving object appears more red when it is moving away from the observer. This is taken to mean that stars in distant galaxies are moving away from us when they exhibit the *red shift*.

drugs and pharmacology *drugs* are substances which, when introduced into an animal's body, produce some kind of effect or response. Most drugs are given to help cure illnesses or other medical conditions and there are a great number of different kinds. *Pharmacology* is the name of the scientific study of all aspects of drugs and medicines including their preparation, uses, properties and effects. Drugs may be given in a variety of different ways: 1. by mouth (orally) as capsules, tablets liquid; 2. by injection; 3. as a cream or ointment applied to the skin; 4. by inhalation (sometimes using an inhaler); 5. by means of skin patches or insertion just beneath the skin and 6. suppositories which are placed via the anus into the end of the digestive tract (the rectum). New drugs are rigorously tested before their use is allowed but many occur naturally in plants. Caffeine (in coffee and tea) and alcohol are examples of drugs which are in social use.

ductility and malleability ductility is the property of metals or alloys that allows them to be drawn out into a thin wire and although their shape is permanently changed they retain their strength and do not crack. *Malleability* is similar but is the property that allows metals and alloys to have their shape altered by hammering, rolling or similar process, into thin sheets.

Most metals are ductile, notable examples being copper and gold. The same metals are very malleable and gold can be produced as very thin gold leaf which is 2μm (micrometres) thick. The high ductility and malleability of metals is due to their molecular structure, in which the lattice can be greatly altered before the atoms are torn apart and the metal breaks.

dyes (or dyestuffs) are substances with a strong colour that can be fixed to material to be dyed, such as fabrics and fibres, plastics, etc. The synthetic dye manufacturing industry began in 1857 when Perkin & Sons set up a factory to produce mauveine. At that time the wool and cotton trade was undergoing vast expansion and demand for dyes was heavy. In the past dyes had been made mainly from plants but mauveine was soon followed by the production of other synthetic dyes. Alizarin appeared in 1869,

Congo Red in 1884 and indigo in 1897. Now dye production is a vast industry undertaken in complex chemical plants.

ear *see* HEARING.

ecdysis and moulting *ecdysis* is the process of shedding skin. It is undergone by a group of invertebrate animals and it enables them to grow. It is a characteristic of arthropods such as insects, spiders and crabs which possess a tough, outer shell. At the start of ecdysis a hormone is released under the influence of which the new shell (or *exoskeleton*) begins to form beneath the old one. In addition some materials are reabsorbed from the old exoskeleton and these can then be used again. Eventually, the old exoskeleton splits and the animal extracts itself from its former covering. To begin with the new exoskeleton is very soft and the animal is often vulnerable at this stage. It then expands, often involving the animal taking in air or water to increase its body size and it hardens by the incorporation of a special substance called *chitin* (or *calcium* salts in crabs). The animal is thus larger than it was before and may undergo this process several times during the course of its life (*see also* METAMORPHOSIS).

Moulting is a term which is sometimes used to describe ecdysis. However, more familiarly, it is applied to the loss of fur or hair or feathers which often takes place in vertebrate animals, especially in the spring.

echo is when a reflected sound is heard a short time after the original sound was made. There is a delay between making a sound and hearing its echo because it takes the sound waves a little time to travel the distance (light travels so quickly that it does not exhibit this phenomenon). The time delay can be used in echo-sounding machines to locate the sea bed or submerged objects. SONAR (Sound Navigation Ranging) is such a device that operates with high frequency sound, collecting the returning waves that have been reflected from submerged objects. In all such cases, the distance can be calculated from the time taken for the sound to return. Echo-sounding equipment is used in ships and boats and *radar* is a similar principle but uses microwaves.

In small spaces, particularly rooms and halls, the echo time may be very short and the echo is not heard but becomes mixed up with the original sound, and the whole sound seems to be extended. This is called *reverberation* and may be a problem in concert halls where walls and ceilings may have to be modified to reduce the effect.

egg an egg, also known as an *ovum* (*pl.* ova), is the female reproductive cell. An egg may have a hard outer shell, as in birds and turtles, and is usually surrounded by one or more protective layers called membranes. After the egg is fertilised by a male sex cell (*sperm*), it divides into several cells which become an embryo. The embryo is nourished by a supply of food from the yolk within the egg. Some eggs contain very little yolk whereas others, such as those of birds, have a large amount which enables a chick to grow quite large before it hatches. Eggs may be extremely small, as in female mammals, which keep the developing embryos inside their bodies. The young of mammals are supplied with all that they need from the body of the mother and grow until they are ready to be born. There are two exceptions to this, the duck-billed platypus and spiny anteater, which are unique among mammals in that they lay eggs (*see* REPRODUCTION).

elasticity is the property of any material such that it stretches when forces are applied and recovers its original form when the forces are removed. To stretch a spring or other elastic material a stretching force must be applied to both ends. As the stretching force is increased, the extension becomes greater and up to a certain point the extension is proportional to the force. However, there is a limit to this proportional response and beyond a material's *elastic limit*, it is permanently stretched and will not return to its original length. *Hooke's Law* records this physical relationship but applies only to materials if the elastic limit is not exceeded. All materials are elastic to some extent but in many cases the extension is a very small amount.

electricity is a general term to cover the energy associated with electric charges, whether static or dynamic. In a simple circuit the *potential difference* between the battery terminals (i.e. the difference in potential) causes a current to flow. Current is measured in ampères and potential difference in volts. Batteries supply *direct current* but the electricity supply to homes and offices is *alternating current.* Power stations generate electricity by means of massive alternators (*see* GENERATOR) driven by turbines which are themselves driven by steam from coal, gas or oil-fired boilers (or heat from a nuclear reactor). The alternators generate a current of 20,000 amps at a voltage of 25,000 volts, which passes through a transformer and then into overhead power cables at a reduced current but a higher voltage-up to 400,000 or 400 kilovolts. The current is reduced to minimise the power losses due to heating in the long cables. The cables feed the nationwide network (the *Grid*), and power from the Grid is distributed by substations where transformers reduce the voltage to 240 volts for ordinary consumption. Heavy industry uses supply at 33,000 volts and light industry 11,000 volts. *See also* STATIC ELECTRICITY.

electrocardiogram (ECG) and **electroencephalogram (EEG)** are both records of the electrical activity in the heart and brain respectively. The

ECG is recorded on an electrocardiograph connected through leads to pads on the chest and legs or arms. It often indicates abnormal heart activity and is therefore a useful diagnostic tool.

The EEG records the brain's electrical activity on an electroencephalograph. Electrodes placed on the scalp record activity, (brain waves) of which there are four types associated with particular phases of activity or rest.

electrolysis is the chemical decomposition (breaking down) of a substance in solution or molten state when an electric current is passed. The solution is called an *electrolyte* and it permits the passage of a current because it forms ions in solution. A strong electrolyte, e.g. sulphuric acid, undergoes complete ionisation. When the current passes through the solutions the ions move to the electrodes of opposite charge; the *cathode* being negatively charged and attracting positively charged ions (*cation*); the *anode* being positively charged and attracting *anions*, which are negatively charged ions. At the electrodes the ions give up their charges to form atoms or groups. Gases are liberated, and solids deposited.

electromagnet is a magnet created by passing a current through a coil of wire that is wound round a soft iron core; the core becomes a magnet while the current is on. The coil of wire is called a *solenoid*. This magnetic effect of electric current was discovered by Hans Christian Oersted (1777–1851), a Danish scientist. There is a cumulative magnetic effect because in producing a magnetic field, the coil magnetises the core, which produces a magnetic field that can be about a thousand times stronger than the field from the core alone.

Electromagnets are clearly useful because the magnetic field generated can be controlled easily. They are used in televisions to control the electron beams in the CATHODE RAY TUBE, and also in devices such as switches, electric bells, loudspeakers and in the earpiece of the telephone.

electromagnetic waves come from a number of sources and are the effect of oscillating electric and magnetic fields. The wavelength of these waves varies but all travel through free space (a vacuum) at approximately $3 \times 10^8 ms^{-1}$ (300,000 kilometres per second), which is the speed of light. The *electromagnetic spectrum* contains waves from low frequency/long wavelength radio waves (long wave) through microwave, infrared and the visible spectrum to ultraviolet X-rays and the short wavelength/high frequency gamma rays.

Electromagnetic waves are generated when particles with an electrical charge change their energy, e.g. when an electron changes orbit around a nucleus. It also happens when electrons or nuclei oscillate and their kinetic energy changes. A large change in energy produces high frequency/ short wavelength radiation.

Radio waves are the longest in the spectrum and are used to transmit sound and pictures. Microwaves have wavelengths of a few centimetres and have numerous uses. *Infrared* (IR) waves are generated by the continuous motion of molecules in materials, and hot objects give out most. When an electric fire is switched on the infrared radiation is felt in the heat. As objects become hotter and hotter, their molecules vibrate more rapidly and the wavelength of the radiation becomes shorter. Eventually it impinges on the visible spectrum and the object appears 'red-hot'. *Ultraviolet* (UV) radiation occurs beyond the violet end of the visible light spectrum, is a component of sunlight and is emitted by white-hot objects. Ultraviolet light from the sun converts steroids in the skin to essential vitamin D but an excess of UV light can be harmful. However, much of the sun's ultraviolet radiation is stopped by the Earth's ozone layer (*see* **GG**: OZONE LAYER). *Gamma rays* are very short wavelength radiation released during radioactive decay and are the most penetrating of all radiations.

electronics is an important area of science and technology that deals with electrical circuits using SEMICONDUCTORS, DIODES, TRANSISTORS, etc. and other devices in which the movement of electrons is controlled to create switches and other components. Technology has advanced so much in recent years that electronic circuits can fit onto a single *silicon chip* and highly complex circuits are constructed on *printed circuit boards* where individual components are linked by metal traces printed on the board and through which the current flows.

electroscope is an instrument used in physics for the detection of small electrical charges. It consists of a metal cap joined to a rod which projects down into a case. At the bottom of the rod is a gold leaf. When a charged object touches the cap, some charge is transferred to the rod and gold leaf and because like charges repel each other, the gold leaf rises. When it is charged, the electroscope can be used to determine whether the charge on an object is positive or negative.

element a pure substance that comprises atoms of the same kind and which cannot be broken down into simpler substances in ordinary chemical reactions (nuclear reactions can, however, alter elements). There are 103 elements known to us, of which 92 occur naturally and the rest have been created in the laboratory. Indeed scientists continue to experiment and occasionally claim the existence of another element.

Elements combine together to form compounds and under normal conditions all but two elements (bromine and mercury) are either a solid or a gas. The elements are classified by their atomic number into the periodic table (*see* PERIODIC TABLE), which comprises groups and periods with similar properties and behaviour. *See also* Table of Elements in appendix 1 on pages 233 and 234.

elementary particles (or *fundamental particles* or *subatomic particles*) are the basic particles and building blocks of which all matter is made. The three key particles in all atoms – electrons, neutron and protons - have now been supplemented by new particles. Essentially two types are thought to exist, *leptons* and *hadrons*, and these are identified by the different ways in which they interact with other particles. Leptons include the electron and the *neutrino*, the latter having no charge and virtually no mass. The neutrino was originally proposed on the basis of theory, to preserve the physical laws of mass, energy and momentum, and it has since been established experimentally. The proton and neutron are called hadrons, although they are not truly elementary particles, and it is now thought that these are composed of real elementary particles called *quarks*. Quarks have become part of a highly elaborate theory of hadron structure in which hadrons occur in two forms, *baryons* and *mesons*, the first comprising three quarks and the latter two plus a quark and its antiquark (*see* **SA**: ANTIMATTER). In addition, quarks have properties termed 'flavour' and 'colour charge', producing a highly complex character for each particle. Although this theory seems to be generally accepted by physicists, quarks have yet to be confirmed experimentally.

embryo the stage in the development of a new plant or animal that follows on from the fertilisation of an egg by a sperm. It is most often used to describe the young of a mammal before birth while they are developing within the mother, and, in birds, to the growing chick while it is still inside the egg. Doctors define an 'embryo'as the stage in the development of a human being, from two weeks after fertilisation until two months, and after this the word 'foetus' is used (*see* REPRODUCTION).

embryology the branch of biological or medical study that is concerned with all aspects of the growth and development of EMBRYOS.

emulsion *see* COLLOID.

endocrine system this is the name given to a network of small organs (known as *glands*) within the body of an animal, which are responsible for the production of chemical signalling substances called hormones. A hormone is released into the bloodstream and travels in the body until it reaches its target cells or organ somewhere else, where it causes a response to occur. There are several endocrine glands in the body of a human being including the *pituitary* gland (at the base of the brain), the *thyroid* gland (in the neck), and the paired *adrenal* glands (one above each kidney). The male and female sex organs (the *testes* and *ovaries*), are also endocrine glands which produce hormones that are responsible for the changes which occur at puberty and control fertility. (*See* HORMONE, REPRODUCTION.)

energy is the capacity to do work, and there are many different forms of energy: light, heat, sound, electrical, kinetic, potential and more, and all are measured in joules (J). *Kinetic energy* is possessed by moving objects and for a mass m, with a constant speed v, the kinetic energy is $\frac{1}{2}mv^2$. So a ball kicked by a footballer has kinetic energy which it loses when it hits the net of the goal, pushing the net outwards. Objects have *potential energy* by virtue of their position, that is, they have been moved and when released can do work. Hence a stretched spring, a car at the top of a hill, or a weight on a shelf all have potential energy. The energy is defined as mgh where m is the mass which is raised through a height h and g is the acceleration of free fall. *Thermal energy* (sometimes called heat energy) is that kinetic and potential energy possessed by an object's molecules and it rises with an increase in temperature. *Electrical energy* is that stored in batteries, and *electromagnetic waves* and sound waves also possess energy.

The law of conservation of energy states that energy cannot be created, nor can it be destroyed, however it can be changed from one form to another. This means that in any action all energy can be accounted for. This may be a simple procedure such as throwing a ball where chemical energy in the arm launches the ball which then has kinetic energy. Depending upon the throw it may have potential energy if the ball stops momentarily before falling, again with kinetic energy. Then when it hits the ground the kinetic energy becomes sound and thermal energy.

engines are machines that convert energy into work, and fuel undergoes combustion to supply the energy. Petrol and diesel engines use the chemical energy from their fuels and electric motors use electrical energy stored in a battery or from a generator. The human body is also an engine, and food is the fuel. There are essentially two types of engine: those in which the combustion is internal as in the internal combustion engine, and those where the fuel is burned outside the engine itself-external combustion.

Engines are used to power all sorts of vehicles such as boats, aeroplanes and cars and although the internal combustion engine is not particularly efficient, it does provide a means of turning fuel into mechanical work very rapidly indeed. In the 1940s a British engineer, Frank Whittle, invented the gas turbine or *jet engine*. Air enters the front of the engine, is compressed and then enters a combustion chamber where liquid fuel is burnt. The energy produced expands the gas and shoots it out where it provides both thrust for motion and energy to drive the turbine which operates the compressor.

The *efficiency* of an engine is a ratio of the work provided for the energy put in. In general, most systems that burn fuels are very inefficient because so much energy is lost as heat. As a percentage, the efficiency of petrol and diesel engines is 25% and 35% respectively, while power stations are only around 30% efficient in producing electrical energy. Although electric motors are in themselves about 75% efficient, the process supplying the electrical input energy is only around 30% efficient.

entomology the specialised branch of biology which is concerned with the study of insects. A person who studies insects is called an entomologist.

entropy is a measure of the disorder or randomness of a system which tends always to increase. The increase is because at every stage of energy transfer, some energy is wasted and the greater the disorder, the higher is the entropy. One result of entropy is that heat always flows from a hot to a cold body and this is the basis of the second law of thermodynamics which can be rewritten as: any system will always undergo change so as to increase the entropy.

enzyme enzymes are naturally-occurring protein molecules that are found in all living things, and which act as catalysts (i.e. they speed up and activate chemical reactions, *see* CATALYSIS) within cells. Enzymes are very specialised and each only acts on a certain substance. Also, conditions of temperature and acidity or alkalinity have to be just right or the reaction will not take place.This is one of the reasons why a stable body temperature is maintained in mammals.

Some enzymes are involved in breaking down processes, e.g. digestive enzymes such as *ptyalin* which is present in saliva and breaks down starch to sugar. Others are involved in reactions to build up more complex molecules from simpler ones such as in tissue growth.

equilibrium is when a system, whether chemical or physical, remains the same over time. In physics an object is in equilibrium if all the forces acting on it are equal and opposite. However, there are three equilibrium states. If a system returns to equilibrium position after being moved slightly, then it is in stable equilibrium, e.g. tipping slightly a box with a wide base. Unstable equilibrium is when the system moves from equilibrium when moved slightly, e.g. a pencil 'stood' on its point, and neutral equilibrium is when a movement results in a new equilibrium position, as with a ball. In chemistry equilibrium is reached in a chemical reaction when the proportion of reactants and products is constant, as the rate of the forward and reverse reactions is the same. Equilibrium is affected by changes in temperature, pressure or concentration of the reactants.

eucaryote the type of cell found in all plants and animals (but not bacteria or blue-green algae (cyanobacteria) in which the nucleus is bound within a membrane. *See also* PROCARYOTE.

evaporation is the process that occurs when a liquid turns into a vapour. Heat accelerates the process, which happens because some molecules near the surface of the liquid gain sufficient kinetic energy (*see* ENERGY) to overcome the attractive forces of the liquid's molecules and escape into the surrounding atmosphere. During the process of evaporation from a container, the temperature of the liquid falls until heat is replaced from heat in the surroundings. This is the reason why swimmers feel cold when leaving the water – heat energy is taken from the body, converted into kinetic energy enabling some water molecules to escape.

evolution the gradual change, over a long period of time, of one species of animal or plant. The organisms eventually acquire characteristics that are different from those of the ancestral species. This is able to occur, firstly, if there has been genetic mutation that allows for different information to be passed on from a parent to its offspring. Secondly, if the offspring (one or several) that received the different characteristic proves better suited to its environment than other members of the species then it is more likely to survive and reproduce. In this way the new characteristic tends to be preserved while those individuals not possessing it are more likely to die out. These changes are very small and take place slowly over many thousands of years, but it is thought that all living organisms have evolved from different ancestors in this way. The study of fossils (*see* **GG**: FOSSILS) has helped in the understanding of how this may have taken place in particular species. *See also* DARWIN AND NATURAL SELECTION, CHROMOSOME AND DNA.

Hominoid evolution

excretion the name given to the process by which an ORGANISM gets rid of the waste products of METABOLISM and eliminates them from its body. It differs from the process of getting rid of food waste, which is called egestion and is concerned with eliminating material that has been taken in. Excretion gets rid of waste products manufactured within the organism itself. The main waste products are CARBON DIOXIDE, water and nitrogen-containing substances from the breakdown of PROTEIN.

One way that these are disposed of is by diffusion or leakage to the outside (in plants and simple animals) either from a single cell or through the body. Higher animals have developed specialised organs for excretion of waste products, and these include gills, lungs and kidneys.

expansion *see* CONTRACTION AND EXPANSION.

explosives are substances or mixtures that, when heated or subjected to a shock or a blow, release a very large amount of energy very violently. The chemicals are actually undergoing rapid decomposition, producing large volumes of gas and quantities of heat. Explosives have numerous uses, both military and civil. In construction they are used for clearing land and blasting new cuttings through rock, in mining, quarrying and tunnelling, and also to demolish large structures, e.g. old cooling towers or multi-storey buildings.

extinction when a plant or animal species dies out completely this is called extinction, and it has occurred many times to thousands of plant and animal species in the course of the Earth's history. There have been times of mass extinctions, e.g. at the end of the Palaeozoic geological era (*see* **GG**: GEOLOGICAL TIMESCALE), about 248 million years ago, when it is thought about 90% of species ceased to exist. A further similar event took place some 65 million years ago, in the early Tertiary period, when the dinosaurs became extinct. Until the appearance of modern man, which was recent in terms of geological time (about 100,000 years ago), extinctions could be described as 'natural', occurring because of the processes of evolution. Mass extinctions were probably brought about by climatic (especially temperature) changes, volcanic activity and possibly collision of asteroids with the Earth. Man's impact upon the Earth has been enormous as whole environments have been changed by tree felling, development of modern agriculture and industry and by pollution. Sadly, the extinction of many species which used to inhabit the Earth has been brought about by the destructive activities of human beings.

extrusion is a manufacturing process used in the production of shaped metal but particularly plastic goods. It is the most economical of plastic shaping methods and the products are simple in shape and have features in just two dimensions so that they can be extruded in the third, continuous, dimension. Pipes and gutters, strips, tubes, fibres can all be produced in this way. The essence of the process is a large screw which receives grains or pellets of plastic which have been heated and compressed and the melt is then forced out through a die which gives the section its shape. PVC foam can also be produced by extrusion.

In the extrusion of metal a block is forced by a ram out through a die. Some metals are extruded while cold but most are heated to increase the malleability (*see* DUCTILITY and MALLEABILITY).

eye *see* SIGHT.

fats are a group of naturally-existing compounds known as *lipids*. They are composed of combinations of one molecule of a substance called glycerol and three of fatty acids. They are found widely in plants and animals and are very important as long term energy stores having twice the number of calories as carbohydrates. In mammals there is a layer of fat deposited beneath the skin which provides insulation, preventing heat loss from the body. This is an absolutely vital provision for many animals, enabling some to inhabit the coldest regions of the Earth, e.g. seals, polar bears and penguins. These fat reserves enable some animals, e.g. bears and hedgehogs, to hibernate through the cold winter months and when they emerge in the spring they must immediately replenish their fat stores. The layer of fat beneath the skin helps to cushion the body against injury and at deeper levels it is stored as fatty (adipose) tissue.

fermentation is a process carried out by certain micro-organisms, e.g. yeast, bacteria and moulds which break down organic substances (those containing carbon, hydrogen and oxygen) into simpler molecules, producing energy. Alcoholic fermentation is a process which has been harnessed by man for centuries, and in this yeast converts sugar to alcohol and carbon dioxide, and it is used to produce such drinks as wine, beer and cider. Fermentation is one of the processes now used in biotechnology and is important in the manufacture of cheese, yoghurt and bread. Also, and most importantly, it is used in the production of drugs such as antibiotics and in GENETIC ENGINEERING.

fertilisation is the fusion or joining together of the male (sperm) and female (egg or ovum) sex cells which is the essential part of sexual reproduction. Fertilisation describes the process in which the two cells come together to become one and it sets in motion a chain of events, (involving further cell division and growth) which eventually gives rise to a new individual. It is a common event in both plants and animals and enables genetic 'mixing' to occur as the new organism receives its characteristics from each parent. In many animals, e.g. most fish, fertilisation is described as *external* as the eggs are laid outside the body and sperm are shed over them. In many other animals, e.g. mammals, fertilisation is *internal* as the male sex cells are released inside the body of the female.

fertilisers are chemicals added to the soil to improve crops and their yield and the growth of plants and flowers. Fertilisers replace the nutrients in the soil that are extracted by growing plants. Modern farming is very intensive and natural processes are unable to provide all the necessary nutrients required. In addition to carbon, hydrogen, oxygen there are other *essential elements* such as nitrogen, phosphorus, potassium, calcium, magnesium and sulphur; plants require *trace elements* (perhaps in parts per million quantities) such as iron, boron, manganese, zinc, copper, molybdenum and chlorine. Artificial fertilisers make up a lot of the deficits in these elements.

Ammonium sulphate is an important nitrogenous fertiliser (i.e. nitrogen supplying) and other chemicals used include sodium nitrate, urea and ammonia. *Superphosphates* contain phosphorus, the chemical used being calcium hydrogen phosphate, $Ca(H_2PO_4)_2$.

It is essential that fertilisers are used correctly and that they are not overused as the excess nutrients can have detrimental effects on the land, and particularly on streams and rivers. As the nutrients drain into water they encourage the growth of algae and surface plants which choke the stream and results in a lack of oxygen in the water which eventually kills animal and plant life beneath the surface.

filters and filtration a filter is a device for separating solids or particles suspended in solution from the liquid, and filtration is the separation process. It may also involve removing particles from a gas. There are numerous materials which are used as filters; filter paper – a pure cellulose paper used in laboratories; cloth and paper filters are used in engines to clean oil and air; crushed charcoal and sand are used in industry and in the medical field dialysis machines use membranes as filters to cleanse the blood of patients with defective kidneys.

The *filtrate* is the clear liquid that results from filtration while the solid particles left are called the *residue*.

flash point is the lowest temperature at which certain liquids give off sufficient flammable vapour to produce a brief flash when a small flame is applied. The term is used particularly for products such as petrol which vaporise very easily, because it is for all practical purposes the temperature at which petrol burns. It is important to be aware of this when petrol is used, transported or stored.

The same applies to industrial solvents such as toluene, benzene, ethanol, etc. which have flash points up to 13°C. Benzene has a melting point of about 5°C but will generate an explosive vapour while solid.

flight a few specialised groups of animals possess particular features which enable them to fly and these include insects such as beetles, flies, dragonflies and butterflies and birds and bats. In beetles, the forewings are hardened and form protective covers for the rear pair of flying wings which are moved in co-ordination and these are the most ancient group known to have possessed flight. Bees and wasps also have two pairs of flying wings which are hooked together and move as one. Similarly, in butterflies, the two pairs of wings are overlapped and move as a single pair and are covered with numerous minute scales. Insect wings are extensions of the outer covering (*cuticle*) of the middle part of the body (*thorax*) behind the head. They are membranes with veins running through them, and are moved by large flight muscles which bend the thorax out of shape. As they move up and down the angle of the wings in relation to the body alters which allows for lift on both the up and down strokes of the beat.

In birds and bats the wings are modified forelimbs or arms. In bats the membranous wings are a layer of skin spread between the long forelimbs and fingers and the body and hindlimbs. Birds possess several adaptations for flight including a lighter skeleton than other vertebrate animals, fewer organs to reduce weight and aerodynamic wings with modified flight feathers.

flotation and buoyancy buoyancy is the upward thrust felt by an object in a fluid and is equal to the weight of the fluid displaced (*see* ARCHIMEDES' PRINCIPLE). An object in water experiences this upthrust because although the object is under pressure on all sides from the liquid, the pressure is greatest where the water is deepest, i.e. underneath the object. Hence an object will float if the upthrust is more than its weight and the *law of flotation* states that a floating object will displace its own weight of the fluid in which it floats. Thus if a block is floated in water and then in a less dense fluid, it will float lower in the less dense fluid to displace a greater volume.

This principle applies to ships, and because salt water is denser than fresh water a ship floats lower in fresh water. Water temperature also affects density and therefore affects flotation. All ships have a line marked on their side (the *Plimsoll line*) which indicates the point beyond which the ship cannot be loaded. This is particularly important for a ship sailing from cold salt water to warm, less salty water.

flowers are the reproductive organs of a group of plants called *Angiospermae* (or *Anthophyta*) which are the flowering plants. They vary greatly in size from the very small and insignificant to the large and magnificent, showing an enormous range of colours and patterns of petals. Before the flower bud opens it is usually tightly folded and enclosed by green, leaf-like structures called *sepals*. These together make up an outer supporting structure for the flower called the *calyx*. When the flower bud opens the coloured petals expand and the sepals may wither and fall off. Petals may attract insects to the flower for pollination, but the actual reproductive parts are contained inside them. These are the *stamens* which are the male organs and the *carpels* which are female and contain egg cells or *ovules*. These structures are supported at the base by a portion of the flower called the *receptacle*. Following FERTILISATION, the ovules eventually form seeds.

food chain in simple terms, a food chain is the route by which energy is transferred through a number of organisms by one eating another from a lower level (called a *trophic* level). At the base of the chain are the primary producers which are the green plants. These are able to use energy from the sun to manufacture food substances from carbon dioxide and water. These food substances (glucose, cellulose and starch) are made use of by animals at the next level in the chain. The herbivores which eat the green plants are known as primary consumers. These in turn are eaten by carnivores (flesh-eating animals) which are called secondary consumers. There may be more than one level of secondary consumer (a flesh-eater may itself be eaten by a larger carnivore) ending up with animals at the end of the chain, e.g. lions, which are not preyed upon and are called the top predators. However, when these and all organisms die, they are eaten by scavenging animals and the remains eventually broken down by micro-organisms so none of the energy is lost but is used again. Food chains are often highly complicated and all of those that exist in a given environment are inter-linked and form a food web. A food chain should be perfectly balanced with many more organisms at the lower levels than at the higher ones. Sometimes the natural balances are upset and this may be due to human interference. For example, in Britain there are no large carnivores such as wolves because they were hunted and killed off during the Middle Ages. In Scotland red deer numbers are too high and (although the situation is complicated) these would, at one time, have been hunted by wolves.

fluids are substances that flow easily and readily alter their shape in response to outside forces. Liquids and gases are both fluids. Liquids have freely-moving particles which tend to be restricted to a single mass, but gases expand to fill their containing space and they do not maintain the same volume. These properties of fluids are very useful in many ways, particularly in industry where machines utilise fluid or gas-filled chambers or cylinders to operate mechanisms, e.g. the braking system on a car.

Hydrostatic is the term applied to a machine using fluid pressure, and *pneumatic* is a system that uses compressed air, e.g. air-brakes, pneumatic drills and other tools.

food additives are chemicals added to foods by manufacturers to improve a particular property whether it is colour, shelf-life, taste or appearance. In addition to colourings and preservatives there are anti-oxidants to stop re-action of the food with oxygen, sweeteners, flavour enhancers (e.g. sodium glutamate), emulsifiers, pH adjusters and many more.

There is now a regulatory system in Europe whereby each additive that can be used in food is given a number and it is then listed on the packaging. Although the vast proportion of these compounds cause no problems, some do create side effects in some people. *Tartrazine* is a well-known example. It is a yellow colouring agent but can cause hyperactivity in children and also skin complaints and breathing problems. Other *E factors* may cause dizziness, vomiting or muscular weakness.

food preservation is the prevention of food spoilage through chemical decomposition and action of micro-organisms. It is generally achieved by the sterilisation of the food which destroys any bacteria by heating in sealed containers (canning), or by pickling, drying, freezing, smoking, etc. Pickling, drying and salting are methods that were used over history and these kept foods through the use of agents (acid, i.e. vinegar, and smoke) in which bacteria would not survive, or by the removal of water (essential to the growth of bacteria) as in drying.

These established methods have been supplemented by more modern techniques such as canning and freezing and also *freeze-drying*. Freeze-drying is used for numerous foods, notably coffee (and has been used for some time in the medical, veterinary and pharmaceutical fields) and perishable foods. The process involves freezing, producing ice from the liquid content of the material and then *sublimation*, i.e. the ice is extracted as vapour at low pressure and temperature. Foods preserved in this way can be kept for very long periods.

Another recent innovation is that of *irradiation* in which food is subjected to ionising radiations (radioactivity) to kill micro-organisms. The technique is still under scrutiny and not everyone is fully convinced that it is suitable.

force is the push or pull upon a body which may cause it to move, stop moving or alter direction of motion. Force is defined as the mass of a body multiplied by its acceleration. If the mass is in kilograms and the acceleration in metres per second per second (m/s²) then the force is in *newtons*. An object will continue to move at a constant speed and in a straight line unless another force acts upon it. For example, a craft in space under the influence of no forces will maintain the same speed in the same direction and would need a force to change its direction. This is the basis of *Newton's first law of motion* which states that an object will continue in a state of rest or uniform motion in a straight line unless an external force acts upon it. The second law of motion relates to momentum and the third law can be given concisely as to every action there is an equal, opposite reaction.

On Earth, we have to contend with friction and gravity but objects can move at a constant velocity or be at rest if forces acting on them are balanced. So an aeroplane can maintain a constant air speed because lift and weight are balanced, as are thrust and air resistance. However, should any of these constituent forces change then the velocity of the aeroplane would change.

formula (*plural* **formulae**) in mathematics or physics is a law or relationship denoted by symbols and figures and possibly expressed in algebraic (*see* ALGEBRA) form.

In chemistry it is a type of shorthand notation that enables a substance to be written in terms of elements and molecules using letters to represent the elements (*see* SYMBOLS). There are three types of chemical formula: an *empirical formula* shows the simplest ratio of atoms present in a compound, e.g. butane has the empirical formula C_2H_5, although it is really C_4H_{10}. The number and type of atoms present is shown in the *molecular formula*, in the case of butane, C_4H_{10}, which means there are four carbon and ten hydrogen atoms in every molecule. The *structural formula* indicates the structure of a molecule and shows the bonds between atoms.

fossils *see* **GG**: FOSSILS.

freezing is the change in a material's state from liquid to solid brought about by reducing its temperature. The temperature at which this change occurs is called the *freezing point*. For pure substances the freezing point is the same as the *melting point*. The freezing point varies enormously between materials as the following table shows:

hydrogen	-259°C	mercury	-39°C	argon	-189°C
oxygen	-218°C	water	0°C	silicon	1410°C
nitrogen	-210°C	sodium	98°C	carbon	3550°C

Impurities reduce the freezing point, e.g. salt reduces the freezing point of water and this property is exploited in car engines by adding *antifreeze* to the coolant to avoid freezing in winter.

frequency represented by the symbol f is the number of complete wavelengths (*see* WAVE) of a wave motion, per second. Frequency is measured in hertz (Hz) and is calculated from the formula; $c = f \lambda$, where c is the speed of the wave, and λ (lambda) is the wavelength. In the *electromagnetic* spectrum there is a large range of frequencies from low frequency radio waves to very high frequency gamma rays.

Sound waves are very different from light waves, and the human ear can hear sounds with frequencies between 20 Hz and 20, 000 Hz (or 20 kHz). A different frequency is heard as a different sound with high frequencies being sounds of high pitch. The scientific pitch of middle C on the piano has a frequency of 256 Hz and the Cs below and above are 128 Hz and 512 Hz, although when a piano is tuned these frequencies are changed slightly.

friction is the force that acts against motion, trying to stop materials and objects sliding across each other. A moving object will tend to slow down due to friction, and a force has to be exerted to keep it moving. The force required will differ depending upon the surface and the nature of the material moving across it. Friction is higher between solids (or a solid and liquid) than between solids and air.

The reason for friction is that rough surfaces have minute projections which restrict movement, and also there is a tendency for molecules to stick together under pressure. Friction in solids can be divided into *static friction* and *dynamic friction*. If an object is being pushed across a surface, the static friction is the maximum force, applied just before the object moves while the dynamic friction is that in action when the object is moving and it is much less than the static friction. There is also *fluid friction* when an object moves through a liquid or a gas. The effects of friction can be seen all around us the difficulty of pushing a heavy box across the floor; being able to walk and run because of the friction between our shoes and the ground; a car's tyres gripping the road and a train's wheels gripping the rails. In all these cases, friction causes the loss of energy as heat, something that applies to all machines.

fruit a fruit develops from the ovary (*see* EGG) of a flower and is given the name when it is mature and ripe. It contains the seeds and there are two main kinds, dry, e.g. an acorn and succulent or juicy, e.g. a tomato. The fruit is the means by which the seeds, which will become new plants, are protected until they are ready to be dispersed. Most juicy fruits are eaten by animals and the seeds pass through the digestive system without harm and are scattered in the droppings to grow elsewhere. Dry fruits often split open to release the seeds which may be shot out explosively, be carried away by wind or water, or cling to the fur of animals to drop off elsewhere. There are several different kinds of juicy fruit including a berry (e.g. blackberry) which is an *aggregate* fruit formed from one flower, but with lots of seeds) a pineapple which is a *multiple fruit* formed from a cluster of flowers and a cherry, a *simple fruit* also known as a drupe containing a stone surrounding the seed. Many of the food plants that we think of as vegetables are actually fruits, e.g. peas, beans and marrows. Pears and apples are known as *pomes* and they and some other kinds of fruit such as straw-berries are also called *false fruits*. This is because the fruit does not just develop from the ovary of the flower but also from the receptacle (*see* FLOWERS).

fuel is a material that stores energy and upon combustion will release that energy. Fossil fuels (*see* GG: FOSSIL FUELS) are the most widely used and account for most of the world's energy supply, with petroleum being the largest contributor. When these fuels are burnt (oil, gas, coal) energy is released and the other products are carbon dioxide, water and a variety of other gases and solids that depend upon the original composition or purity of the fuel. Nuclear fuels such as plutonium and uranium are unstable and release large amount of energy in nuclear reactions.

fuel cell is a cell that generates electricity directly by the conversion through electrochemical reactions, of fuels (gas or liquid) fed into the cell. The two components required are a fuel and an oxidant which are supplied to the electrodes and invariably a catalyst is used (*see* CATALYSIS). Fuels used include hydrogen (H_2), hydrazine (N_2H_4), ammonia (NH_3), and methanol (CH_3OH) and the oxidant is usually oxygen (O_2) or air. The electrolyte (*see* ELECTROLYSIS) in the cell can be a solution or solid, or special ion-exchange resins which, as the name suggests, contain ions that can be replaced by other ions.

Fuel cells have been used on spacecraft. In these, hydrogen and oxygen are combined to produce electricity and water is formed as a very useful byproduct. However, the efficient fuel cells have failed to gain a foothold for use in industry.

fungus (Kingdom *Fungi*) all fungi are simple ORGANISMS which may be one CELL or exist as threads (or *filaments*) of many cells. They were once classified as simple plants but as they contain no chlorophyll and cannot photosynthesise, they are now placed in their own kingdom-fungi. Fungi absorb their food from other organic material and are vital in the breakdown and recycling of organic substances. They are essential in that they make minerals available to the roots of growing plants. Fungi are vital organisms for man, being used in the processes of biotechnology and fermentation. Some are harmful causing diseases in plants and animals, others are parasites and a few are edible, e.g. mushrooms. The scientific study of fungi is called *mycology*.

fuse is a very useful, protective device for electrical circuits. Most electrical appliances have their own fuse in the plug and in addition circuits, whether domestic or industrial, have fuses.

In all circuits there is the possibility of a fault developing and too much current flowing, which could damage the circuit or cause a fire. The fuse is placed in the circuit to avoid this possibility. The commonest form of fuse is a short piece of thin wire encased in a small glass tube with metal ends which overheats, melts and breaks if too high a current flows through it. It is placed in the live wire of the circuit so that if a fault develops, the current is switched off. The fuse value is greater than, but as close as possible to the current that usually goes through the appliance; 3 amp and 13 amp fuses are commonest.

More recently, *circuit breakers* have replaced fuses. These are switches which automatically break the circuit in the event of an overload and they can be reset when the fault has been eliminated.

galvanising is a process whereby one metal is coated with a thin layer of another, more reactive metal. It offers protection to the coated metal and iron and steel are often treated in this way. Galvanising is done in two ways, by dipping into molten zinc or by electrodeposition, i.e. electrolysis. When iron or steel is dipped into zinc, a little aluminium or magnesium is added to prevent a zinc iron alloy forming, because this is very brittle.

With electrodeposition, the object to be coated is connected to the cathode (*see* ELECTROLYSIS) and zinc ions from the electrolyte coat the object while current flows. The layer of zinc then protects the underlying metal because corrosion affects it before the iron or steel beneath.

galvanometer is an instrument used to measure small currents and is often called a *milliammeter* if its scale is calibrated accordingly. It uses the physical property that a wire in a magnetic field experiences a force when a current passes through the wire. The current to be measured passes through a coil in a magnetic field and as a result the coil turns, and in turn it moves a pointer across the scale. This is called the *moving coil galvanometer*. The movement of the coil is resisted by springs and it comes to rest when the force generated by the coil in the magnetic field is balanced by the springs. The higher the current, the greater the force generated and the further the pointer moves across the scale.

Although galvanometers are used a lot and can be converted for use as an ammeter or voltmeter, many modern versions are digital instruments.

gas is the fluid state of matter (solid and liquid being the others). Gases are capable of continuing expansion in every direction because the molecules are held together only very loosely. A gas will therefore fill whatever contains it and because the molecules move around rapidly and at random, they bump into each other and the walls of the container which results in a PRESSURE being exerted on the walls. If a certain amount of gas in a container is put into another container half the size, the pressure doubles (if the temperature is constant). Also, heating a gas in a container increases the pressure. It can be seen therefore that the temperature, pressure and volume of a *fixed mass* of gas are all related and many years ago, early experimentation with gases resulted in three *gas laws*, which when combined can be stated as:

$$\text{For a fixed mass of gas, } \frac{pv}{T} \text{ is constant}$$

Where p is pressure, v is volume and T is temperature. The three laws individually are

$\dfrac{p}{T}$ =	constant if v is unchanged	the Pressure law
$\dfrac{v}{T}$ =	constant if p is unchanged	Charles' law
pv =	constant if T is unchanged	Boyle's law

Only an *ideal gas* obeys these laws exactly and no gas can be considered ideal in this sense, although many approach this point at medium pressures and temperatures.

gas turbine is a type of internal combustion engine used in aircraft and ships, which is often called the *jet engine* because it involves the production of a jet of hot gas which provides the propulsion. The engine was invented by Frank Whittle, a British engineer, in the 1940s (*see* ENGINES).

The jet engine produces a forward force by thrusting out gas behind and it takes in large quantities of air for this purpose. The air also supplies the oxygen needed for combustion of the fuel. The air intake is therefore at the front of the engine, and behind is the compressor which consists of a number of blade-like fans. The compressor forces air under high pressure into the combustion chamber where the fuel (kerosene) burns to produce a hot gas which expands and is thrust out of the rear of the engine, creating a forward thrust on the engine. This gas passes through the turbine before being expelled providing the rotational force to turn the compressor.

Geiger counter (**Geiger tube** *or* **Geiger-Müller tube**) is an instrument that can detect and measure ionising radiations, mainly alpha, beta and gamma rays. It was named after the German physicist Hans Geiger (1882–1945). It is made of a sealed and enclosed tube with a fine wire down the centre of the tube. The tube is filled with argon gas at low pressure and the wire is the anode and the tube forms the cathode. The end of the tube is covered by a mica window through which the radiations pass. When a particle with a charge (or gamma rays) enters the tube, the argon is ionised into electrons and positive *ions* which move to their respective and opposingly charged electrodes and for a moment the gas conducts and a small current flows in the circuit. This is registered by a *ratemeter* (or *scaler*) and can be converted to a series of clicks.

generator is a machine that produces an electric current from mechanical motion. It is based upon the principle of electromagnetic induction (*see also* ELECTROMAGNET). If a coil in a magnetic field is rotated, a current is generated (induced) as the coil cuts through the magnetic field. As the coil completes its rotation, it cuts the field in the opposite direction and an induced current flows in the opposite direction. This is the basis of an alternating current generator, or *alternator*. To enable the coil to continue turning, carbon brushes form the connection between the coil and the outside circuit by rubbing against slip rings fixed to the ends of the coil. To generate direct current from a generator, the device is fitted with a *commutator* and instead of having two slip rings the generator has one ring which is split (i.e. the split ring, or commutator) and the coil ends connect to each half. Then every time the coil passes the split the connections are reversed and current flows in a constant direction to the outside circuit.

genes *see* CHROMOSOMES AND GENES.

genetics and genetic engineering genetics is the name given to the branch of science which deals with the study of *genes* and *chromosomes* and the way in which characteristics are passed on from parents to offspring (called heredity). It is one of the most important areas of modern scientific study especially in helping us to gain an understanding of how certain hereditary diseases and disorders are passed on. Also, it enables new strains of organisms with useful characteristics to be bred more easily. Genetic engineering is the term given to the modification by human beings of an organism's genetic make-up and this is done in two main ways. Firstly, DNA from one organism might be transferred to another where it would not normally occur. This has been carried out in the fight against various diseases and is a technique within BIOTECHNOLOGY. An example is the gene that codes for the HORMONE insulin in human beings which has been inserted into the cells of certain bacteria. The bacteria have been harnessed to produce insulin which is then used to treat diabetes. Secondly, DNA from two different organisms has been combined to produce an entirely new species. It is this second area of research which has caused a great deal of concern and fears that harmful organisms might be produced. Hence it is subject to extremely strict regulation and controls so that all the organisms involved remain securely within the laboratory.

geometry is a branch of mathematics that deals with the properties of lines, curves and surfaces. It includes the study of planar (flat) figures such as the circle and triangle and also three-dimensional figures such as the sphere and cube. Geometry (meaning measurement of the Earth) was first used in the measurement of land areas and today it is the basis of much calculation undertaken by engineers, builders and architects.

Co-ordinate geometry is where points, lines and shapes are represented by algebraic (*see* ALGEBRA) expressions. In two dimensions the plane containing a point is represented by x and y axes at right angles to each other which meet at the origin, O. The position of a point can then be defined by two distances, one along the x and one along the y axis, which intersect at the point in question. Lines are represented by equations, whether straight or curved. The values given to the particular position of a point are its *Cartesian co-ordinates.*

A well-known *theorem* (a rule proven by reasoning) in geometry is *Pythagoras' theorem* which states that in a right-angled triangle, the (area of the) square on the hypotenuse (the longest side opposite the right angle) equals the sum (of the areas) of the squares on the other two sides.

gestation and birth is the period of time in a mammal between fertilisation of the egg and birth of the young which, in human beings, is also called *pregnancy.* The gestation period is characteristic of the species concerned and varies from 18 days in the mouse to 9 months in human beings and 18 to 23 months in the Indian elephant. Usually, larger mammals have longer gestation periods and their offspring require care for a greater length of time before they can live independently. Following fertilisation of the egg in a mammal such as man, cells divide rapidly to become an embryo which becomes attached, by means of a special organ called the *placenta*, to the wall of the *womb* (*uterus*). The placenta allows oxygen and food to pass to the baby through a connecting cord called the *umbilical cord*.

When the gestation period is completed and the baby is ready to be born, the process of birth takes place. This is triggered off by hormones which cause the womb to contract by means of the powerful muscles which are present in its wall. The baby is gradually forced through the birth canal (*vagina*) to the outside and afterwards the placenta is also shed. Most mammals eat through the umbilical cord (but it is cut after a human birth) and the portion which is left attached to the baby soon dries, shrivels and drops off leaving a mark called the *umbilicus* or navel.

Human fetus at 35–38 weeks development

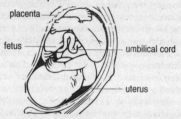

Animals which give birth to live young as described above are called *viviparous*, whereas those which lay eggs that develop and hatch outside the mother's body (e.g. birds and some reptiles) are called *oviparous*. Some animals keep their eggs inside the body for protection. The young are nourished within the egg and not by the body of the mother and these animals (e.g. some fish, reptiles and insects) are called *ovoviviparous*.

gills *see* LUNGS.

gland *see* ENDOCRINE SYSTEM.

glass is the hard transparent material from which windows, bottles, jars and glasses, lenses and laboratory ware is made. There are several types of glass but the essential ingredient in all is silica (SiO_2).

Man-made glasses appeared about 4000 BC in Egypt and by 1500 BC it had developed into both an art and a technology. Glass science was then

not developed until the work of numerous scientists including Michael
Faraday (1791–1867), then later Carl Zeiss (1816–1888) and Ernst Abbé
(1840–1905). Over 30 elements had been used in experimental glasses by
the turn of this century and now 70 have been tried but just three commercial
systems account for nearly all glass production (*see* CERAMICS).

The raw materials are heated in a furnace forming a red-hot liquid. A
blob of this molten glass on the end of a 'blow-pipe' can be blown into
intricate and beautiful shapes by glass-blowers. However, most glassware
is produced from moulds (for bottles, etc.) and sheet glass is made by
floating molten glass on a bed of molten tin. Glass is used in many ways
and its properties can be altered by the processing or by addition of other
materials.

glycerol (or glycerin) is a sweet-tasting, viscous (thick, syrupy) liquid with
no colour or smell. It belongs to the alcohol group but has a structure similar to a sugar. Its formula is $HOCH_2CH(OH)CH_2OH$ and it is derived syn-
thetically from propane (C_3H_6), or as a byproduct in the production of
soap. It occurs naturally in plants and animals as a component of stored
fats. It is an extremely useful compound and is used in the manufacture of
ice cream, sweets and other foodstuffs, toilet preparations, resins and explosives. It also has the useful property that it can absorb up to 50% of its
weight of water vapour which means it can be used as a moisturising agent.

gold and the noble metals gold is a bright yellow metal and a good conductor of electricity and heat. It is soft and malleable (*see* DUCTILITY) and can
be produced as very thin (even see-through) leaf or drawn out into wire
and it is very resistant to corrosion. Of course its primary use for thousands of years has been in the making of jewellery and coins, and today its
value is fundamentally important to the financial stability of the world's
currency markets.

Gold occurs as nuggets or veins or smaller particles in quartz or in
streams after it has been weathered out of its original site. It is also found
in the residue after copper has been purified by *electrolysis*. It is extracted
from ore by dissolving the gold in potassium cyanide (KCN) solution (the
cyanide process) or by the amalgamation process which involves treatment with mercury to form an amalgam which is processed further.

In addition to the applications mentioned above, gold is used in dentistry,
photography, medicine, in electrical contacts (in microchips) and conductors. The purity or fineness of gold is measured in *carats*, which are parts
of gold in 24 parts of the alloy. Thus pure gold is 24 carat. Jewellery is
often made of 9 carat gold, in which the remaining 15 parts are copper.

Gold is also one of the *noble metals*, with silver, platinum etc. and all have similar properties.

graph is a drawing or picture that represents data and numerical values, or shows the mathematical relationship between two or more variables. Often this takes the form of plotting (positioning) points at a certain place, relative to two values measured along axes at right angles to each other (*see cartesian co-ordinates* in GEOMETRY). A *histogram* is a type of graph consisting of a number of blocks drawn with reference to two axes such that the area of each block is directly proportional to the value of the frequency. A *bar graph* looks similar to a histogram but the height of the block is then the relevant factor. A *pie chart* is another graphical method of representing data in which a circle is divided into different sized sectors where the angle of the sector is proportional to the size of the sample, expressed as a percentage.

An example of a bar graph

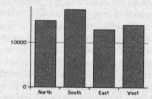

gravity or gravitational force is the downward pull exerted by the material making up the Earth. A gravitational attraction exists between all objects and this will increase with their mass and with a lessening of the distance between them. Although this attraction is always present, in most instances it is so very small as to be unnoticeable and the attraction which dominates is that of the Earth, which affects objects on its surface (*see* WEIGHT). If gravity is thought of as a gravitational field exerting a force on a mass, the value of that field strength, g, can be calculated as almost 10 m/s^2 (metres per second, per second). This means that a falling object near the Earth's surface accelerates at 10 m/s^2; alternatively a mass of one kilogram near the Earth's surface has a force acting on it due to gravity, of 10 N (newtons).

Gravity on the Moon is about one sixth of that on Earth, hence although an astronaut's *mass* remains the same, his or her weight is much less.

growth the process by which living organisms increase in size and often in weight. It is brought about by cells dividing and often becoming more specialised to form the bulk of a particular tissue or *organ*. All organisms have a maximum size which is determined by their genetic make-up and the growth process is controlled by HORMONES. Once the individual has reached its full size there is no more growth but cell division occurs to repair and replace worn out or damaged tissues. Growth often occurs in spurts as can be seen in the development of a human child. A baby grows fastest during the first six months of life and there is a further growth spurt at the time of adolescence.

habitat *see* **Natural History**.

hair a hair is any fine outgrowth from the surface of a plant or animal. Hairs are found on many living organisms and may be used for a variety of different purposes. The hair or fur of mammals is composed of dead cells in which a substance called *keratin* has been laid down. It is used for insulation to keep the animal warm and may occur in a variety of colours. The colour is determined by the presence and amount of a certain dye or *pigment* known as *melanin*. The base of each hair is embedded in the skin and has a tiny muscle attached to it. In cold conditions the hair is raised by these muscles to stand up straight and this traps a layer of air which has a warming effect. People notice this happening when they have 'goose pimples' in response to the skin feeling cold.

halogens are the elements fluorine, CHLORINE, BROMINE, iodine and astatine which form a group in the PERIODIC TABLE. They are the extreme form of the non-metals and show typical characteristics forming covalent diatomic molecules, i.e. form molecules of two atoms, e.g. Br_2. At room temperature fluorine and chlorine are gases, bromine is a volatile liquid and iodine a volatile solid. Astatine exists only as short-lived, radioactive isotopes. The reactivity increases from iodine to fluorine and the latter reacts with all elements save helium, neon and argon to form compounds. Halogens occur naturally in salt deposits and as IONS in sea water.

haploid *see* CELL DIVISION.

hard water is water that does not readily produce a lather with soap (*see* DETERGENTS AND SOAP) because of dissolved compounds (carbonates, sulphates and chlorides) of calcium, magnesium, sodium and iron. The use of soap results in the formation of a scum due to a chemical reaction between the metal IONS and fatty acids in the soap, producing salts. Water that does produce a good lather is called soft water.

Temporary hardness is one of two types and is due to water passing over carbonate-rich rocks such as chalk or limestone. This produces metal hydrogen carbonates which dissolve in the water and upon boiling these salts form insoluble carbonates which in a kettle results in kettle fur. This leaves the water soft. *Permanent hardness* is caused by metal sulphates (calcium or magnesium sulphates or chlorides) and cannot be removed by boiling. Special ion-exchange water softeners must be used in this case.

hearing the means by which animals are able to receive and decode sound waves which is usually closely related to balance, especially in vertebrates. Specialised small organs called RECEPTORS, which are often hair-like, vibrate in response to sound waves. This triggers off an electrical impulse in a sensory nerve (one which travels to the brain) which is in contact with the receptor (or receptors). The information is transmitted to the brain where it is decoded and interpreted as sound. In many invertebrates sound receptors may be relatively simple structures. However, in other animals such as mammals, complex and specialised organs, the ears, are used to detect sound.

The human ear

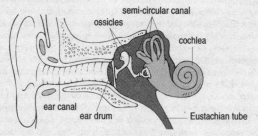

Fish have simpler ears than mammals and also a *lateral line system* which has sensory cells along the body, both of which are used for hearing. Amphibians (frogs and toads), reptiles and birds possess ears with a simpler structure than those found in mammals.

Lateral line system

heart *see* CIRCULATION.

heat is ENERGY, and is measured in JOULES. It is stored in materials as vibrations of the molecules and the vibration increases with temperature. Heat travels by CONDUCTION, CONVECTION and by electromagnetic RADIATION and material states, i.e. whether something is liquid, solid or gas, depends upon the heat available. In a solid the molecules are attracted together and this overcomes the kinetic energy possessed by virtue of the molecules vibrating. If energy is put in and the molecules can be separated enough to become free, then the solid becomes a liquid. The work done in separating the molecules is called the *latent heat of fusion.* Similarly, the *latent heat of vaporisation* is the heat required to turn a liquid into gas. When these changes are reversed, the material gives out heat.

The human body generates heat from food and the liver is a major heat-producing organ. Muscles also generate heat as a byproduct during activity.

heat exchanger is used to transfer heat from one fluid (i.e. a liquid or gas) to another without the fluids coming into contact. Heat exchangers are used a great deal to cool machines, e.g. the radiator in a car engine, or to conserve heat in an industrial (often chemical) process so that it can be used elsewhere in the process.

helium is one of the INERT GASES (or noble gases), so called because it has a stable electronic configuration and no chemical reactivity as such. It occurs naturally in very small quantities and being non-inflammable is used as an inert atmosphere for arc welding, for airships and balloons, in gas lasers and with oxygen as the atmosphere for deep sea divers. Helium liquefies below 4K (-269°C) and is used extensively in *cryogenics* – the study of materials at very low temperatures.

Helium has no colour, taste or smell and was named after *helios*, the greek for Sun. It is formed in stars such as the Sun as hydrogen nuclei are pressed together in the processes of nuclear fusion (*see* NUCLEAR FISSION AND FUSION).

herbivore any animal that feeds on plants, e.g. the familiar grazing mammals such as cows, sheep and horses.

heredity the passing on of characteristics from parents to offspring which is accomplished through the transfer of genes (*see* CHROMOSOMES AND GENES). Some of the basic laws of heredity were studied and worked out by an Austrian monk, Gregor Mendel (1822–1884) who carried out experiments with pea plants. He noticed that some characteristics were dominant over others, e.g. tallness is dominant to shortness in these plants. The study of genetics during this century has established that there are *dominant* and *recessive* genes for many characteristics and this is particularly important in some inherited diseases. A dominant gene is one which will always be seen in the offspring. A recessive gene will only be seen if it is present as a 'double dose', i.e. one from each parent. *See also* DNA, GENETICS.

hertz *see* FREQUENCY.

holography is a method of recording and then projecting a three-dimensional image using light from a LASER but without the need of a camera. A single laser beam is split into two by a special mirror, with half the beam continuing straight through the mirror onto photographic film. The other part of the beam is reflected by the mirror onto the object in question and then onto the film. The two beams produce an interference pattern, or *hologram* on the film which when illuminated with laser light recreates a three-dimensional image of the object. A screen is not required and the light forms an image in mid-air.

There are now holograms that do not need laser light to produce an image, for example, some credit cards have holograms that work with reflected daylight.

homing *see* NH.

hominid *see* NH.

hormone an organic substance produced in minute amounts by special cells within plants and animals, which acts as a 'chemical messenger' causing a powerful response somewhere else in the body. In mammals, hormones are produced and released (secreted) by special small organs called glands (the *endocrine* glands), and travel in the bloodstream. The site at which they produce a response is called the 'target,' (*see* ENDOCRINE SYSTEM).

horsepower is a measure of power which originates from the time when steam engines began to replace horses. The name was coined by James Watt (1736–1819) the British engineer and one horsepower is equivalent to about $^3/_4$ kW, or more accurately, 746 W. It has become the standard practice to measure engine power in *brake horsepower*. This is horsepower measured by means of the resistance offered by a brake and shows the useful horsepower that can be produced by an engine. A typical car develops around 90–100 brake horsepower (bhp) while an articulated lorry develops 400 or 500 bhp.

horticulture this refers to the cultivation of all kinds of garden and greenhouse plants including flowers, vegetables and fruit. Horticulture is concerned with the breeding of new varieties of plants by propagation and seed production. Many of our food plants, especially fruit and vegetables, result from the techniques of horticulture.

hybrid *see* **breeding**

hydraulics is the study of fluid flow, and the practical application of the dynamics of liquids in science and engineering. Hydraulics is thus a very important subject as it is relevant to the design of harbours, canals, dams or the study of the flow of water in pipes. *Hydraulic machinery* is operated, and the power transmitted using the pressure of a liquid. Such machines use the properties of liquids that they cannot, for all practical purposes, be squashed and when pressure is applied to a confined liquid, the pressure applies to all parts of the liquid. The transference of a force through the liquid is arranged in such a way as to produce a greater force in the machine, e.g. in a hydraulic car jack.

hydrocarbons are *organic* compounds (*see* CHEMISTRY) that contain only CARBON and HYDROGEN. There are many different hydrocarbon types and they form one of the most important groups of organic compounds. There is a fundamental division into two groups based on structure: *aliphatic* hydrocarbons comprise carbon atoms in open chains and in addition to the main groups such as alkanes (the paraffins), this term includes all compounds made by the replacement of atoms in a molecule. *Aromatic* hydrocarbons are characterised by a ring structure made up of six carbon atoms as found in BENZENE (C_6H_6). These are also called closed-chain or cyclic compounds.

Aliphatic hydrocarbon groups include the *alkanes*, with a general formula C_nH_{2n+2}, e.g. ethane C_2H_6. The first four compounds in the series are gases, then liquids and the higher members (above $C_{16}H_{34}$) are waxy solids. Alkanes are the main components of petroleum and in general they are quite resistant to chemical action. The *alkenes* have the formula C_nH_{2n} and resemble the alkanes, but are more reactive. They are used as fuels and in the manufacture of other substances, e.g. alcohols and glycerols. The *alkynes* (or acetylenes) have triple bonds between two carbons, and a general formula of C_nH_n. Acetylene is a well-known member of this series.

hydroelectricity is ELECTRICITY that is generated from water moving from a high to a low level. If a river or lake is dammed to form a large reservoir then the water is held back, high above the original river level, and the body of water has enormous *potential* ENERGY. To turn this into electrical energy the vast concrete dam contains a tunnel down which water can be directed and at the foot of the tunnel, before the water rejoins the river, the force of the flow is used to turn the blades of a large turbine linked to a generator, thus creating electricity.

Some power plants of this nature are called *pumped storage schemes* in which water flows through the day from a high level to a low level reservoir to generate electricity and at night when demand for electricity is low, water is pumped back up to the higher level ready for supply the next day.

hydrogen and the hydrides hydrogen is the lightest element and forms molecules comprising two atoms, H_2. It occurs free and is widely distributed in water (H_2O), organic matter (HYDROCARBONS and CARBOHYDRATES) and minerals. The ordinary hydrogen atom has a nucleus of one proton, with one electron. There are other ISOTOPES and in addition to *protium*, there is *deuterium* which contains one neutron and tritium, containing two neutrons.

Hydrogen is manufactured by the ELECTROLYSIS of water and is produced in the treatment of petroleum with catalysts (*see* CATALYSIS). It is explosive over a wide range of mixtures with oxygen and because of this is no longer used in ballooning (where it has been replaced by HELIUM). It is used in numerous industrial processes including the production of methanol and ammonia and in metallurgy.

Hydrogen reacts with most elements to form HYDRIDES of which there are several different types. Some are ionic and salt-like while most of the nonmetals form covalent compounds (*see* BONDS), e.g. methane, CH_4. There are then many more complex compounds. Hydrides are often used as catalysts in hydrogenation reactions, i.e. the addition of hydrogen to a substance, frequently used in the refining of petroleum.

hydrometer is an instrument used for measuring the relative DENSITY of a liquid. It is a quick and convenient tool, although not as accurate as some other methods. The hydrometer consists of a tubular stem with a weighted bulbous base. It floats in the liquid to be measured and the density can be read from the graduated scale on the stem. The narrow stem ensures that small changes in density create readily visible changes in the reading. Hydrometers are used in checking the quality of beer and also in testing the level of charge in a car battery, because the relative density of the acid in a battery varies with the available charge.

hydroxides are compounds that contain the OH group which is present as the hydroxyl ion OH^-. ALKALIS are the hydroxides of metals and are strongly basic. Hydroxides such as caustic soda (NaOH), potassium hydroxide (KOH) and ammonium hydroxide (NH_4OH) are commonly used in industry in the production of soap, detergents, bleaches, paper and many other items.

hypertonic and hypotonic a hypertonic solution is one which has a higher *osmotic* pressure (*see* OSMOSIS) than another, or a standard, with which it is being compared. Hypotonic is the opposite, i.e. it has a lower osmotic pressure than the solution to which it is compared. *Isotonic* solutions are those with the same concentration. These concentration differences are important in cells (*see* OSMOREGULATION).

immune system the natural defence system which operates within a vertebrate animal to protect it from infections, caused mainly by such microorganisms as BACTERIA and VIRUSES. The cells which operate the immune system are the white blood cells or *leucocytes* of which there are a number of different types. The immune system is provoked into action by the presence of 'foreign' PROTEIN substances which are called *antigens*. Many substances are antigens but they are commonly found on the surface of bacteria and viruses. When the white blood cells encounter antigens in the body, they produce special proteins called *antibodies* which trap the foreign material. The antibody and antigen are locked together like two pieces of a jigsaw puzzle and are eventually 'eaten up' by other cells of the immune system called *macrophages*. More antibodies are rapidly produced by the cells and will always recognise, and be ready to bind to, the antigens. In this way, the animal becomes *resistant* to a particular disease and this is the basis of vaccination.

A *Vaccination* is a preparation of a virus or bacteria which causes a particular disease is treated to kill it or make it harmless, but it still provokes the production of antibodies (an immune response) when it is injected into the bloodstream. These antibodies are then always available to attack any live micro-organisms of that type which the animal might encounter in the future.

Particular antibodies are produced to each kind of antigen and the immune system operates in two ways. Firstly, there is the inborn or *natural immunity* present from birth which is not specialised and operates against almost any substance that threatens the body. Secondly, there is *acquired immunity* which is the situation described above and brought about by an encounter with a particular foreign substance.

indicators are substances used to detect the presence of other chemicals. Most often an indicator is used in the laboratory to show the pH of a liquid, i.e. its acidity or alkalinity. Indicators are used in *titrimetry* which is the fast reaction of two solutions to an end point determined by a visual indicator and the two solutions are commonly an acid and a base.

The simplest indicator is *litmus paper* which shows red in acid and blue in alkali. *Universal indicator* is a mix which shows a gradual series of colour changes over a range of pH. However, most such indicators operate over a narrower pH range, e.g. methyl orange is red below pH 3.1 and changes to orange and then yellow as the pH reaches 4.4

Another group, called *redox indicators*, show different colours depending upon whether they are oxidised or reduced (*see* OXIDATION AND REDUCTION). The change occurs over a narrow range of electric potential within the system under study.

inductance is when a circuit carrying an electric current is characterised by the formation of a magnetic field. Similarly a current can be made to flow when the position of the magnetic field moves relative to the circuit (*see* ELECTROMAGNET, GENERATOR). The unit of inductance is the henry (H), named after the American physicist Joseph Henry (1797–1878) who was a pioneer in this field. Due to inductance a change in the current within one circuit can cause a current to flow in a nearby circuit. This is because if current flows through a circuit containing a coil, a magnetic field is created and an adjacent coil, in a separate circuit but within the magnetic field, experiences an *induced current*.

inert gases are the gases in group 0 of the PERIODIC TABLE, known also as the *noble gases*. These are helium, neon, argon, krypton, xenon and radon and they make up approximately 1% of air, by volume, with argon the most abundant. As their name suggests, these elements are chemically unreactive, due to their stable electronic configuration. They can be extracted from liquid air by fractional DISTILLATION and helium occurs in natural gas deposits. Their stability makes them useful in many applications, e.g. helium and argon are used as inert atmospheres for welding, in light bulbs and fluorescent lamps. Helium in its liquid form is important in low temperature research.

inertia the property of a body that causes it to oppose any change in its velocity, even if the velocity is zero. An object at rest requires a FORCE to make it move, and a moving object requires a force to make it slow down or accelerate or change direction. Isaac Newton (1642–1727) called this resistance to a change of velocity inertia. The greater the mass of a body, the higher is its inertia.

infection and toxin an infection is a disease or illness which is caused by the invasion of a micro-organism which, because it is able to do this, is called a PATHOGEN. In animals and man most pathogens are bacteria or viruses but in plants a wide range of fungi are pathogenic. A high standard of hygiene is the best means of preventing infections from occurring, and sometimes people who are sick with an infectious disease require special isolation, nursing and care.

There are a number of ways in which a pathogen can enter an animal's body. 1. It might be breathed in; 2, it may enter the bloodstream through a cut or wound; 3, it might be carried by a blood-sucking insect such as a mosquito which passes the pathogen on when it bites or stings; 4, it may be present on food (called contaminated) which is then eaten; 5, in drinking water, particularly that which is contaminated by sewage and 6, through sexual intercourse-a sexually transmitted disease.

Often the illness is caused not by the micro-organism itself but by a poison, known as a *toxin*, which it produces and this is especially true of bacteria.

infinity is the term used to describe a number or quantity which has a value that is too large to be measured. For example, outer space is regarded as infinite since it has no limits. By convention, infinity (designated by the symbol ∞) is the result of dividing any number by zero. If a value is so small as to be incalculable, it can be written as negative infinity (-∞) and it is called infinitesimal.

infrared and **ultraviolet** *see* ELECTROMAGNETIC WAVES.

injection moulding is an industrial process, similar to EXTRUSION, used for the production of plastic mouldings. Granular or powdered plastic is fed into a hopper which feeds into a screw mechanism. The heat generated by the screw and outside heaters produces a plastic melt by the time it reaches the end of the screw. The melt is then injected or forced through a nozzle into a cool mould and pressure is maintained while the entrance to the mould is blocked by solidified melt. The moulding is then released and the process is repeated. Most injection moulding machines run automatically and large quantities can be produced at low cost.

instinct *see* BEHAVIOUR.

insulation is the means of preventing the passage of heat or heat loss by conduction, convection or radiation (it also applies when an electric current is prevented from passing). There are many ways of providing thermal insulation, the commonest example being the insulating materials used in houses to reduce heat loss. Cavity walls can be filled with foam, roof spaces lined with fibreglass or polystyrene beads and windows can be double glazed.

A vacuum prevents conduction and convection and this property is utilised in a vacuum flask to retain heat in hot drinks. There are several examples of natural insulation, notably the fur and feathers of mammals and birds respectively.

insulator *see* CONDUCTOR.

intelligence the ability of animals to learn and understand and so to be able to live effectively in their surroundings. Human beings are considered to be the most intelligent of animals and this ability depends upon GENETIC make-up and environment. The potential for developing a person's intelligence is considered to be at its greatest during childhood, especially in the early years. Also, it is thought to be important to use intellectual abilities throughout life in order to exercise our intelligence to its full power.

invertebrate animals are those 'without a backbone' or rather which lack an internal SKELETON. They make up 95% of animal species and show many different kinds of specialisations which allow them to adopt all sorts of lifestyles and habitats.

ion is an ATOM or MOLECULE that is charged due to the loss or gain of an electron or electrons. A *cation* is positively charged and an *anion* negatively charged. *Ionisation* is the process that results in ions and it can occur in a number of ways including a molecule breaking down into ions in solution, or the production of ions due to the bombardment of atoms by radiation. During ELECTROLYSIS, ions are attracted to the electrode with an opposite charge.

iron is a metallic element in group 8 of the PERIODIC TABLE, which in its pure form is silver-white. It is a common component of minerals in clays, granites and sandstones and is a dominant element in meteorites. It occurs naturally as several minerals: magnetite (Fe_3O_4), haematite (Fe_2O_3), limonite ($FeO(OH)_nH_2O$), siderite ($FeCO_3$) and pyrite (FeS_2). In combination with copper it occurs as chalcopyrite, $CuFeS_2$. Pure iron melts at 1535°C and is extracted from its ores by the BLAST FURNACE process.

Iron is a widely used metal, in combination with other metals. Cast and wrought iron (*see* CAST IRON) are both used extensively but most iron goes into the production of STEEL.

Iron is also of biological significance because it is essential to the red blood cells. These cells contain the pigment *haemoglobin* which is made up of the iron-containing pigment haem and the protein globin. Haemoglobin is responsible for the transport of oxygen around the body, hence if there is insufficient iron in the diet anaemia may result.

irradiation is the exposure of an object to radiation which may be electromagnetic radiation such as X-rays or gamma rays. The radiation may also come from a radioactive source. Above a certain level radiation harms organisms and this principle is adopted when using irradiation as a technique for food preservation. Very specific irradiation is used in medicine when obtaining an X-ray or in the use of ionising radiations to treat cancer.

isomers are chemical compounds with the same molecular formula, i.e.

same composition and molecular weight, but which differ in their chemical structure. This property is called *isomerism*, of which there are two types. *Structural isomers* differ in the way that their atoms are joined together whether it be changes in the arrangement of carbon atoms in the chain or the position of a group or atom on the chain or ring. *Tautomerism* is a special case of structural isomerism which is termed dynamic. This is because a compound exists as a mixture of two isomers in equilibrium and removal of one isomer results in conversion of the other to restore the equilibrium. The other type of isomerism is *stereoisomerism* in which isomeric compounds have atoms bonded in the same way but arranged differently in space. One type of stereoisomerism is *optical isomerism* due to asymmetry of the molecules and in this case the isomers differ in the direction in which they rotate a plane of polarised light (*see* POLARISATION OF LIGHT).

isotope is one of several atoms of the same element that have the same ATOMIC NUMBER (i.e. same number of protons) but differing numbers of neutrons in the nucleus (affecting their atomic mass). The chemical properties of isotopes are therefore the same, only physical properties affected by mass differ. Most elements exist naturally as a mixture of isotopes but can be separated upon their slightly different physical properties. For laboratory purposes MASS SPECTROMETRY is often used. *Radioisotopes* are isotopes which emit RADIOACTIVITY and decay at a particular rate, e.g. carbon -14.

Chemical symbols can be used to show the different configurations of isotopes, thus for hydrogen there are three isotopes:

	Protium ordinary hydrogen	Deuterium	Tritium
protons	1	1	1
neutrons	0	1	2
electrons	1	1	1
symbol	$_1^1 H$	$_1^2 H$	$_1^3 H$

When deuterium replaces hydrogen in a water molecule, the resulting compound is called *heavy water*.

joule (J) is the unit for measurements of ENERGY and WORK. It is equal to a force of one newton moving one metre (one newton is the force required to give a mass of one kilogram an acceleration of one metre per second, per second). The unit is named after the British physicist James Prescott

Joule (1818–89) who investigated the link between mechanical, electrical and heat energy.

One thousand joules is called a kilojoule. Energy used to be measured in *calories*, one calorie being 4.1868 joules.

kidney *see* OSMOREGULATION.

kiln is a furnace or large oven that has many uses. The most obvious is its use for drying, baking and hardening clay objects such as plates, cups and similar domestic items, but also bricks and other building components and by in processing by the minerals extraction industry. Kilns vary in size depending upon their use and modern models are heated by gas or electricity.

laboratory any room or building that is especially built or equipped for undertaking scientific experiments, research or chemicals manufacture. The study of physics, chemistry, biology, medicine, geology and other subjects usually involves some work in a laboratory and each is equipped with special instruments.

A chemical laboratory typically contains balances for weighing samples, bottles of chemicals including dangerous acids, a vast array of glassware (test tubes, flasks etc.) and bunsen burners. The *bunsen burner* is a gas burner consisting of a small vertical tube with an adjustable air inlet at the base to control the flame. The flame produced by burning the hydrocarbon gas/air mix has an inner cone where carbon monoxide is formed and an outer fringe where it is burnt. When the gas is burnt completely the flame temperature is very high, around 1450ºC. The burner was invented by Robert Wilhelm Bunsen (1811–99), a German scientist.

laminates are materials produced by bonding together under pressure two or more different materials. Plastics are commonly used in this way, bonded to chipboard or another building board, to make kitchen units and worktops and other items of furniture. Wood, such as *plywood*, is made of veneers bonded together which is in effect a laminate. Laminated plastics are composites made up of plastics and reinforcing or strengthening materials, e.g. carbon fibres, glass fibres. Glass sheet can also be made in laminated form with layers of glass joined by tough plastic, and these are used for security glass, sound insulation, fire resistance, etc. The overriding feature of laminates is that the combination of materials, albeit in thin sheets, produces a composite material that is much stronger than the individual components alone.

larva and metamorphosis a larva is a young or immature form of an animal that looks and often behaves differently from the adult. There may be several larval stages, and this is a common feature of invertebrate animals.

Familiar larvae are those of butterflies and moths (caterpillars), those of flies (maggots) and those of many marine animals, huge numbers of which make up PLANKTON. Larvae can feed and lead an independent life but (with one or two exceptions) are not able to reproduce. Usually an animal passes through several larval stages before undergoing a process known as *metamorphosis* to become an adult. In insects, the final larval stage is a *pupa* or *chrysalis*, during which all activities such as feeding and walking cease. The body is enclosed within an outer case and, under the influence of HOR-MONES, it gradually changes to become an adult. Usually, there is a break-down of some of the larval tissues, which are then re-used, and some of the cells that were inactive in the larva divide to form the body of the adult. When the process is complete, the pupal case splits and the adult emerges.

laser is an acronym for *l*ight *a*mplification by *s*timulated *e*mission of *ra*dia-tion and is a device that produces an intense beam of light of one wave-length (*monochromatic*) in which the waves are all in step with each other (*coherent* light). In its simplest form a ruby crystal shaped like a cylinder is subjected to flashes of white light from an external source. The chro-mium atoms in the ruby become excited through absorbing photons of LIGHT and when struck by more photons, light energy is released. One end of the cylinder is mirrored to reflect light back into the crystal and the other end is partially reflecting, allowing the escape of the coherent light. The ruby laser produces pulses of laser light and is called a *pulse laser*.

Lasers have also been constructed using INERT GASES (helium and neon mixed; argon alone) and carbon dioxide. These are called *gas lasers*, and produce a continuous beam of laser light. Lasers are being used for an in-creasing number of tasks including printing, communications, COMPACT DISC players, cutting metals, HOLOGRAPHY and for an ever-widening range of surgical techniques in medicine. Lasers are also used in shops at the checkout, to read BAR CODES.

learning *see* BEHAVIOUR.

lens is a device that makes a beam of rays passing through it either converge (meet at a point) or diverge. Optical lenses are made of a uniform transpar-ent medium such as glass or a plastic and they refract the light (*see* REFRAC-TION). They are either convex (thickest in the middle) or concave (thickest at the edges) in shape and lenses can be made with combinations of these profiles or one side may be flat (plane). Light rays that pass through a con-vex lens are bent towards the *principal axis* (or optical axis-the line join-ing the centre of curvature of the two lens surfaces), and away from the axis with a concave lens. The *focus* is where the light rays are brought together at a point and the focal length is the distance of the focus from the centre of the lens.

A convex lens forms a small image of the object which is inverted (upside down) and on the opposite side of the lens. This is called a *real image* and can be seen on a screen. As an object in the distance is brought nearer to a convex lens the image moves away from the lens and becomes larger. The image formed by a concave lens is always upright, smaller than the object and it is a *virtual image*, that is it cannot be projected because although the rays of light appear to come to the observer from the image, they do not actually do so.

Lenses can be found in many optical instruments including the camera and the telescope and also in the human eye (*see* SIGHT).

lever a simple machine which at its simplest consists of a rigid beam which pivots at a point called the *fulcrum*. A load applied at one end can be balanced by an *effort* (a force) applied at the opposite end. There are three classes of lever depending upon the position of fulcrum, load and effort. The fulcrum may be between the effort and load (sometimes called a first-class lever); if the load is between the fulcrum and effort it is second class; and a third class lever has the effort between the fulcrum and load. Examples of these are pliers, a wheelbarrow and the shovel on a mechanical digger.

Although the work done by both effort and load must be equal, it is possible by moving a small effort through a large distance to move a very large load, albeit through a small distance.

light is ELECTROMAGNETIC WAVES of a particular wavelength which are visible to the human eye. Objects can only be seen if light reflected from them or given off by them reaches the eye. Light is given out by hot objects and the hotter the object the nearer to the blue end of the spectrum is the light emitted. The Sun is our primary source of light and the light travels at almost 3×10^5 (300, 000) km/s through space. The light waves are made up of packets or quanta (*singular*, quantum) of energy, called *photons*. Every photon can be considered to be a particle of light energy, the energy increasing as the wavelength shortens.

White light is actually made up of a range of colours. This can be shown by passing a very narrow beam of light through a prism. Because the individual colours have different wavelengths they are refracted by differing amounts and the resulting *dispersion* produces the characteristic *spectrum*.

A beam of light can often be seen particularly if a torch is shone on a misty night or in a dark room where there is smoke, or if sunlight highlights dust particles. In each case the edge of the beam indicates that light travels in straight lines and because of this a shadow forms when an object is placed between a light source and a flat surface.

light bulbs consist of a glass bulb within which is a filament of tungsten. When a current is passed, the tungsten glows white hot, giving out light. Tungsten is used because it has a very high melting point (3410°C) and because the thin wire of the filament would burn up quickly in air, the bulb contains argon and/or nitrogen to provide an inert atmosphere. Only a small proportion of the energy of a light bulb is given out in the form of visible light. Fluorescent lights are often used because to achieve the same illumination, they use only a third of the power. Fluorescent lamps, or strips, contain a vapour, e.g. mercury, under low pressure. Electrons from an electrode bombard the mercury atoms making electrons move into a higher orbit around the mercury nuclei. When the electrons move back into their normal orbit, ultraviolet light is given off which causes a coating on the tube to glow. Neon and other INERT GASES are used for this purpose, as is sodium.

lightning conductor was invented by the American statesman and scientist Benjamin Franklin (1706–90). It is made of a metal rod (often copper) attached to the top of a building and which is then connected by cable to a metal plate buried in the ground. If and when lightning strikes, the lightning conductor provides a suitable path for electrons to move to the ground, without causing damage to the building. The ground, or as it is known, the *earth*, has an unlimited capacity to accept electrons. A lightning conductor may also help reduce the possibility of lightning striking. This is because there is a flow of IONS from the point of the conductor which lowers the charge induced on the roof by the thundercloud. The result is that some of the charge on the cloud is cancelled out, lowering the risk of a strike.

linear equation is an equation in which the variables in the equation are not raised to any power (squared, etc.) but may have a coefficient. Thus $y = mx + c$ is a linear equation and the slope of the line plotted has a gradient m and c is the value where the line crosses the y-axis. This is known as the *intercept*. Sets of linear equations are used in engineering to describe the behaviour of structures.

linear motor otherwise known as a *linear induction motor*, relies essentially upon the principle of electromagnetic induction, that is when current flows through a coil, magnetic forces cause the coil to spin. In the linear motor, electromagnets are laid flat and when a current is passed, a metal bar skims across them, i.e. it becomes a method of propulsion. Linear motors are now used in trains that do not run on conventional rails, but 'float' over a guiding rail due to the magnetic fields generated.

liquid is a fluid state of matter that has no definite shape and will take on the shape of its container. A liquid has more kinetic energy than a solid but less than a gas, and although it flows freely the molecules stick together to form drops, unlike gases which continue to spread out whenever possible. Liquids can form solids or gases if cooled or heated but many substances such as oxygen, nitrogen and other gases will only form liquids if cooled a great deal or put under pressure.

liquid crystals are substances that are liquids which on heating become cloudy and in this state they show alignment of MOLECULES in an ordered structure, as in a crystal. At higher temperatures still there is a transition to a clear liquid. The application of a current disrupts the molecules, causing realignment and optical effects, darkening the liquid and this property has been exploited for use in displays. *Liquid crystal displays* are used in calculators and watches and also in thin thermometers which work by laying a strip containing the liquid crystals on a child's forehead and the temperature is shown by the segments of crystal changing colour.

liver the liver is a large and very important organ present in the body of vertebrate animals, just below the ribs in the region called the ABDOMEN. It is composed of many groups of liver cells (called lobules) which are richly supplied with blood vessels. The liver plays a critical role in the regulation of many of the processes of METABOLISM. A vein called the hepatic portal vein carries the products of digestion to the liver. Here any extra glucose (sugar) which is not immediately needed is converted to a form in which it can be stored known as glycogen. This is then available as a source of energy for MUSCLES. PROTEINS are broken down in the liver and the excess building blocks, (amino acids), of which they are composed, are changed to ammonia and then to urea, a waste product which is excreted by the kidneys. Lipids, which are the products of the digestion of fat, are broken down in the liver and CHOLESTEROL, an essential part of cell membranes, some hormones and the nervous system, is produced. Bile, which is stored in the gall bladder and then passed to the intestine, is produced in the liver. In addition, poisonous substances (toxins) such as alcohol are broken down (detoxified) by liver cells. Important blood proteins are produced and also substances which are essential in blood clotting. Vitamin A is both produced and stored in the liver and it is a storage site for vitamins D, E and K. Iron is also stored and some hormones and damaged red blood cells are processed and removed.

logarithm abbreviated to log, is a mathematical function first introduced to render multiplication and division with large numbers more simple. However, the advent of calculators and computers has reduced the former dependency on logs. The basic definition is that if a number x is expressed as a *power* (i.e. the number of times a quantity is multiplied by itself) of another number, y, that is $x = y^n$, then n is the logarithm of x to the base y, written as $\log y x$.

There are two types of log in use; *common* (or Briggs') and the *natural* (or Napierian). Common logs have base 10, $\log_{10} x$. Addition of the logs of two numbers gives their *product,* while subtraction of two numbers' logs is the means of division. Natural logs are to the base e where e is a constant with the value 2.71828. The two logs can be related by the function:

$$\log_e x = 2.303 \log_{10} x$$

loudspeaker is a device for turning an electric current into sound and is found in radios, televisions, and many other pieces of equipment that output sound. The commonest design is the *moving-coil loudspeaker*. This consists of a cylindrical magnet with a central south pole surrounded by a circular north pole producing a strong radial magnetic field. There is also a coil sandwiched between the two poles of the magnet which is free to move forwards and backwards and a stiff paper cone that is fastened to the coil. Because the wire of the coil is positioned at right angles to the magnetic field, when current flows through the coil, it moves.

When an alternating current passes through the coil it moves forwards and backwards and the paper cone vibrates resulting in sound waves.

lubricants are a vital group of materials used in modern industry to make surfaces slide more easily over each other, by reducing FRICTION. Without *lubrication* surfaces grind against each other, producing wear and this can shorten the working life of a machine or engine. In the main, lubricants are liquid in form and are made from oil. However, there are other liquid lubricants (vegetable and mineral oils), plastic lubricants (fatty acids, soaps) andsolids, such as graphite and talc. Vehicle engines use oil as a lubricant and turbines for aircraft use synthetic fluids. Main synthetic lubricants are silicones, polyglycols, esters and halogenated (*see* HALOGENS) HYDROCARBONS.

Greases made from a liquid lubricant with a thickening agent are also used to combat wear where temperature and shearing forces apply. A petroleum oil forms the base, and a soap mixture the thickener, often with additives such as graphite, glycerine or fatty acids.

luminescence is when a body gives out light due to a cause other than a high temperature. It is due to a temporary change in the electronic structure of an atom, and involves an electron taking in energy and moving to a higher orbit in the atom which is then re-emitted as light when the electron falls back to its original orbit. The energy required to promote the electron to a higher orbit may come from light (*photoluminescence*) or from collisions of the atoms with fast particles (*fluorescence*). When materials continue to give out light after the primary energy source has been removed, this is called *phosphorescence*.

This phenomenon of luminescence is put to use in the CATHODE RAY TUBE of TELEVISIONS. It also occurs in nature and is called BIOLUMINESCENCE.

lungs and gills lungs are the sac-like organs which are used for RESPIRATION in air-breathing vertebrate animals. In mammals a pair of lungs are situated within the rib cage in the region of the body behind the head known as the thorax. Each lung is made of a thin, moist membrane which is highly folded, and it is here that oxygen is taken in to the body and carbon dioxide is given up. The lungs do not have muscles of their own but are filled and emptied by the muscular movement of a sheet-like layer dividing the thorax from the abdomen, known as the DIAPHRAGM. The diaphragm flattens, which reduces the pressure in the thoracic cavity enabling the lungs to expand and fill with air (inhalation). When the diaphragm muscles relax it arches upwards forcing air out of the lungs (exhalation). This is accompanied (and the effect made greater) by outward and inward movement of the ribs which are controlled by other (intercostal) muscles. Gills, which are present in many invertebrate animals and also in fish, are organs which fulfil the same function as lungs.

In mammals such as man, air enters through the nose (and mouth) and passes into the windpipe or TRACHEA which itself branches into two smaller tubes called bronchi (*singular* bronchus). Each bronchus goes to one lung and further divides into smaller, finer tubes known as bronchioles. Each bronchiole is surrounded by a tiny sac called an alveolus (*plural* alveoli) formed from one minute fold of the lung membrane. On one side of the membrane there is air and on the other there are numerous tiny blood vessels called capillaries. Deoxygenated blood, that is, blood which contains little oxygen, is brought via a branch of the pulmonary artery to each lung. The artery divides many times eventually forming capillaries surrounding the alveoli. In the same way, other capillaries unite and become larger eventually forming the pulmonary veins which take oxygenated blood back to the heart. The heart pumps it around the body. CARBON DIOXIDE passes out from the capillaries across the alveoli into the lungs and oxygen passes into the blood in the opposite direction, this process being known as gaseous exchange. The numerous folds of the membrane forming the alveoli increase the surface area over which this is able to take place.

The human respiratory system

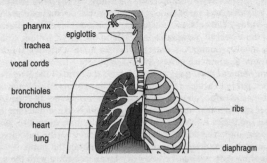

pharynx
epiglottis
trachea
vocal cords
bronchioles
bronchus
heart
lung
ribs
diaphragm

lymph system is a network of fine tubules occurring throughout the body of a vertebrate animal. In places the tubules are swollen to form lumps of tissue known as *lymph nodes* or glands.

This network transports the lymph – a colourless, watery fluid which is mainly water but also contains white blood cells (called *leucocytes* and *lymphocytes*) PROTEIN and digested fats. The lymphocytes are an essential part of the body's IMMUNE SYSTEM and collect in the lymph glands and nodes. In the event of an infection these cells multiply rapidly and this often causes a swelling which can be felt through the skin. (An example of this is the adenoids and tonsils which often become enlarged in the case of an infection of the nose or throat.) Lymph, which contains waste matter from cells, drains into the tubules from all the tissues of the body. It is filtered when it reaches the lymph nodes, where bacteria and other foreign and waste material are destroyed. The lymph tubules finally drain into two major lymphatic vessels that empty into veins at the base of the neck. The circulation of lymph is by muscular action rather than by the beating of the heart and it is essential in the transport of digested fats as well as in the immune system.

In children, white blood cells are produced in the thymus gland but this shrinks as adulthood is reached. In adults, white blood cells are produced in the bone marrow, spleen and lymph nodes.

machine is basically a means of overcoming resistance at a point by applying a FORCE at another point. Although a machine does not reduce the amount of work to be done to achieve a task, it does allow the work to be done more conveniently.

There are six *simple machines* in the study of physics. These are the wheel and axle, wedge, LEVER, PULLEY, screw and the inclined plane. Each in its own way can be used for a particular task-the lever or pulley to raise a load, the wheel to transport a load and so on. More complex machines usually involve the input of energy either for modification or for driving a mechanism to achieve a task.

The *mechanical advantage* of a machine is the ratio of the load moved to the effort put in to achieve the movement. The *velocity ratio* is the distance moved by the effort divided by the distance moved by the load. An inclined plane, or *ramp*, doesn't appear very much like a machine but it is because it enables a load to be taken gradually to a height to which the load could not have been lifted vertically. In this case the velocity ratio is essentially the length of the ramp over the height of the ramp.

Mach number is the speed of a body expressed as a ratio with the speed of sound. It was named after an Austrian physicist Ernst Mach (1838–1916). If the Mach number is below 1 then the speed is *subsonic*; above 1 is *supersonic* and as an aircraft increases its speed to go over Mach 1 it is said to *break the sound barrier*. *Hypersonic* is when speeds are in excess of Mach 5. Most passenger airliners travel subsonically but Concorde flies at Mach 2. Certain military planes reach over Mach 3.

The noise associated with breaking the sound barrier is a *sonic boom*. A subsonic aircraft produces pressure waves in front of itself and these waves travel at the speed of sound. A supersonic aircraft overtakes the pressure waves creating a shock wave like a cone with the point of the cone at the nose of the aircraft. The shock wave creates a typical double bang which can be strong enough to damage buildings.

magnetism is the effective force which originates within the Earth and which behaves as if there were a powerful magnet at the centre of the Earth, producing a magnetic field. The magnetic field has its north and south poles pointing approximately to the geographic north and south poles and a compass needle or freely swinging magnet will align itself along the line of the magnetic field. With the correct instrument it can also be seen that the magnetic field dips into the Earth, increasing towards the poles.

A *bar magnet* has a north and south pole, so named because the pole at that end pointing to the north is called a north-seeking pole, and similarly with the south pole. When dipped in a material that can be magnetised, such as iron filings, the metal grains align themselves along the magnetic field between the poles of the magnet. Some materials can be magnetised in the presence of a magnet, e.g. iron and steel. Iron does not retain its magnetism, but steel does. These are called *temporary* and *permanent magnets*. A more effective way to produce a magnet is to slide a steel bar into a solenoid (coil) through which current is passed and magnetism is *induced* in the steel (*see* ELECTROMAGNET).

In addition to iron, cobalt and nickel can also be magnetised strongly and these materials are called ferro-magnetic. Non-metals and other metals such as copper, seem to be unaffected by magnetism, but very strong magnets do show some effect.

The origin of magnetism is unknown, but is attributed to the flow of electric current. On the electronic scale within magnetic materials it is thought that electrons act as minute magnets (because electrons carry a charge) as they spin around their nuclei in atoms. In some elements, this electron spin is cancelled out but in others it is not and each atom or molecule acts as a magnet contributing to the overall magnetic nature of the material.

A bar magnet

magnetometer is an instrument for measuring the strength of a magnetic field. The *deflection magnetometer* consists of a long magnetic pointer pivoted on a short magnet. The pointer swings along a scale, allowing small deflections of the magnet to be measured. Other versions have a small coil which generates a voltage on moving through a magnetic field. More complex and sensitive magnetometers are used for special purposes, for example, it is possible to tow a magnetometer behind an aircraft to detect changes in the Earth's magnetic field that may be due to mineral deposits, including oil.

magnification is the ratio of the size of the image to the object in an optical magnifying system. Magnification of an object can be achieved by simple means, e.g. a hand lens or *magnifying glass* which is merely a convex LENS. A far greater magnification can be achieved by using a *compound microscope* which consists essentially of two convex lenses with a short focus, called the objective and the eyepiece. The two lenses are at opposite ends of a tube beneath which is a stage upon which the sample (object) is placed. Magnifications of several hundred can be obtained with this microscope. For greater magnification still (above 1500) an electron microscope is used.

The *electron microscope* uses a beam of electrons striking the object. In the *transmission electron microscope* (*tem*) the electron beam passes through a thin slice of the sample and the resulting image is formed by the scattering of the beam which is enlarged and focused on a fluorescent screen. The *scanning electron microscope* (*sem*) actually scans the surface of the sample and the image is created by secondary electrons which are emitted from the sample. Scanning does not magnify the object as much as transmission electron microscopy, but the image is three-dimensional. Magnifications up to 200,000 can be achieved with *tem*.

Microscopes are used throughout science and engineering, often with modifications to fulfil a particular role. They are used for studying plant and animal tissue, rock samples to determine the minerals and structures present, metals and non-metals to determine structure, and much more.

malleability *see* DUCTILITY.

mammals *see* **Natural History**.

maser stands for *m*icrowave *a*mplification by *s*timulated *e*mission of *r*adiation and is a microwave amplifier/oscillator that works in a similar way to the LASER and, after it was discovered, prompted the research that resulted in the laser. An atom already in an excited state, because of absorption of energy, gives out a photon because of absorption of further energy. The 'active' material of the maser is therefore built up to an excited state and enclosed to generate a wave of just one frequency. The microwaves produced can also be used in a clock because of their very precise frequency.

mass *see* WEIGHT.

mass number is the total number of *protons* and *neutrons* in the nucleus of an ATOM. Atoms of a particular element may have differing mass numbers because of different numbers of neutrons in the nucleus, i.e. they are ISOTOPES.

mass spectrometry is a technique to analyse samples to determine the elements in a compound or the various isotopes in an element. The *mass spectrometer* bombards the sample with high energy electrons, producing charged IONS, and fragments that are neutral. The ions are then deflected in a magnetic field that separates them according to their mass, and then pass through a slit to a collector. The output is a printed chart (a *mass spectrum*) containing a series of lines or peaks, where each peak corresponds to a particular ion and its mass. If isotopes are being identified, the mass spectrometer provides the mass and relative amount of each isotope.

Mass spectrometry is used for the identification and structural analysis of organic compounds and the determination of elemental traces in inorganic materials.

mathematical symbols in addition to the well-known symbols of arithmetic, such as = (equals),-(minus), + (plus), x (multiplied by) and ÷ or / (divided by), there are many other useful symbols that permit the shorthand writing of scientific formulae, equations and statements. These are used in mathematics, physics, chemistry, astronomy, geology and others scientific and engineering disciplines. A sample is shown below:

$\pm$	plus or minus	Σ	the sum of
$>$	greater than	α	proportional to
$<$	less than	$\approx$	similar or equal to
$\geq$	greater than or equal to	$\equiv$	equivalent to
$\leq$	less than or equal to	$\therefore$	therefore
$=$	equal by definition	$\because$	because

mathematics is the science of relationships that involve numbers and shapes and has been around for thousands of years since the ancient Egyptians used geometry in construction. It is divided into two main categories – *pure* and *applied mathematics*. Pure mathematics includes algebra, arithmetic, geometry, trigonometry and calculus (*see individual entries*). Applied mathematics verges on to other subject or parts of subjects and includes statistics, mechanics, computing and mathematical aspects of topics such as thermodynamics, astronomy and optics.

matrix (*plural* **matrices**) is an array of elements, that is, numbers or algebraic symbols, set out in rows and columns. It may be a square or a rectangle of elements. Matrices are very useful for condensing information and are used in many ways, for example in solving simultaneous LINEAR EQUATIONS (simultaneous equations are two or more equations with two or more unknowns which may have a unique solution). The order of a matrix refers to the number of rows and columns, thus;

A = [2 1 3] has one row and three columns while

$B = \begin{bmatrix} 2 & 6 \\ 1 & 4 \end{bmatrix}$ has two rows and two columns

Matrices with one row are called *row vectors* and similarly *column vectors* are so named because they have just one column.

Only matrices of the same order can be added or subtracted and to be multiplied the second matrix must have the same number of columns as the first has rows. The multiplication is carried out by combining the rows and columns of each matrix to form a new matrix where the various elements are the products of the rows of the first and the columns of the second matrices.

matter is any substance that occupies space and has mass and is the material of which the universe is made. Matter exists normally in three states: gas, liquid and solid. Most substances can be made to exist in all three states at different temperatures, thus by cooling a gas it eventually becomes liquid and then a solid. *Plasma* is considered a fourth state and consists of a high temperature gas of charged particles (electrons and IONS). Although it contains charged particles, a plasma is neutral overall, but it can support an electric current. Stars are made of plasma, but it finds applications in the study of controlled nuclear fusion (*see* NUCLEAR FISSION and NUCLEAR FUSION).

mechanics is the part of physics that deals with the way matter behaves under the influence of forces. It involves:

dynamics the study of objects that are subjected to forces that result in changes of motion.

statics the study of objects subjected to forces but where no motion is produced.

kinematics the study of motion without reference to mass or force but which deals with velocity and acceleration of parts of a moving system.

Newton's law of motion (*see* FORCE) forms the basics of mechanics except at the atomic level, when behaviour is explained by QUANTUM MECHANICS.

meiosis and mitosis *see* CELL DIVISION.

melting point *see* FREEZING.

membrane a membrane is a thin sheet of tissue widely found in living organisms. It covers, lines or joins cells, organelles (small organs), organs and tissues, and consists of a double layer of lipids (fats) in which protein molecules are suspended. Water and fat-soluble substances are able to pass across a membrane but sugars cannot. Other substances or ions are actively carried across a membrane by a complex system known as *active transport*.

memory a function of the brain in animals that enables information to be stored and brought back for use later. Several areas of the brain (such as the temporal lobes) are involved in memory, and although, in humans, this function has been widely studied it is not entirely understood. Placing information in the memory involves three stages – registration, storage and recall. The information is committed either to the *short term memory* or the *long term memory*. It tends to fade quickly from the short term memory if not needed but, if used often, is transferred to the long term memory. Information is usually lost (forgetfulness) during the process of retrieval or recollection. Sometimes this can be helped if the circumstances in which the information was registered can be recreated. This is a technique which is used by the police when they are trying to gain information (which might have been only fleetingly seen) from witnesses at the scene of a crime.

metabolism is the name given to all the chemical and physical processes which occur in living organisms. These are of two kinds, *catabolic* (or breaking down) as in the digestion of food, and *anabolic* (or building up) as in the production of more complicated MOLECULES from simple ones. All these processes require energy and ENZYMES in order to take place. Plants trap energy from the sun during PHOTOSYNTHESIS and animals gain energy from the consumption of food. The metabolic rate is the speed at which food is used or broken down to produce energy, and this varies greatly between different species of animals. In people, children have a higher metabolic rate than adults and more energy is required by someone during hard work than by someone who is at rest.

metal fatigue is the structural failure of metals due to repeated application of stress, which results in a change to the crystalline nature of the metal. *Stress* is force per unit area and when it is applied to a material, a *strain* is developed, that is a distortion.

metallurgy is the scientific study of metals and their alloys. It includes the extraction of metals from their ores and their processing for use. *Extractive metallurgy* deals with production of the metals from their ores and *physical metallurgy* the structure of metals and their properties.

metals are materials that are generally ductile, malleable (*see* DUCTILITY), dense with a metallic lustre (or sheen) and usually good conductors of heat and electricity. There are about 80 metals in all, some of which occur as the pure metal, but most are found as compounds in rocks and deposits. Pure metals are used for certain applications (e.g. GOLD in jewellery and copper in electrical goods) but it is usually the case that mixtures of metals (ALLOYS) provide the properties required for specific applications.

Metallic elements are generally electropositive, that is they give up electrons to produce a cation (e.g. Na⁺) in reactions. When reacting with water, bases are produced. Elements that show some features of both metals and non-metals are called METALLOIDS or semimetals, e.g. arsenic, bismuth and antimony.

metamorphosis *see* LARVA.

methane is the first member of the alkane (*see* HYDROCARBONS) series, and has the formula CH4. It is a colourless, odourless gas and the main component of coal gas and a byproduct of decaying vegetable matter. It is the primary component of natural gas and occurs in coal mines where mixed with air it forms highly explosive *firedamp*. It is highly flammable and is used in the manufacture of hydrogen, ammonia, carbon monoxide and other chemicals.

metric system is a system of measurement of weights and measures based upon the principle that levels of units are related by the factor 10, i.e. it is a decimal system that began with the metre. There are now seven basic units of measurement: metre, second, kilogram, ampere, kelvin, candela (light) and mole and each has a standard value and is defined very precisely. *See also* SI UNITS.

microbiology and micro-organism microbiology is the scientific study of all aspects of the life of micro-organisms or microbes. These organisms are so called because they can only be seen with a microscope. They include bacteria, viruses, yeasts and moulds, many of the (largely single-celled) organisms called protozoa (*see* PROTISTA) and some algae and fungi. Many of these organisms are highly significant for man because of their use in BIOTECHNOLOGY and GENETIC ENGINEERING and also because some cause diseases of various kinds. The study of microbiology has advanced significantly along with the technological development of microscopes, particularly the electron microscope and also with more advanced laboratory facilities.

microphone is a device for changing sound into electric current. It is essentially the reverse process to that which happens in a LOUDSPEAKER. In a moving coil microphone, sound waves cause vibration in a diaphragm made of paper or plastic and this moves a small coil which rests in the field of a cylindrical magnet. A small current is *induced* in the coil due to it moving through the magnetic field and this can be amplified and output through a loudspeaker. A variety of microphones are now in use: *carbon microphone* where the diaphragm changes the resistance in a carbon contact; *condenser microphone* and a crystal microphone which relies upon the PIEZOELECTRIC EFFECT in crystals.

microwaves are electromagnetic waves with wavelengths of a few centimetres or less. Microwaves are used for communications, e.g. via satellites, and intense beams are produced in a MASER. Microwaves are easily deflected and as they have a shorter wavelength than radiowaves, they are suitable for use in radar systems because they can detect small objects. Heat is produced when microwaves are absorbed and this effect is utilised in microwave ovens. A unit called the MAGNETRON generates the microwaves and these impart their energy to the water in the food, producing heat and the cooking effect.

mirror an object or surface that reflects light. Mirrors are made from glass coated with a thin metallic layer but polished metal surfaces have the same effect. When light strikes a mirrored surface, it is reflected in a particular way, according to the laws of REFLECTION. A plane mirror has a flat surface which bounces back light, creating an image 'behind' the mirror. Curved mirrors are convex or concave. Concave mirrors produce a magnifying effect if the object is sufficiently near to the mirror, but distant objects are smaller and inverted. Convex mirrors produce upright images that are smaller than the object. Concave mirrors are used in car headlights while convex mirrors are often used for driving mirrors because they produce a wide angle of view.

mitochondrion (*pl.* mitochondria) a type of rod-shaped organelle found in the cytoplasm (cell contents except for the nucleus) of EUCARYOTIC cells which is surrounded by a double membrane. Mitochondria have been called the 'power houses' of the cell as they are very important in the generation of energy in a form called ATP. ATP production is the end result of cellular respiration and provides energy for all metabolic processes. As mitochondria are the sites where this takes place, they are especially abundant in cells which require lots of energy such as those of muscles. Mitochondria contain a form of DNA, structures called ribosomes in which proteins are manufactured with numerous enzymes, each specific to a particular metabolic process.

molecule and mole a *molecule* is the smallest chemical unit of an element or compound that can exist independently. It consists of atoms bonded together in a particular combination, e.g. oxygen, O_2, is two oxygen atoms and carbon dioxide, CO_2, is on carbon and two oxygen atoms. Molecules may contain thousands of atoms. Gases, organic compounds, liquid and many solids consists of molecules but some materials, e.g. metals and ionic substances are different and comprise changed atoms or IONS.

The *mole* is the unit of substance that contains the same number of elementary particles as there are in 12 grams of carbon. One mole of a substance contains 6.023×10^{23} molecular atoms, or ions, or electrons.

momentum is the property of an object defined as the product of its velocity and mass and it is measured in kgm/s. Momentum is related to force as follows:

force = the rate of change of momentum.

Changes in momentum occur mainly due to the interaction between two bodies. During any interaction the total momentum of the bodies involved remains the same, providing no external force, such as FRICTION, is acting. Newton's second law of motion states that the rate of change of momentum of a body is directly proportional to the force acting and occurs in the direction in which the force ends.

If a body is rotating around an axis then it has *angular momentum* which is the product of its momentum and its perpendicular distance from the fixed axis.

Momentum can be seen around us all the time, but one of the most obvious examples is the collision of balls on the snooker table.

monera the biological kingdom in which all the organisms have PROCARYOTIC cells and are the bacteria and cyanobacteria (formerly called blue-green algae). *See* PROCARYOTE.

motors (electric) the basic principle behind most common electric motors is that when current is passed through a coil in a magnetic field, a turning effect is produced. In a d.c. (direct current) motor a coil rotates between the poles of a permanent magnet and is connected to a battery via carbon brushes which contact a split ring or *commutator*. The commutator reverses the current direction every half-turn of the coil ensuring that the coil continues to rotate (*see also* GENERATOR). Motors are used in many different devices and pieces of equipment, such as hair-dryers, mixers and food processors, drills and so on. Such motors operate from an a.c. (alternating current) supply and in this case an electromagnet is used because it can match the change in current and yet maintain a constant turning effect. In addition, the smooth and reliable running of these motors is ensured by: the incorporation of several coils at different angles each connected to a set of commutator pieces; several hundred turns of wire in each coil, on a soft iron core (as *armature*) which becomes magnetised, increasing the strength of the magnetic field; the poles of the magnet are shaped into a curve creating a magnetic field that is almost radial, giving a constant turning force (*see also* INDUCTANCE).

muscle a special type of tissue which is responsible for movements in the

body of an animal and which often works by pulling against the hard SKEL-
ETON. Muscle cells are elongated and arranged as bundles (called fibres)
and in mammals there are three types controlled by different parts of the
nervous system. *Voluntary* or striated muscle operates limbs and joints and
is under the conscious control of the will. Each muscle fibre consists of
smaller elongated *fibrils* (myofibrils) and these either lengthen and become thinner, or shorten and become fatter, as they slide over one another,
depending upon whether the muscle is contracting or relaxing. *Involuntary* or smooth muscle is not under conscious control but is regulated by a
special part of the nervous system (called the *autonomic nervous system;
see* NERVOUS SYSTEM). These muscles work automatically and are
responsible for the contractions of the gut, and of the womb at the time of
birth. This type of muscle also occurs at various other sites within the
body. *Cardiac muscle* is the third specialised kind and is responsible for
the beating of the heart which continues throughout life. This muscle is
involuntary but the rate of beat is affected by activity of an important
nerve called the vagus nerve. The *pacemaker* is a collection of specialised
cardiac muscle cells situated in the wall of the right atrium (one of the
upper chambers of the heart). These cells are under the control of the
autonomic nervous system and produce the contractions which stimulate
the rest of the heart to contract.

mutation any change which occurs in the DNA in the chromosomes of cells.
Mutation is one way in which genetic variation occurs and allows natural
selection to operate (*see* GENETICS). This is because any alteration in the
sex cells may produce an inherited change (mutation) in the characteristics
of later generations of the organism. Mutations occur naturally during the
time when DNA is copying itself, as in cell division although they are
relatively rare and most are harmful or lethal. They can occur much more
frequently following exposure to certain chemicals and radiation (X-rays),
and these agents are known as *mutagens*. A *mutant* is an organism which
shows the effects of a mutation.

mycology the name given to the scientific study of all aspects of the life of
FUNGI.

natural selection *see* DARWIN AND NATURAL SELECTION.

nervous system a network of specialised cells and tissues which is present
in all multicellular animals to a greater or lesser degree (with the exception of sponges). The activity of the nervous system consists of electrical
impulses which are caused by the movement of chemical (sodium and potassium) IONS. The nervous system includes RECEPTORS, which receive in-

formation from the surrounding environment and are called *sensory*. These are concerned with the senses such as sight, sound, touch and pressure and they transmit the information which they detect along nerves (called sensory nerves) and these travel to the central nervous system. In the simpler animals such as invertebrates, this often consists of a paired nerve cord with swellings along its length called *ganglia* (*sing.* ganglion). In vertebrate animals, the central nervous system is highly complex and consists of the brain and spinal cord. Within the central nervous system all the information is decoded and, if appropriate, a response is initiated. This often consists of a signal being sent outwards along a nerve (called a motor nerve) which travels to a muscle causing a contraction to occur. In vertebrates, a part of the nervous system is concerned with the control of the involuntary or smooth MUSCLE of the body. This is called the autonomic nervous system and consists of two divisions, the *sympathetic* and *parasympathetic* which act in opposite ways (antagonistic). It is sometimes called *involuntary* because its activity regulates the internal environment of the body and it supplies the smooth muscle (heart, gut, etc.) and glands with their motor nerve supply.

A nerve is made up of numerous nerve cells or 'neurons'. some nerves are sensory, others are motor and yet others are mixed carrying both types of neurons. Each neuron has a cell body (containing the neucleus) and many fine projections called 'dendrites'. Dendrites from surrounding neurons are able to communicate with one another across a gap called a 'synapse'. A long, fine projection runs out from the neuron cell body and this is called an 'axon'. It may be surrounded by a fatty sheath (called a 'myelin sheath') which is restricted at intervals at sites which are known as 'nodes of Ranvier'.

The nervous system

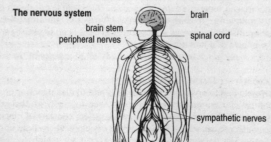

brain
brain stem
peripheral nerves
spinal cord
sympathetic nerves

nitrides are very similar compounds to CARBIDES and form hard materials with high melting points. Metals such as titanium, chromium, vanadium, zirconium and hafnium are used and these result in nitrides with high hardness, resistance to molten metals and a high corrosion resistance. As such they are used in crucibles for melting metal, protective coatings for moving surfaces and cutting tools.

nitrogen is a colourless gas existing as a diatomic molecule, N_2. It occurs in air (75% by weight), and as nitrates, ammonia and in PROTEINS. It is relatively unreactive at room temperature but reacts with some elements on heating. It is used extensively in the production of ammonia in liquid form as a refrigerant (its melting point is -210°C) and as an inert atmosphere. It is obtained industrially by the fractionation of liquid air.

Nitrogen is a vital element in the life cycle of both plants and animals and there is a regular circulation, called the *nitrogen cycle*. Bacteria take nitrogen from the atmosphere (*nitrogen fixation*) and plants use nitrate ions (NO_3^-) from the soil. The nitrogen is incorporated into plant tissue, which is then eaten by animals. The nitrogen is returned to the soil by the decomposition of dead plants and animals and by excretion.

nose *see* SMELL.

nuclear energy is the energy produced by the controlled decay of radioactive elements. Upon decay, an element such as uranium releases energy as heat which can be harnessed – the energy given off per atom is thousands and thousands times more than during burning. However, the decay often has to be accelerated by bombarding the material with neutrons.

NUCLEAR FISSION is the splitting of such atoms and is the way in which electricity is generated for nuclear power. In a *nuclear reactor* heat from the nuclear reactions heats water into steam, which drives the turbines. The core of a reactor contains the nuclear fuel, which may be uranium dioxide with uranium-235. Neutrons produced by the fission reactions are slowed down by a graphite core to ensure the *chain reaction* continues. The graphite core is called the *moderator*. *Control rods* of boron steel are lowered into or taken out of the reactor to control the rate of fission. Boron absorbs neutrons, and so if rods are lowered there are fewer neutrons available for the nuclear fission, and the reactor core temperature will fall. This is a *thermal reactor*. In a *fast breeder reactor*, low grade uranium surrounds the core, and impact from neutrons creates some uranium-239, which forms plutonium, which itself can be used as a reactor fuel. *Nuclear fusion* (*see* NUCLEAR FUSION) has not yet been harnessed for commercial power production.

Nuclear energy has the benefit of producing a lot of energy from a small amount of fuel. It doesn't produce gases that contribute to the *greenhouse effect* (*see* **NH**: GREENHOUSE EFFECT), but the waste produced is very dangerous and must be stored or treated very carefully.

nuclear fission nuclear fission is the splitting process that results when a neutron strikes a nucleus of, for example, uranium-235. The nucleus splits into two and releases more neutrons and a lot of energy. A *chain reaction* develops when the neutrons go on to split further nuclei, and the energy released becomes enormous.

nuclear fusion is where two nuclei are combined to form a single nucleus with an accompanying release of energy. Ordinarily nuclei would repel each other because of the like electrical charge, and so very high collision speeds have to be used, which in practice means the use of incredibly high temperatures.

Because thermal energy (*see* ENERGY) has to be supplied before the nuclear reactions occur, fusion is often called *thermonuclear fusion*. Fusion occurs in the Sun and, in an uncontrolled way, in the *hydrogen bomb*, but it is technically very difficult to control in the way that nuclear fission is managed.

nuclear reactor *see* NUCLEAR ENERGY.

numbers our numbers are based on Arabic numerals, which in turn were based on a Hindu system, and the system is constructed upon powers of ten, i.e. the decimal system (*see* DECIMAL NUMBERS). BINARY NUMBERS use the base two and are used extensively in computer programs. *Real numbers* include all *rational numbers* (whole numbers, or integers, and fractions) and *irrational numbers*, that is those that cannot be expressed as an exact fraction, e.g. some square roots such as 2, 5 and values such as the constant π (pi). *Complex numbers* are those written in the form $a + ib$ where a and b are real numbers and i is the square root of -1.

A *prime number* is a number that can be divided only by itself and 1, such as 2, 3, 5, 7, 11, 13, 17, 19, 23. There is an infinite number of prime numbers, and over the years mathematicians have spent much time trying to find a general method for calculating primes. A *surd* is an expression that contains the root of an irrational number and that can never be expressed exactly (e.g. 3 = 1.7320508 . . .).

oestrous cycle *see* REPRODUCTION.

oils are greasy liquid substances obtained from animal or vegetable matter or mineral sources, and they are complex organic compounds. There are also many synthetic oils. There are basically three groups of oils: the *fatty oils* from animal and vegetable sources; *mineral oils* from petroleum and coal; and *essential oils* derived from certain plants. Typical vegetable oils are extracted from soya beans, olives, nuts and maize. The essential oils are volatile (evaporate quickly) and are used in *aromatherapy* and in making perfumes and flavourings. Examples are peppermint oil, clove oil, oil of wintergreen and rose oil.

Mineral oils are actually fossil fuels and come under the general term of petroleum.

omnivore any animal that eats both plant and animal material, e.g. human beings (*compare* CARNIVORE and HERBIVORE).

optical fibres are made of very thin glass rods, which are flexible. When light rays enter one end of the fibre it is reflected completely within the fibres, being reflected from side to side until it emerges at the other end. Bundles of fibres are called *light pipes*, and they have several very important uses. Surgeons use them to see inside the body of a patient, often without the need for an incision. Also the pipes can carry an enormous number of telephone calls, where the calls are coded and sent along the fibres as pulses of LASER light. Another remarkable feature of optical fibres is that the light exits almost as strongly as it entered, even if the path is several kilometres, and this eliminates the need for numerous stations to boost the signal as required with ordinary telephone cables.

organ and tissue a tissue is a collection of cells within an ORGANISM, which are specialised to perform a particular function. An *organ* is a distinct and recognizable site or unit within the body of an organism that consists of two or more types of tissue. It is specialised in terms of its structure and function, and, in animals, examples include the kidneys, liver, skin and eyes. In plants, flowers, stems, roots, leaves and flowers are all organs. An *organelle* is a structure within a cell that performs a particular function and is surrounded by a membrane to separate it from other cell contents, e.g. the nucleus and MITOCHONDRIA.

organism any living creature including micro-organisms, plants and animals. There are very many different kinds of organism with new species being discovered all the time. At the other end of the scale, over the course of the Earth's history, numerous types of organism have become extinct. *Biotic* is an adjective relating to life or living things (hence *biota*, the plant and animal life of a region). Thus, for any organism, the other organisms around it make up the biotic environment.

osmoregulation this describes any process or mechanism in animals that regulates the concentration of salts (e.g. sodium chloride) and water in the body. Depending upon the environment it inhabits, there is a tendency for water to pass into or out of an animal's body by *osmosis*. Water tends to pass into the body of an animal which inhabits fresh water as the concentration of salts within its body is higher than that outside. Animals have a variety of structures to rid the body of excess water. In simple organisms (e.g. single-celled ones) an organelle called a *contractile vacuole* fills with water and expels it to the outside through a pore in the cell membrane. In marine animals there is a tendency to lose water from the body to the surrounding environment where the concentration of salts is higher. In vertebrate animals, whether the problem is one of water gain or loss, the kidneys are the main osmoregulatory organs. In land-dwelling animals, the outer covering of skin or cuticle forms a barrier to excess water gain or loss but many other mechanisms are also at work (including kidneys, sweating, panting, behavioural responses) so that a correct water/salt balance is maintained.

In humans, there is a pair of kidneys situated at the back of the abdomen and these are responsible for cleaning the blood and removing waste products which are then excreted. The kidney contains numerous tubules called nephrons, each with an expanded cup-shaped portion at one end called the Bowman's capsule. Behind this there is a folded length of tubule, known as the proximal convoluted tubule then a straight hairpin-shaped loop, the loop of Henle, and finally another looped portion called the distal convoluted tubule. Blood enters the Bowman's capsules from tiny capillaries which form a knot, called the glomerulus, inside the cup. This blood is brought to the kidney by the renal artery. Water and waste substances pass along the length of the nephrons and this is known as filtrate. Useful substances, including water and salts are reabsorbed. Many capillaries surround the nephrons and cleaned or filtered blood eventually leaves the kidney in the renal vein. The distal convoluted tubules, containing the waste products which have not been reabsorbed, empty into a collecting duct and final processing takes place. The liquid which is left, known as *urine* enters the ureter which is a narrow tube leading to the *bladder*.

osmosis is the process whereby molecules of solvent (usually water) move through a semi-permeable membrane to the more concentrated solution. This is due to the size of the molecules compared to the holes in the membrane. The holes permit the small water molecules through but not the larger solvent molecules so there is a tendency for the molecular concentrations to approach equality. *Osmotic pressure* is the pressure that must be applied to prevent osmotic flow.

Osmosis is an important mechanism in living organisms in the movement of water across cell membranes and particularly in the uptake of water by plant roots. Certain mechanisms have also evolved to prevent too much water entering cells causing rupture, or leaving cells, causing shrinkage.

oxidation and reduction are processes that occur during chemical reactions. *Oxidation* is the gain of oxygen or loss of electrons from the reactant. Oxidation can occur in the absence of oxygen as it can also be represented by the loss of hydrogen. Similarly, *reduction* is the loss of oxygen or gain of electrons from one of the reactants, and also the gain of hydrogen.

oxygen is a colourless, odourless gas vital for the respiration of most life forms. It is the most abundant of all the elements forming 21% by volume in air, almost 90% by weight of water and nearly 50% by weight of rocks in the crust. It is manufactured by the fractional DISTILLATION of liquid air and on heating reacts with most elements to form oxides. It is used extensively in industry for steel making, welding, rocket fuels and in chemical synthesis (forming other chemicals).

paint is a liquid made up of the pigment (the coloured material) in SUSPENSION within a non-volatile and a volatile part. The non-volatile oil or resin holds the pigment in place, while the volatile part enables the paint to be applied easily and it eventually evaporates (and may be water or a HYDROCARBON solvent). When applied to a surface the liquid evaporates leaving the pigment as an adhesive skin. Many paints are oil-based and are waterproof when dry and may contain additives to speed drying or improve coverage. Linseed oil was used with a thinner and a drier but synthetic compounds are now commonly used. Paints based on water are emulsions (*see* COLLOID), hence emulsion paint. These are often acrylic resins or polyvinyl acetate in water.

Of course, the earliest examples of paint were obtained from natural materials. Now there are special paints for particular purposes, e.g. anti-fouling paint to stop the growth of barnacles on a ship's hull.

pancreas an important gland present in VERTEBRATE animals situated behind and just below the stomach. It has two functions as it produces both digestive ENZYMES and the hormones insulin and glucagon which regulate the amount of sugar present in the blood. The digestive enzymes produced include trypsin, which breaks down protein; amylase which digests starch and lipase which aids in the digestion of fats. These are produced in an alkaline fluid which counteracts the acid effect of the stomach's gastric juice. The pancreatic juice, with its enzymes, passes through a tube or duct into the first part of the small intestine below the stomach which is called the *duodenum*.

paper consists of sheets of hydrated cellulose fibres derived from wood pulp. Pulp is made from timber mechanically or chemically. The mechanical method is simpler and more economical but produces weaker, poorer quality papers (e.g. newsprint).

parasite and symbiosis a *parasite* is an organism which obtains its food by living in or on the body of another living organism, without giving anything in return. The organism on which the parasite feeds is known as the *host*. Usually, the parasite does not kill the host as its future depends upon their mutual survival. However, sometimes a host species can become so seriously ill or weakened by the presence of the parasite that it dies. Parasites are of two kinds: *ectoparasites* attach themselves to the host's surface or skin and examples include the blood-sucking headlice, ticks and fleas. *Endoparasites* live inside the host's body, often within the gut or muscle, and examples are tapeworms, roundworms and liver flukes. Parasitic plants usually twine themselves around their host. They send projections, called haustoria (*sing.* haustorium) into the sap of the host to draw up water and food substances. A parasitic plant of this type is the dodder which lacks leaves and CHLOROPHYLL and cannot PHOTOSYNTHESISE. Others, such as the mistletoe, are partial parasites, able to photosynthesise but obtaining minerals and water from the host.

Some other organisms live together in a way which brings mutual benefit rather than harm, and this type of relationship is called *mutualism*. Sometimes one organism benefits while the other remains unharmed and this is termed *commensalism*. These three types of relationship between organisms-parasitism, mutualism and commensalism usually of two different species-are grouped together and called *symbiosis*.

particle accelerator is a machine for increasing the speed (and therefore the kinetic energy) of charged particles such as protons, electrons and helium nuclei by accelerating them in an electric field.

Accelerators are used in the study of subatomic particles. To split an atom, particles travelling close to the speed of light are required. There are two types of accelerator *linear* and *cyclic*. Linear acceleration, or *linacs*, have to be very long, up to several kilometres, and consist of rows of electrodes separated by gaps. The ions in the beam accelerate across each gap due to a high frequency potential between alternate electrodes. *Cyclic accelerators* use a magnetic field to bend the path of the charged particles. The *cyclotron* is an example in which energies of several million electron volts are imparted to the particles as they travel along a spiral path between D-shaped electrodes. The *synchrotron* is another example. In the cyclic accelerators the stream of charged particles is accelerated to the required level and then deflected out of the ring.

pasteurisation is the process named after the French chemist and biologist, Louis Pasteur (1822–95). It involves the partial sterilisation of food and kills potentially harmful bacteria. Milk is an obvious example. If it is heated to 62°C for 30 minutes, it kills bacteria that could cause tuberculosis and it increases the shelf life by delaying fermentation because other bacteria have also been killed or damaged. An alternative treatment involves heating milk to 72°C for 15 seconds. Higher temperatures still are used to produce 'long-life' milk. Pasteurisation is also used with beer and wine, to eliminate any yeast which would create cloudiness in the drink.

pathogen and pathology a *pathogen* is any organism that causes disease in another organism. Most pathogens that affect humans and other animals are BACTERIA or VIRUSES, but in plants a wide range of fungi also act as pathogens. *Pathology* is the medical science and speciality in which the area of study is the causes of diseases and the ways in which these affect the body. Pathology relies on the use of powerful MICROSCOPES to study samples, and also on the techniques of MICROBIOLOGY.

periodic table is an ordered table of all the ELEMENTS arranged by their ATOMIC NUMBERS, i.e. the number of protons and electrons in an atom. The arrangement means that elements with similar properties are grouped near to each other. The horizontal rows are called *periods* and the vertical rows are *groups*. Elements with the same number of electrons in their outer shell behave in a similar way and this is the basis of the vertical group. Moving from left to right along the periods corresponds to the gradual filling of successive electron shells and an increase in the size of the atom.

The elements and their symbols are listed in appendix 1 on pages 233 and 234.

pesticides are chemical poisons designed to kill insects (*insecticides*), weeds (*herbicides*), fungi (*fungicides*) and other pests. Until the advent of organic pesticides in the 1930s the compounds used were inorganic mixtures such as Bordeaux mixture (copper sulphate and lime) and calcium arsenate. Some naturally-occurring organic insecticides were also used, such as pyrethrum produced from the flowers of the chrysanthemum. Now most are organic, save for some well-known examples such as DDT.

Fungicides traditionally contained sulphur, or copper or mercury although the toxicity of mercury has led to a decline in its use. Now there are a number of organic compounds and many are *systemic* i.e. they actually enter the plant. *Herbicides* are the single most important group of pesticides, as they kill weeds which compete with crops for light and nutrients and which may be sources of other pests and diseases. Herbicides may be selective (killing only certain plants) or total (non-selective) and in the main are complex organic chemicals. *Insecticides* are very important in controlling insects that consume or destroy crops, and also in limiting diseases spread by insects, such as malaria and sleeping sickness. There are naturally-occurring insecticides, for example, nicotine, derris and pyrethrum, and synthetic compounds which form the greater proportion. Synthetic varieties include organochlorines, organophosphates and carbamates.

petrochemicals are chemicals derived from crude oil (petroleum) and natural gas which are used to manufacture an enormous range of compounds and materials including plastics, drugs, fertilisers, solvents and detergents. Over 90% of synthetic organic materials come from these sources. A major factor in the development of petrochemicals was the dramatic rise of the motor car in the early part of this century, and the discovery of oil in large quantities. The hydrocarbons left from petroleum after the removal of the gasoline meant that producers and government sought ways of using these chemicals and consequently production of organic chemicals from these sources grew dramatically.

Petroleum is a complex mixture and *distillation* produces a number of *fractions*. The operations undertaken in a *refinery*, to produce lighter fractions, are *cracking* and *reforming*. Catalytic cracking, which has replaced the old thermal process is an accelerated decomposition of middle to higher fractions over a solid catalyst usually consisting of zeolites. Catalytic reforming, which uses a platinum or platinum/rhenium catalyst, is undertaken at about 500°C and 7 to 30 atmospheres pressure. Various reactions occur simultaneously with straight-chain alkanes being converted to isomers and gasoline of a higher octane number being produced. There are other processes, including hydrocracking, steam cracking and steam reforming, which are implemented to act on a particular feedstock to produce certain chemicals.

pH of a solution is a measure of that solution's acidity or alkalinity. It shows the concentration of hydrogen IONS (H⁺) in an aqueous solution and is the negative logarithm (to base 10) of H⁺ concentration calculated with the formula:

$$pH = \log_{10} (1/H^+)$$

The scale ranges from 1 (very acidic, e.g. concentrated hydrochloric acid) through the neutral point of 7 (pure water) to 14 (very alkaline, e.g. CAUSTIC SODA). Since pH is a logarithmic value, one unit of change is equivalent to a tenfold change in the H^+ ion concentration. The pH of solutions is checked by means of INDICATORS.

pharmacology *see* DRUGS AND PHARMACOLOGY.

pheromones a pheromone is a chemical substance that acts as a communication signal between individuals of the same species. Pheromones are found widely throughout the animal kingdom and have a number of different functions, e.g. sexual attraction (common in insects) and marking of territory (used by many mammals either by urine spraying as in dogs and members of the cat family, or by means of special scent glands often on the head or bottom). Pheromones act as *external hormones* and have been shown to be effective at very low concentrations. They are often organic acids or alcohols which are usually termed *volatile* because their effect is short-lived. Pheromones are important in techniques of biological control.

phosphorus is a non-metal which occurs naturally as compounds and mainly as calcium phosphate ($Ca_3(PO_4)_2$), but also the mineral apatite. Phosphorus has several forms: red, white and black (a property called *allotropy*) and the white form is the most reactive. It is obtained by heating calcium phosphate with sand and carbon in an electric furnace.

Phosphorus is essential to life because calcium phosphate is a vital component of animal bones. It is also important in the compounds that it forms, which are used in fertilisers, the manufacture of glass and china ware, matches, detergents, special steels and foods and drinks.

photochemistry is the study of chemical reactions brought about by light. Only light that is actually absorbed will produce any effects and it is necessary to determine which parts of the spectrum are appropriate. The essential step in a photochemical reaction is the raising of an atom or molecule to an excited state by the absorbed light. Ultraviolet light is often the vehicle for such reactions and radiation from the far ultraviolet can break chemical bonds. However, the light may not actually produce a reaction directly. The excited molecule may emit the energy absorbed, affecting a neighbouring molecule which then undergoes a reaction.

Absorbed light may act as a catalyst or supply energy which renders a reaction possible. PHOTOSYNTHESIS is an example of a photochemical reaction.

photoelectric cell (or *photocell*) is a device used for the detection of light and other radiations. One type of cell, the *photoemissive cell*, makes use of the *photoelectric effect*. This is when light energy striking a substance causes energy to be transferred to electrons in the substance. When light above a certain (threshold) frequency is used, photoelectrons are generated and can create a current in a circuit. The photoemissive cell is in effect a light-powered electric cell and comprises a metal base and a transparently thin metal layer coated with selenium. Light entering the cell causes electrons to be released from the selenium and they move across a barrer to the metal layer, setting up a potential difference which can be used to drive a current. Cells of this nature can be used on solar cells and in camera light meters.

The other types of photoelectric cell are *photovoltaic* and *photoconductive* and are used to detect ultraviolet and infrared radiation, respectively.

photography is the process of capturing an image on photographic film (or plates) by means of LENSES in a *camera*. The earliest cameras produced images on metal or glass plates. Cameras consist essentially of a box with a variable aperture and a timed shutter through which light enters after which it is focused by lenses onto the light-sensitive film. The film is coated with an emulsion containing a silver halide (chloride or bromide) and on exposure to light the silver becomes easily reduced and when the film is developed a black deposit of fine silver gives a negative image. By further exposure of the negative and an underlying sensitive paper to light, a positive image is produced which is fixed and washed, producing a photograph.

photon *see* LIGHT.

photosynthesis and transpiration *photosynthesis* is the complicated process by which green plants use the energy from the sun to make carbohydrates from carbon dioxide and water, releasing oxygen as a result. There are two stages known as the *Calvin Cycle* and the *Light Reactions* of photosynthesis which are very complex but result in the production of sugars and starch. Photosynthesis can only occur if light trapping pigments are present, and the main one of these is CHLOROPHYLL which is green-coloured and occurs in stems and leaves. Chlorophyll captures light energy and this initiates a series of energy transfer reactions which enable simple organic compounds to be made from the splitting of carbon dioxide and water. Photosynthesis is the basis of all life on Earth and regulates the atmosphere as it increases oxygen concentration while reducing the carbon dioxide concentration. *Transpiration* is the loss of water in the form of vapour through pores, known as *stomata*, in the leaves of plants. As much as one sixth of the water taken up by the roots can be lost in this way. The transpiration rate is affected by many environmental factors such as temperature, light and carbon dioxide levels (i.e. whether photosynthesis is taking place), humidity, air currents and water uptake from the roots. Transpiration is greatest when a plant is photosynthesising in warm, dry, windy conditions.

phototropism the response by plants in the form of growth movement to the presence of light. Plant shoots show *positive phototropism* as they grow towards the light but roots tend to display *negative phototropism* because they grow away from the light source. Phototropism is caused by *auxin* (a plant growth HORMONE). The hormone is more abundant on the dark side of the plant and this side is induced to grow more by elongation of cells resulting in a curving towards the light.

physics is the study of matter and energy, and changes in energy without chemical alteration. Physics includes a number of topics such as magnetism, electricity, heat, light and sound (*see individual entries*). The study of modern physics also encompasses QUANTUM THEORY, atomic and nuclear physics (i.e. subatomic particles and their behaviour (*see* ELEMENTARY PARTICLES) and physics of NUCLEAR FISSION AND FUSION). As the research into topics has expanded over recent years, so new subjects begin to develop often on the boundaries of two major disciplines. This has happened in geophysics (geology and physics), biophysics (biology and physics) and astrophysics, which combines astronomy with physics.

physiology the study of all the METABOLIC functions of animals and plants including the processes of RESPIRATION, REPRODUCTION, EXCRETION, working of the NERVOUS SYSTEM, PHOTOSYNTHESIS, etc. It covers all aspects of the life of organisms and may be one specialised area of research or broadly based.

piezoelectric effect is the effect within certain crystals whereby positive and negative charges are generated on opposite faces when the crystal is subjected to pressure. The charges are reversed if the crystal is put under tension and the whole effect is reversible, i.e. the application of an electric potential produces an alteration in size of the crystal. Quartz is the commonest piezoelectric crystal and very pure crystals grown in the laboratory can be cut to vibrate at one frequency when a voltage is applied. The vibrations are used in watches and enable near perfect time to be kept. The piezoelectric effect is also used in crystal microphones and pickups. Other crystals that show the effect are Rochelle salt (sodium potassium tartrate) and barium titanate.

pig iron *see* CAST IRON.

pigments are compounds that produce colour and occur naturally in plants and animals. In plants, *chlorophyll* imparts a green colour, and animals contain *melanin*, which produces the black or brown colour of hair or skin. *Carotenoids* are plant pigments, orange, red and yellow, that occur in carrots and tomatoes.

Synthetic pigments are used to colour plastics, textiles, inks, etc. Pigments are different from dyes and tend to be insoluble and occur as particles and many are inorganic:

Colour	Pigment
white	titanium dioxide
	lead carbonate and sulphate
	zinc oxide and sulphide
red/brown	iron oxides
	red lead
	cadmium red, orange, scarlet
yellow	iron oxides
	lead, zinc and cadmium chromates
blue	ultramarine (an aluminosilicate with sulphur)
black	carbon

pitchblende is an important ore of uranium, a mineral called Uraninite, made up primarily of uranium oxide. It is also the principal source of radium. The uranium in it decays to form radioactive radium and radon gas.

plankton very small organisms, often microscopic and including both plants and animals, which drift in the currents of oceans and lakes. The plants (or *phytoplankton*) consist mainly of single-celled algae (*Bacillariophyta*) called *diatoms* which photo-synthesise and form the basis of food chains. The animals (or *zooplankton*) include the *larval* stages of larger organisms, some protozoans (Kingdom PROTISTA) and small creatures called copepods which are related to crabs (*see* NH: CRUSTACEA). Plankton provide food for many larger animals, e.g. whales, and are of vital importance in the FOOD CHAIN.

plants Kingdom *Plantae* forms one of the major kingdoms of life. Plants are distinguished from animals by their ability to manufacture food by PHOTO-SYNTHESIS. This type of nutrition is termed *autotrophic* whereas that of animals, relying on taking in food from outside, is called *heterotrophic*. The photosynthetic cells of plants contain organelles (*see* ORGAN) called *chloroplasts* which contain the pigment CHLOROPHYLL and this traps light energy from the sun. Plant cells have walls (absent in animal cells), and the main substance of which these are composed is a carbodyhydrate called CELLULOSE. Plant cells store carbohydrate in the form of *starch* whereas animal cells store it as glycogen.

There are twelve divisions of the plant kingdom (the same as phyla in animals). In three of these divisions, there is no true system of structures or tubes to transport water and food. These are called *non-vascular* plants and include mosses, liverworts and hornworts. In the other divisions this *vascular tissue* is present but they are further divided into those which produce *seeds* and those which do not. The *seedless plants* are the horsetails, ferns, club mosses and whiskferns. The seed plants are divided into two groups, the *Gymnosperms* which produce 'naked' unprotected seeds, e.g. the conifers, and the *Angiosperms* (or *Anthophyta*), the flowering plants. These are the ones most familiar to us and are the most complex among plants, producing seeds within special protective coverings.

Most plants have sexual REPRODUCTION and many are also able to reproduce asexually. In the plant life cycle an *alternation of generations* occurs with a *sporophyte* generation which is *diploid* (i.e. has the full number of CHROMOSOMES) producing the *gametophyte generation* which is *haploid* (half the number of chromosomes). The sporophyte generation is nearly always the most prominent form, and in most plants the gametophyte is represented by very small structures.

Flowering plants are either *monocotyledons*, with one seed leaf or *dicotyledons*, with two. Some flowering plants are called *annuals* as they grow from seed, produce flowers and die. *Perennials* grow up from the same root stock year after year even though the leafy parts die back during the winter.

plastics is a group name for mainly synthetic organic compounds which are mostly POLYMERS, formed by polymerisation that can be moulded when subjected to heat and pressure. There are two types: *thermoplastics* (e.g. PVC or polyvinyl chloride) which become plastic when heated and can be heated repeatedly without changing their properties; *thermosetting plastics* such as phenol/formaldehyde resins lose their plasticity after being subjected to heat and/or pressure. Plastics are moulded and shaped while in their softened state and then cured by further heat (thermosetting e.g. epoxy resins, silicones) or cooling (thermoplastics e.g. perspex and polythene).

The first synthetic plastic was *Bakelite*, invented in 1908. Since then the plastics industry has become vast and an enormous range of domestic, leisure, industrial and commercial items are now produced. Plastics can be shaped by blow moulding, vacuum forming, EXTRUSION and INJECTION MOULDING and they are used extensively in composite materials and LAMINATES.

plutonium *see* NUCLEAR ENERGY.

pneumatics refers to the use of compressed air, usually to power machines. A supply of air is piped to the pneumatic motor which commonly features a piston within a cylinder. Compressed air pushes the piston one way and a spring or air pressure pushes it back, producing a hammer action used in drills for mixing or construction.

The greatest benefit of pneumatic tools over electrically-powered tools is that there is no chance of electric shocks or sparks which could cause a fire or explosion in certain circumstances.

polarisation of light is when light is made to vibrate in one particular plane. Light normally consists of waves vibrating in many directions and because it is electromagnetic radiation there is an electric and a magnetic field vibrating at right angles to each other. If light is polarised, the electric field vibrations are confined to one plane (*plane polarised light*) called the plane of vibration and the magnetic vibrations are in one plane at right angles, the plane of polarisation.

pollen pollen grains are the male sex cells (*gametes*) of flowering PLANTS. They occur in small pollen sacs contained within a structure called the *anther*, which is part of the male reproductive organ of the flower. The anther occurs on the end of a thin stalk called the stamen. Pollen grains and their female equivalents, the *embryo sacs*, are the *gametophyte generation* (*see* PLANTS) in flowering plants.

pollination is the transfer of pollen from an anther to a stigma. This is part of the female reproductive organ of the flower, the other portions being the *style* and *ovary* which together make up a *carpel*. The ovary contains one or more *ovules* which develop into seeds. Pollen may be transferred by means of the wind, insects, birds, water, etc. and the grains vary in shape according to the method of pollination used by the plant. Wind-pollinated plants have light, smooth grains while insect-pollinated ones have grains which are rough or spiny. This is called *cross-pollination* as the pollen is transferred from one flower to another of the same species. *Self-pollination* is where pollen is transferred from an anther to a stigma in the same flower.

polygon is a term used in GEOMETRY to describe a closed plane (i.e. two-dimensional) figure with three or more straight line sides. Common polygons are figures such as the triangle, quadrilateral and hexagon. A square is a regular polygon where the sides and all angles are equal.

For a polygon with n sides, the sum of the interior angles = $180°$ $(n-2)$. Except for the triangle and square, polygons are named after their number of sides so a ten-sided figure is called a *decagon*. Polygons are common around us, whether in a natural form as in honeycomb, or the faces of crystals or man-made as with tiles and nuts and bolts.

polymer a large, usually linear molecule that is formed from many simple molecules called *monomers*. Synthetic polymers include PVC, Teflon, polythene and nylon while naturally-occurring polymers include starch, cellulose (found in the cell walls of plants) and rubber (*see individual en-*

tries). Early versions of polymers were modified natural compounds. The first fully synthetic polymer to be developed was *Bakelite* (*see* PLASTICS) followed by urea-formaldehyde and alkyd resins in the late 1920s. Polyethylene (that is polythene) was first produced by ICI on a commercial basis in 1938 and the Dupont company in America produced the first nylon in 1941. Many synthetic polymers are produced from alkenes (*see* HYDROCARBONS) in reactions called addition polymerisations which are rapid and require only relatively low temperatures. Condensation polymerisation is another means of producing polymers e.g. the nylons (polyamides) and the silicones (polysiloxanes) in which some molecule (often water) is removed at each successive reaction stage.

potassium is an alkali metal that is silver white and highly reactive. In fact, it reacts violently with water and therefore in nature occurs only as compounds. It occurs widely in silicate rocks as alkali feldspar, in blood and milk and in salt beds and as potassium chloride in sea water. Potassium is an essential element for plants and it is added to the soil by farmers, as FERTILISERS (such as potash). Fertilisers are the primary use of potassium but it is also used in making batteries, ceramics and glass.

power is the rate at which WORK is done. It is also regarded as the rate at which energy is converted. The unit of power is the *watt* (W) which is measured in joules per second. Thus if a machine does 10 joules of work every second, it has a power output of 10W. Electrical power can be calculated from the product of the voltage and the current.

Power is important because many routine processes and functions require energy to do work, whether it concerns an engine, light bulbs or our bodies. In most cases, when energy is expended some escapes or is lost, e.g. engines lose energy in vibrations and heat.

pressure is the force exerted per unit area of a surface. The pressure of a gas equals the force that its molecules exert on the walls of its container, divided by the surface area of the vessel. The pressure of a gas varies with temperature and volume (*see* GAS) and the pressure in a liquid or in air equals the weight of liquid or air above the area in question and therefore as the depth increases, the pressure will also increase. This explains why air pressure decreases with height (*see* ATMOSPHERE). If force is measured in N (newtons) and area in m^2 (square metres), pressure is N/m^2 or *pascals* (Pa).

primates an order of mammals which includes monkeys, lemurs, apes and humans. Primates have highly mobile hands and feet due to the presence of thumbs and big toes which can grasp. They also have a large brain (especially the part called the *cerebrum*) and are very intelligent.

prism is a solid figure that is essentially triangular in shape (resembling a wedge) and made of a transparent material. It is used in physics to deviate or disperse a ray in optical instruments or laboratory experiments. If a narrow beam of white light passes through a prism it is split into a range of colours – the *spectrum*. The light is split because each of the colours is refracted by a different amount, because each is light of a different *wavelength* (*see* WAVE).

probability is the chance of something happening, or the likelihood that an event will occur, expressed as a fraction or decimal between 0 and 1 (or as odds). If something is absolutely certain, the probability is 1; if it is impossible, then the probability is 0, and all probabilities lie within these two figures. Thus if a coin is flipped, there is an equal chance of gaining 'heads' and 'tails', i.e. one chance out of two for heads or tails giving a probability of $1/2$ or 0.5. The probability of a particular number coming up on rolling a dice is one in six, i.e. 1/6 or 0.1666, and it is 0.5 for rolling an even number (3 possibilities out of the 6 numbers).

procaryote any *organism* which has a nucleus that is <u>not</u> surrounded by a true membrane. These organisms all belong to the Kingdom MONERA and are the BACTERIA and blue-green *algae* (*cyanobacteria*). They have a single chromosome and do not undergo meiosis or mitosis (*see* CELL DIVISION) but reproduce ASEXUALLY by a method called *binary fission*. In this, the whole cell divides and each 'daughter' cell receives a copy of the single parental chromosome. Procaryotes are very important organisms, vitally involved in all life-sustaining processes. A few are disease-causing organisms, but others are used in BIOTECHNOLOGY. They were the first organisms to evolve being the only life forms on Earth for about 2 billion years.

protein and amino acid a protein is a type of organic (*see* CHEMISTRY) compound of which there are many different kinds, and it usually contains nitrogen and sulphur. The individual MOLECULES are made up of building blocks called *amino acids* arranged in long chains (known as *polypeptide* chains). There are 20 different amino acids but a huge number of possible arrangements in a polypeptide chain or protein. Most proteins consist of more than one polypeptide.

protista a biological kingdom containing numerous different kinds of simple organisms, most of which are single cells. They are the simplest eucaryotic (*see* EUCARYOTE) organisms because they are usually unicellular (single-celled). However, since each protist is able to carry out lots of different functions within its one cell, and many are highly complex, some have the most elaborate of all cells. Most protists have extensions or projections out from the *cytoplasm* of the cell, called cilia, (*sing.* cilium) or flagella (*sing.* flagellum), which are used for movement. These may not be present at all stages of the life cycle but usually occur at some time or other. All protists can reproduce asexually and some also have sexual reproduction. They are important organisms in the PLANKTON and hence significant in food chains. Most require oxygen for RESPIRATION and so are called *aerobic*. Some are PHOTOSYNTHETIC (i.e. they are *autotrophic* and make their own food), others are *heterotrophic* (i.e. they absorb or ingest food) and yet others combine the two, a condition known as *mixotrophic*. Protists inhabit a wide range of environments. Many are free-living but others live inside cells and tissues of other organisms as PARASITES or in other relationships (known as *symbiosis*).

pulley is one of the six varieties of simple MACHINE. It is a wheel with a groove around the edge around which a rope can be passed. An individual pulley, suspended on an axle may make lifting a load a little easier but in general several pulleys are combined in a *block-and-tackle* system to enable the lifting of larger loads that would not normally be feasible. A rope wound around the pulleys in such a system can be pulled a long way to raise a heavy load a short distance.

pumps are machines that move gases and liquids. A basic pump is the force, or reciprocating pump in which a piston moves in and out of a cylinder. Fluid or gas is taken into the cylinder on one stroke and pushed out through a valve when the piston moves in the opposite direction. A bicycle pump or a water pump are examples of this type.

Pythagoras' Theorem *see* GEOMETRY.

quantum mechanics is the system of mechanics that facilitates an explanation of the structure of the atom and the behaviour of small particles within atoms (*see* ATOM). The electronic structure of the atom comprises a nucleus around which electrons orbit at various levels. Putting energy into an atom causes electrons to move temporarily into a higher orbit, through absorption of the energy. When the electron returns to its original orbit, light energy is given off as a *quantum* or PHOTON. This principle, called *quantum theory* was discovered by Max Planck (1858–1947) and it was realised that all electromagnetic radiations can be thought of in this way, i.e. a photon is a quantum of electromagnetic radiation.

quantum numbers a set of four numbers used to describe atomic structures (*see* ATOM and QUANTUM MECHANICS). The principal quantum number (n) defines the shells (or orbits) which are visualised as orbitals (that is, a charge cloud which represents the probability distribution of an electron).

The orbit nearest the nucleus has 2 electrons and $n = 1$. The second shell contains 8 electrons (and $n = 2$) and so on, the maximum number of electrons in each shell being defined by the formula $2n^2$. The orbital quantum number (l) defines the shape of the orbits and these are designated s, p, d and f, the letters arising purely for historical reasons. The magnetic orbital quantum number (m) sets the position of the orbit within a magnetic field and s is the spin quantum number. The latter is based upon the assumption that no two electrons may be exactly alike and pairs of electrons are considered to have opposite spin.

The quantum numbers n, l and m are related and allow the electronic structure of any atom to be determined.

quantum theory *see* QUANTUM MECHANICS.

radiation (thermal) is a process by which heat is transferred from one place to another. Objects give out infrared waves and hot objects may also emit light into the ultraviolet region. Some surfaces are better emitters and absorbers of thermal radiation. Dull black surfaces are better at absorbing and emitting thermal radiation than white or silver surfaces. The nearer to a silver, mirror-like finish is a surface, the greater will be the reflection and lower the absorption of radiation.

Vacuum flasks, silver body blankets and greenhouses all make use of this property. In the case of the greenhouse, the glass permits light and short wavelength infrared radiation through from the Sun, which warms the air and the plants. The plants re-emit radiation, but of a longer wavelength and this does not pass through the glass, but is reflected back into the greenhouse, helping to maintain the higher temperature.

radio uses electromagnetic waves to send and receive information without wires (hence the former term wireless, for the radio). It includes, in its widest sense, radio, television and radar. Radiowaves are created in an antenna or aerial by making electrons oscillate. Long and medium waves are sent around the world by bouncing them off the *ionosphere* (a layer of charged particles in the upper atmosphere) but VHF (very high frequency) and UHF (ultra-high frequency waves for television) waves require a straighter path between the receiver and the transmitting aerial because these waves are not reflected by the ionosphere. Similarly, the longer wavelengths can diffract around hills and other obstacles, unlike the short wavelength VHF and UHF waves.

When a receiver is tuned to the frequency of the appropriate wave sent from the transmitter, it can amplify and rectify the signal to produce a varying current which matches the frequency of the sound wave at the microphone. This current is then used to work a loudspeaker, thus reproducing the original sound.

radioactivity means that a material naturally gives out radiations while undergoing spontaneous disintegration. The (nuclear) radiation given out by a radioactive material is one of three types: α – particles (alpha), ß – particles (beta) or gamma (γ) rays and each is a different entity with varying effects.

Radioactivity was discovered in 1896 by Henri Becquerel who found that uranium salts emitted some form of radiation capable of ionising the air and also capable of affecting a photographic plate, through its wrapping. Further work determined the properties of the three types of radiation.

An *alpha particle* is a helium nucleus (2 protons and 2 neutrons, He^{2+}), and it has a strong ionising effect but little penetration, having a range in air of a few centimetres. *Beta particles* are electrons moving at different speeds, in some cases almost at the speed of light. They have a negative charge, and although their ionising effect is very weak, they are more penetrating, with a range in air of about one metre. Beta particles can be stopped by a few millimetres of aluminium. *Gamma rays* are short wavelength electromagnetic waves with little ionising effect but greatest penetration. They are never completely absorbed, but lead 25mm thick reduces their intensity to half. Radioactive materials can give one or a combination of radiation types.

Radioactive decay is the emission of particles by an unstable nucleus, which in so doing becomes another atom. The decaying nucleus is the parent, the resulting nucleus is the daughter, which together with particles emitted are called the decay products. During decay, nuclei disintegrate randomly but at a different set rate for different atoms. The *half-life* of a radioactive *nuclide* (i.e. the radioactive form of an element) is the time taken for half the atom to decay, i.e. for the activity to fall by half. For example, uranium-238 has a half-life of 4.51×10^9 years; radium-226, 1620 years; and sodium-24, 15 hours; and radon-220 just 52 seconds.

rainbow is the characteristic display of the colours of the spectrum, which may form a large arc of a circle. The Sun must be behind the viewer for the rainbow to be seen. Light enters droplets of water in the sky and is refracted and internally reflected. Because the raindrop acts like a prism, the light is split up into the constituent colours.

receptor a special type of animal cell, which is called *excitable* because it is sensitive to a particular type of stimulus. When the receptor cell is *excited*, electrical impulses are sent along a (sensory) nerve to the central nervous system. Some receptors respond to factors or stimuli outside the animal's body, and others are present internally. Receptors are sensitive to a variety of different stimuli and are often called after the *sense* that they detect. Examples are *proprioreceptor* (pressure, movement or stretching within the body), *chemoreceptor* (chemicals), *mechanoreceptor* (touch) and *photoreceptor* (light). Receptors may be grouped together within a special organ, such as the ear, which detects sound waves and also controls balance and posture.

recording media there are many ways in which sounds and pictures can be recorded. One medium that is fast being replaced by new technologies is the vinyl record. These are plastic discs upon which the sound is recorded in a groove cut in the disc. The sound to be recorded is fed via microphones to cutters operated by electromagnets. Thus, when a stylus is placed on the record, it vibrates along the groove, and the vibrations are turned into electric currents to operate loudspeakers.

Magnetic tape can be used for recording sound (audio tape) or pictures (video tape) and consists of a plastic tape coated with magnetic particles, often iron oxide or chromium dioxide for higher quality. Recordings are made by magnetising the tape in a specific way. It is a flexible medium as it can be re-used and edited.

More recent media include the compact disc, which is a form of laser disc and has a very large capacity, often used in the storage of computer data.

rectifier *see* DIODE.

reflection light striking a surface may be reflected but in most cases the reflections are in all directions. When the surface is smooth, e.g. a mirror, an image is produced. When light is reflected from a surface it follows certain laws. The incoming (*incident*) ray makes an angle (angle of incidence) with the line drawn at 90° to the surface (the normal) equal to the angle of reflection which is the angle between the normal and the *reflected* ray. This encompasses the *laws of reflection*. A *reflector* is any surface that reflects electromagnetic radiation.

refraction is the bending of, most commonly, a light ray when it travels from one medium to another, e.g. air to water. The refraction occurs at the point where the light passes from one material to another and is caused by the light travelling at different velocities in the different media. The incident (*see* REFLECTION) ray passing into a material becomes the refracted ray and in an optically more dense medium is bent towards the normal to the interface. The two angles – of incidence and refraction – are related by *Snell's Law* which states that the ratio of the sines (*see* TRIGONOMETRY) of the two angles is constant for light passing from one given medium to another. The value of the ratio of the sines of the angles is called the *refractive index*, measured when light is refracted from a vacuum into the medium.

refrigeration *see* EVAPORATION.

relativity is the theory developed by Albert Einstein (1879–1955) and which is made up of two parts. The *special theory* states that the speed of light is the same for all observers, whatever their speed, that is light from an object travels at the same velocity whether the object is moving or stationary. Nothing may move faster than the speed of light. Further important implications of this theory are that the mass of a body is a function of its speed, and Einstein derived the *mass-energy equation*, $E = mc^2$ where c is the speed of light. As a result of this theory the concept of *time dilation* was proposed which essentially means that for someone travelling at very great speed, time passes much more slowly for them that it does for a stationary observer.

The *general theory of relativity* relates to gravity. Matter in space is said to cause space to curve so as to set up a gravitational field and gravitation becomes a property of space. The validity of Einstein's theories has been tested with experiments in modern atomic physics.

reproduction the production of new individuals of the same species either by *asexual* or *sexual* means. The term usually refers to sexual reproduction which involves the joining together (called *fusion*) of special sex cells, one of which is female (the egg or *ovum*) and the other is male (e.g. *sperm* in animals and pollen in flowering plants). The sex cells of any organism are known as *gametes*. Many organisms produce gametes within special reproductive organs. In the flower of a seed plant, the male sex organs are the stamens which produce pollen. The *carpels* are female and produce *ovules* which later develop into seeds after *fertilisation*. Gametes are special cells which contain half the number of chromosomes (called haploid, *see* CELL DIVISION) of the parent. When a male and female gamete join together (*fusion*), fertilisation takes place and a single cell (now called a zygote) is produced which contains the full number of chromosomes (diploid). This goes on to produce a new individual, usually by a process of many cell divisions. In mammals (and many other animals), the male sex organs are the *testes* and the female ones are the *ovaries*. These reproductive organs (also called *gonads*), are specialised structures, the cells of which produce the sperm and ova under the influence of hormones. Most adult female mammals have a reproductive cycle, called an *oestrous cycle*, during which time the eggs develop and the animal becomes ready to mate (a period known as *heat* or *oestrus*). Mating occurs at the time when the animal is most likely to become pregnant. Some mammals have a definite *breeding season* and only one oestrous cycle in a year (*monoestrous*). Others have several cycles and are *polyoestrous*. In female humans, the *menstrual cycle* replaces the oestrous cycle. Mating usually results in the fertilisation of one or more egg. The cells rapidly divide and become embryos which grow and develop inside a muscular, bag-like organ called the *uterus* or womb. The animal is now said to be *pregnant*. A special organ of pregnancy, called the *placenta*, develops and this attaches the embryos to the uterus by a cord called the *umbilical cord*. This provides for the passage of food, oxygen and some other substances (e.g. vitamins and antibodies) to the embryos while waste products, (mainly carbon dioxide and urea), pass in the opposite direction and are removed by the mother's blood circulation. When the young are fully developed they are *born*, which means that they are pushed to the outside through a passage leading from the womb called the *vagina*. This is brought about by contractions of the muscles in the wall of the uterus under the influence of hormones. Immediately after birth, the placenta is also pushed out.

resistance (R) is measured in *ohms* and is the potential difference between the ends of a conductor divided by the current flowing. Superconductors apart, materials resist the flow of current to varying degrees, and some of the electrical energy is thereby converted to heat. The resistance of a wire depends on the ability of the material to conduct electricity, and the dimensions of the wire. In general, a short wire has less resistance than a long one and a thick wire less resistance than a thin one.

Resistors are devices made to produce resistance and they control the current in a circuit. They are found in radios, televisions and similar pieces of equipment. A variable resistor is called a *rheostat* and by means of a sliding contact can alter the current flowing. Wires used in circuits have a low resistance to minimise heat loss, but in some cases thermal energy is required, as in heating elements for electric kettles, fires, immersion heaters and cookers. Nichrome wire is commonly used for such applications.

resonance is the creation of vibrations in a system, such that it is vibrating at its natural frequency, due to vibrations of the same frequency being received from another source. Resonance occurs in many instances; the strings of an instrument, columns of air in a wind instrument and even an engine causing vibrations in a bus or van.

respiration and ventilation *respiration* is often used to mean *breathing* but more correctly it is a metabolic (*see* METABOLISM) process which occurs in the cells of an organism. It is the process by which living cells release energy by breaking down complicated organic substances (food molecules) into simpler ones using enzymes. In most organisms, respiration occurs in the presence of oxygen and is called *aerobic*, with water and carbon dioxide produced as waste products and energy released. Some organisms (e.g. a number of species of bacteria and yeasts) do not require oxygen but use alternative chemical reactions. This is known as *anaerobic respiration* and it is possible for it to occur for a short time in the muscles of mammals when these are being very hard worked. However, it is short-lived and results in the build up of a substance called *lactic acid* which causes muscular *cramps*. *Ventilation* is the actual process of breathing or drawing air in and out of an animal's body. Various mechanisms and structures are involved in different animals, using muscles to pump air in and out (*see also* LUNGS AND GILLS).

rubber is a high molecular weight polymer which occurs naturally, being obtained from the tree *Hevea braziliensis*. It is an elastic solid from the latex (a colloid of rubber particles in a watery base) of the tree which contains about 35% rubber. After straining, the latex is coagulated and the raw rubber is 'compounded' and other substances are added to increase strength and it is then *vulcanised* (heated with sulphur) to increase the cross-linking in its structure. This provides more elasticity and the rubber becomes less sticky. Natural rubber is a form of polyisoprene $-(CH_2.CH : C(CH_3) : (H_2)_n$.

Synthetic rubbers are polymers of simple molecules and include butyl rubber, neoprene, styrene-butadiene rubber and silicone rubber. Butyl rubber is used for the inner tubes of tyres; styrene-butadiene for car tyres; and silicone rubbers for applications requiring temperature stability, water repellence and chemical resistance.

salt is the common name for sodium chloride, NaCl. It occurs in sea water and in hot climates shallow ponds of sea water are left to evaporate to dryness, providing deposits of salt. Significant salt deposits were formed in the geological past and are now mined (*see* **GG**: EVAPORITE). In chemistry, a salt is produced by the reaction of equivalent amounts of an acid and a base, with the production of water. Salt molecules contain metal atoms with one or more non-metal atoms and are named from the acid and base from which the salt is formed, e.g. hydrochloric acid and sodium hydroxide produce sodium chloride.

saturated solution is a solution of a substance (solute) that exists in equilibrium when there is excess solute present (*see* SOLUTIONS). Heating a saturated solution allows more to dissolve producing a *supersaturated solution*. Cooling or loss of solvent will cause some of the solute to come out of solution, i.e. it will crystallise.

seed *see* FLOWERS *and* PLANT.

semiconductors materials, such as SILICON, that can act as a conductor of electricity or an insulator. Pure semiconductors are insulators when cold and allow current to pass when heated although at room temperature they conduct only poorly. However, by *doping* them, with small amounts of other substances, semiconductors can be made to conduct. Depending upon the material used for doping, a p- or n-type semiconductor is created (*see* DIODE).

Semiconductors may be compounds or elements. In addition to silicon, germanium selenium and lead telluride are used. Diodes, rectifiers and transistors all utilise semiconductors, as do silicon chips used in microprocessors.

sense organ *see* RECEPTOR.

sight the sense of sight is possessed by many animals. Some simple, single-celled (unicellular) organisms have cells which are sensitive to light, but cannot be said to 'see' in the way we understand it. They have *eyespots* which contain pigments (called *carotenoids*) and these are sensitive to light. They cause the cell or organism to move in a particular way in response to light. Other invertebrate animals have more complicated eyes, ranging from a fairly simple type called ocelli (*sing.* ocellus) to a more advanced kind known as a *compound* eye. Compound eyes are a feature of many Arthropod invertebrates (spiders, insects, beetles, etc.) and give very good vision especially in some insects, e.g. dragonflies and flies. Squids and octopuses (which are molluscs), have eyes that are similar to those of vertebrate animals and have excellent powers of vision.

The eyes of vertebrates are almost spherical balls filled with fluid, and contained within bony sockets in the skull. Light enters the eye through the transparent *cornea* and is bent (or refracted) as it passes through a small space filled with a fluid, the *aqueous humour*. The light passes through the *pupil* which is a hole in the centre of the coloured *iris*. The light rays pass through the lens and on through a larger cavity filled with fluid called the *vitreous humour*. The lens bends the light rays and focuses them so that they form an *image* on the layer at the back of the eye which is called the *retina*. The retina contains the actual light receptors (photoreceptors). These are pigment-containing cells of two types, *rods* and *cones*. The pigments undergo chemical changes (*bleaching*) in light of different wavelengths and this generates electrical impulses which travel to the brain along a special sensory *optic nerve*. Cones contain pigments which allow for colours to be detected and there are about 6 million in a human retina. Rods are sensitive in very dim light and allow for night vision but do not detect colour. The human retina contains about 125 million of these. Most mammals are nocturnal and have poor colour vision, but keen night sight is allowed for by the large number of rods that are present.

silicon is a non-metallic element and the second most abundant in the Earth's crust. It does not occur as free silicon, but is found in abundance as numerous silicate minerals including quartz (SiO_2). Silicon is manufactured by reducing SiO_2 in an electric furnace but further processing is necessary to obtain pure silicon. When doped with boron or phosphorus it is used in semiconductors, (*see also* DIODE). Quartz and some silicates are used industrially to produce glass and building materials. Silicon melts at 1410°C. *Silicones* are polymers built on SiR_2O groups (where R is a hydrocarbon). Simpler substances are lower melting point oils, which are used as lubricants. More complex varieties are solid and very stable and are used as electrical insulators.

siphon is a bent tube, shaped like an upside-down U, and it can be used for transferring liquid from a higher to a lower level. One end of the tube is placed in the higher container, and the other end is primed by sucking. When the liquid flows through the tube, the end is placed in the lower container and the flow continues even though the suction is no longer there. The liquid flows due to a pressure difference between the two ends of the tube.

SI Units (Système International d'Unités) is a system of units agreed internationally. It comprises seven basic units and some supplementary units with a larger number of derived units. It also established the prefixes used for decimal multiples where the practice is to raise to 10 by a power that is a multiple of three.

basic units		derived units		
m	metre	Bq	becquerel	(radioactivity)
kg	kilogram	C	coulomb	(electric charge)
s	second	F	farad	(capacitance)
A	ampere	Gy	gray	(ionising radiation)
K	kelvin	H	henry	(inductance)
mol	mole	Hz	hertz	(frequency)
cd	candela (light)	J	joule	(work or energy)

skeleton the whole structure that provides a framework and protection for an animal's body and within which organs are protected and muscles are attached. In many invertebrates there is an *exoskeleton* which may have to be shed to allow for growth (*see* ECDYSIS AND MOULTING).

Other invertebrates add to the outer edge of their exoskeleton to allow for growth, e.g. molluscs such as snails. Other animals have an *endoskeleton* which lies inside the body. Vertebrate animals have a skeleton made up of numerous bones and cartilage. In mammals over 200 bones are present, some of which are joined by *ligaments* while others are fused together. Both types of skeleton are flexible due to the presence of joints which allow for the movement of limbs, etc.

Snails have a shell hardened by calcium (*calcareous*), in arthropods the skeleton is hardened by the presence of a substance called *chitin* and in crabs and lobsters the shell (carapace) is hardened with chitin and calcium salts.

skin an important organ which forms the outer covering of a vertebrate animal. There may be a variety of structures protruding from the surface of the skin (i.e. hair, fur, feathers or scales) depending upon the type of animal. The skin provides a protective layer for the body, helping to cushion it in the event of accidental knocks and preventing drying out. Also, skin helps to maintain the correct body temperature. When the body is hot the many small blood vessels in the skin, the *capillaries*, widen allowing more blood to flow through them, and heat is lost to the outside by radiation. Sweat *glands* present in the skin secrete a salty fluid which evaporates from the surface and forms another cooling mechanism. If the body is cold, the capillaries contract to decrease blood flow and conserve heat. The layer of fat in the skin has a warming effect and small erector muscles attached to hair roots contract to raise the hair. The hairs trap a layer of air which helps to warm the body. Skin is a physical barrier to harmful substances or organisms which might otherwise enter more easily. In humans the outer layer of skin is called the epidermis. The layer beneath the epidermis, the dermis, contains many receptors sensitive to pain, touch, pressure and temperature and these connect with sensory nerves (*see* NERVOUS SYSTEM) relaying messages to the brain. Hence skin is very important in enabling an animal to live within its environment. The outer layer is dead and is continually being shed and replaced by cells from underneath. In amphibians (frogs, toads, etc.) the skin has to be kept moist and there is some exchange of gases (oxygen in and carbon dioxide out) through the surface.

A cross-section of human skin

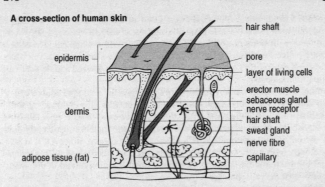

- hair shaft
- epidermis
- pore
- layer of living cells
- erector muscle
- sebaceous gland
- nerve receptor
- dermis
- hair shaft
- sweat gland
- nerve fibre
- adipose tissue (fat)
- capillary

sleep a period of deep rest shown by many animals during which the metabolic rate (*see* METABOLISM) is lowered, awareness is reduced and the body is relaxed. Most animals sleep but some need more than others. Adult humans require about eight hours sleep each night. Other animals, (e.g. some grazing mammals), need only a few minutes sleep at any one time. Many animals are easily and rapidly awakened from sleep and this is more likely in those which are hunted as prey. There is a change in the electrical activity of the brain of a person entering into sleep and this can be recorded, producing a trace called an *electroencephalogram* (EEG). *Alpha* brainwaves are produced when an adult person is awake and *delta* waves during sleep. At the onset of sleep, low frequency waves of high amplitude are produced (known as *slow wave sleep*). These are interrupted by short periods of high frequency, low amplitude waves, during which time the person may be restless and show rapid eye movements behind closed eyelids. This is known as Rapid Eye Movement (REM) sleep and it is the time when dreaming occurs. A person who wakens during REM sleep remembers dreams but otherwise these are usually forgotten. The part of the brain especially involved in the control of sleep is called the *reticular formation*.

smell a keen sense of smell or *olfaction* is characteristic of many animals. This is achieved by special receptors (*chemoreceptors*) which are able to detect chemicals carried in the air or dissolved in water. They may be grouped together within *olfactory organs* such as the *nose* of vertebrates. The lining or *epithelium* of the *nasal cavity* contains *olfactory cells* which respond to chemical molecules dissolved in the moisture of the surface mucous membranes. These cells are neurones (*see* NERVOUS SYSTEM) which connect with branches of the *olfactory nerve* within a special area of the brain called the *olfactory bulb*. The olfactory nerve transmits the information to the *cerebral cortex* of the *brain* where it is decoded and detected as a particular smell.

sodium is an alkali metal which occurs widely – its principal source being sodium chloride (salt) in sea water and salt deposits. It is obtained by electrolysis of fused sodium chloride, but does not exist in its elemental form because it is highly reactive. When prepared, the metal is sufficiently soft to be cut with a knife and it is a silvery white colour. However, it reacts violently with water and rapidly with oxygen and the halogens. It is essential to life, particularly in the biological mechanism involved in the transmission of nerve impulses.

It forms numerous compounds with diverse uses and is itself used as a heat-transfer fluid in reactors. Compounds and their uses include: hydroxide, numerous uses; benzoate, antiseptic; carbonate, in glass, soap and other manufacturing processes; chlorate, herbicide; citrate, medicinal; hypochlorite, bleaches; nitrite, in dyes; and many more.

The other alkali metals are lithium (Li), potassium (K), rubidium (Rb), caesium (Cs) and francium (Fr). Francium is radioactive, and caesium is extremely reactive.

sodium hydroxide *see* CAUSTIC SODA.

solar cell is an electric cell that produces electrical energy from light. It is based upon a SEMICONDUCTOR device, called a photoelectric cell, which creates a small current because of the movement of electrons. Solar cells are ideal for use in spacecraft to power electronic equipment, but to produce an appreciable output cells have to be put into panels. In this way they are used to complement domestic heating systems.

solid a state of matter in which the component atoms, ions or molecules maintain a constant position relative to each other. Some solids are *crystalline*, with a regular and repetitive arrangement of atoms, while others are totally disordered (amorphous – no shape). When solids are heated, their atoms absorb the energy and vibrate more. Eventually the energy intake is sufficient to break down the structure, and it melts to form a liquid. A few solids go directly from solid to gas, they *sublime*, e.g. solid carbon dioxide.

solution a mixture of two or more components producing a single, homogeneous phase from which there is no settling out. The term usually applies to a solution of a solid in a liquid, and often the liquid is water (producing an *aqueous* solution). However, it is possible to have solutions of gases in liquids, gases in solids, liquids in liquids, and solids in solids (a solid solution).

The *solute* is the substance that dissolves to make a solution, and the *solvent* is the substance in which the solute dissolves. The solvent is usually a liquid, and water is the commonest. *Solubility* is the concentration of a saturated solution, i.e. the maximum amount of one substance dissolved in another.

A *solid solution* is when two or more elements share a common crystalline framework. The composition can vary, although within limits, and two types of solid solution are found. A substitutional solid solution is when atoms of one element are replaced by another, e.g. nickel and copper; an interstitial solid solution is when small atoms rest in lattice spaces of the structure, as with carbon in metals. Minerals commonly exhibit solid solutions.

sonar *see* ECHO.

sound the effect upon the ear created by air vibrations with a frequency between 20 Hz (hertz) and 20 kKz (20,000 Hz). More generally, sound waves are caused by vibrations through a medium (whether gas, liquid or solid). One of the commonest sources of sound is a loudspeaker. When it produces sound, the cone vibrates, producing a series of compressions in the air. These are called longitudinal progressive waves, that is the oscillations occur in the same direction that the wave is travelling (*see* WAVE). The sound waves so produced enter the ear causing pressure changes on the ear drum, causing the brain to register the sound. Most items produce sound when they vibrate or are moved or banged together, but sound can only be transmitted through a medium and it cannot travel through a vacuum.

The speed of sound varies with the material it is travelling through, moving most quickly through solids, then liquids and gases. In air, sound travels at approximately 350 m/s. The speed increases with temperature, but is unaffected by pressure. Frequency of sound waves relates to *pitch*; high frequencies produce a sound of high pitch, e.g. a whistle at 10 kHz, while low pitch is caused by low frequencies, e.g. a bass voice at 100 Hz. Sound intensity is measured in *decibels* (db) and it is a logarithmic scale. Ordinary conversation might register 40-50 decibels, traffic 80 and thunder 100 while jet aircraft can exceed 125 dB.

specific gravity *see* DENSITY.

specific heat or specific heat capacity is the heat required by unit mass to raise its temperature by one degree, that is the gain in thermal energy divided by mass and temperature. The units are joules per kgK. The specific heat capacity varies with the material and metals have a much lower value than, for example, water. This means that much more energy is required to create a 1K (1°C) rise in 1kg of water than in 1kg of copper:

water	4200 joules required per kgK
ice	2100 " " "
aluminium	900 " " "
glass	700 " " "
copper	400 " " "

If the specific heat capacity of a substance is known, and its mass, it is possible to work out the thermal energy (heat) required to give a certain temperature rise.

spectroscopy the study of spectra using *spectroscopes* (this includes spectrometers and spectrographs, etc.). Light emitted from a hot object, or given out by a substance upon excitation can be analysed. The light or radiation passes through an analyser or *monochromator* which usually incorporates a prism to split the light into its components. This enables monochromatic light (light of a specific wavelength) to be studied. An alternative is to use a filter which absorbs unwanted frequencies. The light then passes into a detector, and there are numerous types, some employing a photoelectric cell.

Spectrometry is used to study light from the stars and also extensively in chemistry.

spore and sporophyte a small reproductive structure, usually consisting of one cell only, which detaches from the parent and is dispersed. If environmental conditions are favourable it grows into a new individual. Spores are commonly produced by fungi and bacteria, but also occur in all groups of green land plants especially *ferns, horsetails* and *mosses*. The sporophyte is the phase in the life cycle of a plant that produces spores. The sporophyte is *diploid* but it produces haploid spores (*see* CELL DIVISION). It may be the dominant stage in the life cycle of a plant (as in the seed plants) or be mainly dependent upon the gametophyte structure for water and nourishment as in mosses (*Bryophyta*). (*See also* GAMETE AND GAMETOPHYTE).

starch is a *polysaccharide* found in all green plants. Polysaccharides are a large group of natural carbohydrates in which the molecules are made from simple sugars (*monosaccharides*) of the form $C_6H_{12}O6$ (hexoses) or $C_5H_{10}O_5$ (pentoses). Starch is built up from chains of glucose ($C_6H_{12}O_6$)

units arranged in two ways, as amylose (long unbranched chains) and amylopectin (long cross-linked chains). Potato and some cereal starches contain 20–30% amylose and 70–80% amylopectin. Amylose contains 200-1000 glucose units while amylopectin numbers about 20. Starch is formed and broken down in plant cells and is stored as granules and it occurs in seeds. It is insoluble in cold water and is obtained from corn, wheat, potatoes, rice and other cereals by various physical processes. It is used as an adhesive for sizing paper and has many uses in the food industry.

static electricity is electricity or electric charges, at rest. The structure of the atom is visualised as having electrons 'orbiting' a central nucleus and this means that in some materials, electrons can be removed by rubbing with a cloth. When, for example, a Perspex rod is rubbed with a woollen cloth, the cloth pulls electrons away from the rod, becoming negatively charged and leaving the rod positively charged. The reverse happens when the cloth is rubbed on a polythene rod, the rod becoming negatively charged. No charge is created, it is just that charges are separated. Charges on materials can be registered using the gold-leaf electroscope and, as with other phenomena involving charges, unlike charges attract while like charges repel. (*See also* VAN DER GRAAFF GENERATOR.)

statistics is the part of mathematics that deals with the collection, analysis, interpretation and presentation of quantitative data. It involves processing data with a view to predicting future outcomes, based upon the information available. Probability plays an important role in statistics. The figures can be presented in numerous graphical ways but it is important to select relevant features to illustrate a point, i.e. statistics can be very misleading, depending upon how they are presented. Statistics are used extensively by manufacturers, in medical research, insurance and, of course, in politics.

steel is iron that contains up to 1.5% carbon in the form of *cementite* (Fe_3C). The properties of steel vary with iron content and also depend upon the presence of other metals and the production method. *Alloy steels* contain alloying elements while *austenitic steel* is a solid solution of carbon in a form of iron and is normally stable only at high temperatures but can be produced by rapid cooling. *Stainless steel* is a group of chromium/nickel steels which have a high resistance to corrosion and chemical attack. A high proportion of chromium is necessary (12–25%) to provide the resistance and a low carbon content, typically 0.1%. Stainless steel has many uses: cutlery, equipment in chemical plants; ball bearings and many other items of machinery.

stroboscope is an instrument that is used to view rapidly moving objects. By shining a flashing light onto a revolving or vibrating object, the object can be made to appear stationary providing the frequency of the flashes of light match the revolutions or vibrations of the object in question. This technique is used in engineering to examine, for example, the blades of a propeller, or an engine part. It is also used to set the ignition timing in a car engine.

sulphur is a yellow, non-metallic element that exhibits *allotropy*, i.e. exhibits several physical forms. It is widely distributed in both the free state and in compounds (*see* SULPHUR COMPOUNDS), forming sulphates, sulphides and oxides, amongst others. It is manufactured by heating pyrite or purification of the naturally-occurring material. The primary use of sulphur is in the manufacture of sulphuric acid (H_2SO_4), but it is also used in the preparation of matches, dyes, fireworks, fertilisers, fungicides and the photographic industry.

sulphur compounds are very common, and include sulphates such as gypsum ($CaSO_4.2H_2O$) and anhydrite ($CaSO_4$). Metal sulphides often form minerals e.g. FeS_2 iron pyrite (also chalcopyrite, $CuFeS_2$) from which the elements can be separated. Sulphur forms several oxides including sulphur dioxide (SO_2), one of the primary gases causing acid rain. Sulphuric acid is the commonest product of sulphur and is a very strong and corrosive acid that is used very widely in the manufacture of dyestuffs, explosives and many other products.

superconductor is a material which shows practically no resistance to electric current when maintained at temperatures approaching absolute zero (which is -273°C). Each material has a critical temperature above which its behaviour is normal, resistance decreasing with falling temperature. At the critical temperature, the resistance disappears almost to nothing. If a current is induced in superconducting material by a changing magnetic field, then the current will continue to flow long after its source has been removed. Metals such as aluminium, lead, and tin become superconducting as do some ceramics, and the phenomenon has been applied to electromagnets because large currents can flow without the supply of large amounts of energy. Other potential uses of superconductors include larger and faster computers, and the transmission of electricity without heat loss.

surface tension is the 'tension' created by forces of attraction between molecules in a liquid resulting in an apparent elastic membrane over the surface of the liquid. This attraction between molecules of the same substance is called *cohesion* and the result is that it tries to pull liquids into the smallest possible shapes. This can plainly be seen in water which forms round droplets and also supports the feet of insects on ponds and puddles. The same phenomenon is demonstrated by a needle on a piece of blotting paper which is then placed gently on water. When the paper absorbs sufficient water to sink, the needle remains afloat, because of the surface tension of the water. Droplets of mercury show the same effect, forming compact globules on a surface.

Adhesion is when molecules of two different substances are attracted to each other, as shown by water wetting glass. This attraction is also responsible for the *meniscus* formed where water meets glass. The meniscus is the upward-curving surface of the water upon meeting the glass. Mercury forms a meniscus curving down because its cohesion is greater than its adhesion with glass (*see also* CAPILLARY ACTION).

suspension is a two-phase system with denser particles distributed in a less dense liquid or gas. Settling of the particles is prevented or slowed down by the viscosity of the fluid or impacts between the particles and the molecules of the fluid. Fog is a suspension of liquid particles and smoke a suspension of solid particles.

symbiosis describes various relationships between organisms, usually two different species, which co-exist to the benefit of at least one of the parties involved. In *mutualism* both parties benefit and neither is harmed. In *commensalism* one party benefits and the other is unharmed but in *parasitism*, one organism thrives at the expense of the other (*see also* PARASITE).

symbols in chemistry are used to represent elements, atoms, molecules, etc. Each element has its own symbol of one or two letters (*see* PERIODIC TABLE), thus fluorine is F, and chlorine is Cl. Symbols are used further in formulae, i.e. the shorthand representation of a compound, for example NaCl is sodium chloride. The formula can then be used in equations to represent chemical reactions and processes, e.g.

$$NaOH + HCl \ \text{Æ} \ NaCl + H_2O$$

This formulae states that caustic soda and hydrochloric acid, when combined, will react to form sodium chloride and water.

Symbols are used elsewhere, particularly in the sciences, to provide a convenient shorthand, e.g. prefixes in decimal numbers (*see* SI UNITS), concepts in physics such as *m* for mass and *I* for electric current and in mathematics where a letter or figure represents a word or sentence.

symmetry is the property of a geometrical figure whose points have corresponding points reflected in a given line (axis of symmetry), point (centre of symmetry) or plane. Symmetry is closely related to balance in nature and many forms exhibit bilateral symmetry, humans included. Symmetry is very evident in crystals that have grown in ideal conditions because then the crystals faces are apparent and most crystals exhibit several symmetrical features (*see also* CRYSTALLOGRAPHY).

synthetic fibres are used widely in producing cloth and for reinforcements in composite materials. They are manufactured from polymers or modified natural materials and the first synthetic fibres, e.g. *rayon*, were made from cellulose. Rayon is produced from wood fibre treated with alkali and carbon disulphide and it is then extruded into a bath of sulphuric acid to harden the fibres. Completely synthetic fibres include: *nylons* which are polyamides, and are used in textiles, insulation and cables; *polyesters*, used in textiles and film and also for reinforcement in boats etc; *acrylics* and *glass fibres* which are incorporated in resins to increase strength.

There are inorganic fibres such as alumina (Al_2O_3) and glass wool many of which are used in insulation and packing. Asbestos was used for the production of fire resistant textiles but it is being replaced because it is hazardous to health.

tannin *see* CAFFEINE AND TANNIN.

taste and taste bud *taste* is one of the senses and is enhanced by that of smell. Hence if a person has a cold, he or she is not able to taste things properly.

The organs of taste are called *taste buds* and are situated on the tongue and sides of the mouth. They consist of groups of cells which are able to detect four different tastes – salt, sweet, bitter and sour. All the flavours which we detect are combinations of these in different proportions and the taste buds for each are grouped together in various parts of the tongue. Substances can only be tasted if they start to dissolve in the saliva of the mouth, hence certain hard materials have no taste at all.

teeth are hard structures used by animals for biting and chewing food and also for attacking, grooming and other activities such as behavioural displays. In the more advanced vertebrate animals the teeth are collected in the *jaws* but fish and amphibians (frogs and toads) have teeth all over the *palate* (roof of the mouth). Teeth evolved from the scales of cartilaginous fish and are adapted according to the lifestyle of the animal. In mammals a tooth consists of a central *pulp cavity* supplied with nerves and blood vessels, surrounded by a layer of *dentine* and an outer thickness of enamel. Enamel is extremely hard to resist wear and decay. The *root* of the tooth is embedded in a socket in the jaw bone. Four different types of teeth are present – molar, premolar, canine and incisor – but the numbers and arrangement differ between animals. This is known as *dentition*. Also, *jaw of carnivore* – carnivores have well-developed canine teeth for biting and the last premolars (upper jaw) and first molars (lower jaw) have cusps with sharp, cutting edges for shearing through flesh. These are called *carnassial teeth*.

Jaw of herbivore – herbivores have large, ridged premolars and molars for grinding vegetation and incisors for cutting through stems.

Rodent jaw – in rodents the upper and lower jaws contain a single pair of long incisors which grow continuously throughout the animal's life. These are adapted for gnawing and there is an absence of enamel on the back which means that they wear to a chisel-like cutting edge.

telegraph an early device for transmitting messages first developed in the late 1700s. By the mid 19th century the technique had been refined so that information was sent along a wire as electrical pulses. Samuel Morse (1791–1872) introduced his code in which each letter of the alphabet was represented by a different set of pulses. Telegraph messages were also used to control train movements and eventually the Post Office formed a network. The telegraph gradually faded into history when it became possible to use the telephone on an international basis.

telephone is an instrument that enables speech to be transmitted by means of electric currents or radio waves. It was invented by Alexander Graham Bell (1847–1922) in 1876 and a public service was begun three years later after Bell brought his invention to the UK. The modern telephone consists of a mouthpiece containing a thin diaphragm of aluminium which moves with the sound of speech. This movement presses carbon granules which produces a surge of current and in the earpiece of the receiving set, these surges are changed back into sound. An electromagnet reacts to the current charges and vibrates a diaphragm, thus reproducing the voice of the speaker.

television is the transmission of moving image by electrical means and the television set is essentially a complex cathode ray tube. The tube consists of an electron gun and a screen that fluoresces and the beam of electrons is deflected by magnetic coils. On a black and white screen, the picture is composed of lines as the spot moves across the screen and the spot is also moved down the screen, although at a slower rate. The result is that 25 images per second are shown on the screen, which to the human eye appears to be a moving picture.

Producing colour pictures is much more complex. There are three electron guns for red, green and blue and the screen is coated with thousands of tiny strips of the same colours which, when struck by electrons, glow in combination to produce a colour picture. Accurate targetting of the strips is achieved by a *shadow mask* through which the electron beams are fired.

The pictures and sounds are converted by cameras and microphones into electrical signals which are sent to transmitting aerials. Receiving aerials then pick up the signal, pass them to the television set where they form pictures and sound.

temperature is a measure of an object's overall kinetic energy. When an object is cold, its molecules, atoms or ions have less *kinetic energy* – its temperature is lower. Although molecules do not stop moving altogether, at -273˚C they possess the minimum possible energy. This is *absolute zero* and this temperature cannot be exceeded. The temperature scale which has -273˚C (actually -273.15˚C) as its zero is called the *Kelvin* scale. The degrees are the same size as centigrade degrees, but the temperatures are stated as figures without the degree. In addition to the centigrade (or *Celsius*) scale which has water freezing at 0˚ and boiling at 100˚, there is the *Fahrenheit* scale where the respective temperatures are 32˚F and 212˚F.

tempering is the process whereby (usually) steel is heated to a particular temperature and then cooled quickly in oil or water. The heating permits stresses in the metal to be relieved and results in a toughened, less brittle material.

tensile strength of a material is the force that is required to stretch it until it breaks. It is measured using a special machine upon which the 'breaking' force can be read from a dial. Since tensile strength is the force per unit area, the breaking force is divided by the material's cross-sectional area. The units are newtons per square metre.

thermocouple is a device for measuring temperatures and consists of two different types of metallic wire joined at both ends. The temperature is measured at one join and the other join is kept at a fixed temperature. A temperature difference between the two joins causes the metals to produce a small electric current which can be metered. Thermocouples are used in furnaces because they have a range up to about 1600˚C. The two metals used are often copper and *constantan*, the latter being a copper/nickel alloy which has a constant resistance irrespective of the temperature.

thermodynamics is the study of laws affecting processes that involve heat changes and energy transfer. Heat transfer from one body to another, the link between heat and work and changes of state in a fluid all come within the field of thermodynamics, it is the prerequisite to analysis of work by machinery. There are essentially three *laws of thermodynamics*. The first law says that heat is a form of energy and is conserved and any work energy produced in a closed system must arise from the conversion of existing energy, i.e. energy cannot be created or destroyed. The second law states that the entropy of any closed system cannot decrease and if the system undergoes a reversible process it remains constant, otherwise it increases. The result of this is that heat always flows from a hot body to a cooler one. The third law states that absolute zero (*see* TEMPERATURE) can never be attained.

thermometer an instrument used to measure temperature. The basis of a thermometer is a property of a substance that varies reliably with temperature, e.g. expansion. Thermometers that utilise a liquid in glass are based upon the property that liquids expand slightly when they are heated. Both mercury and alcohol are used and when the bulb at the base of the thermometer's stem is heated, the liquid expands up the stem to create a reading. More sensitivity is gained by using a narrower tube. This is the case with *clinical thermometers* where the scale covers just a few degrees on either side of the normal body temperature of 37°C.

thermostat *see* BIMETAL STRIP.

tissue *see* ORGAN.

titanium is a malleable and ductile silvery-white metal that melts at 1660°C. It occurs as the minerals rutile (TiO_2) and ilmenite ($FeTiO_3$) and is obtained by reducing titanium chloride ($TiCl_4$) with magnesium. It is characterised by its lightness, strength and high resistance to corrosion and is used in alloy form (with aluminium, manganese, chromium and iron) in the aircraft industry. It is also used in missile manufacture, engines and chemical plant.

touch the sense of touch is made possible by specialised sets of receptors which are located in the SKIN and also in muscles and other internal areas of an animal's body. Touch has different elements including pressure, pain and temperature. The receptor cells which detect pain and pressure tend to be concentrated in certain areas (e.g. fingertips) and distributed less thickly elsewhere. Sensory receptor cells are associated with the hairs covering an animal's body so that the slightest movement of air can be detected. The sense organs involved in touch are specially adapted to respond to a particular sensation. Different nerve pathways are used to transmit the information to the brain where it is decoded and detected.

trace elements is a term used both in biology and geology. In biology it refers to an element that an organism requires in very small quantities.

These elements may be necessary for the formation or action of vitamins, enzymes and hormones.

transformer is a device for changing the voltage of an alternating current. It is based upon the principle of mutual induction whereby an alternating current passing through a coil (the primary) on a soft iron core induces current flow in another (secondary) coil on the core. The primary and secondary coils form a transformer. Transformers can be made to step-up or step-down a voltage by varying the number of turns in the coils. For example, if the primary coil has ten times the number of turns compared to the secondary, then the voltage in the secondary is one tenth that of the supply, and the associated current increases tenfold.

Transformers have many uses but practical versions are not 100% efficient and some energy is lost as heat. Huge transformers are used in the mains power supply between the power station and the domestic supply. Current generated at a power station goes through a step-up transformer, creating voltages of up to 400,000 volts, at much reduced currents (thus minimising heat loss) for transmission through the power lines of the grid. Power from the *grid* then goes to substations where transformers step the voltage down by a series of transformers to 132,000 volts, then 33,000V (for heavy industry), then 11,000V for light industry and finally 240V for offices and homes.

transistor is a SEMICONDUCTOR that can be used for three functions: as a switch, a rectifier and as an amplifier. A transistor consists essentially of a semi-conductor chip of silicon which is doped (*see* DIODE *and* semiconductor) to form two p-n junction diodes back to back (p-type diode is silicon doped with boron; n-type is doped with phosphorus). Current cannot flow through a transistor unless a small current is applied to the p-type region of the semiconductor called the *base* circuit, but when this current is applied an enlarged current flows in the output or *collector* circuit. A transistor can be used to amplify current changes and practical amplifiers contain several transistors, as used in radio, to increase currents to output a signal through the loudspeaker.

Because a current must flow in the base circuit to allow current to flow in the collector circuit, a transistor can be used as a switch and is turned on and off by a change in the base current.

trigonometry is the branch of mathematics, used in surveying and navigation, that involves the study of right-angled triangles including problem-solving involving the calculation of unknown sides and angles from known values.

It involves the use of the *trigonometrical ratios*, sine, cosine and tangent. In the right-angled triangle below the ratios are:

$$\sin \theta = \frac{\text{opposite}}{\text{hypotenuse}} = \frac{yz}{xy}$$

$$\tan \theta = \frac{\text{opposite}}{\text{adjacent}} = \frac{yz}{xz}$$

$$\cos \theta = \frac{\text{adjacent}}{\text{hypotenuse}} = \frac{xz}{xy}$$

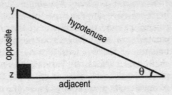

ultrasound (or ultrasonic waves) is sound with a frequency beyond the range of human hearing, i.e. around 20,000 Hz. Ultrasound is used extensively in industry and medicine. It is used to detect faults and cracks in metals and to test pipes; it can clean surfaces due to the rapid, small vibrations; in ultrasonic welding, soldering and machining; and in medicine ultrasound is used to scan a growing foetus and also to destroy kidney stones or gall stones. A recent development is the use of ultrasound in chemical processes, to initiate reactions in the production of food, plastics and antibiotics. Ultrasound can make chemical processes safer and cheaper as it eliminates the need for high operating temperatures and expensive catalysts.

vaccination *see* IMMUNE SYSTEM.

vacuum is defined as a space in which there is no matter. In practice a perfect vacuum cannot be achieved although interstellar space comes very close indeed. Also, special equipment in the laboratory can reach very low pressures, but in general vacuum is taken to be air or gas at very low pressure, 10^{-4} mm Hg or lower.

The *vacuum flask* uses a vacuum to help keep liquids or gases cold or hot. It was invented by James Dewar at the end of the 19th century and it consists of a double-walled glass bottle. A vacuum is created between the glass walls, and the surfaces are silvered so that together, transfer of heat by convection and radiation is reduced to a minimum.

valency is the bonding potential or combining power of an atom or group, measured by the number of hydrogen ions (H^+, or equivalent) that the atom could combine with or replace. In an ionic compound, the charge on each ion represents the valency e.g. in NaCl, both Na^+ and Cl^- have a valency of one. In covalent compounds (*see* BONDS), the valency is represented by the number of bonds formed. In carbon dioxide, CO_2, carbon has a valency of 4 and oxygen 2. The *valency electrons* of an atom are those in the outermost shell that are involved in forming bonds and are shared, lost or gained when a compound or ion is formed, i.e. they determine the chemical reactivity.

The *electronic theory of valency* explains bonds through the assumption that specific arrangements of outer electrons in atoms (outer shells of eight electrons) confers stability (as with the inert gases, which have such a structure) through the transfer or sharing of electrons. Thus with the combination of sodium with chlorine, sodium has one electron in the outer shell, which it loses (to form the Neon stable structure) to chlorine, giving it also a stable structure, in this case, that of Argon.

Van der Graaff generator is a machine that provides a continuous supply of electrostatic charge (*see* STATIC ELECTRICITY) and which can build up a very high voltage. It consists essentially of a hollow metal sphere supported on an insulating tube. A motor-driven belt of rubber or silk carries charge (positive or negative) from the driving roller up the moving belt to the sphere, where the charge collects. Very high voltages (up to 13 million volts) can be produced and in conjunction with high voltage X-ray tubes and other equipment, these voltages are used in research to split atoms. The apparatus was named after the American physicist R. J. Van der Graaff (1901–67).

velocity is the rate of change of an object's position, i.e. the speed at which an object travels. Velocity provides both the magnitude (size) and direction of travel (per unit time) and and such is called a *vector quantity*. The units are metres per second (ms^{-1} or m/s). On plotting a graph of distance moved, against time, a straight line would represent an object moving at constant velocity. However, it is usually the case that velocity changes with time, in which case an object is said to be accelerating (or decelerating). *Acceleration* is the gain in velocity of an object divided by the time taken to achieve the gain and the units are metres per second, per second. As with velocity, it is a vector quantity. Graphical plots of velocity against time are useful because the gradient of the line plotted is equal numerically to the acceleration and the area under the graph represents the distance moved.

The *terminal velocity* of an object falling through air, for example, is the constant velocity reached when the object's weight is matched by the air resistance.

vertebrate any animal with a backbone including fish, amphibians, reptiles, birds and mammals.

virus the smallest kind of micro-organism which is completely parasitic (*see* PARASITE) and exists and reproduces within the cells of a host organism. Most, but not all viruses cause diseases in plants, animals and even bacterial cells. Viruses operate by invading and taking over the metabolism of the cells which they inhabit and using the metabolic processes to reproduce. Diseases caused by viruses include influenza, herpes, AIDS, mumps, chicken pox and polio, and possibly some cancers.

viscosity is a property of fluids that indicates their resistance to flow. Oil is more viscous than water and an object will take much longer when falling through oil than when it falls through water. All fluids show this resistance to shear forces but a perfect fluid would be non-viscous. Viscosity measurements can be used to find the molecular weight of polymers.

vitamins a group of organic substances that are required in very small amounts in the human diet to maintain good health. A lack of a particular vitamin results in a *deficiency* disease. There are two groups of vitamins; those which are fat-soluble including A, D, E and K and those which are water-soluble, C (ascorbic acid) and B (Thiamine).

The six vitamin groups are as follows;

A or *Retinol*
Source   green vegetables, dairy produce, liver, fish oils
Needed for the manufacture of rhodopsin-a pigment needed by the rod cells of the eye for night vision. Also for the maintenance of the skin and tissues
Deficiency night blindness and possible total blindness

B **complex** (including Thiamine, Riboflavin, Nicotinic acid, Pantothenic acid, Biotin, Folic acid, B_6, Pyroxidine, B_{12} [cyanocobalamin], Lipoic acid)
Source   green vegetables, dairy produce, cereal, grains, eggs, liver, meat, nuts, potatoes, fish
Needed for the manufacture of red blood cells, for enzyme activity and for amino acid production. Also for maintaining the fatty sheath (myelin) around nerves
Deficiency Beri beri (B_1 deficiency) anaemia and deterioration of the nervous system (B_{12} deficiency)

C **(ascorbic acid)**
Source   citrus fruit, green vegetables.
Needed for maintaining cell walls and connective tissue. Aiding the absorption of iron by the body
Deficiency scurvy-affects skin, blood vessels and tendons

D

Source   fish oils, eggs, dairy produce

Needed for controls calcium levels required for bone growth and repair.

Deficiency Rickets in children-deformation of the bones. Osteomalacia in adults-softening of bones

E

Source   cereal grains, eggs, green vegetables

Needed for maintenance of cell membranes

Deficiency unusual as common in the diet

K

Source   leafy green vegetables, especially spinach, liver

Needed for clotting of blood

Deficiency rare as it is also manufactured by bacteria in the gut

volt (V) is the SI unit of potential difference. It is defined formally as the difference of potential between two points on a conducting wire that is carrying a current of one ampere when the power given out between these points is one watt. The voltage across battery terminals is a measure of the potential energy given to each coulomb of charge and a potential difference of one volt exists if each coulomb has one joule of potential energy, so there is a potential difference of 6 volts if each coulomb is given 6 joules of potential energy.

water is the normal oxide of hydrogen, H_2O, and is found in one form or another in most places on Earth. It can occur in solid, liquid or gas phases, forms a large part of the Earth's surface, and is vital to life. Natural water is never absolutely pure, but contains dissolved salts, organic material, etc. Pure water freezes at 0°C and boils at 100°C and has its maximum density of 1gm/cm³ at 4°C. It occurs in all living organisms and has a remarkable combination of properties in its solvent capacity (i.e. its ability to dissolve so many substances), chemical stability, thermal properties and abundance. Water has an almost unlimited range of uses and can provide power through hydroelectric schemes.

watt *see* POWER.

wave is a periodic displacement that repeats itself and a mechanism of transferring energy through a medium. In the simple waveform shown the *amplitude* is the maximum distance moved by a point from its rest position as the wave passes. The *wavelength* is the length of one complete wave.

    The origin of a wave is vibrating particles which store and release energy while their average position remains constant, as it is only the wave that travels. Waves are either *longitudinal* with oscillations occurring in the direction of wave travel (e.g. sound), or *transverse* because the oscillations are from side to side, at 90° to the direction of travel (e.g. light).

The *wave equation* relates frequency (*f*) and wavelength (λ):

$$c = f\lambda \quad \text{where c is the speed of the wave}$$

All forms of wave show the properties of reflection, refraction, interference and diffraction. Electromagnetic waves have these properties but have one additional feature in that they can travel through a vacuum.

A waveform

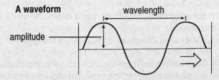

weight is the gravitational force of attraction exerted on an object by the Earth and although such an attraction exists between all objects, it is so infinitesimally small as to be non-existent and the Earth is so massive that its attraction dominates. Weight is a force, measured in newtons (N), and is the force that makes an object accelerate downwards when falling to the Earth's surface. The weight of an object is therefore dependent upon its distance from the Earth, and the further away it is, the smaller the pull of the Earth and the less is the object's weight.

Mass is a measure of the quantity of matter that a substance possesses and it remains constant, but the weight of an object varies. A constant mass will therefore have different weights depending upon the gravitational effect of nearby bodies. The weight of a constant mass on Earth will be approximately six times greater than its weight on the Moon and in space the weight of that same mass would be zero. Because weight on Earth is directly proportional to mass; any instrument that measures one property also measures the other.

work is done when something is moved by a force. It is also a transfer of energy, i.e. energy is changed into a different form when work is done. Work is measured in the unit of energy, the joule and is calculated as the force, multiplied by the distance moved in the direction of the force. One joule of work is done when a force of one newton is moved through one metre, *in the direction of the force*.

X-rays are electromagnetic waves with a short wavelength (approximately 10^{-10}-10^{-8}m) and are produced when electrons moving at high speed strike a target, are stopped very quickly and X-rays are emitted. They were discovered in 1895 by Röntgen. He found that wrapped photographic plates left near a working cathode ray tube became fogged as if they had been exposed to light and he called this unknown radiation X-rays. In fact X-rays were being emitted as electrons hit the anode and walls of the cathode ray tube.

Atoms of all elements give out characteristic X-rays when hit by electrons. The stream of electrons colliding with the atom displaces electrons from inner orbitals and vacant places are then filled by electrons from the outer orbital, which give out energy as they move down. X-rays have the properties of electromagnetic radiation and also penetrate solid matter, cause ionisation (by removal of electrons from atoms), make some materials fluoresce and, as mentioned, they affect photographic film. These properties render X-rays both useful and hazardous. Their ionisation effect damages living tissue, but by using very small doses, they can be used in medicine to take X-ray photographs of the body. The extent to which the rays are absorbed depends upon the density and the atomic weight (or relative atomic mass, *see* ATOMIC NUMBER) of the material; the lower these factors, the more easily will the rays penetrate. The greater density of bone means it is possible to take an X-ray photograph because the flesh appears transparent while the bones are opaque.

X-rays are also used in industry for checking joints in metal and examining flaws. They are also used in *X-ray diffraction* (or X-ray crystallography) which is an analytical tool in geology, crystallography, and biophysics. X-rays directed at the sample are diffracted off the planes of atoms in the crystal. By repeating the procedure and then calculating the spacing between atomic planes, a representation of the crystal's structure can be determined. In this way the structure of some proteins and nucleic acids has been analysed.

yeast *see* FERMENTATION.

zoology the scientific study of animals.

zygote *see* REPRODUCTION.

Appendix 1 — Element Table

Element	Symbol	Atomic Number	Element	Symbol	Atomic Number
Actinium	Ac	89	Fermium	Fm	100
Aluminium	Al	13	Fluorine	F	9
Americium	Am	95	Francium	Fr	87
Antimony	Sb	51	Gadolinium	Gd	64
Argon	Ar	18	Gallium	Ga	31
Arsenic	As	33	Germanium	Ge	32
Astatine	At	85	Gold	Au	79
Barium	Ba	56	Hafnium	Hf	72
Berkelium	Bk	97	Helium	He	2
Beryllium	Be	4	Holmium	Ho	67
Bismuth	Bi	83	Hydrogen	H	1
Boron	B	5	Indium	In	49
Bromine	Br	35	Iodine	I	53
Cadmium	Cd	48	Iridium	Ir	77
Caesium	Cs	55	Iron	Fe	26
Calcium	Ca	20	Krypton	Kr	36
Californium	Cf	98	Lanthanum	La	57
Carbon	C	6	Lawrencium	Lr	103
Cerium	Ce	58	Lead	Pb	82
Chlorine	Cl	17	Lithium	Li	3
Chromium	Cr	24	Lutetium	Lu	71
Cobalt	Co	27	Magnesium	Mg	12
Copper	Cu	29	Manganese	Mn	25
Curium	Cm	96	Mendelevium	Md	101
Dysprosium	Dy	66	Mercury	Hg	80
Einsteinium	Es	99	Molybdenum	Mo	42
Erbium	Er	68	Neodymium	Nd	60
Europium	Eu	63	Neon	Ne	10

Element	Symbol	Atomic Number	Element	Symbol	Atomic Number
Neptunium	Np	93	Selenium	Se	34
Nickel	Ni	28	Silicon	Si	14
Niobium	Nb	41	Silver	Ag	47
Nitrogen	N	7	Sodium	Na	11
Nobelium	No	102	Strontium	Sr	38
Osmium	Os	76	Sulphur	S	16
Oxygen	O	8	Tantalum	Ta	73
Palladium	Pd	46	Technetium	Tc	43
Phosphorus	P	15	Tellurium	Te	52
Platinum	Pt	78	Terbium	Tb	65
Plutonium	Pu	94	Thallium	Tl	81
Polonium	Po	84	Thorium	Th	90
Potassium	K	19	Thulium	Tm	69
Praseodymium	Pr	59	Tin	Sn	50
Promethium	Pm	61	Titanium	Ti	22
Protactinium	Pa	91	Tungsten	W	74
Radium	Ra	88	Uranium	U	92
Radon	Rn	86	Vanadium	V	23
Rhenium	Re	75	Xenon	Xe	54
Rhodium	Rh	45	Ytterbium	Yb	70
Rubidium	Rb	37	Yttrium	Y	39
Ruthenium	Ru	44	Zinc	Zn	30
Samarium	Sm	62	Zirconium	Zr	40
Scandium	Sc	21			

Computers

Computers have become important to nearly every aspect of our lives and with the advent of the internet they will facilitate communication and interaction on a global scale. This section of *The Pocket Encyclopedia* explains some of the common terms, concepts and developments in computing and information technology. The cross-references, given in SMALL CAPITALS, will enable you to relate these terms to one another.

access to locate and retrieve the information, whether data or program instructions, stored on a disk or in a computer. Nowadays the term usually refers to the amount of time it takes to transfer information from one source to another, and is called the *access time*. It is measured in NANOSECONDS for memory chips, in MILLISECONDS for data transfer from the hard disk. Typical access times for hard disks on personal computers range between the fast (9ms) and the slow at around 100ms. The access time is determined by the time required for the disk heads to move to the correct track (the *seek time*) and then to settle down (the *settle time*) and the time needed for the sector to move under the head (*latency*).

AI *see* ARTIFICIAL INTELLIGENCE.

ANSI is the acronym for the *A*merican *N*ational *S*tandards *I*nstitute, a non-governmental organisation founded in 1918 to approve the specification of data-processing standards in the USA. It is also responsible for the definition of high-level programming langauges.

APL (A Program Language) a high-level programming language, designed for handling engineering and mathematical functions, and as a notation for communication between mathematicians. It is quick, efficient, and well suited to 'what if' applications.

application program a computer program that performs specific tasks such as letter-writing, design, statistical analysis etc.

architecture is the particular selection, design and inter-connection of the principal components of a computer system. Normally it refers to the physical structure of a computer and the manner in which its components are connected. It is also common to use the term as a logical description of the components in a system.

artificial intelligence (AI) is the ability of an artificial mechanism to exhibit intelligent behaviour by modifying its actions through reasoning and learning from experience. Artificial intelligence is also the name of the research discipline in which artificial mechanisms that exhibit intelligence are developed and studied. It was first discussed by the British mathematician Alan Turing, who is regarded as one of the founders of the subject.

In recent years artificial intelligence has been used in the development of 'expert systems', which use knowledge-based information to make seemingly rational decisions. However, this rationale is limited to a specific knowledge area. It is generally accepted that AI has not met its objectives and the necessary solutions are probably many, many years away.

ASCII *A*merican *S*tandard *C*ode for *I*nformation *I*nterchange. It is one of several standard sets of codes, devised in 1968, which define the way information is transferred from one computer to another. It is one method of representing binary code, whereby specific binary patterns are represented by alphanumeric codes. The standard ASCII code contains 96 upper and lower case characters and 32 control characters that are not displayed.

asynchronous a commonly used mode of transmitting data over telephone lines. In this method of data transmission, the length of time between transmitted characters may vary. It is not dependent on the timing of the host processor being in synchronous operation with the sending processor, and therefore requires the use of start and stop bits to signal the beginning and end of each character. Asynchronous communication is used by people developing personal computers because normal telephone lines can be used.

auxiliary storage or **secondary storage** is storage other than the main computer memory, e.g. magnetic media such as hard or floppy disks and tapes that store data after the power supply is switched off.

back-up is the term given to the duplication of files that are stored on magnetic media, such as disk, tape or diskette. It is considered essential practice to make back-up copies of all data in case of accidental loss.

BASIC *B*eginner's *A*ll-purpose *S*ymbolic *I*nstruction *C*ode is one of the most popular computer programming languages. It was developed at Dartmouth College in the USA in 1964. BASIC is available on a wide range of computer platforms and is one of the easiest languages in which to program. It is normally an interpretive language, with each statement being interpreted and executed as it is encountered. It can also be a compiled language, with all of the statements being compiled into machine code before execution. Early versions of BASIC were criticised for not encouraging structured programming. New versions of BASIC, i.e. Visual Basic, are very powerful indeed.

baud is a measure of telecommunications transmission speed, denoting the number of discrete signal elements that can be transmitted per second. Devised by the French telecommunications pioneer, J.M. Baudot, the baud rate is the standard way of representing information in telex and telegraph communications. It commonly refers to the changes in signal frequency per second and not bits per second unless at low baud rates (300) where it is equal to bits per second. At higher rates, the number of bits per second transmitted is higher than the baud rate, and one change in the electrical state of the circuit represents more than one bit of data. So 1200 bits per second can be sent at 600 baud.

bi-directional describes a device, usually a printer, that is capable of printing from right to left as well as from left to right. There are also bi-directional printer ports capable of sending and receiving data. Serial cables are bi-directional, as they are capable of transmitting and recieving information.

binary the language of all computers in which all numbers, letters and special characters are represented by ones and zeroes. It is called base two notation. *See* **ST**: BINARY NUMBERS.

bit is short for *bi*nary dig*it*, the smallest unit of information in a digital computer. It has a value of '0' or '1', which represents yes/no and either/or choices. A collection of eights bits is called a BYTE.

bitmap is the term given to a method of storing graphics information in memory in which a BIT is devoted to each pixel (picture element) on screen. A bitmap contains a bit for each point or dot on a video display, and can allow for fine resolution because each point on the display can be addressed. Unfortunately all bitmapped graphics require a great deal of memory, often in excess of one megabyte. A bitmapped font is a font for screen and/or printer in which every character is made up of a pattern of dots, and to allow display or printing a full record must be kept in the computer's memory. Again this leads to a memory-intensive process.

boot is the computer program routine designed to make the computer ready for use. To 'boot the system' or 'to initialise it' is to make it ready for normal use. In modern computers booting the system loads its operating system into memory, and prepares it to run application programs. Within the ROM of a computer is a program that is started when the power is switched on, and this tells the computer to search for the computer's operating system. This is called a *cold boot*. A *warm boot* is achieved either by pressing the reset button on newer IBM computers and compatibles or by pressing Ctrl/Alt/Del simultaneously. This is usually done to unlock the system.

buffer is an electronic memory storage device that is used for temporary storage of data passing in or out of the computer. A common use for a buffer is as a temporary holding area between a slow-moving device and a fast-moving device, e.g. between a computer and a printer. A buffer therefore allows different parts of the computer system to operate at optimum speeds.

bug is a hardware or software error. The term 'bug' was first coined in early computer days when a singed butterfly was found to have caused a malfunction in the MARK I computer. A programming error may be serious and can cause the computer to perform incorrectly or even to CRASH.

byte a combination of BITS used by the computer to represent an alphabetical character, a numerical digit or special character. A page of text will require slightly more bytes than there are characters to store it, to include spaces, control characters, etc. A large document will therefore need very many bytes, and a great many computers have millions of bytes (megabytes) of memory. Units that are used most often are the kilobyte and megabyte, representing 1000 and 1 million. These are however inaccurate because a kilobyte is actually 1,024 bytes and a megabyte 1,048,576 bytes.

CAD is the acronym for *C*omputer *A*ided *D*esign, a special software that can create and manipulate complicated and detailed graphics shapes in the same manner in which an architect or designer might do. The draughtsperson using CAD can change, edit, save and reprint drawings without having to redraw everything over again. Until quite recently CAD was within the realm of dedicated computer systems only, but the increased speed, memory and processing power of modern systems means that it can now be undertaken on more ordinary machines. It is used in many disciplines, including architecture, interior design and civil engineering.

capacity is the amount of text or data that may be stored in a computer or on magnetic media.

CD ROM (*C*ompact *D*isk *R*ead *O*nly *M*emory) is a system invented by Phillips in 1983. CD ROM can store much larger amounts of data than conventional storage. Although slower than hard disks, a CD ROM will store in excess of 600Mb of data. They are very useful for the storage of archival data. Video and sound can also be stored on a CD disk, making possible MULTIMEDIA applications.

central processing unit *see* CPU.

character a single letter, number, space, special character or symbol that can be made to appear on screen by using the keyboard.

character set the full set of numbers, punctuation marks, alphabetic characters and symbols that a particular computer system uses and that a printer is capable of producing.

chip a tiny chip or wafer of silicon (*see* **ST**: SILICON) that contains minute electronic circuitry and forms the core of a microprocessor or computer. After the initial discovery of semiconductors (*see* **ST**: SEMICONDUCTOR), technological advance was rapid. Early INTEGRATED CIRCUITS duplicated the functions of a number of electronic components, but now it is possible to create chips that contain unimaginable numbers of components – in fact, 16 million on one chip smaller than the tip of your finger. Chips can be mass-produced, and after their design, which is undertaken on an enlarged circuit diagram, the circuitry is transferred to plates called photomasks. Using a succession of photomasks, the chip is coated with materials that result in several layers of doped silicon, and it then forms the equivalent of a highly complex electronic circuit.

COBOL *CO*mmon *B*usiness *O*riented *L*anguage. One of the most commonly used computer programming languages for large mainframe business applications. It has never achieved the popularity of BASIC on smaller computers such as PCs. For large businesses, however, it became the choice for invoicing, salary records and stock control because its programs are easy to read and amend. Its function is to store, retrieve and process such data and was therefore useful in automating such processes.

command is an instruction or set of instructions that will start or stop an operation in a computer program, e.g. RUN, PRINT, EXIT.

compatibility is a characteristic of word or data-processing equipment that permits one machine to accept and process data prepared by another machine without conversion. It commonly refers to data, but also can refer to hardware such as printers, monitors, e.g. IBM-compatible. To be really compatible, it should be possible for a PROGRAM or PERIPHERAL to run on a system with no modification and with everything running as intended.

computer is an electronic data processing device, capable of accepting data, applying a prescribed set of instructions to the data, and displaying the result in some manner or form.

A computer system with
screen, processor box,
mouse and keyboard

configuration the machines that are interconnected and programmed to operate as a computer system. Typically, this includes a CPU with keyboard, VDU, printer and some form of DISK DRIVE. It also refers to the setting up of a computer system or program to ensure that it matches the needs of the user. Configuration has to be performed at the outset, and while modern applications software has automated the procedure to some extent there are certain elements that have to be done manually. Once established, the set-up is saved in a configuration file that should not be erased or altered.

console is the terminal that is used to control the computer system. It is applied as a descriptive term to a control device on large mainframe systems. The word 'console' is also used to describe the keyboard and display in personal computer systems.

CPU (central processing unit) is the core of a computer system, which contains the circuits needed to interpret and execute instructions and perform the basic computer functions. At one time it was used to describe the box that housed the electronics of the computer system. Its modern description is the INTEGRATED CIRCUIT that makes use of VLSI (Very Large Scale Integration – up to 100,000 transistors on one chip) to house the control transistors for the computer system.

crash the unplanned termination of an application in which the computer fails to respond or 'freezes'.

cursor is an indicator on the screen of a VDU, used by a computer to direct a user to the starting position, to enter data. It can be a small line, a square of light on the screen, or an arrow symbol, and can be controlled by use of the MOUSE or the arrow keys on the numeric pad on the right-hand end of the keyboard.

daisy wheel the print wheel for a *daisy wheel printer*, which produces 'letter quality' printing. It does this by rotating a print element resembling a wheel with spokes. Each spoke contains two characters of the alphabet. Daisy wheel printers were once the first choice but have now been overtaken by the technology of printing that has made inkjet, bubble-jet and laser printers more readily available.

data is jargon for information – groups of facts, concepts, symbols, numbers, letters or instructions that can be used to communicate.

database is a file of information (data) that is stored on a computer in a structured manner and used by a computer program such as a database management system (DBMS). Information is usually subdivided into particular data FIELDS, i.e. a space for a specific item of information.

DBMS (database management system) a software system for managing da-

tabase storage, access, updating and maintenance. Users can edit the database, save the data, and extract reports from the database using the DBMS.

data processing is the preparing and storing, handling or processing of data
through a computer.

dedicated line a communications cable line that is dedicated exclusively to
a particular communication function, e.g. a line may be dedicated in a
building to connect up a number of computers.

density is a measure of the amount of information (in BITS) that can be
stored on magnetic media such as a FLOPPY DISK. Single density allows for
a measured quantity, but there is also double density. Quad density or high
density uses very fine-grained magnetic particles, and although they are
more expensive to produce than double density, they can store one megabyte or more on a single disk.

desktop publishing *see* DTP.

dial-up the process of locating and retrieving information over telephone
lines.

dip switches a collection of small 'on' and 'off' switches used to select op-
tions on circuit boards without having to modify the hardware. They are
frequently found inside printers to control vertical spacing and other variable functions, and in computers and other electronic devices. Dip stands
for *dual in-line package* and it is the complete unit of plastic that contains
the circuit and leads for fitting into the device.

directory is the table of contents of a computer file system, which allows
convenient access to specific files. A directory is an area of disk that stores
files. It is common practice to store the files from one particular application in a directory so that they do not get mixed up with other files. Files
can then be recognised by their name. When a directory is called up on
screen it usually provides several items of information:

volume label	a name given when a disk is formatted.
file name	the title given to a file, consisting of up to 8 characters with a three character file extension that often identifies the software program in which the file was created.
file size	the size of a file is given in bytes.
date	the date when the file was last opened and modified.
time	the time when the file was last changed.
space free	the number of bytes of space left on the disk.

disk drive the piece of hardware and electronics that enables information to
be read from and written to a disk. The recording and erasing is performed

by the READ/WRITE HEAD. The circuitry controlling the drive is called the disk drive controller.

diskette an alternative name for a FLOPPY DISK.

DOS (disk operating system) the program responsible for communications between the computer and PERIPHERALS, such as the DISK DRIVE, PRINTER or the MONITOR. It controls and manages all the peripherals connected to the computer system. It therefore must be the first program to be loaded when the computer is switched on. The commonest operating system is MS-DOS (produced by Microsoft Corporation in the USA), which was introduced in 1981.

dot matrix the means of printing characters used in a dot matrix PRINTER. It is an impact technology, and as such is comparatively noisy when compared to the non-impact printers such as ink-jet or laser. A dot matrix image is created by a number of pins striking a ribbon and forming the image on the paper. Printers with just 9 pins produce poor quality output, and although there are versions with more pins, which give better quality, they come second to the newer technologies for effect. They are fast, however, and are still much used for large volume repetitive work.

double-sided disk a type of FLOPPY DISK with both surfaces available for storage of data.

down time is the time when computer equipment is not available for use because of hardware or software malfunction.

DTP (desktop publishing) is the software and hardware that make possible the composition of text and graphics as would normally have been done by a printer or in a newspaper office. Desktop publishing requires the use of a computer, laser printer, and various software programs to prepare and print documents. It is possible to produce anything from a single page of text to advertisements, pamphlets, books and magazines. Computer-aided publishing has been possible since the early 1970s for organisations willing to invest large sums of money, e.g. traditional printers or publishing houses. Desktop publishing as a function of personal computers (PCs) became possible on a broad scale only in 1985, with the introduction of the first relatively inexpensive laser printer producing 'letter quality' type and visuals.

A basic desktop publishing system allows its printer to produce print by employing a variety of fonts and type sizes, type justification, hyphenation, and other typesetting capabilities offered by DTP software programs. Page layouts, based on a template, can be set up on the computer monitor and transferred, as seen on the monitor, to the printer. Many types of graphics can be created, and the system may also incorporate art and photographs from sources inside the computer. The command codes for producing text and graphics are comparatively simple. Some computers use symbols and a pointer controlled by the mouse; others use word and letter commands. A basic DTP system includes a microcomputer, a laser printer that is able to print at 300 or more dots per inch (dpi), word processing software and a page description language; a software program that enables its user to position, size, and manipulate blocks of type and pictures.

In contrast to professionally printed matter, 300 dpi provides relatively low resolution. More complex laser printers or the use of an added phototypesetting unit produces finer quality print and illustrations. The addition of a computer-connected scanner allows the use of text and visual material from other sources.

dumb terminal is a computer terminal that has little or no memory or computing capability of its own and must rely on the computer for memory and processing.

dump is the process of transferring the contents of memory in one storage device to another storage device or item of hardware, e.g. it may be a dump from disk to printer, disk to tape or screen to printer. Dumps are often performed when programmers are debugging programs.

electronic mail (email) is a method of sending messages from one computer to another via the telephone line or via network cabling. Common on networked computer systems, electronic mail can also be used to send information from any suitable computer to any other suitably equipped computer anywhere in the world. The increasing use of electronic mail is seen to offer an alternative to the traditional methods of working in offices or administration centres. It is not necessary for the recipient to be there to receive a message and there are other advantages – email is effective in terms of time, distance is no object, and it is very flexible.

error message is a message displayed on a screen that indicates that the computer has detected an error or malfunction. *Error trapping* is the ability of a program to recognise and almost anticipate an error and then carry out a preset course of action in response to the error.

ESC (escape) is a non-printing character or keyboard control key that causes an interruption in the normal program sequence. Within a software program it is usually pressed to cancel a command or operation.

execution the process of carrying out the individual steps called for by the program in a computer.

fax (short for **facsimile**) a fax machine is a device capable of transmitting or receiving an exact copy of a page of printed or pictorial matter over telephone lines in, usually, less than 60 seconds. Facsimile transmission in some form has been available since the end of the 19th century but remained a relatively specialised communications device until the development of sophisticated scanning and digitising techniques in computer and communications technologies, and the establishment of standards that made it possible for all fax machines to communicate with one another over ordinary telephone lines.

Most contemporary fax machines conform to a set of standards, known as Group III, that were implemented in 1980 and require digital image scanning and data compression. Machines built to conform to Group III standards can transmit data at a maximum 9,600 bits per second (bps). To transmit, the original document is fed into the machine, where it is scanned by a mirror-and-lens-aided device, or, in some faxes, by a series of light-emitting diodes (LEDs). Light and dark picture elements – pixels, or pels – are described digitally, and the message is shortened by compressing much of the white space. The receiving machine, which is addressed through its telephone number, translates the code it receives back into a pattern of greys, blacks and white. The reconstituted message is printed out on heat-sensitive paper, using techniques similar to those for copying machines. Some fax machines can actually double as copiers, and modern machines use ordinary paper, which eliminates the use of heat-sensitive paper that browns over a period of time.

An example of a standard fax machine

field a defined group of characters or numbers, e.g. a customer number, a product description, a telephone number or address, within a specific space in a database program.

fixed disk a HARD DISK that cannot be removed from its housing or interchanged.

floppy disk is a removable, secondary medium of storage for computers. The disks are made of a plastic that is coated with a magnetic material (of which the main component is ferric oxide) and the whole thing is protected by a rigid plastic case ($3^1/_2$-inch disks) or plastic envelope ($5^1/_4$-inch disks). The disk rotates within its cover, and an access hole allows the READ/WRITE HEAD of the disk drive to record and retrieve information. There is a *write-protect notch* on the disk cover, which can be set so that the disk drive cannot change the disk, it can only read the data stored there. The $5^1/_4$-inch disks are more susceptible to damage than the $3^1/_2$-inch disks and have been virtually superseded. Floppy disks are an essential part of any computing system because they are the means of installing software, backing up files and transferring data between users if no others means exists. The storage capacity of a disk varies and depends on the size, the density of the magnetic particles coating the disk's surface and the drive used.

font a complete set of letters, numbers, special characters and punctuation marks of a particular size and for one identifiable typeface, whether roman or bold (the weight), italic or upright (the posture). The term is often used to refer to a family of fonts or typefaces, although this is technically incorrect. Fonts come as bitmapped (*see* BIT MAP) or OUTLINE fonts.

format is the preparation of hard or floppy disks for use by laying down clearly defined recording areas (*see also* INITIALISE). The format is the way in which the magnetic pattern is laid down on the disk. In particular programs, e.g. a spreadsheet, the format is the overall arrangement of labels and values in the separate cells of the spreadsheet. This may relate to the layout of decimal numbers or the alignment of entries within columns. A similar concept applies to database management and word processing programs. In the latter the format encompasses all aspects of the typeface, page layout (numbering, headers and footers) and paragraph styles.

function any single operation of a computer or word processor (e.g. editing). Also within certain programs, such as spreadsheets, a procedure that is stored in the program and that will perform a particular sequence of operations or calculations to produce an end result.

function keys are special purpose keys on the keyboard of a word processor or computer system that enable the user to perform a particular task or execute a command that might otherwise take several keystrokes.

graphical user interface (GUI) the part of the software program that communicates and interacts with the user by means of pull-down menus (*see* MENU), *dialog boxes* (a box on screen that presents information and offers choices to the user about a particular function or process) and ICONS. The GUI makes computers easier to use because people recognise and respond to graphic representations of concepts, etc, much more readily than if they have to read words. Microsoft WINDOWS utilises this system to great effect.

hard disk a fixed disk that forms a storage medium within the computer. It was developed in 1973 by IBM and initially called the Winchester disk, but early versions were very expensive. Today they are a standard component of just about every computer, and their mass production has reduced the price enormously. At the same time, the capacity has risen dramatically, from the early sizes of 10, 20 and 40 megabytes to several hundred megabytes and even one gigabyte (that is one billion or 1,073,741,824 bytes or 1000 megabytes).

The hard disk includes the storage medium and the read/write head and the electronics to connect it to the computer. There are several disks or platters, which revolve at 3600rpm, and the head floats just above the disk surface to eliminate wear. The large capacity of hard disks means that several software programs can be installed on one machine plus innumerable data files. However, hard disks may fail and it is important to back up data regularly.

hardware the physical equipment such as a computer's CPU, disk drive(s), VDU, magnetic tape unit and printer – in fact, anything that can be connected to the computer.

head crash the physical impact of a disk head on the disk, resulting in damage to its surface and a serious equipment malfunction that usually destroys data stored on the disk. It was relatively common on older systems, but modern high-tolerance engineering ensures that head crashes rarely occur.

icon is a symbol on screen that represents something or some process/function in the computer. Icons are used in a GRAPHICAL USER INTERFACE, and the image of an icon resembles the result of choosing that particular option or command. Programs resident within WINDOWS use icons for tasks such as opening files (small pictures of files), printing (a printer), discarding files (a dustbin), and so on. Icons can also represent software programs.

index hole is a hole punched in a floppy disk and detected electro-optically to indicate the beginning of the first sector.

information technology (IT) a jargon term used to describe all computer, telecommunications and related technology that is concerned with the handling or transfer of information. IT is a vast field incorporating the collection, handling, storage and sending/communication of information.

initialise to start up or set up the basic conditions. When disks or diskettes are initialised, they are formatted to accept data that will be stored later.

input the information to be entered into a computer system for subsequent processing. An input device is any peripheral that provides a means of getting data into the computer. It thus includes the keyboard, mouse, modem, scanner, etc.

input/output a general term for the equipment and system that are used to communicate with a computer, commonly called I/O. It ensures that program instructions and data readily go into and come out of the central processing unit.

integrated circuit (IC) a module of electronic circuitry that consists of transistors and other electronic components, usually contained on a rigid board. A variety of boards are plugged into a computer to enable it to perform its various tasks.

integrated software a group of software packages, each with a logical relationship to the other components. For example, a typical integrated package may include a word processor, a SPREADSHEET, a DATABASE, a graphics application and perhaps a communications application. The common link will be that all these applications will operate in a similar manner, and it will be possible to transfer data between them.

interface essentially a connection with associated electronic circuitry that permits two devices to be interconnected and to communicate.

Internet a worldwide system of linked computer NETWORKS. It links computers with different operating systems and storage techniques. There is no main source of information or commands as it was designed to operate even if one network was destroyed.

IT *see* INFORMATION TECHNOLOGY.

k abbreviation for *kilo* as in kilometres. It actually means 1000, but in the computer world it is used rather more loosely because 1 kilobyte is actually 1024 bytes. It is commonly used to refer to the relative size of a computer's main memory. 64K is equal to approximately 64,000 characters of information.

log on and **log off** the procedure by which a user begins or ends working at a computer terminal or system. In MS-DOS logging on means the process of activating a drive. In networks a password may be necessary to log on to the system.

machine language a binary language that all computers use. Machine code uses the lowest form of coding, binary, to instruct the machine to change the numbers in memory locations. All other computer languages must be *compiled* from their high-level code into machine code before the programs can be executed.

magnetic media any of a wide variety of disks or tapes coated or impregnated with magnetic material, on which information can be recorded and stored. The magnetic coating is repositioned when influenced by a magnetic field and the READ/WRITE HEAD emits a magnetic field when writing to the disk or tape that produces a positive or negative charge corresponding to that item of data. When reading, the head senses the charges and decodes them. Disks are used universally but for very high capacity storage, magnetic tape is ideal.

mailbox within the ELECTRONIC MAIL system, a disk file or memory area in which messages for a particular destination (or person) are placed. Modern bulletin-board communications systems use a mailbox metaphor to store messages for electronic mail users. The *bulletin board* system is a telecommunications utility that facilitates informal communication between computer users.

main memory *see* RAM.

mainframe refers to any large computer, such as an IBM or Cray. They do not use the same ARCHITECTURE as small desktop computers and are intended for use by many people, usually within a large organisation. To begin with the term referred to the large cabinet that held the central processing unit and then referred to the large computers developed in the 1960s that could accommodate hundreds of DUMB TERMINALS. Now there is a difference in the use of the word, and mainframe applies to a computing system that serves the needs of a whole organisation.

MBASIC Microsoft's original BASIC programming language, now superseded by QBASIC and Visual Basic.

megabyte one million BYTES (characters) of information. The common storage measurement for memory and hard disks, e.g. 4Mb of RAM, with a 210Mb hard disk drive.

memory the circuitry and devices that accept and hold binary numbers and are capable of storing data as well as programs. Memory must be installed in all modern computer systems. It is the computer's primary storage area, e.g. RAM (random access memory), as distinguished from the secondary storage of disks. Typical memory devices are SIMMS (*Single In-line Memory Modules*), which plug into the *motherboard* of the computer. SIMMS are plug-in modules that contain all the necessary chips to add more RAM to a computer. The motherboard is the large circuit board that contains the central processing unit, the RAM, expansion slots and other microprocessors.

menu a list of operator action selections displayed on a VDU. A user is presented with a menu that will give a choice of commands or applications. Menus make the computer system easier to use. A *pull-down menu* is a selection of commands that appears after a command on the menu bar of a program has been selected. A command or action is selected and often another menu will appear. The term originated with the idea started by Macintosh. *Menu-driven software* contains programs that proceed to the next step only when the user responds to a menu prompt.

microchip *see* MICROPROCESSOR.

microcomputer is traditionally the smallest size of computer, of desktop size. The modern use of the term includes any small computer system. In many ways the term has lost its relevance, and its meaning has been somewhat blurred by technological developments. Initially it referred to any computer that has certain key units on one integrated circuit, called the MICROPROCESSOR. The first personal computers, designed for single users, were called microcomputers because their CPUs were microprocessors. However the distinction between a micro and a MINICOMPUTER has all but disappeared, and many microcomputers are now more powerful than the mainframes of a few years ago.

microprocessor or **microchip** an electronic device (integrated circuit) that has been programmed to follow a set of logic driven rules. It is essentially the heart of any computer system.

microsecond one millionth of a second.

millisecond one thousandth of a second.

minicomputer a computer system usually smaller than a mainframe but larger than a microcomputer and designed for many users.

modem (*MO*dulator-*DEM*odulator) a device that will receive data from a computer, automatically translate it into codes that can be transmitted over normal telephone lines and then be reformatted by another modem on the receiving computer. The modem is an extremely important device, enabling communication and transfer of data all over the world. In order that modems facilitate communication between computers, both must conform to the same PROTOCOL.

module is a part of a program or set of programs capable of functioning on its own.

monitor *see* VDU.

mouse an input device that controls the on-screen CURSOR. Movement of the mouse on the desktop causes a similar movement of the cursor around the computer screen.

multimedia a system of presenting information as sound, text and graphics and based upon the computer. An essential component is interactivity and involvement of the user. Software systems provide encyclopedic collections of graphics, pictures and text and even moving images. Inevitably the memory requirements are huge, and a CD-ROM drive is a necessity.

network is the interconnection of a number of terminals or computer systems by data communication lines. It may consist of two or more computers that can communicate between each other. Networks for personal computers differ according to scope and size. *Local area networks* (LANs) usually connect just a few computers (although it may be more than 50), perhaps in order that they can share the use of an expensive peripheral. Large systems are called wide area networks (WANs) and use telephone lines or similar media to link computers together. In general, LANs cover distances of a few miles, and some of the largest versions are found in universities and large companies. Each user has a workstation capable of processing data, unlike the DUMB TERMINALS of a multi-user system.

non-impact printer a printer that produces textual output on plain or special paper without contact between the printing mechanism and the paper. Typical examples are inkjet, bubble-jet or laser printers. Most are capable of high quality print.

OCR (*O*ptical *C*haracter *R*ecognition) an information processing technology that can convert readable text into computer data. A SCANNER is used to import the image into the computer, and the OCR software converts the image into text. No one software package provides a foolproof conversion of text, but the more sophisticated ones have various means of highlighting queries and even recognising certain unclear characters once the user has responded to the first case. It is a useful tool for inputting large amounts of typewritten or already printed text for editing and changing.

off-line refers to equipment that is not under the direct control of the CPU. A printer may be in an off-line state when it is switched on but not capable of receiving data from the computer.

on-line refers to the operation of terminals and peripherals in direct communication with (and under the control of) the CPU of a computer, i.e. switched on and ready to receive data.

operating system (OS) a suite of computer programs (systems software) that control the overall operation of a computer. Operating systems perform the housekeeping tasks, such as controlling the input and output between a computer and peripherals, and accepting information from the keyboard or other input devices. Common operating systems are MS-DOS (*see* DOS), OS/2, UNIX, XENIX. OS/2 (*Operating System/2*) was developed ultimately by IBM, although initially it was a joint development with Microsoft. When Microsoft devoted its energies to the improvement of

WINDOWS, IBM took OS/2, and it has now gained more acceptance although it is nowhere near rivalling WINDOWS. UNIX is written in language C and was developed by AT&T Bell Laboratories in the 1970s. It can be used on computers from personal computers to mainframes, and it is suited to multi-user systems. XENIX was produced by Microsoft Corporation for use on IBM-compatible computers.

outline font is a font for printer and screen in which each character is generated from a mathematical formula. This produces a much smoother outline to a character than can be obtained from a bitmapped font (*see* BITMAP). The use of mathematical formulae means that characters can be changed in size quite easily, and only one font need reside in the computer memory.

output most computer output comes in the form of printed reports, letters and other printed data, or information sent to a mass storage device, such as a hard disk drive or a tape drive. But the most common output form is the image on the screen. *Output devices* are computer peripherals, such as a printer, a magnetic tape drive or floppy disk, that will acccept information from the computer.

parameter is a step in any program sequence that will cause the program to take a specific course of action. It is a value that is added to a command to ensure the task is undertaken in the desired manner. For example, to format the disk in drive A one would type FORMAT A: – the A: is the parameter of the FORMAT command.

Pascal a computer language originally designed for the teaching of structured programming. It is popular in colleges and schools and is used as a teaching language and in the development of applications. It is simlar to BASIC in that the computer is told what to do by statements in the program – it is a *procedural language*. It has some disadvantages in that it is too slow for large-scale development and commercial versions are changed sufficiently to make them individually isolated.

password a code, assigned to a program or set of files for security purposes, that allows the user to gain access to the file or program. It may have certain levels, allowing some users the facility of read-only while others may also write and copy files.

path the means of pointing to the exact location of a file on a computer disk. It uses a hierarchical structure of directories in which files are stored. It is the name given to the location of the file using the directory structure. A file called THISYEAR, for example, stored on the C drive in a directory called ACCOUNTS has the path C:\ACCOUNTS\THISYEAR.

PC *see* PERSONAL COMPUTER.

peripheral a generic term for equipment that is connected to the computer. These are external (to the CPU) and include such devices as external disk drives, printers, modems, CD-ROMS, scanners and VDUs.

personal computer (PC) a MICROCOMPUTER that can be programmed to perform a variety of tasks for home and office. They can be part of a large database or a small NETWORK. The boundary between the PC and formerly specific computing set-ups such as workstations and minicomputers is now very blurred. *Workstations* are powerful computers for use by designers, architects and engineers, and feature computer-aided design (CAD) software. PCs are now evolving to this level of sophistication, and similarly are in many instances performing the functions asked of a MINICOMPUTER.

port a plug or socket along which data may be passed into and out of the computer. Typically, each input and output device requires its own separate port. Most computers have a parallel and a serial port. The *parallel port* is a high-speed connection to printers while the *serial port* enables communication between the computer and serial printers, modems and other computers. In addition to receiving and transmitting data, the serial port also guards against data loss.

printer the device that produces hard copy. Printers vary enormously in quality of output, speed, fonts available, and so on. In addition to DAISY-WHEEL and DOT MATRIX printers, which are called *impact* printers and have distinct disadvantages in terms of flexibility and quality, there are the NON-IMPACT PRINTERS. Ink-jet printers create text and graphics by spraying ink onto the page, and there is always some risk of smudging the image. Although their resolution and quality does not approach that of laser printers, they do tend to be less expensive. Laser printers use a process similar to that of photocopiers, whereby ink powder is fused into the paper.

To begin with, the major disadvantage of laser printers was their high cost, but with the advent of reasonably priced machines the benefit of high quality print, quiet running and built-in fonts is more widely available. There are other types of printer available, e.g. thermal, but they do not form a significant part of the market.

A laser printer

processing is the normal operation of the computer acting upon the input data according to the instructions of the program in use.

program a set of instructions arranged for directing a digital computer to perform a desired operation or operations. Programmers use a variety of high-level programming languages, such as BASIC, C and Fortran, to create programs (*see* PROGRAM LANGUAGE). At some stage the program is converted to machine language so that the computer can carry out the instructions. Computer programs fall into one of three categories:

system programs	the programs required for the computer to function. They include the operating system (e.g. MS-DOS).
utility programs	the programs that help keep the computer system functioning properly, providing facilities for checking disks, etc.
application programs	the programs that most people use on their computers, such as word processing, database management, desktop publishing, graphics, and many more.

program language a language that is used by computer programmers to write computer routines, e.g. COBOL, BASIC, Fortran, PASCAL, C. The *high-level programming languages*, such as BASIC, C, Pascal, are so called because the programmer can use words and arrangements of words that resemble human language, and this leaves the programmer free to concentrate on the program without having to think of how the computer will actually carry out the instructions. The language's *compiler* or *interpreter* then turns the programmer's instructions into machine language that the computer can follow.

protocol the conventions or rules that govern how and when messages are exchanged in a communications network or between two or more devices. There are many different protocols, but communicating devices must use the same protocols in order to exchange data.

QWERTY keyboard the standard typewriter/computer keyboard, denoted by the letters on the top line of characters. It was originally developed to slow down typists to stop the manual typewriters jamming the keys. There are now alternatives to QWERTY keyboards that enable faster use and easier learning. One such system is the *Dvorak keyboard*, which places the most frequently used letters together.

RAM (*R*andom *A*ccess *M*emory) also known as main or internal memory, it refers to the memory that can be, and is, altered in normal computer operations. The RAM stores program instructions and data to make them available to the central processing unit and the CPU can write and read data. Application programs use a part of the RAM as a temporary place of storage allowing modification of the file in use until it is ready for storage permanently on disk. Any work in the RAM that has not been saved will be lost if the power fails.

random access the retrieval of information randomly from any part of the computer memory or from magnetic media, which means that the computer can reach the information straight away.

read to retrieve information stored on magnetic media and transfer it to the memory of the computer.

read/write head the part of a disk drive that actually reads data from, and writes data onto, a disk by travelling backwards and forwards over the surface of the disk.

robot an electromechanical device that may perform programmed tasks and is commonly used in automated factories to perform repetitive functions. The first industrial robots were developed in the early 1960s although they consisted of little more than an automated hand. Japan subsequently invested heavily in robots, and other countries have now followed suit.

ROM (*Read Only Memory*) The part of a computer's internal memory that can be read but not altered. It contains the essential programs (system programs) that neither the computer nor user can alter or erase. The instructions that enable the computer to start up come from the ROM, although the tendency now is to put more of the operating system on ROM chips rather than putting it on disk.

run is to execute a program.

scanner a piece of hardware that copies an image or page into a computer by creating a digital image. A scanner works by bouncing a beam of light off the paper and recording the reflected light as a series of dots similar to the original image. If the dots are created as a variation of 16 grey values, the scanner is using a *tagged image file format* (TIFF), otherwise a *dithered* image is created. A dithered image is a simulation of a *halftone* image, composed of shading created by the size and density of dots (e.g. light areas will be made up of small dots spaced apart). Digital halftones become distorted when they are sized. Scanners are available in three basic types: a flatbed scanner, a hand-held scanner and a drum scanner. A flatbed scanner is used to transport text and graphics from paper into a digitised form. A hand-held scanner performs the same function but can be held by the hand. A drum scanner is used to create colour separation film.

An example of a flatbed scanner

secondary storage *see* AUXILIARY STORAGE.

sector a pie-shaped division of the magnetic surface on a disk that separates information into individual sections or zones. Data can be stored in these sectors and read by the disk drive. A unit of storage of one or more sectors is called a *cluster*.

software the series of programs that are loaded into the computer's internal memory and tell the computer what particular function to perform (*see also* PROGRAM).

speech recognition an information processing technology in which the spoken word is converted into signals that can be recognised by speech recognition software and converted into commands for the computer to follow.

spreadsheet a program that creates an on-screen worksheet which is a series of rows and columns of blocks (or *cells*), into which values, text and formulae can be placed. The spreadsheet is recalculated whenever a change to a cell's value of formula is made.

stand-alone the term applied to a computer system that is self-contained with only the hardware and software required by the user.

syntax the set of rules that govern the way in which a command or statement is given to the computer so that it recognises the command and proceeds accordingly.

system is all the necessary hardware and software required in an installation, all of which is interconnected and set up to work together (CPU, disk drives, monitor, printer, keyboard, and so on).

track one of a number of concentric circles on a floppy or hard disk. The track is encoded on the disk during formatting and is a particular area on the disk for data storage. *Tracks per inch* (tpi) is a measure of the density of data storage on floppy disks, higher figures representing a greater capacity for data.

UNIX *see* OPERATING SYSTEM.

user-friendly jargon term for a system that is easy to learn and operate. A user-friendly program often involves the use of menus rather than commands that have to be remembered; help that is available on-screen at the touch of a key; error messages with some explanation of the fault and solution; prompts when performing potentially damaging procedures, e.g. questions such as 'Do you really want to ...' when deleting a file. Applications software also comes with numerous manuals including, one presenting the basics of a program in a way that is easily understood.

VDU (*Visual Display Unit*) or **monitor** or **video display terminal** this resembles a television screen and produces a visual picture of computer input or output. There is some concern that the electromagnetic radiation (*see* ST ELECTROMAGNETIC WAVES) given out by monitors may be hazardous. Monitors emit X-rays, ultraviolet radiation, electrostatic discharge and electromagnetic fields, but it is not proven that these emissions are dangerous to users. However, some studies have indicated that at a distance of 18 inches the radiation from monitors is less than that of the background and this, and the use of low radiation monitors, is being included in regulations for workers using computers.

volatile storage storage of which the contents are lost when power is removed, e.g. the RAM.

Windows (Microsoft Windows) is a comprehensive software facility that utilises the GRAPHICAL USER INTERFACE features that were once the domain of the Macintosh. These include pull-down menus (*see* MENU), a variety of accessories, and the powerful facility of moving text and graphics from one program to another via the clipboard (an area for temporarily storing items that have been copied from one area and that are to be pasted elsewhere). It is possible to run several programs at once, each within a separate window, and to move from one to the other very quickly. All applications that run within the Windows system have a common way of working with windows, dialog boxes, etc.

word processing a method of document preparation, storage and editing, using a microcomputer/personal computer. Word processing is the most widespread computing application (*see* APPLICATION PROGRAM), primarily because of the ease with which documents can be amended before printing.

workstation *see* PERSONAL COMPUTER.

Sport

This section of the *Pocket Encyclopedia* gives an explanation of the origins and development of the most popular international sports, along with a brief account of the major sporting events and competitions. The cross-references, given in SMALL CAPITALS, will enable you to relate each of these events to the relevant sport.

Admiral's Cup *see* YACHTING.

American football has its origins in the undisciplined ball games introduced by the early colonists to America. The basic rules of the modern game were established by college teams, and the first professional game was played in Latrobe, Pennsylvania, on 31 August 1895. Today it is America's most popular spectator sport.

The most important game of the American football season is the *Super Bowl*, contested by the winners of the two divisional leagues, the NFC (NPL before 1970) and the APC (APL). Inaugurated in 1966-7, it is now America's greatest sporting event.

America's Cup *see* YACHTING.

archery is an ancient skill that was first established as a competitive sport in the mid-19th century. The first national meeting was held in York in 1844, and the Grand National Archery Society, which still governs the sport, was founded in 1861.

The sport was included in the OLYMPIC GAMES from 1900 to 1908 and again in 1920, and was reintroduced in 1972 with team events added in 1988. The *World Championship* takes place every two years and is contested on a knockout basis.

association football has its origins in ancient ball games played in various parts of the world, but much of the game's development came in England. Three British monarchs banned the sport at various times for its disruptive influence until it began to be organised in the 19th century. The first attempts at framing a set of rules for football were made in the mid-19th century by a group of representatives of the English public schools and universities. Out of their meetings the Football Association (FA) was founded in 1863, and the 11 players per side game became standard soon afterwards.

Association football pitch

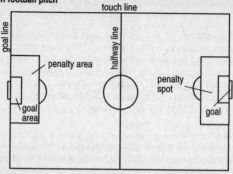

The international governing body, the Fédération Internationale de Football Association (FIFA), was founded in Paris in 1904. By 1992 it had over 180 members. International games have been played since 1872 when amateur teams representing Scotland and England first met for a friendly match in Glasgow. The first international championship was contested by the four home nations and lasted from 1883 to 1984.

The first *World Cup* for the Jules Rimet Trophy was contested by 13 nations in Uruguay in 1930, and has since been held every four years (except 1942 and 1946). In 1934 a qualifying tournament was introduced. Brazil kept the original trophy after their third victory in 1970, and teams now compete for the FIFA World Cup. Host nations qualify automatically for the final stages of the tournament.

The *European Championship*, originally called the European Nations Cup, took its present name in 1968. Held every four years, the championship is contested over a two year period. The teams compete for the Henri Delaunay Cup, named after the former General Secretary of UEFA.

The *European Champion Clubs' Cup* is popularly known as the European Cup. It is an annual knockout competition first held in 1955/6 for the best league champions of all UEFA affiliated countries. Since 1991/2 a Champions' League has been included, together with a number of qualifying stages, and the structure of the competition is now more flexible.

The *European Cup-Winners Cup* is open to winners of domestic senior cup competitions in UEFA-affiliated countries. Originally the final play-off was decided over two games, but this changed in 1963, and it is now one game.

The *UEFA Cup* is competed for over two legs on a home and away basis. Originally called the International Industries Fairs Inter-Cities Cup, or Fairs Cup, it was established in 1955, and the first competition took three years to complete. It became the UEFA Cup in 1971.

The *English Football League* was established in 1888/9 by twelve clubs from the Midlands and North of England. By 1958 there were four divisions and 92 clubs, and this set-up was retained until 1993 when the top 22 clubs formed the FA Premier League and the three divisions of the Football League succeeded the original Divisions 2 to 4.

The *English FA Cup* competition was established as the Football Association Challenge Cup with 15 teams from across Britain entering first competition. It is contested annually on a knockout basis and since 1923 the final has been played at Wembley Stadium.

The *English League Cup* was first contested in 1960, it was not until 1970 that all 92 league teams competed. It was first sponsored in 1982 by the Milk Marketing Board and is now known as the *Coca-Cola Cup*.

The *Scottish Football League* was founded in 1890, two years after the English Football League. It was restructured in 1975/6 when the Premier Division, with the top ten clubs, was established with the remaining clubs divided into Divisions 1 and 2. A further restructuring in 1994 introduced a four-league system with ten teams in each.

The *Scottish FA Cup* was initiated at a meeting of eight clubs hosted by Queen's Park in 1873, in order to establish a competition in Scotland similar to the English FA Cup.

athletics are thought to have originated in the ancient Greek OLYMPIC GAMES around 1370 BC. Organised events in England began in the mid-19th century, with the first regular competition taking place at Exeter College, Oxford, in 1850.

The most important competitions in international athletics are the Olympic Games and the *World Championships*. There are also a number of events, such as the IAAF (International Amateur Athletic Federation) World Cup, the European Cup and the World Indoor Championships.

The first *World Championships* for athletics alone were held in 1983 in Helsinki, Finland. They are now held biennially.

British Open *see* GOLF.

badminton originated either from Badminton Hall in Gloucestershire, *c.*1870, where it was played by the family and guests of the Duke of

Beaufort, or from a game played in India around the same time. The modern rules of the sport were established in India, however, where it was very popular for a time among British Army officers. The Badminton Association was founded in England in 1893 and the International Badminton Federation in 1934.

The most important competitions are the Thomas Cup (men), the Uber Cup (women) and the *World Championships*, all of which are held biennially. In recent years teams from Indonesia, China and Japan have dominated international competition.

baseball according to American folklore the game was invented by a West Point cadet, Abner Doubleday, in 1839. A game of the same name, however, is known to have been played in England prior to 1700, and it is more likely that baseball evolved from such popular bat and ball games as cricket and rounders.

The first rules of the modern game were established in 1845 by Alexander Cartwright Jr, and the professional game developed almost entirely in North America where there are two 'major' leagues, the American (AL) and the National (NL), founded in 1901 and 1876 respectively.

The *World Series* is a best-of-seven contest held annually between the winners of the two professional baseball leagues. It was first played in 1903 and is now one of America's most popular sporting events. In 1992 the Toronto Blue Jays became the first non-American team to win the series when they defeated the Atlanta Braves.

At international level South American teams dominate. The most successful country is Cuba, which has won the World Amateur Championships 20 times since it was established in 1938. Baseball has also been a demonstration sport at six OLYMPIC GAMES and became a medal sport for the first time in 1992.

basketball in its present form was invented in 1891 by Dr James Naismith, a sports instructor from Springfield, Massachussets, although games bearing a strong resemblance to basketball have been played for thousands of years. Early games in America featured large numbers of players but the 5-a-side standard was agreed in 1895 and the first league established three years later.

In the USA there are now 23 professional basketball teams, and it is one of America's most popular spectator sports, with televised games attracting large audiences.

The *NBA Championship* is contested annually by the 23 professional basketball teams in the USA. The teams are divided into two conferences,

Eastern and Western, which are subdivided into the Western and Atlantic Divisions and the Midwest and Pacific Divisions respectively. A series of play-offs decide the champions.

At amateur level it is popular around the world and has been included in the OLYMPIC GAMES since 1936 (the women's game was included in 1976). *World Championships*, first held in 1950 (men) and 1953 (women), are staged every four years and have been dominated in recent years by teams from the USA and the former Yugoslavia.

biathlon is one of the most physically demanding combination sports. Competitors ski over a prepared course carrying a small-bore rifle and stop for either two or four shooting competitions, standing and prone. Men compete over 10km and 20km, and women over 7.5km and 15km. There is also a relay event, which is 4 x 7.5km with every member shooting once.

Men's biathlon has been included in the OLYMPIC GAMES since 1960 and the women's event since 1992. There is also a World Cup and a World Championship, both contested annually.

billiards is believed to have evolved from the game of *paillemalle*, played on grass. It was popular in the 15th century, and Louis XI, king of France (1461–83), is known to have had a table. Today there are world professional and amateur championships, played annually and biennially respectively.

bobsleigh and *toboggan* racing was pioneered by a group of Swiss enthusiasts who organised the first known bobsleigh races in the 1880s. The first two luge runs were built in 1879 at Davos in Switzerland.

There are now bobsleigh events in the OLYMPIC GAMES for two and four man teams and for single man luge toboggans.

bowls the rules of the modern game were framed in 1848–9 by a Scottish solicitor, William Mitchell, although similar games were played as early as the 13th century. There are now two types of greens, the 'crown' and the 'level', the former is almost exclusive to the north of England, while the latter played mostly in the UK and Commonwealth countries.

The *World Outdoor Championships* were established in 1966 for men and 1969 for women. They are held every four years, with singles, pairs, triples and fours events. The Leonard Trophy is presented to the overall best men's team.

boxing is one of man's oldest physical contests. The first organised boxing match is thought to have taken place in the late-17th century when the Duke of Albemarle organised a fight between his butler and his butcher. The modern rules, which introduced gloves, were set out in 1867 by the 8th Marquis of Queensbury (who gave his name to them). The first world championship fight took place in New York in 1884 with Jack Dempsey beating George Fulljames in New York for the middleweight title.

In boxing today there are four different governing authorities, all with their own weight classes, titles and fight regulations. This naturally leads to confusion, especially as all four governing bodies recognise world champions. The four are: the World Boxing Association (founded 1960), the World Boxing Council (1963), the World Boxing Organisation (1988) and the International Boxing Federation (1983).

The weight categories accepted by the WBC ar as follows:

Weight	Limit	Also known as
Heavy	>190 lbs.	
Cruiser	190 lbs.	Junior Heavy (WBO)
Light Heavy	175 lbs.	
Super Middle	168 lbs.	
Middle	160 lbs.	
Super Welter	154 lbs.	Junior Middle (WBO, IBF, WBA)
Welter	147 lbs.	
Super Light	140 lbs.	Junior Welter (WBO, IBF, WBA)
Light	135 lbs.	
Super Feather	130 lbs.	Junior Light (WBO, IBF, WBA)
Feather	126 lbs.	
Super Bantam	122 lbs.	Junior Feather (WBO, IBF, WBA)
Bantam	118 lbs.	
Super Fly	115 lbs.	Junior Bantam (WBO, IBF, WBA)
Flyweight	112 lbs.	
Light Fly	108 lbs.	Junior Fly (WBO, IBF, WBA)
Straw	105 lbs.	Mini Fly (WBO, IBF, WBA)

Calcutta Cup *see* RUGBY UNION.

canoeing as a sport can be attributed to an English barrister, John MacGregor, founder of the Royal Canoe Club in 1866. In the sport today there is flat and wild water competition featuring kayaks (double blade) and Canadian canoe (single blade). It has been included in the OLYMPIC GAMES, with several different categories, since 1936.

Commonwealth Games are held every four years and are contested by representatives of the British Commonwealth. The original idea for the games was suggested by the Rev. J Astley Cooper in the magazine *Greater Brit-*

ain in 1891. The first British Empire Games were held in 1930 in Canada, and four sports were contested by representatives from Great Britain, Canada, Australia and New Zealand.

Known as the Commonwealth Games since 1970, recent Games have included ten sports. Athletics and swimming are obligatory, and the other eight are selected from 15 recognised sports, with two demonstration sports also chosen.

County Championship *see* CRICKET.

cricket the precise origins of cricket are unclear although games with a bat and ball were played as long ago as the 13th century. The first match in which scores were kept was contested in 1744 by England and Kent. The Marylebone Cricket Club (MCC), founded in 1787, remained the governing body for the sport until the formation of the Cricket Council in 1968.

The Imperial (International from 1965) Cricket Conference (ICC) was formed in 1909 and now has nine Test-playing members, 19 associate members and five affiliated members. The nine full, test-playing members are England, Australia, West Indies, India, Pakistan, New Zealand, Sri Lanka, South Africa (ceased to be a member in 1961, readmitted in 1992) and Zimbabwe (from 1992).

The first Test match was played in Melbourne in 1877 between Australia and England, and the first in England was played by the same nations three years later, although in both these contests neither side was truly representative of its country.

Cricket fielding positions

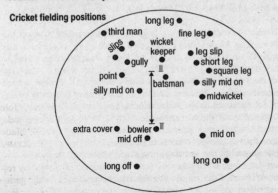

English *County Championship* cricket began with the first recorded match between counties, contested by Kent and Surrey, in 1709. The first county to be declared county champion was Surrey in 1827. From 1827 to 1889 the champions were decided on the basis of fewest matches lost, and Kent, Surrey and Sussex dominated. Since 1890 the championship has been contested on a points system.

cross-country running was first staged with an international field in 1903 at Hamilton Park Racecourse in Scotland. The World Cross-Country Championships are now held annually with the senior events being run over 5km and 12km courses for women and men respectively.

cycling the first treadle-propelled bicycle was invented by Scottish blacksmith, Kirkpatrick Macmillan, in 1839, but it was not until the more refined *velocipede* was built by Pierre Michaux of Paris, in 1861, that there was any popular interest in bicycle racing. The first club was the Liverpool Velocipede Club, which was formed in 1867, and the first race (over 1200 metres) took place in Paris a year later.

It has been included in the OLYMPIC GAMES since 1896, and there are currently nine events in the programme, including sprint, pursuit, time trials, and individual and team road-racing events.

The *Tour De France* is the most famous cycle race in the world. First held in 1903, it is now one of the world's most popular spectator events. The course changes every year but always includes a number of mountain stages as well as time trials. It is held over a three week period. The longest race has been over 5745 km (3569 miles).

Davis Cup *see* TENNIS.

Diving as a competitive event, diving began in Britain in 1893 when the Amateur Swimming Association established a 'plunging' contest. It was included in the Olympic Games in 1904, although women divers were not allowed to compete until 1912. There are three events; the 1m springboard; the 3m springboard and the 10m platform. Divers are judged only on their execution of the dive, although the degree of difficulty of the dive is taken into account in the value allocated to it.

English FA Cup *see* ASSOCIATION FOOTBALL.

English Football League *see* ASSOCIATION FOOTBALL.

English League Cup *see* ASSOCIATION FOOTBALL.

European Championship *see* ARCHERY, ATHLETICS, BADMINTON, BOWLS.

European Cup *see* ASSOCIATION FOOTBALL.

European Cup-Winners Cup *see* ASSOCIATION FOOTBALL.

European Super Cup *see* ASSOCIATION FOOTBALL.

equestrianism although horse-riding is many thousands of years old, competition jumping became popular only in the late 19th century with the first 'horse show' held in Dublin in 1867. Dressage competition evolved from French and Italian horsemanship academies in the 16th century, while the three-day event has its origins in cavalry endurance tests.

Equestrian events have been included in the OLYMPIC GAMES since 1912, but the first competition to combine all six equestrian disciplines – show jumping, three-day eventing, dressage, carriage driving, endurance riding, and vaulting – was the *World Equestrian Games*, first held in Stockholm in 1990. The second Games were held at the Hague in 1994.

fencing has its origins in the duelling of the Middle Ages, although fighting with swords had been practised as a sport in older civilisations.

There are three types of sword used today: the *foil*, the *epée* and the *sabre*. Each is a separate discipline with a different set of rules applicable to it in competition:

weapon	weight	target
epée	770 grams	whole body
foil	500 grams (maximum)	upper body
sabre	500 grams	upper body and head

Fencing has been included in all OLYMPIC GAMES, and these tournaments count as World Championships in Olympic years. Women first competed in the 1924 Games.

football *see* AMERICAN FOOTBALL; ASSOCIATION FOOTBALL.

golf although the precise origins are unclear, it was in Scotland that the popular pastime was first properly organised and the first club established. The earliest rules of the game were drawn up in 1754 by enthusiasts in St Andrews, who went on to form the Royal and Ancient Golf Club there. In 1764 18 holes was declared as the standard round, but it was not until 1919 that the Royal and Ancient, who had decided the number, was formally recognised as the supreme authority in golfing matters.

In professional golf the most important, and financially rewarding, competitions are the British Open, the US Open, the US Masters and the US PGA. These are played annually at different courses except the US Masters, which is always played at the Augusta National course in Georgia.

Although not offering the same high levels of prize money, there is also a well-established masters' series in women's golf. These are the US Women's Open, the LPGA Championships, the Nabisco Dinah Shore and the Du Maurier Classic.

The *British Open* was first played over three 12-hole rounds at Prestwick, Scotland, in 1860. Prestwick hosted the first 12 Opens, and all subsequent championships have been played over various seaside links courses around Britain. Prize money (totalling £10) was introduced in 1863.

The *Ryder Cup* was launched in 1927, following a successful match between the USA and Great Britain. It is now held biennially with the teams taking it in turn to play host. The Great Britain team was succeeded by a Great Britain and Ireland team in 1973, which in turn was succeeded by a European team in 1979.

Grand National *see* HORSE RACING.

Grand Prix *see* MOTOR RACING.

Grand Slam *see* RUGBY UNION.

gymnastics although the origins of gymnastics can be traced back to the ancient civilisations of Greece, Persia, China and India, as a modern competitive sport it has been developed primarily in Eastern European countries. The first national federation was formed in Germany in 1860, and gymnastics were included in the first modern OLYMPIC GAMES in 1896, although women's events were not introduced until 1928.

The apparatus used in modern gymnastics differs for men and women. Men use the parallel bars, horizontal bar, pommel horse, rings, and horse vault. Women use asymmetrical bars, the beam, and the horse vault. Both men and women also perform floor exercises.

The *World Championships* were established in 1903 for men and 1934 for women. Both are now held biennially.

Modern rhythmic gymnastics for women use ropes, hoops, ribbons and balls in musically accompanied floor exercises, and have been included in the OLYMPIC GAMES since 1984.

handball is similar to football, only played with the hands rather than the feet. It was first played at the end of the 19th century in Germany, and it has remained popular in that country.

At the 1936 OLYMPIC GAMES it was played by 11-a-side teams outdoors, but when it was reintroduced in 1972 it was as a 7-a-side indoor event. World Championships take place every four years, and a European Cup for national champions is contested annually.

hang gliding as a modern sport was pioneered by Otto Lilienthal in Germany in the late 19th century. The distances travelled and the duration of flights have increased dramatically in recent years with developments in technology and design. The first *World Championships* in 1975 were unofficial; in 1976 they became official and are now held biennially.

hockey was played in primitive form in ancient civilisations, and tomb drawings in the Nile Valley suggest it could be as much as 4000 years old. The modern game became popular in the mid 19th century when many public schools took up the sport.

The most successful teams at international level have traditionally been from India and Pakistan, although recently European teams have dominated the major competitions. The IHF World Cup and the Champion's Trophy are the premier competitions, and the sport has been included in the OLYMPIC GAMES since 1908.

horse racing has its origins in warfare, hunting and chariot racing with the earliest reference to prize money being the purse of gold offered by Richard I in 1195. The oldest known racecourse in Britain is on the Roodee at Chester, which staged its first meeting in 1540. The Jockey Club was formed in 1750, and the first steeplechase was run in 1752 in Cork, Ireland.

There are two kinds of modern racing, flat racing and jumping, with the latter divided into steeplechasing and hurdle racing. The most important flat racing events in Britain are the five English Classics: the Derby, the Oaks, the St Leger and the 1000 and 2000 Guineas. Other famous races held annually include the series of Irish and French Classics, the Coronation Cup at Epsom and the Ascot Gold Cup at Royal Ascot.

In National Hunt Racing, the *Grand National* and the *Cheltenham Gold Cup* are the two most important events in the British calendar. The Grand National is the oldest and most famous steeplechase in the world. It has been run at Aintree, Liverpool, every year since 1847 with the exception of the war years. The current course takes in 30 fences over two circuits, and is four miles and four furlongs long. The only horse to have ever won the Grand National three times is Red Rum (1973, 1974, 1977).

hurling is one of Ireland's oldest competitive sports but standardised only since the foundation of the Gaelic Athletic Association in 1884. The hurl, or stick, is similar to the hockey stick only flat on both sides. The All-Ireland Championship has been held annually since 1887.

ice hockey was developed in Canada in the late 19th century with the first club founded in Montreal in 1880. World Championships have been held annually since 1930 with teams from North America, Scandanavia and Eastern Europe dominating in recent years. It has been included in the Olympic Games, since 1920.

ice skating is over 2000 years old and first became popular in the Netherlands, although the first known skating club was formed in Edinburgh in the mid-18th century. The first artificial ice rink was opened in London in 1876.

The modern sport can be divided into two: figure skating and speed skating. The *World Championships* are contested in both disciplines. Figure skating has been included in the OLYMPIC GAMES since 1908, and speed skating was introduced into the 1924 Games (1960 for the women's event).

International Championships *see* RUGBY UNION.

judo was developed from several different schools of Japanese martial arts. The first training school was founded in Shitaya in 1882 by Dr Jigoro Kano. 'Ju' means 'soft', and the sport relies on speed and skill as opposed to brute force. Classes in judo are divided into *kyu* (pupil) and *dan* (master) grades, differentiated by different coloured belts.

Kyu grades – 1st brown, 2nd blue, 3rd green, 4th orange, 5th yellow.

Dan grades – 1st–5th black, 6th–8th red and white, 9th–11th red, 12th white.

It has been included for men in the OLYMPIC GAMES since 1964 (except 1968) and for women since 1992. There are currently twelve weight divisions.

lacrosse was originally played by North American Indians and was taken up by French settlers, who called it *baggataway*. The modern crosse, or playing stick, evolved from the early implement used by the Indians, which was a curved stick with a net fitted at one end. The women's game evolved separately from that played by men, and they both now have *World Championships*.

lawn tennis *see* TENNIS.

modern pentathlon, as it was introduced at the 1912 OLYMPIC GAMES, consists of horse riding, fencing, shooting, swimming and cross-country running.

For many years the sport was dominated by members of the military forces, and military lore explains the origins of the modern format thus: a messenger has to ride on horseback, fight with sword and pistol, swim a river and run on foot to complete his journey. The format of the sport has been amended by the Olympic Committee and instead of being competed for over three or more days it is staged over one day.

motor cycling the earliest motorcycle race was held in 1897 at Sheen House in Richmond over an oval course of one mile. The *World Championship* races began in 1949 with classes for 50cc, 125cc, 250cc, 350cc, 500cc bikes and sidecars. In road-racing the most important series is the Isle of Man TT races, first held in 1907. Motocross, or *scrambling*, is a specialised branch of racing with competitors negotiating undulating dirt tracks on specially adapted machines. A *World Championship* is held annually.

motor racing was inevitable with the invention, and rapid growth in popularity, of the motor car. The first known race took place in Paris in 1887 and was won by Count Jules Felix Philippe Albert de Dion de Malfiance, riding a steam quadricycle.

The most important class of racing, that of Formula One, held its first *World Championship* in 1950, although the first Grand Prix was run in France in 1906. Other notable competitions are the Le Mans circuit (for touring cars), the Indy Car World Series (16 races in North America and Australia), and the many long-distance 'rally' events held around the world.

The *World Championship Grand Prix* was inaugurated in 1949. The first Grand Prix was held at Silverstone, England, and won by the Italian Giuseppe Farina. Grand Prix races are now staged all over the world, and points are awarded for finishing places, which count towards the World Championship.

NBA Championship *see* BASKETBALL.

netball is a 7-a-side game played primarily by women. It was developed in the USA at the end of the 19th century. A *World Championship* has been held every four years since 1963. In recent years these have been dominated by teams from Australia and New Zealand.

Olympic Games were first staged every four years at Olympia, 120 miles west of Athens in Greece, with the earliest recorded games being held in 776 BC. The games grew in size and importance and reached the peak of their fame in the 5th and 4th centuries BC, when events included running, jumping, boxing, wrestling, discus and chariot racing.

The final games of the ancient era were held in AD 393, before the emperor of Rome, Theodosius I, decreed their prohibition because they were disapproved of by the early Christians.

The first modern Games were instigated by a Frenchman, Pierre de Fredi, Baron de Coubertin. His efforts to bring back the principle of the ancient Games and re-establish the high sporting standards of the early Greeks led to the formation of the International Olympic Committee in 1895 and thence to the staging of the 1896 Games in Athens.

rowing the earliest established sculling race, the *Dogget's Coat and Badge*, was instituted in 1715 by the Irish humorist Thomas Dogget and was rowed from London Bridge to Chelsea. The first regatta was held on the Thames at Putney in 1775.

Rowing has been a part of the OLYMPIC GAMES since 1900, and *World Championships* have been held every year since 1962.

The famous University Boat Race, contested annually between teams from Oxford and Cambridge universities, was first held on the River Thames in 1829. The Putney to Mortlake course, over a distance of 6779 metres (4 miles 374 yards), which is currently used, has not changed since 1863. At present Cambridge leads as the winning team. The only dead heat in the history of the race was recorded in 1877.

rugby league originated as a breakaway from RUGBY UNION in 1895 when the governing body refused to let northern clubs pay players who were losing their Saturday wage in order to play. Today it is most popular in the north of England, Australia, New Zealand and France. The most important tournaments in England are for the Premiership Trophy and the Challenge Cup. Both are contested annually.

A rugby league *World Cup* was played every three years from 1954 to 1975, when the tournament was renamed the International Championship. The World Cup was revived in 1985.

rugby union is thought to have originated at Rugby School, England, as the modern game can supposedly be traced back to the moment when one William Webb Ellis picked up the ball and ran with it during a school football match in November 1823. The first club was formed at Guy's Hospital in London in 1843 and the Rugby Football Union (RFU) was established in 1871. The Fédération Internationale de Rugby Amateur (FIRA) was founded in 1934. Membership reached 49 nations in 1992. The international Rugby Football Board (IRFB) was founded in 1886. The members are: Wales, England, Scotland, Ireland, France, New Zealand, Australia and South Africa.

At international level the annual *International Championship* and the recently established *World Cup* are the most important events. The first Rugby Union World Cup tournament was played in Australia and New Zealand in 1987 by 16 national teams and won by New Zealand. The second was played in Britain and France in 1991 and won by Australia. The third World Cup was held in South Africa in 1995 and won by the host nation.

Since 1888, a home nations select team, the British Lions, has toured Australia, New Zealand.

The *International Championship* was first contested by the home nations in 1884, with France joining to make it the 'Five Nations' tournament in 1910. Each team plays each other once during the season.

The *Grand Slam* is the beating of all four other nations in one season's games, and the *Triple Crown* is awarded to the home nation team that beats the other three. The *Calcutta Cup* is played for by England and Scotland.

Ryder Cup *see* GOLF.

Scottish FA Cup *see* ASSOCIATION FOOTBALL.

Scottish Football League *see* ASSOCIATION FOOTBALL.

shooting the first shooting club, the Lucerne Shooting Guild was formed around 1466 and the first recorded match held in Zurich in 1472. It has been a feature of the OLYMPIC GAMES since the first modern games in 1896.

skiing the home of the sport is undoubtedly Scandinavia, where the first competitive slalom was held in Murren in 1922.

There are two kinds of competitive skiing; *Nordic*, which is cross-country or jumping, and *Alpine*, which is racing on prepared slopes. Nordic skiing has been included in the OLYMPIC GAMES since 1924, and *World Championships* have been held biennially since 1939. Alpine skiing has been an Olympic sport since 1936 and *World Championships* have been held biennially since 1939.

snooker it is generally thought that Colonel Sir Neville Chamberlain concocted the game of snooker in 1875 at Madras in India. The name *snooker* is taken from the nickname given to first year cadets at the Royal Military Academy, Woolwich. The first rules were established by The Billiards Association in 1900.

Snooker *World Championships* were first held in 1926. The tournament was discontinued in 1952 and not restored until 1964. In 1969 it became a knockout contest. Since 1979 all finals have been held at the Crucible Theatre in Sheffield.

squash was developed at Harrow School in England in the early 19th century. It was originally a game for practising the game of rackets but using a softer, squashy ball. The Squash Rackets Association was formed in 1928, and this became the World Squash Federation in 1992.

The *World Open Championship* was first held in 1976. Since 1979 they have been contested annually by men (annually since 1990 for women).

Super Bowl *see* AMERICAN FOOTBALL.

surfing was originally a Polynesian activity. Although a popular pastime in countries such as Australia and America for some time, it was not developed as a sporting activity until the late 1950s and early 1960s. The *World Amateur Championships* were first held in 1964 and the *World Professional Championships* in 1970. There has been a Grand Prix circuit for professionals since 1976, organised by the Association of Surfing Professionals (ASP).

swimming the earliest references to competitive swimming occur in 36 BC in Japan. In Britain, organised competitive swimming was introduced only in 1837 when the National Swimming Society was formed.

It has been an integral part of the OLYMPIC GAMES since 1896, and water sports now include diving, water polo, synchronised swimming and swimming using breaststroke, butterfly, front crawl and backstroke over different distances.

World Championships, separate from the Olympics, were first held in 1973 and are now staged every four years. The seventh World Championships were held in Rome in 1994.

table tennis was originally known as *ping-pong* and was widely played in England in the early part of the 20th century. The modern game grew in popularity when textured rubber mats were attached to the faces of the wooden bats, allowing the players to put spin on the ball. The International Table Tennis Federation was founded in 1926, and the *World Championships* have been held since 1927. In recent years Chinese players have dominated. The Swaythling Cup is awarded to the winning men's team and the Corbillon Cup to the winning women's team.

tennis evolved from the indoor game of *real tennis* and is thought to have first been played at the end of the 18th century. It was patented by Major Wingfield, regarded as the 'father' of the game, who claimed to have invented lawn tennis at his country house in Wales, in 1874. The Marylebone Cricket Club (MCC) later revised the major's rules, and in 1877 the All-England Croquet Club added Lawn Tennis to its title.

The All-England Championships at Wimbledon have been held since 1877 and are regarded as the most prestigious tennis championships played on grass in the world. Since 1922 they have been contested on a knockout basis.

To achieve the *Grand Slam* in international tennis is to hold the titles to all four major tournaments simultaneously. These tournaments are: Wimbledon, the French Open, the Australian Open and the US Open.

The *Davis Cup* was established in 1900 by American player Dwight F. Davis as an international challenge match. Since 1972 a World Group of 16 nations have played-off for the Cup. Each match is decided over two pairs of singles and a doubles.

test cricket *see* CRICKET.

toboggan *see* BOBSLEIGH.

Tour De France *see* CYCLING.

UEFA Cup *see* ASSOCIATION FOOTBALL.

University Boat Race *see* ROWING.

volleyball was invented by sports instructor William Morgan in 1895 and was originally intended for those who found basketball too strenuous. The game quickly spread from North America around the world, reaching Britain in 1914. An International Federation was founded in 1948, and the sport has been included in the OLYMPIC GAMES since 1964.

A *World Championship* was first staged in 1949, and the event has been held every four years since 1952. In recent years teams from the USA, Russia and China have dominated.

walking has been included in the OLYMPIC GAMES since 1906. It is defined as 'progression by steps so that unbroken contact with the ground is maintained'. Road walking is now more common than track walking, and the current Olympic distances for men 20km and 50km.

water polo originally known as 'football in the water', the sport was developed in Britain in the late 19th century. It was given official recognition in 1885 by the Amateur Swimming Association Great Britain and has been included in the OLYMPIC GAMES since 1900. A *World Championship* was first held separately from the *World Swimming Championships* (*see* SWIMMING) in 1991.

water skiing was pioneered by Ralph Samuelson on Lake Pepin, Minnesota, in 1922. Competition today is divided into the events of trick skiing, slalom and jumping. The *World Championship* has been held biennially since 1949.

weightlifting competitions go back to the Chou Dynasty in China and were an integral part of the ancient OLYMPIC GAMES.

The sport has been included in the modern Games since 1896. Contests are decided by the aggregate of two forms of lifting: the snatch, and the clean and jerk. In 1993 it was decided by the International Weightlifting Federation to introduce a new set of 10 weight categories. These are:

   Men   54kg, 59kg, 64kg, 70kg, 76kg, 83kg, 91kg, 99kg, 108kg, >108kg
   Women   46kg, 50kg, 54kg, 59kg, 64kg, 70kg, 76kg, 83kg, >83kg

Whitbread Round the World Race *see* YACHTING

Wimbledon *see* TENNIS.

Winter Olympic Games although ICE SKATING was included in the 1908 Olympic Games, the first international competition to feature a variety of winter sports was not held until 1924. This event, called the International Winter Sports Week, was later ratified by the International Olympic Committee as being the first Winter Olympic Games.

Since 1994 the Winter Games are have beenn held in the middle of the four-year Olympic cycle. The 2002 Winter Olympic Games will be held in Salt Lake City in the USA.

World Cup *see* ASSOCIATION FOOTBALL, RUGBY LEAGUE, RUGBY UNION.

World Championship *see individual sports.*
World Equestrian Games *see* EQUESTRAINISM.
World Open Championship *see* SQUASH.
World Outdoor Championship *see* BOWLS.
World Series *see* BASEBALL.

wrestling was one of the most important events in the ancient OLYMPIC GAMES and has been included in the modern Games since 1896. There are two styles: Greco-Roman and freestyle, with the main difference being that in Greco-Roman the use of the legs is prohibited. A *World Championship* was first staged in 1904, and it is now an annual event in non-Olympic years.

yachting as a sport is thought to have begun in the 17th century in the Netherlands, then the world's greatest maritime power. The first recorded yacht race took place in 1661 when Charles II challenged the Duke of York to a race on the River Thames.

Yachting has been included in the OLYMPIC GAMES since 1900, and there have been variations in the number of different classes through the years because of changes in technology and design.

The *Admiral's Cup* was first held in 1957 and is now held biennially. National three-boat teams compete over a six-race series combining inshore and outshore racing. The races take place in the English Channel, at Cowes and in the Solent, and culminate in the Fastnet race from Cowes to Fastnet Rock, off the Irish coast, and back. The *America's Cup* is an international challenge competition for large yachts. It gained its name in 1851 when the Royal Yacht Squadron presented a trophy to be awarded to the winner of a race around the Isle of Wight. The race was won by the schooner *America*. The Cup was later offered as a challenge trophy by the New York Yacht Club. Yachts from Britain, Canada and Australia competed for it unsuccessfully 24 times before it was won by an Australian yacht, *Australia II*, in 1983. The catamaran *Stars and Stripes* regained it for the United States in 1987, and it has remained there despite two further challenges and a legal battle concerning the use of a catamaran against a monohulled vessel.

The *Whitbread Round the World Race*, inaugurated in 1973, is held every four years and is the longest race in the world. Starting and finishing at Portsmouth in England, the competitors have to sail via the Cape of Good Hope and Cape Horn, a distance of some 32,000 nautical miles (increased in 1990 from the original distance of 26,180 nautical miles). The race is conducted as a handicap, with different classes of yacht competing.

Art, Music and Literature

This section of *The Pocket Encyclopedia* defines and explains the major terms and movements in art, music and literature. Cross-references, in SMALL CAPITALS, will enable you to relate one term to another and develop a comprehensive understanding of the cultural world.

A the sixth NOTE of the SCALE of C; it is the note to which instruments of an orchestra are usually tuned (*see* TUNING).

abbreviations are employed in music for terms of expression, *f.* for FORTE; as arbitrary signs, such as two DOTS on either side of an oblique line for repetition of a group of NOTES; or as numerals, which serve as shorthand symbols for various CHORDS in FIGURED BASS.

absolute music *or* **abstract music** instrumental music that exists purely as music and does not attempt to relate to a story or image.

absolute pitch *or* **perfect pitch** the sense by which some people can exactly identify, or sing without an accompanying instrument, any NOTE they hear.

abstract art art that intentionally avoids representation of the observed world. Abstraction has long been a feature of the decorative arts and to a large degree continues to dominate 20th-century art.

abstract expressionism art that is based on freedom of expression, spontaneity and random composition and is characterised by loose, unrestrained brushwork and often indistinct forms, usually on large canvases. The works may or may not be FIGURATIVE. The term mainly applies to an influential art movement of the 1940s in New York. Inspired by SURREALISM, the movement represented a breakaway from the REALISM hitherto dominant in American art and went on to influence European art in the 1950s.

abstract music *see* ABSOLUTE MUSIC.

Absurd, Theatre of the a form of theatre, developed in the 1960s, that characterises the human condition as one of helplessness in the face of an irrational, 'absurd' universe. Absurdist drama reacts strongly against the conventions of naturalism

a cappella *or* **alla capella** (*Italian*) literally 'in the chapel style'; it is a term that has come to mean unaccompanied choral singing.

accent the emphasis given to specific notes to indicate the RHYTHM of a piece of music.

acciaccatura (*Italian*) an ornamental or auxiliary NOTE, normally the SEMITONE below, played just before, or at the same time as, a regular note. From the Italian *acciacciare*, to crush.

accidental a NOTE in a piece of music that departs by one or two SEMITONES from the KEY SIGNATURE. It is indicated by a SHARP, FLAT or NATURAL sign before it. An accidental holds good throughout a BAR unless contradicted.

accompaniment music supporting a soloist or CHOIR. An accompaniment may be provided by an orchestra, organ or, most usually, a piano.

accordion a portable REED ORGAN. Air is forced through the reeds by means of bellows that are operated by the player's arms, and notes and chords are played by pressing buttons. The piano accordion has a keyboard (operated by the right hand) for playing MELODY notes, and buttons (operated by the left hand) for simple CHORDS. The accordion is associated with informal or FOLK music, but it has been used by serious composers.

Acmeist group a school of Russian poetry which first emerged in Leningrad in 1911. In part a reaction to the more obscure aspects of SYMBOLISM, the group proclaimed the virtue of clarity of expression. It was founded by the poet Anna Akhmatova (1889–1966).

acoustic guitar *see* GUITAR.

acoustics (1) a branch of physics that is concerned with SOUND. The main characteristics of a sound are its PITCH, intensity, RESONANCE and quality. (2) the characteristics of a hall or auditorium that enable speech and music to be heard without the sounds being distorted. In a concert hall with good acoustics, sounds from the stage can be heard clearly in all quarters.

acrostic a type of poem, in which the initial letters of each line form a word reading downwards.

action (1) the mechanism of a keyboard instrument that links the keyboard to the strings or, in the case of an ORGAN, to the PIPES and STOPS. (2) the gap between the strings and FINGERBOARD of a stringed instrument as dictated by the height of the BRIDGE.

action painting a form of ABSTRACT EXPRESSIONISM in which paint is applied to canvas through a series of actions/movements by the artist. It may involve dancing, cycling or rolling on the canvas to spread and mix wet paint.

act tune *or* **curtain music** an instrumental piece of music that is played between the acts of a play while the curtain is down. *See also* ENTR'ACTE; INTERLUDE; INTERMEZZO.

adagietto (*Italian*) (1) 'slow' but not as slow as ADAGIO. (2) a short composition in an adagio TEMPO.

adagio (*Italian*) (1) 'at ease', i.e. at a slow TEMPO. (2) a slow movement.

adagissimo (*Italian*) 'very slow'.

added sixth a frequently used chord created by adding the sixth note from the ROOT to a MAJOR or MINOR TRIAD; for example, in the key of C major, A is added above the triad of C-E-G.

additional accompaniments new or revised PARTS for extra instruments written by later composers and added to 17th- and 18th-century works in order to increase fullness.

ad libitum (*Latin*) literally 'at pleasure' and usually abbreviated to AD LIB. In music, the term is used to indicate that, when playing a piece, a performer can: (a) alter the TEMPO or RHYTHM; (b) choose an alternative PASSAGE by the composer; (c) improvise a CADENZA; and (d) include or omit a passage if he or she so chooses.

a due corde (*Italian*), **à deux cordes** (*French*) 'on two strings'; when applied to music for stringed instruments, the term means that a piece should be played on two strings, not just on one.

Aeolian harp a type of ZITHER which has strings of similar length but of different thickness. The instrument is not actually played but left outside to catch the wind; different CHORDS are sounded according to the speed of the wind, which makes the strings vibrate faster or slower (*see* VIBRATION). The name is derived from Aeolus, who was the Greek god of the wind.

Aeolian mode a MODE that, on the PIANO, uses the white NOTES from A to A.

Aesthetic movement a cultural movement which developed in England in the late 19th century, characterised by a very affected and mannered approach to life and the arts, a fondness for orientalism and decadence, archaic language and pseudo-medievalism. Oscar Wilde (1854–1900) is the most prominent literary figure of merit associated with the movement.

aesthetics an area of philosophy concerning ideals of taste and beauty and providing criteria for critical study of the arts. The term was coined in the mid-18th century by the German philosopher Alexander Baumgarten (1714–62). In the 20th century it came to include a wider theory of natural beauty.

affettuoso (*Italian*) 'tender' or 'affectionate', i.e. an indication that a piece of music should be played with tender feeling.

African art a term generally used to describe African tribal art in the countries south of the Sahara desert. Much of this art is of a group nature, in that it has a cultural and religious significance at its heart rather than individual ambition. Examples of typical art forms include richly carved wooden masks and figures. Body art is also important in tribal ritual and may involve scarring, tattooing or disfigurement of parts of the body, although it can also make use of paint, beads and feathers.

agitato, agitatamente (*Italian*) literally 'agitated', 'agitatedly', i.e. an indication that a piece should be played restlessly or wildly.

air (1) a simple TUNE or SONG. (2) a melodious BAROQUE composition.

Alberti bass a simple accompaniment to a MELODY consisting of 'broken' or spread CHORDS arranged in a rhythmic pattern.

Albumblatt (*German*) literally 'album leaf'; a popular title given by 19th-century composers to short, instrumental compositions (often for the PIANO) and of a personal nature.

Aldeburgh Festival an annual music FESTIVAL held in June, which was founded by the composer Benjamin Britten (1913–76) and the tenor Peter Pears (1910–86) at Aldeburgh, Suffolk, in 1948.

aleatory music music which contains unpredictable or chance elements so that no two performances of a piece are ever similar.

alienation effect an effect which is supposed to occur upon an audience when the audience is reminded by action, dialogue or song that it is in fact an audience watching a play, and not, for example, waiting for a bus. The intention is to confront the audience with the artificiality of dramatic representation, through devices such as interrupting the action to address the audience, or by bursting into song, or by stylising the stage set or action.

alla (*Italian*) 'in the style of'.

alla breve (*Italian*) (1) an instruction that a piece of music should be performed twice as fast as the NOTATION would suggest. (2) 2/2 TIME.

allargando (*Italian*) literally 'getting broader', i.e. an indication that a piece should be played grandly whilst at the same time getting slower.

allegory in literature a form of narrative in which the characters and events symbolise an underlying moral or spiritual quality, or represent a hidden meaning beneath the literal one expressed. Bunyan's (1628–88) *Pilgrim's Progress* is the greatest English-language example of a sustained allegory.

allegro (*Italian*) literally 'lively', i.e. in a quick TEMPO. The term is often used as the title of a bright composition or MOVEMENT.

alphabet the letters used in music as they occur in the natural SCALE are C, D, E, F, G, A, B. The oldest HARPS and shepherd PIPES are believed to have had seven TONES, to which the Greeks gave the names of letters, A being the lowest. Greek NOTATION became highly complicated with the development of the MODES, and Pope Gregory the Great (540–604) changed church notation, again employing the first seven letters, indicating the lower OCTAVE by capitals, and the upper by small letters. NOTES were gradually added to the lower A, and when the modern scale was adopted in the 16th century, the lowest tone had become C instead of A.

al segno (*Italian*) 'to the sign' (i.e. to a standard symbol used in musical notation). The term is used in two ways: it can instruct the player either to go back to the sign and start again, or to continue until the sign is reached.

alt an abbreviation of the Latin phrase *in alto,* which means 'high'. It is used for the NOTES in the OCTAVE rising from G above the TREBLE CLEF; the notes in the octave above that are said to be *in altissimo.*

alto (*Italian*) 'high' (1) the highest adult male VOICE, which is now used only in male-voice CHOIRS. (2) an addition to the name of an instrument to indicate that it is one size larger than the SOPRANO member of the family; for example alto CLARINET. (3) a low female voice that has a greater compass than the male alto voice (usually, and more properly, called CONTRALTO).

Amati the name of a famous family of violin-makers who worked in Cemona, Italy, in the 16th and 17th centuries.

Ambrosian chants a collection of CHANTS or PLAINSONG, used in Milan Cathedral, which are named after St Ambrose (*c.* 340–97), Bishop of Milan, who greatly influenced church singing and may have introduced the ANTIPHONAL singing of the Syrian church. Despite bearing his name, the earliest surviving chants were composed long after his death.

American organ *or* **cabinet organ** a REED ORGAN, similar to a HARMONIUM except that air is sucked, rather than blown, through the reeds.

amoroso (*Italian*) 'lovingly', indicating that a piece should be played with warm affection.

amplifier any device, particularly if electric, which renders a sound louder.

anabasis (*Greek*) a succession of ascending tones.

anacrusis (*Greek anakrousis*, literally 'a prelude') an unstressed NOTE or grouping of notes at the beginning of a musical PHRASE; it can also mean an unstressed syllable at the beginning of a SONG.

Ancients, The a group of Romantic artists working in England between 1824 and the early 1830s. Samuel Palmer (1805–51), the English painter and engraver, was a leading member of the group. Their work was mainly pastoral in theme.

ancora (*Italian*) 'again', 'yet' or 'still', as in *ancora forte* meaning 'still loud' and *ancora più forte* meaning 'yet louder'.

andante (*Italian*) 'going' or 'moving'; it is usually used to indicate a moderate TEMPO or a walking pace. *Più andante* means 'moving more' or slightly faster. Andante is sometimes used as a title for a moderately slow piece of music.

andantino (*Italian*) 'less slow' (i.e. slightly faster) than ANDANTE.

Anfang (*German*) 'beginning'; *Anfangs* means 'from the beginning'.

anglaise (*French*) short for *danse anglaise* or 'English dance', i.e. a lively dance in quick time, such as a HORNPIPE.

Anglican chant a characteristically English way of setting to music prose, psalms and canticles, in which the number of syllables per line can vary. To accommodate this irregularity, the first NOTE of each musical PHRASE is a RECITING NOTE which is timeless and is used to sing as many syllables as necessary before moving on to notes which are sung in time and which normally carry one syllable each. It is basically a simple form of GREGORIAN CHANT.

Anglo-Saxon art a term for works of art produced in England between AD 5 and 1066. The major source of surviving artefacts is the 7th-century excavation site at Sutton Hoo, and much of the Anglo-Saxon jewellery collection at the British Museum comes from there. The abstract plant and animal designs show the influence of Celtic art typical of Anglo-Saxon craft.

Angry Young Men a rather imprecise term used in mid-1950s Britain to denote a group of English writers who had little in common apart from vaguely leftish sympathies and a hatred of English provincialism and intellectual pretentiousness ('madrigalphobia'). *Look Back in Anger* by John Osborne (1929–94) is typical of the work of the Angry Young Men.

anima (*Italian*) 'soul' or 'spirit', as in *con anima,* which means that a piece should be played 'with soul' or 'with emotion'.

animato (*Italian*) 'animated'.

animo (*Italian*) 'spirit'.

animoso (*Italian*) 'spirited'.

answer the second entry of the main SUBJECT (theme) of a FUGUE which is played a FIFTH higher or lower than the first entry. In a *real answer,* the subject and answer are identical; in a *tonal answer,* the intervals in the answer are changed.

anthem the Anglican equivalent to the Roman Catholic MOTET. An anthem is usually an elaborate musical setting of non-liturgical words sung by a church CHOIR without the congregation; SOLO parts are common and accompaniment by an ORGAN is usual.

anticipation the sounding of a NOTE (or notes) of a CHORD before the rest of the chord is played.

antiphon the sacred words, sung in PLAINSONG by two CHOIRS, before and after a PSALM or CANTICLE in a Roman Catholic service.

Antique, The remains of ancient art, in particular Greek and Roman statues, which were taken as a standard of classical order and beauty in the representation of the human form by RENAISSANCE and NEOCLASSICAL artists.

anvil a percussion instrument consisting of steel bars that are struck with a wooden or metal mallet. It is meant to sound like a blacksmith's anvil being struck with a hammer.

a piacere (*Italian*) 'at pleasure', meaning that the performer of a piece of music is permitted to take a certain amount of liberty, particularly with TEMPO, while playing it. *See also* AD LIBITUM.

appassionato, appassionata (*Italian*) 'impassioned' or 'with passion or feeling', hence the title *Sonata appassionata* which was given to Beethoven's Piano Sonata in F Minor (Op. 57).

applied art art that serves a useful purpose or that ornaments functional objects; often a synonym for *design*. Subjects included under this term are architecture, interior design, ceramics, furniture, graphics, etc. These are usually contrasted with the *fine arts* of painting, drawing, scupting, and the division became more distinct at the time of the Industrial Revolution and the emergence of AESTHETICS. This division is still a matter of debate.

appoggiando (*Italian*) 'leaning'; when applied to NOTES, this implies that they should pass very smoothly from one to the next.

appoggiatura (*Italian*) a term for a 'leaning' NOTE (*see also* APPOGGIANDO), indicated in the SCORE. (1) a *long appoggiatura* is a note of varying length that is different from the HARMONY note. (2) a *short appoggiatura* is a very short note of indefinite length, sometimes accented, sometimes not. (3) a *passing appoggiatura*, as used in the 18th century, normally occurs when the principal notes of a MELODY form a sequence of THIRDS and it is played before the beat.

aquarelle a French term for WATERCOLOUR painting, where a water-based paint is applied to dampened paper in thin glazes that are gradually built up into areas of tone.

aquatint an etching technique where a resin-coated metal plate is placed in a bath of acid that bites into the resin, producing a pitted surface. The finished print resembles a watercolour wash, and the technique of overlaying separate plates of different colours can be used to build up a range of depth and colour. The process is often combined with linear ETCHING.

arabesque (1) a florid treatment of thematic music. (2) a lyrical piece of music that employs an exaggerated and elaborate style.

Arcadia a region of ancient Greece which became the archetypal setting for rural bliss and innocence in the arts. Virgil's *Eclogues* in the 1st century BC established the use of Arcadia as a literary device for this purpose, but the ironic undertone in Virgil's work (Arcadia is largely barren) is usually missing from later writers' use of the myth.

archet (*French*) a BOW, such as is used to play a stringed instrument.

archi (*Italian*) 'bows', a term that refers to all stringed instruments played with a BOW.

arco (*Italian*) the singular of ARCHI. It is the usual instruction to play with the BOW after playng PIZZICATO.

ardito (*Italian*) 'bold', 'energetic'.

aria (*Italian*) a SONG or AIR. Originally the term was used for any song for one or more voices but it has come to be used exclusively for a long, SOLO song as found in ORATORIO and OPERA.

arioso (*Italian*) 'like an aria'. (1) a melodious and song-like RECITATIVE. (2) a short air in an OPERA or ORATORIO. (3) an instrumental piece that follows the style of a vocal arioso.

arpeggio (*Italian*) 'HARP-wise', i.e. an indication that the NOTES of a CHORD should be played in rapid succession, as they are on a harp, and not simultaneously.

arrangement an adaptation of a piece of music for a medium different from that for which it was originally composed.

ars antiqua (*Latin*) the 'old art', i.e. music of the 12th and 13th centuries as opposed to **ars nova**, the new style of music that evolved in the 14th century.

Art Autre *or* **Art Informel** a name coined by art critic Michel Tapie in *Un Art Autre* (1952); he used it to describe nongeometric ABSTRACT EXPRESSIONISM.

Art Deco the decorative art of the 1920s and 1930s in Europe and North America, originally called *Jazz Modern*. It was classical in style, with slender, symmetrical, geometric or rectilinear forms. Major influences were ART NOUVEAU architecture and ideas from the ARTS AND CRAFTS MOVEMENT and the BAUHAUS. The simplicity of style was easily adaptable to modern industrial production methods and contemporary materials, especially plastics. This resulted in a proliferation of utility items, jewellery and furniture in an elegant streamilned form, as well as simplification and streamlining of interior decor and architecture.

Art Nouveau a style of decorative art influential and popular between 1890 and World War I in Europe and North America. Art Nouveau was primarily a design style with its main effects being seen in applied art, graphics, furniture and fabric design, and in architecture. In the fine arts it represented a move away from historical realism, but was not as vigorous or dominant as IMPRESSIONISM or CUBISM. Art Nouveau design is characterised by flowing organic forms and asymmetrical linear structures, although architectural and calligraphic forms were more austere and reserved. Its principal exponents were the Scottish architect and designer Charles

Rennie MacKintosh (1868–1928) and the American designer Louis Comfort Tiffany (1848–1933).

Arts and Crafts Movement an English movement in the decorative arts towards the end of the 19th century. It was based on the ideas of the art critic John Ruskin (1819–1900) and the architect Augustus Pugin (1812–52), with reference to the medieval guilds system, and took its name from the Arts and Crafts Exhibition Society formed in 1888. The motive was to re-establish the value of handcrafted objects at a time of increasing mass-production and industrialisation. Designers in the movement, with a variety of styles, attempted to produce functional objects of an aesthetically pleasing nature. The most active and important leader of the movement was William Morris (1834–96).

ascription *see* ATTRIBUTION.

Ashcan School a group of American painters of urban realism between 1908 and 1918. Their aim was to declare themselves primarily American painters, and they painted what they saw as American life, rejecting subject matter of academic approval.

assai (*Italian*) 'very', as in *allegro assai*, 'very fast'.

atelier the French term for an artist's studio. In 19th-century France, an *atelier libre* was a studio where artists could go to paint a model.

a tempo (*Italian*) 'in time', a term that indicates that a piece should revert to its normal TEMPO after a change of speed.

athematic music music that does not have any THEMES or TUNES as such; it is concerned with exploring the unconventional possibilities of sounds.

atonal music music that is not in any KEY.

attacca (*Italian*) 'attack', i.e. start the next MOVEMENT without a pause.

attribution *or* **ascription** the assigning of an unsigned picture to a painter, using similarity of style or subject as the basis.

aubade (*French*) 'morning music', as opposed to a SERENADE.

augmentation the lengthening of the time values of NOTES in melodic parts with the result that they sound more impressive and grand. The opposite of augmentation is DIMINUTION.

augmented interval the INTERVAL formed by increasing any perfect or MAJOR interval by a SEMITONE.

augmented sixth a CHORD based on the flattened SUBMEDIANT that contains the augmented sixth interval.

augmented triad a TRIAD of which the FIFTH is augmented.

a una corda (*Italian*) 'on one string' (*compare* A DUE CORDE), meaning left-hand PEDAL (of a piano), i.e. reducing the volume.

autograph in art, a term used to denote a painting by one artist only, and not assisted by pupils or assistants.

autoharp a type of ZITHER in which CHORDS are produced by pressing down KEYS (1) that dampen some of the strings but let others vibrate freely.

Automatistes a Canadian group of painters formed in the 1950s whose ideas were based on the spontaneity of creativity.

avant-garde (*French*) 'vanguard', a term applied to music (or any other art) that is considered to break new ground in style, structure, or technique.

B (1) the seventh note of the scale of C major. (2) abbreviation for bass or for Bachelor (as in B. Mus., Bachelor of Music).

baby grand the smallest size of grand PIANO.

Bach trumpet a 19th-century valved TRUMPET which was designed to make it easier to play the high-pitched parts that were originally composed by BACH and his contemporaries for a natural (unvalved) trumpet.

back the lower part of the sounding box of string instruments, connected in VIOLS to the sounding board or belly by a sound post set beneath the bridge. Its construction and material vitally affect the quality of the TONE (3) produced.

bagatelle (*French*) 'trifle', a short, light piece of music, usually for piano.

bagpipes a reed instrument in which air is supplied to the PIPE or pipes from an inflated bag. Bagpipes are known to have existed for 3000 years or more and hundreds of different types are found today. The best known form of bagpipe is played in Scotland and consists of a *bag* which is inflated through a pipe and is held under the arm; a CHANTER (a REED pipe with finger holes) on which the MELODY is played; and several DRONE pipes, each of which is tuned to a different note. Air is rhythmically squeezed from the bag by the arm (and is then replenished with more breath) and is forced out through the chanter and drone pipes.

balalaika (*Russian*) a FOLK instrument of the GUITAR family, with a triangular body. It is of Tartar origin and usually has just three strings and a fretted FINGERBOARD.

ballad a narrative poem or song in brief stanzas, often with a repeated refrain and frequently featuring a dramatic incident. Examples of what has been termed the *literary ballad* began to appear in the 18th and 19th centuries. Notable examples include Samuel Coleridge's (1772–1834) 'Rime of the Ancient Mariner'.

Among the greatest examples of the form are the *Border ballads*, which stem from the violent world of the English/Scottish borders from the late Middle Ages to the 17th century. Representative examples of the Border ballads are the laments 'Sir Patrick Spens' and 'The Bonny Earl of Murray'. The most important collection of Border ballads is that issued by Sir Walter Scott (1771–1832) in 1802–3, *Minstrelsy of the Scottish Borders*.

In music, a ballad is also a sentimental 'drawing-room' song of the late 19th century (sometimes referred to as a *shop ballad* to differentiate it from a broadside ballad) or a narrative song or operatic ARIA.

ballade a type of medieval French poetry, often set to music by TROUBA-DOURS. In music, it is a 19th-century term, coined by Frédéric Chopin (1810–49) for a long, romantic instrumental piece. Chopin wrote four outstanding ballades.

ballad opera popular OPERA composed of dialogue and SONGS with tunes borrowed from FOLK music, popular songs, and sometimes opera.

ballet a dramatic entertainment in which dancers in costume perform to a musical ACCOMPANIMENT. Mime is often used in ballet to express emotions or to tell a story. Ballet has a long history that dates back to before the Middle Ages. In the 16th and 17th centuries, ballets often included singing and consequently were closely linked to OPERA. By the end of the 18th century, however, ballet had evolved more gymnastic qualities and, although it was still included as an integral part in many operas, it also kept a separate existence. In the 19th century, ballet achieved new heights of popularity in France and spread to Italy and Russia where several schools of ballet were established that incorporated traditional dancing into their teaching. The ballet scores of Peter Ilyich Tchaikovsky (1843–93), including *Swan Lake* and *The Sleeping Beauty*, had a massive influence on Russian ballet and greatly added to its international appeal. The Russian choreographer and entrepreneur Sergei Diaghilev (1872–1929) encouraged young composers such as Igor Stravinsky (1882–1971) and Maurice Ravel (1875–1937) to write ballet scores. At the start of the 20th century, ballet became immensely popular in England, assisted by the work of the outstanding British choreographers Sir Frederick Ashton (1904–88) and Sir Kenneth Macmillan (1929–92). In the USA, the choreographer George Balanchine (1904–83) had an equally powerful influence, and many American composers, such as Aaron Copland (1900–1990) and Leonard Bernstein (1918–1990) have since written ballet music.

Ballet is witnessing a new revival; SCORES are being produced by young composers and energetic companies are establishing new dance techniques.

band a term used to describe virtually any group of instrumentalists except a concert ORCHESTRA, for example dance band, JAZZ band, POP band, MILITARY BAND.

banjo a GUITAR-like, stringed instrument of Black American origin. It comprises a shallow metal (sometimes wood) drum with parchment stretched over the top while the bottom is (usually) left open. Banjos can have between four and nine strings, which are played by plucking either with the fingers or a PLECTRUM.

bar (1) a vertical line (bar line) drawn down one or more STAVES of music. (2) the space between two bar lines.

barber-shop quartet a quartet of amateur male singers who perform CLOSE-HARMONY arrangements. The tradition originated in barber shops in New York in the late 19th century.

Barbizon School a group of French landscape painters in the 1840s who based their art on direct study from nature. Their advanced ideas represented a move away from academic conventions and their interest in daylight effects and the bold use of colour helped prepare the way for IMPRESSIONISM.

barcarolle (*French*) a boating song with a rhthm imitating that of songs sung by gondoliers.

bard a Celtic minstrel, part of whose job it was to compose SONGS for his master. Bards traditionally held annual meetings (*Eisteddfods*) in Wales and these have been revived in recent times as competition festivals.

baritone (1) a male voice, midway between BASS and TENOR with a range of approximately two OCTAVES. (2) a BRASS INSTRUMENT of the SAXHORN family.

Baroque a cultural movement in art, music and science in the 17th century. In terms of art history, the area of reference is slightly broader and takes in the late 16th- and early-18th centuries. It specifically indicates the stage between the MANNERISM of the late High RENAISSANCE and ROCOCO, into which Baroque developed. As a style it is characterised by movement, rhetoric and emotion, stemming from the achievements of the High Renaissance, and it represented a reaction away from the attitudes and techniques of MANNERISM. Michelangelo de Caravaggio (1573–1610), was among its leading figures when it first began in Rome, and Rembrandt's work reflected Baroque trends for part of his career. Adjectivally, *baroque* can also be used to describe art from any age that displays the richness and dynamism associated with the movement.

barrel organ a mechanical ORGAN of the 18th and 19th centuries in which air was admitted into PIPES by means of pins on a hand-rotated barrel. It was restricted to playing a limited number of tunes but was nonetheless frequently used in church services. *See also* MECHANICAL INSTRUMENTS.

bass (1) the lowest adult male VOICE. (2) an abbreviation for DOUBLE BASS.

(3) an addition to the instrument name to indicate the largest member of a family of instruments (except where CONTRABASS instruments are built).

bassa (*Italian*) 'low'.

bass-bar a strip of wood glued as reinforcement under the BRIDGE (1) inside the BELLY of instruments of the VIOLIN family.

bass clarinet a single-REED instrument built an OCTAVE lower than the CLARINET, with a crook and upturned bell.

bass clef *see* CLEF.

bass drum a large PERCUSSION INSTRUMENT consisting of a cylindrical wooden hoop which is usually covered on both sides with vellum.

bass flute an ALTO FLUTE with a PITCH a FOURTH lower than a 'concert' or normal flute.

bassoon a double-reed instrument of the 16th century, consisting of a wooden tube doubled back on itself. It has a compass from B flat below BASS CLEF to E on the fourth line of the TREBLE CLEF.

bathos in literature it describes the anti-climax whereby the elevated swiftly descends into the ridiculous. It has been used as a comic parallel to PATHOS.

baton the stick used by a CONDUCTOR to give commands to performers.

batterie (*French*) (*also* **battery**) (1) a 17th- and 18th-century term for ARPEGGIO. (2) the PERCUSSION section of an ORCHESTRA.

Bauhaus a German school of architecture and applied arts founded by the architect Walter Gropius (1883–1969) at Weimar in 1919. One of its aims was to narrow the gap between fine and APPLIED ARTS; another was to focus on architecture as the environment of art. Each student took a six-month foundation course in practical craft skills such as weaving, glass painting and metalwork. Later came a shift in emphasis from craftsmanship towards industrialised mass-production. The Bauhaus was closed by the Nazis in 1933. A number of Bauhaus masters emigrated to the US, where their ideas were influential.

Bayreuth a town in Germany where Richard Wagner (1813–83) arranged for the building of a festival theatre which has subsequently become internationally famous for staging his operas.

beat (1) a unit of rhythmic measure in music, indicated to a CHOIR (2) or ORCHESTRA by the movement of a conductor's BATON. The number of beats in a BAR depends on the TIME-SIGNATURE. (2) a form of 20th-century POPULAR MUSIC with a steady and powerful RHYTHM.

Beat Generation a term invented by Jack Kerouac (1922– 69) to describe a group of American writers, artists and musicians in the 1950s. Notable

Beat writers included Kerouac himself, whose novel *On the Road* (1952) became the 'Beat bible', the poet Allen Ginsberg (1926–1997), and the novelist William Burroughs (1914–). The Beat writers were anti-Western in their values; they dabbled in communalism, loved modern jazz and took drugs.

bebop a JAZZ development of the 1940s in which complex RHYTHMS and harmonic sequences were carried out against rapidly played melodic IMPROVISATION.

Bebung (*German*) 'trembling', i.e. a vibrato effect caused by shaking a finger holding down a KEY (1) of a CLAVICHORD.

Bechstein a company of German piano manufacturers established in Berlin in 1856 by Friedrich Wilhelm Karl Bechstein (1826–1900). Branches of his firm were subsequently formed in France, England and Russia.

bel a unit used to measure the intensity of sound. *See also* DECIBEL.

bel canto (*Italian*) 'beautiful singing', a style of singing characterised by elaborate technique, associated with 18th-century Italian OPERA.

bells (*orchestral*) cylindrical metal tubes (*tubular bells*) of different lengths which are suspended from a frame and struck with a wooden mallet.

belly the upper part of the body or soundbox of a stringed instrument.

ben, bene (*Italian*) 'well', as in *ben marcato* meaning 'well marked', 'well accented'.

berceuse (*French*) a cradle song.

Biedermeier a style in art and architecture in Austria and Germany between 1815 and 1848. It took its name from a fictional character of the time, Gottlieb Biedermeier, who personified the philistine artistic taste of the middle classes. Architecture associated with the style is solid and utilitarian, paintings are meticulous and devoid of imagination.

big band a large BAND, most commonly associated with the SWING era. Such bands were famed for the strong dance RHYTHMS they produced.

Bildungsroman (*German*) 'education novel', a novel that describes the growth of a character (usually based on the author) from youthful naivety to a well-rounded maturity. The term derives from Johann Wolfgang von Goethe's (1749–1832) *Wilhelm Meister's Apprenticeship*. *David Copperfield* by Charles Dickens (1812–70) and *Portrait of the Artist as a Young Man* (1882–1941) by James Joyce are two notable examples in English literature.

binary form a structure, common in BAROQUE music, consisting of two related sections which were repeated. SONATA FORM evolved from it.

bis (*French*) 'twice', 'again'.

bitonality the use of two keys simultaneously.

blank verse a term sometimes used to denote any form of unrhymed verse but normally applied to unrhymed verse in iambic pentameters, i.e. a line of verse with five short-long 'feet'. The form was developed in English by the Earl of Surrey (*c*.1517–47), and reached its highest peak in Shakespeare's plays.

Blaue Reiter, Der (*German*) 'The Blue Rider', the name, taken from a painting by Wassily Kandinsky (1866–1944), of a group of German EXPRESSIONISTS formed in Munich in 1911. Leading members were Kandinsky and Paul Klee (1879–1940), who, although their working styles were diverse, were united by a philosophy of the creative spirit in European art.

Bloomsbury Group a group of artists, writers and intellectuals who lived or worked in the Bloomsbury area of London in the early decades of the 20th century and whose members included Virginia Woolf (1882–1941).

blues a 20th-century Black American SONG or lamentation following an essentially simple form of twelve BARS to each verse. Blues music formed the basis for JAZZ; musicians favoured such instruments as the GUITAR and HARMONICA.

Bluestocking an originally disparaging term denoting members of small, mostly female groups in English 18th-century social life, who held informal discussion groups on literary and scholarly matters. The term derives from the blue stockings worn by a male member of the group, the botanist Benjamin Stillingfleet.

Boehm system an improved system of KEYS (2) and levers for the FLUTE (1) which is named after its German inventor, Theobald Boehm (1794–1881). The system is also applied to other instruments, for example the CLARINET.

bolero (*Spanish*) a moderately fast Spanish dance in triple TIME.

bones a pair of small sticks (originally bones) that are held in the hands and clicked together rhythmically.

bongos pairs of small, upright Cuban DRUMS that are often found in dance BANDS. They are played with the hands.

boogie-woogie a JAZZ and BLUES style of piano playing in which the left hand plays a persistent bass RHYTHM while the right hand plays a MELODY.

Border ballad *see* BALLAD.

bouzouki a Greek stringed instrument with a long, fretted neck. Its six strings are plucked, often as an ACCOMPANIMENT to songs.

bow a wooden stick which is strung with horse-hair and used to play instruments of the VIOLIN and VIOL families.

bowed harp a primitive VIOLIN, dating back to at least the 12th century. It was held on the knee and played vertically.

brace the vertical line, usually with a bracket, which joins two STAVES of music to indicate that they are played together.

brass band a type of BAND, particularly associated with the north of England, which consists of BRASS INSTRUMENTS and DRUMS only. Brass bands have been popular in England since the beginning of the 19th century.

brass instruments a family of WIND INSTRUMENTS which are made of metal but not always brass. Instruments with REEDS and those which used to be made from wood (such as the FLUTE) are excluded. A characteristic of the family is that sound is produced by the vibration of the lips which are pressed into a funnel-shaped MOUTHPIECE. A selection of NOTES can be produced by effectively lengthening the tubing, either with a slide (as in the TROMBONE) or with valves (as in the TRUMPET). Brass instruments include the trombone, CORNET, BUGLE, trumpet, French HORN, TUBA, and EUPHONIUM.

bravura (*Italian*) literally 'bravery', as in a 'bravura passage', a passage that demands a VIRTUOSO display by the performer.

break (1) in JAZZ, a short, improvised, SOLO passage. (2) the point in a vocal or instrumental range where the REGISTER changes.

breve originally the short NOTE of music (*c.*13th century), but as other notes have been introduced, it is now the longest note and is only occasionally used.

bridge (1) a piece of wood that stands on the BELLY of stringed instruments and supports the strings. (2) a passage in a COMPOSITION (1) that links two important THEMES together.

brindisi (*Italian*) 'a toast', a drinking song in an opera during which toasts are often given.

brio (*Italian*) 'vigour', so CON BRIO means 'with vigour'.

brisé (*French*) 'broken'; a term which indicates that a CHORD should be played in ARPEGGIO fashion, or that music for stringed instruments should be played with short movements of the BOW.

broadside ballad *see* ballad.

broken octaves a term used to describe a passage of NOTES that are played alternately an OCTAVE apart.

Brücke, Die (*German*) 'The Bridge', an association of German artists founded in 1905 in Dresden. The name derives from Friedrich Wilhelm Nietzsche's (1844–1900) idea that a man can be seen as a bridge towards a better future, and in this the artists saw themselves as a link with the art of the future, in a move away from REALISM and IMPRESSIONISM. They also wanted to integrate art and life, and lived together in a community in the tradition of the medieval guilds system. Their influences included AFRICAN tribal art and the works of Vincent Van Gogh (1853–90) and the FAUVISTS. Their painting was mainly EXPRESSIONIST, although comprehending a varitey of styles and techniques. They concentrated initially on figures in landscape and portrait, and made use of texture, clashing colour and aggressive distortion to powerful effect. They helped found the NEUE SEZESSION in 1910, then split away and exhibited as a group with Der BLEUE REITER. In 1913 the group disbanded because of conflicts over aims and policies in relation to the development of CUBISM.

brushwork the 'handwriting' of a painter, i.e. the distinctive way in which he or she applies paint, either smoothly or roughly, thinly or thickly, in long strokes or short. Brushwork is individual to a painter.

bugle a simple BRASS INSTRUMENT with a conical tube and a cup-shaped MOUTHPIECE which was widely used for giving military signals.

burla, burlesca (*Italian*) a short and jolly piece of music.

Byzantine music music of the Christian Church of the Eastern Roman Empire which was established in AD 330 and lasted until 1435. It influenced Western Church Music.

C (1) the key-note or TONIC of the SCALE of C major. (2) an abbreviation for CONTRALTO; *con* (with); *col, colla* (with the).

cabaletta (*Italian*) a term for a simple ARIA with an insistent RHYTHM, or an emphatically rhythmical ending to an ARIA or DUET.

cabinet organ *see* AMERICAN ORGAN.

cacophony a discordant muddle of SOUND or DISSONANCE.

cadence literally a 'falling', a term used to describe the concluding PHRASE at the end of a section of music.

cadenza (*Italian*) literally 'cadence', but it has come to have two specific meanings: (1) an elaborate ending to an operatic ARIA. (2) a flourish at the end of a PASSAGE of SOLO music in a CONCERTO.

calando (*Italian*) 'diminishing', i.e. in both volume and speed.

calcando (*Italian*) 'pressing forward', i.e. a term used to indicate an increase in speed.

calypso a kind of song with SYNCOPATED RHYTHMS from the West Indies, notably Trinidad; calypso LYRICS are usually witty and topical, and are often vehicles for political satire.

cambiata (*Italian*) an abbreviation for *nota cambiata*, CHANGING NOTE.

camera (*Italian*) literally a 'room', but in musical terms it refers to a type of music that can be performed in a place other than a church, music hall, or opera house, etc; *see* CHAMBER MUSIC.

campanology the art of bell-ringing or the study of bells.

cancan a Parisian music-hall dance of the late 19th century in quick 2/4 time.

cancel (*US*) *see* NATURAL.

cancrizans a type of music that makes sense if it is played backwards; RETROGRADE MOTION.

canon a COUNTERPOINT composition in which one part is imitated and overlapped by one or more other PARTS, for example, a SOPRANO lead with a TENOR follow-up. In a 'strict' canon, the imitation is exact in every way.

cantabile (*Italian*) 'song-like', a term applied to instrumental pieces indicating that they should be played in a singing style.

cantata originally a piece of music of the BAROQUE period that is sung (as opposed to a SONATA, a piece which is played). It has come to be a term used to describe a vocal or CHORAL piece with an instrumental accompaniment. German cantatas were generally religious works. In many ways, the form is similar to OPERA and ORATORIO, but it tends not to be so elaborate.

canticle a HYMN that has words from the Bible, other than a PSALM.

cantor (*Latin*) a 'singer'; nowadays the term refers to the chief singer in a CHOIR or the lead singer of liturgical music in a synagogue.

canzone, canzona, canzon literally 'song'; a vocal work, or an instrumental piece that is modelled on music for the VOICE.

canzonet (1) a short kind of CANZONE. (2) a type of MADRIGAL or a simple SOLO SONG.

capotasto (*Italian*) the 'head of the fingerboard', i.e. the raised part or 'nut' at the top of the FINGERBOARD of a stringed instrument that defines the lengths of the strings. A moveable capotasto, comprising a wood or metal bar that can be clamped to the fingerboard, is occasionally used on fretted instruments to shorten all the strings at the same time, thus raising the PITCH.

cappella, a *see* A CAPPELLA.

capriccio (*Italian*) 'caprice'; a short, lively piece.

caricature a drawing of a person in which his or her most prominent features are exaggerated or distorted in order to produce a recognizable but ridiculous portrait, possibly suggesting a likeness to another object.

carillon (1) a set of bells, usually in a bell tower, which can be played by electrical or mechanical means to produce a tune. (2) an ORGAN STOP which produces a bell-like sound.

carol originally, any medieval English song with a refrain, but now generally a song associated with Christmas.

cartoon (1) a drawing, or series of drawings, intended to convey humour, satire or wit. Cartoons were commonly used from the 18th century onwards in newspapers and periodicals as a vehicle for social and political comment, and in comic magazines for children and adults in the 20th century. (2) a full-size preparatory drawing for a painting, mural or fresco.

castanets a Spanish PERCUSSION INSTRUMENT comprising two shell-like pieces of wood which are clicked together by the fingers. In orchestras, they are occasionally shaken on the end of sticks.

castrato (*Italian*) an adult male singer with a SOPRANO or CONTRALTO voice produced by castration before puberty. Castrati were popular singers in the 17th and 18th centuries. The practice was abandoned during the 19th century.

catch a ROUND for three or more VOICES. The words are often humorous and frequently contain puns, for example, *Ah, how Sophia* which, when sung, sounds like 'Our house afire'.

Cavalier Poets a loose grouping of lyric poets associated with the court or cause of Charles I during his clashes with the English Parliament and the ensuing Civil War. The most notable poets are Robert Herrick (1591–1764), Thomas Carew (*c*.1595–1640) and Richard Lovelace (1618–*c*.1658).

cavatina (*Italian*) a short and often slow SONG or instrumental piece.

Cecilia, St the patron saint of music who was martyred in the second or third century. Since the 16th century music festivals to commemorate her have been annual events. Her feast day is 22 November.

celesta a small keyboard instrument in which HAMMERS are made to strike metal bars suspended over wooden resonators; the sound produced has an ethereal, bell-like quality.

cello *see* VIOLONCELLO.

cembalo (*Italian*) (1) a DULCIMER. (2) an abbreviation of *clavicembalo*, which is the Italian for HARPSICHORD.

chalk a soft stone, similar to a very soft limestone, used for drawing. *Crayon* is powdered chalk mixed with oil or wax.

chamber music originally, chamber music was a term used to describe any type of music that was suitable for playing in a room of a house as opposed to a church or concert hall. However, it has come to mean music for a small number of instruments (for example, flute and piano) or group of performers (for example, STRING QUARTET, SEXTET, etc.), with one instrument to each part.

chamber orchestra a small orchestra, sometimes solely of stringed instruments, for performing CHAMBER MUSIC.

changing note *or* **cambiatta** a dissonant PASSING NOTE which is a third away from a preceding note, before being resolved.

chanson (*French*) a song for either a SOLO VOICE or a CHOIR. In some contexts it can also mean an instrumental piece of song-like quality.

chant a general term for a type of music which is sung as part of a ritual or ceremony. It is a term which is used particularly for unaccompanied singing in religious services.

chanter the pipe of a BAGPIPE, on which the MELODY is played.

chanterelle (*French*) literally the 'singing one', i.e the highest string on a bowed, stringed instrument (for example, the E string on a VIOLIN).

character piece a term used by composers for a short instrumental piece, such as may attempt to describe a specific mood.

charcoal the carbon residue from wood that has been partially burned. Charcoal will make easily ersable black marks and is used mainly to make preliminary drawings.

charleston a ballroom dance, similar to the FOXTROT.

chest voice the lower REGISTER (2) of VOICE (1), so called because NOTES seem to emanate from the chest. *Compare* HEAD VOICE.

chiaroscuro (*Italian*) literally 'light-dark', used to describe the use of light and shade in a painting, drawing or engraving to convey depth and shape.

chinoiserie the style of Chinese fine art much imitated and mass produced, both in Europe and the Far East. A familiar product of this range is the Willow Pattern pottery range.

chitarrone (*Italian*) a large LUTE.

choir (1) the place, defined by special seats or 'choir stalls', in a large church or cathedral where singers are positioned. (2) a body of singers, such as a male-voice choir, church choir. (3) (US) a section of the orchestra, for example 'brass choir'.

choirbook a large medieval volume that (usually) included both words and music and was designed to be read by various members of a CHOIR (2) while it was stationed on a centrally placed lectern.

choir organ the section of an ORGAN that is played from the lowest MANUAL and is soft enough to accompany a church CHOIR (2).

choral an adjective used to describe music that involves a CHORUS, for example CHORAL SYMPHONY.

chorale a HYMN-tune of the Lutheran Church, dating back to the 15th century.

choral symphony (1) a SYMPHONY in which a CHORUS is used at some point (or, indeed, a symphony written entirely for voices). (2) the popular name of Beethoven's symphony no. 9 in D Minor, which ends with 'An die Freude' ('Ode to Joy') for chorus and soloists.

chord a combination of NOTES played simultaneously, usually not less than three.

chorus (1) a body of singers. *See* CHOIR. (2) music written for a body of singers (usually to follow an introductory piece). (3) a REFRAIN that follows a SOLO verse.

chromatic (from Greek *chromatikos,* 'coloured') a term describing NOTES which do not belong to a prevailing SCALE, for example, in C major all SHARPS and FLATS (1) are chromatic notes. The 'chromatic scale' is a scale of twelve ascending or descending SEMITONES; and a 'chromatic CHORD' is a chord that contains chromatic notes. *See also* TWELVE-NOTE MUSIC.

cimbal, cimbalom *see* DULCIMER.

cittern a pear shaped stringed instrument of the GUITAR family popular from the 16th century to the 18th century. It was similar to the LUTE except that it had a flat back and wire strings, and was easier to play.

clappers virtually any kind of PERCUSSION INSTRUMENT comprising two similar pieces that can be struck together, for example BONES, spoons and sticks.

clarinet a single-REED WOODWIND instrument dating back to the 17th century. It has a cylindrical tube and nowadays comes in two common sizes: B flat and A. It is an instrument common to both CLASSICAL music and JAZZ.

clàrsach (*Gaelic*) a small HARP of the Scottish Highlands and Ireland.

classical (1) a term used to describe a certain form of music which adheres to basic conventions and forms that are more concerned with carefully controlled expression rather than unrestrained emotion. (2) a term used to describe 'serious' music as opposed to popular music.

Classicism a style of art based on order, serenity and emotional control, with reference to the classical art of the ancient Greeks and Romans. It eschews the impulsive creativity and spontaneity of Romanticism in favour of peace, harmony and strict ideals of beauty. *See also* NEOCLASSICISM.

clavecin (*French*) *see* HARPSICHORD.

claves short sticks that are held in the hand and clicked together to emphasise a BEAT (1) or RHYTHM.

clavicembalo (*Italian*) *see* HARPSICHORD.

clavichord a keyboard instrument dating from the 15th century in which the strings are struck by a brass 'tangent' and can be made to sound a note of variable PITCH until the KEY (1) is released.

clavier (1) a practice keyboard which makes no sound save clicks. (2) any keyboard instrument that has strings, for example, the CLAVICHORD, the HARPSICHORD, the PIANO.

clef a symbol positioned on a line of a STAVE which indicates the PITCH of the line and consequently all the NOTES on the stave. Three clefs are commonly used: ALTO (TENOR), TREBLE and BASS.

close harmony HARMONY in which the NOTES of the CHORDS are close together.

In singing, this means that each VOICE remains fairly close to the MELODY.

coda (*Italian*) literally a 'tail', meaning a PASSAGE at the end of a piece of music which rounds it off.

col, coll', colla, colle (*Italian*) literally 'with the', so *col basso* means 'with bass'; *colle voce*, 'with voice'.

collage a piece of art created by adhering pieces of paper, fabric, wood, etc, on to a flat surface.

coloratura (*Italian*) the florid ornamentation of a melodic line, especially in opera.

colour (1) in art, an effect induced in the eye by light of various wavelengths, the colour perceived depending on the specific wavelength of light reflected by an object. Most objects contain pigments that absorb certain light frequencies and reflect others, e.g. the plant pigment chlorophyll usually absorbs orange or red light and reflects green or blue, therefore the majority of plants appear to be green in colour. A white surface is one where all light frequencies are reflected and a black surface absorbs all frequencies. (2) in music, the TONE quality of instruments and voices.

colour field painting a movement begun by abstract EXPRESSIONISTS towards a more intellectual abstraction. Their paintings were large areas of pure, flat colour, the mood and atmosphere being created by the shape of the canvas and by sheer scale.

colourist a term in art criticism referring to an artist who places emphasis on colour over line or form. The term is, however, too vague to be applied consistently.

combination tone a faint (third) NOTE that is heard when two notes are sounded simultaneously; also called a 'resultant tone'.

combo an abbreviation of 'combination', especially a collection of musicians that make up a JAZZ BAND.

comedy a form of drama, usually of a light and humorous kind and frequently involving misunderstandings that are resolved in a happy ending. The first major examples known, those by the Greek dramatist Aristophanes (*c*.448–380 BC), are still among the greatest, and became known as *old comedy*. The roots of Aristophanes' work are ancient, based on fertility rituals, and often involve ferocious attacks on named individuals, e.g., Euripides (480–406 BC) and Socrates (470–399 BC). The so-called *new comedy* developed in Greece is known to us largely through adaptations of lost Greek originals by Roman dramatists. It is this new comedy, based upon Aristotle's (384–322 BC) opinion that the business of comedy is with people of no significance (who can be safely ridiculed), that was to prevail on the stage until the advent of Anton Chekhov (1860–1904), Henrik Ibsen (1828–1906) and August Strindberg (1849–1912), with their downbeat comedies of middle-class life. These latter comedies may loosely be described as *tragicomedies*, although the term is normally reserved to denote those plays of the Jacobean period, for example Shakespeare's *Measure for Measure*. Other notable forms of comedy include the comedy of HUMOURS, the COMEDY OF MANNERS, SENTIMENTAL COMEDY and COMMEDIA DELL'ARTE. *See also* MELODRAMA, *compare* TRAGEDY.

comedy of humours see HUMOURS, THEORY OF.

comedy of manners a form of comedy that features intrigues, invariably involving sex and/or money, among an upper region of society. The central characters are usually witty sophisticates, and there is often much mockery of characters from inferior stations who try to imitate the behaviour of their betters, e.g. a merchant trying to live the lifestyle of a gallant. The form is associated particularly with RESTORATION dramatists such as William Congreve (1670–1729), whose *The Way of the World* (1700) is the finest example of this form.

comic opera an OPERA that has an amusing plot, or (sometimes) an opera that includes some spoken dialogue.

commedia dell'arte a form of Italian comedy, popular from the RENAISSANCE until the 18th century, that used stock farcical characters (such as Harlequin and Columbine) and plots as a basis for improvisation. Actors wore masks representing their particular characters, and were often skilled acrobats.

common chord a MAJOR or MINOR CHORD, usually consisting of a keynote and its third and FIFTH.

compass the musical RANGE of a VOICE or instrument.

composition in art, the arrangement of elements in a drawing, painting or sculpture in proper proportion and relation to each other and to the whole. In music, (1) a work of music. (2) the putting together of sounds in a creative manner. (3) the art of writing music.

compound interval an INTERVAL which is greater than an OCTAVE.

compound time musical TIME in which each BEAT (1) in a BAR is divisible by three, for example 6/8, 9/8 and 12/8 time.

concert a public performance of secular music other than an OPERA or BALLET.

concert grand a large GRAND PIANO that is used in concert halls.

concertina a type of ACCORDION, hexagonal in shape, with small studs at each end which are used as keys.

concertmaster (*US*) the first violinist, or leader of an orchestra.

concerto (*Italian*) (1) originally, a work for one or several voices with instrumental ACCOMPANIMENT. (2) a work for several contrasted instruments. (3) an orchestral work in several movements, containing passages for groups of SOLO instruments (*concerto grosso*). (4) a piece for a solo instrument and an accompanying orchestra.

concert overture an orchestral piece of one MOVEMENT, similar to an opera OVERTURE, but written solely for performance in a concert hall. It originated in the 19th century.

concert pitch the internationally agreed PITCH, according to which A above middle C (in the middle of the TREBLE CLEF) is fixed at 440 hertz (cycles per second).

concitato (*Italian*) 'agitated'.

concord a combination of sounds (such as a CHORD) that are satisfactory and sound agreeable. The opposite of DISSONANCE.

concrete art a term used to describe severely geometrical abstract art.

concrete music *see* MUSIQUE CONCRÈTE.

conducting the art of directing and controlling an ORCHESTRA or CHOIR (or operatic performance) by means of gestures. As well as indicating the speed of a piece, a conductor, who often uses a BATON to exaggerate his or her arm movements, is also responsible for interpreting the music.

conjunct a succession of NOTES of different PITCH.

conservatory a school that specialises in musical training. The term originates from the kind of charitable institutions for orphans, called *conservatorii* in 16th- and 17th-century Italy, where music was taught to a high standard.

consort an old spelling of the word 'concert', meaning an ENSEMBLE of instruments, for example, a consort of VIOLS.

Constructivism a movement in abstract expressionism concerned with forms and movement in sculpture and the aesthetics of the industrial age. It began in post-World War I Russia with the sculptors Antoine Pevsner (1886–1962), his brother Naum Gabo (1890–1979) and Vladimir Tatlin (1885–1953). Their work, which made use of modern plastics, glass and wood, was intentionally nonrepresentational. Their ideas were published in Gabo's *Realistic Manifesto* (1920). Gabo and Pevsner left Russia in 1922 and 1923 respectively and went on to exert great influence on Western art.

Constructivist theatre a form of theatre devised by Vsevolod Meyerhold (1874–1940), Russian theatrical producer and director. By the time the

Bolsheviks came to power in 1917, Meyerhold was recognised as the most prominent exponent of avante-garde ideas and productions on the Russian stage. Among the plays he produced at his Meyerhold Theatre were those of Mayakovsky (*see* FUTURISM). His productions cheerfully abandoned traditional conventions, such as the proscenium arch, and broke plays up into episodic segments. Stage sets were determinedly Constructivist, i.e. they used technological artefacts derived from industrial processes to emphasise the kinetic, active nature of the stage (in large part a development from *Russian Futurism*). Actors were encouraged to think of themselves as 'biomechanisms', and to study circus acrobatics and the conventions of COMMEDIA DELL' ARTE. Meyerhold's ideas inevitably proved intolerable to the Soviet cultural commissars of Socialist realism and he was executed.

continuo (*Italian*) an abbreviation of *basso continuo. See* FIGURED BASS.

contrabass (1) (adjective) an instrument that is an OCTAVE lower than the normal BASS of the family, for example, contrabass TUBA. (2) (noun) a DOUBLE BASS.

contralto the lowest female VOICE, which usually has a range of about two OCTAVES.

contrapuntal relating to COUNTERPOINT.

contratenor the 14th and 15th century word for a *voice* with approximately the same range as a *tenor*.

cor anglais (*French*) literally 'English horn', but it is neither English nor a horn. It is in fact an ALTO OBOE pitched a FIFTH below the standard oboe.

corda (*Italian*) a 'string', as in 'piano string'; the term *una corda* literally means 'one string', an indication to use the 'soft' PEDAL on the PIANO.

cornet (1) a BRASS INSTRUMENT with three valves that has a quality of TONE (3) lying between a HORN and a TRUMPET; it has great flexibility and is often used in MILITARY and JAZZ BANDS. (2) an ORGAN STOP used for playing flourishes.

cottage piano a small upright PIANO.

counterpoint the combination of two or more independent melodic lines that fit together to create a coherent SOUND texture. The CLASSICAL (1) conventions of HARMONY are based on counterpoint.

counter-subject a MELODY, found in a FUGUE, that is CONTRAPUNTAL to the main THEME (SUBJECT), i.e. after singing the subject, a VOICE (2) carries on to sing the counter-subject while the answer is sung.

counter-tenor the highest natural male VOICE (not to be confused with FALSETTO).

country and western a generic term for a form of 20th-century American folk music, originating from the southeast of the USA, with Nashville, Tennessee, as its traditional home. It is usually played by small BANDS using FIDDLES, GUITARS, BANJOS and DRUMS etc. The songs are typically of a sentimental, sometimes tragic, nature.

couplet (1) the same as DUPLET. (2) a two-note SLUR. (3) a SONG in which the same music is repeated for every STANZA.

courante (*French*) short for *danse courante* or 'running dance', a lively Baroque dance in triple time.

crayon *see* CHALK.

crescendo (*Italian*) 'increasing', i.e. getting gradually louder.

croche (*French*) a QUAVER.

crook (1) a detachable section of tubing that was inserted into a BRASS or WOODWIND INSTRUMENT between the MOUTHPIECE and the body of the instrument to give it a different KEY (by increasing the length of the air-column). Performers often had as many as twelve crooks but, the introduction of valved instruments in the 1850s virtually dispensed with their necessity. (2) a curved metal tube between the mouthpiece and the body of large wind instruments such as the BASSOON and BASS CLARINET.

cross rhythms rhythms that appear to have conflicting patterns and are performed at the same time as one another.

crotchet (*US* 'quarter note') a NOTE with a quarter of the time value of a whole note (SEMIBREVE).

Cruelty, Theatre of a form of theatre devised by the French actor and theatre director Antonin Artaud (1896–1948) which uses non-verbal means of communication such as pantomine, light effects and irrational language, to project the pain and loss fostered by the modern world. His aim was to use drama to subvert the idea of art as a set of concepts separate from real life and he has had a lasting effect on Western drama.

crumhorn *see* KRUMHORN.

Cubism an art movement started by Pablo Picasso (1881–1973) and Georges Braque (1882–1963) and influenced by African tribal masks and carvings, and by the work of Paul Cézanne (1839–1906). They moved away from REALIST and IMPRESSIONIST trends towards a more intellectual representation of objects. Hitherto, painters had observed subjects from a fixed viewpoint, but the Cubists also wanted to represent a more cerebral understanding of their subject. The result was an explosion of multi-viewpoint images, often broken up into geometric shapes and realigned to suggest faces full on and in profile together, to explain the three-dimensional variety of an object or to imply movement. Such fragmented images could be highly complicated. Cubism had an enormous and continuing influence on 20th-century art.

cuckoo a short PIPE with a single finger hole; it gives two notes that imitate the sound of the bird.

cue a catchword or note on a score, used to indicate the entrance of a voice or instrument.

curtain music *see* ACT TUNE.

curtall a small BASSOON of the 16th and 17th centuries.

cycle a series or sequence of pieces of music, by a single composer, which have a common THEME or idea.

cymbalo *see* DULCIMER.

cymbals PERCUSSION INSTRUMENTS comprising two metal plates which are held in the hands and clashed together. They are mounted on stands for JAZZ and POPULAR MUSIC DRUM KITS, where they are operated by pedals or struck with sticks.

D (1) the second NOTE of the SCALE of C major. (2) abbreviation for DOMINANT, and for doctor (as in D.Mus., Doctor of Music).

da capo (*Italian*) 'from the head'; it is an instruction to repeat the beginning of the piece (abbreviation: DC).

Dada an art movement that began in Zurich in 1915, its name randomly chosen from a lexicon. Dada represented a reaction to postwar disillusion with established art. Leading figures included Jean Arp (1887–1966) and the poet Tristan Tzara (1896–1963), and when the movement moved to New York, Francis Picabia (1879–1953) and Marcel Duchamp (1887–1968). Its aim was to reject accepted aesthetic and cultural values and to promote an irrational form of non-art, or anti-art. The random juxtapositions of collage and the use of ready-made objects suited their purpose best. A notable example is Duchamp's *Fountain* (1917), which was an unadorned urinal. Dada gave way to NEUE SACHLICHKEIT around 1924 as the artists associated with the movement diversified. It led, however, to the beginnings of SURREALISM and is the source of other movements in ABSTRACT ART, such as ACTION PAINTING.

Danube School a school of German painters who developed the art of landscape painting as a genre in its own right. Its most prominent member was Albrecht Altdorfer (1480–1538) whose work is characterised by a fantastic inventiveness, distortion of figures and brilliant effects of colour and light.

DC *see* DA CAPO.

début (*French*) 'beginning', i.e. a first appearance.

decibel one tenth of a BEL, a unit for measuring SOUND. A decibel represents the smallest change in loudness detected by the average human ear.

Deconstruction *see* STRUCTURALISM.

degree a step of a SCALE; the position of each NOTE on a scale is identified by its degree.

descant (1) a soprano part, sometimes improvised, sung above a HYMN TUNE while the tune itself is sung by the rest of the congregation or CHOIR. (2) (spelt **discant** by music scholars) a general term for all forms of POLYPHONY used from the 12th century.

De Stijl *see* STIJL, DE.

deus ex machina a Latin term meaning 'god from the machine', i.e. a god introduced into the action of a play to resolve some intractable situation in the plot. A device common in both Greek and Roman drama. In Greek drama, the intervention took the form of the god being lowered onto the stage via some kind of stage machinery. The term has come to denote any twist in a plot which resolves or develops the action in an unexpected way.

diapason (1) the term given to a family of ORGAN STOPS which are largely responsible for the TONE of the instrument. (2) (*French*) a TUNING FORK; *diapason normal* means the same as CONCERT PITCH.

diatonic belonging to a SCALE. The diatonic NOTES of a major scale consist of five TONES (T) and two SEMITONES (S), arranged TTSTTTS. *Compare* CHROMATIC.

digital (1) one of the KEYS on the keyboard of a PIANO or ORGAN. (2) in sound recording, a method of converting audio or analogue signals into a series of pulses according to their voltage, for storage or manipulation.

diminished interval a PERFECT or MAJOR INTERVAL reduced by one SEMITONE by flattening the upper NOTE or sharpening the lower one.

diminished seventh chord a CHORD which covers a MINOR SEVENTH diminished by one SEMITONE, i.e. C-B flat diminished to C-A. (This is in fact equivalent to a major sixth, but the term 'diminished seventh' is often used.) It is frequently employed as a means of TRANSITION into another KEY.

diminuendo (*Italian*) 'diminishing', i.e. getting gradually quieter.

diminution the shortening of NOTE TIME-values, so that a MELODY is played more quickly, usually at double speed.

diptych a pair of paintings or carvings on two panels hinged together so that they can be opened or closed.

discord a CHORD or combination of NOTES which creates an unpleasant or jarring sound that needs to be resolved.

dissonance the creation of an unpleasant sound or DISCORD.

distemper an impermanent paint made by mixing colours with eggs or glue instead of oil.

divertimento (*Italian*) an 18th-century term for a piece of music that was intended to be a light entertainment, i.e. a diversion.

divertissement (*French*) (1) a short ballet incorporated into an opera or play. (2) a short piece that includes well-known tunes taken from another source. (3) a DIVERTIMENTO.

divisi (*Italian*) 'divided'; a term used to indicate that, where a PART is written in double NOTES, performers should not attempt to play all the notes but should divide themselves into groups to play them. It is particularly used in music for STRINGS.

division (1) a 17th-century type of VARIATION in which the long NOTES of a MELODY were split up into shorter ones. (2) an obsolete term for long vocal RUNS.

Divisionism *see* POSTIMPRESSIONISM.

'Dixieland' a simple form of traditional JAZZ , originated in New Orleans at the start of the 20th century.

do (*Italian*) *see* DOH.

dodecaphonic relating to dodecaphony, the TWELVE-NOTE SYSTEM of composition.

doh the spoken name for the first NOTE of a MAJOR SCALE in TONIC SOL-FA.

domestic tragedy a form of tragedy that appeared in the Elizabethan period, which focuses on the crises of middle-class domestic life in an unpatronising and sympathetic manner. An early example is the anonymous *Arden of Faversham* (1592).

dominant (1) the fifth NOTE above the TONIC of a MAJOR or MINOR SCALE. (2) the name given to the RECITING NOTE of GREGORIAN CHANTS.

doppio (*Italian*) 'double', as in *doppio movimento*, meaning 'twice as fast'.

Dorian mode a term applied to the ascending SCALE which is played on the white keys of a PIANO beginning at D.

dot a MARK used in musical NOTATION. When it is placed after a NOTE, it makes the note half as long again; when it is placed above a note it indicates STACCATO.

dotted note *see* DOT.

double (1) a word used to describe certain instruments that are built an OCTAVE lower than normal, for example a double BASSOON (also called a *contrabassoon*) is built an octave lower than a standard bassoon. (2) a term used to describe a type of VARIATION found in 17th-century French instrumental music in which MELODY NOTES are embellished with ornamentation.

double bass the largest and lowest-pitched of the bowed string instruments. It used to have three strings but now it has four (sometimes five).

down-beat the downward movement of a conductor's BATON or hand which usually indicates the first BEAT of a BAR.

drama (1) a PLAY for the stage, radio or television. (2) dramatic literature as a genre.

dramatic irony a situation in which a character in a PLAY, NOVEL, etc, says or does something that has a meaning for the audience or reader, other than the obvious meaning, that he or she does not understand. Its use is common in both COMEDY and TRAGEDY.

drone a PIPE that sounds a continuous NOTE of fixed PITCH as a permanent BASS. The BAGPIPES, for example, have several drone pipes. Also, a similar effect produced by stringed instruments fitted with 'drone strings'.

drum a PERCUSSION INSTRUMENT of which there are numerous types, including BASS DRUM, SIDE DRUM, TABOR, TENOR DRUM and TIMPANI. Most drums consist of a hollow metal or wood cylinder over which is stretched a skin. Sound is produced by beating the skin with drumsticks or with the hands.

drum kit a set of DRUMS and CYMBALS arranged in such a way that they can all be played by one person sitting on a stool. Some of the instruments (such as the BASS DRUM) are played with a foot PEDAL, but most are struck with sticks or wire brushes. They are used by JAZZ and POP drummers and can vary enormously in size.

due corde (*Italian*) literally 'two strings'; a term used in VIOLIN music indicating that a PASSAGE that could theoretically be played on one string should nevertheless be played on two to produce the desired effect.

duet a combination of two performers or a composition for such a pair, for example, piano duet.

dulcimer *or* **cymbalo** an ancient instrument introduced to Europe from the East in the Middle Ages. It consists of a shallow box over which strings are stretched. It is placed on the knees and the strings struck with small HAMMERS. In the USA, an instrument like the ZITHER may be called a dulcimer.

dulcitone a keyboard instrument containing TUNING FORKS which are struck with HAMMERS, as in a PIANO.

duplet a group of two NOTES of equal value which are played in the time normally taken by three.

duple time a form of musical TIME in which the number of BEATS in a BAR is a multiple of two, for example 2/4 (2 CROTCHETS) and 6/8 (6 QUAVERS in two groups of three).

dynamic accents ACCENTS which correspond to the regular RHYTHM of a piece of music, as indicated by the TIME SIGNATURE.

E the third note (MEDIANT) of the SCALE of C major.

eighth-note (US) a QUAVER.

electronic instruments a generic term for instruments that convert electrical energy into sound, such as the SYNTHESIZER.

embouchure (1) the mouthpiece of a BRASS or WIND INSTRUMENT. (2) the correct tensioning of the lips and facial muscles when playing woodwind and brass instruments to create good TONE.

encore (*French*) 'again', the call from an English audience (the French equivalent is bis) for more music. If the performance does continue, the additional music is also known as an 'encore'.

end pin *see* TAIL PIN.

engraving a technique of cutting an image into a metal or wood plate using special tools. When ink is applied to the plate, the raised parts will print black and the engraved parts white. The term is also used for a print produced in this way.

enharmonic intervals INTERVALS that are so small that they do not exist on keyboard instruments; an example is the interval from A sharp to B flat.

ensemble (*French*) literally 'together'; a term meaning a group of players or singers, a MOVEMENT in OPERA for several singers, or the precision with which such a group performs together.

entr'acte (*French*) the music played between the acts of a play or OPERA. *See also* ACT TUNE, INTERLUDE, INTERMEZZO.

epic (1) a very long narrative poem dealing with heroic deeds and adventures on a grand scale, as Homer's *Iliad*. (2) a novel or film with some of these qualities.

episode (1) in a FUGUE, a PASSAGE that connects entries of the SUBJECT. (2) in a RONDO, a contrasting section that separates entries of the PRINCIPAL THEME.

epistolary novel a novel in the form of a series of letters written to and from the main characters, sometimes presented by the author in the anonymous role of 'editor'. The form flourished in the 18th century, an example being Samuel Richardson's *Pamela* (1741).

equal temperament a convenient, but technically incorrect, way of tuning a keyboard in which all SEMITONES are considered equal, for example F sharp and G flat are taken to be identical NOTES when theoretically they are not. Such a system makes complex MODULATIONS practicable.

escapement the mechanism in a PIANO which releases the HAMMER, allowing a string to vibrate freely after it has been struck.

etching a technique of making an engraving in a metal plate, using acid to bite out the image rather than tools. Tones of black or grey can be produced, depending on the extent the acid is allowed to bite. The term is also used for a print produced in this way.

étude (*French*) a piece of music evolved from a single PHRASE or idea. Studies are also written purely as exercises to improve technique or FINGERING.

eulogy in literature a work of praise for an individual who is either distinguished or recently deceased. An *elegy* is a poem of lamentation for the dead.

euphonium a large BRASS INSTRUMENT, a tenor TUBA, which is mainly used in BRASS and MILITARY BANDS.

eurhythmics a system of teaching musical RHYTHM by graceful physical movements. It was invented in 1905 by the Swiss composer and teacher Émile Jaques-Dalcroze (1865–1950).

Existentialism a philosophical position based on a perception of life in which man is an actor forced to make choices in an essentially meaningless universe that functions as a colossal and cruel THEATRE OF THE ABSURD. Writers associated with Existentialism include Jean-Paul Sartre (1905–80) and Albert Camus (1913–60), and Samuel Beckett (1906– 89).

exposition (1) in the SONATA FORM, the first section of a piece in which the main THEMES are introduced before they are developed. (2) in FUGUE, the initial statement of the SUBJECT by each of the PARTS.

Expressionism a term, derived from the character of some 20th-century Northern European art. Expressionist works represented a move away from the observational detachment of REALISM and, to an extent, IMPRESSIONIST trends, and were concerned with conveying the artist's feelings and emotions as aroused by his subject. The term expressionist also refers to an expressive quality of distortion or heightened colour in art from any period or place. *See also* ABSTRACT EXPRESSIONISM. In music it is used to imply the expression of inner emotions.

F (1) the fourth note (or SUBDOMINANT) of the scale of C major. (2) in abbreviations, *f* means *forte* (loud); *ff*, *fortissimo* (very loud) and *fp*, *forte piano* (loud and then soft).

fa In the TONIC SOL-FA, the fourth degree in any major scale.

falsetto (*Italian*) an adult male voice, used in the register above its normal range. It has often been used to comic effect in operas.

fancy *see* FANTASIA.

fanfare a flourish of trumpets, or other instruments (for example, the organ) that imitate the sound of trumpets.

fantasia (*Italian*) a piece in which the composer follows his imagination in free association rather than composing within a particular conventional form; when such a piece is played, it can sound as if it is being improvised.

Fauvists a group of French painters, including Henri Matisse (1869–1954) and André Derain (1880–1954), whose style was very vivid and colourful. The term *fauve* ('wild animal') was coined as a form of derogatory criticism. They were less interested in representing what they saw and more concerned to express their own feelings in the boldness and freedom of their compositions. Although Matisse continued to explore Fauvist techniques, the other artists soon diverged, and the movement was fairly short-lived. It was, however, influential in CUBIST and EXPRESSIONIST art.

feminine cadence an ending in which the final chord occurs on a weak beat of the bar and not the more usual strong beat.

fermata (*Italian*) *see* PAUSE.

fiddle (1) a generic term for a range of primitive stringed instruments played with a bow, as used in parts of Asia, Africa and Eastern Europe. (2) a colloquial term for a violin, especially in folk music.

fife a small flute still used in 'drum and fife' bands.

fifth an INTERVAL of five notes (the first and last notes are counted) or seven semitones, for example, from C to G.

figurative art *or* **representational art** art that recognizably represents figures, objects or animals from real life, as opposed to ABSTRACT ART.

figure a short musical phrase that is repeated in the course of a composition.

figured bass the bass part of a composition which has numerical figures written below the notes to indicate how the harmony above should be played. In effect a type of musical shorthand, the bass line and melody are written down while the numbers indicate which chords should be played. The system was used during the 17th and early 18th centuries.

finale (*Italian*) (1) the last movement of a work. (2) the concluding section of an opera act.

fine arts *see* APPLIED ARTS.

fingering a type of notation that indicates which fingers should be used to play a piece of music.

fino (*Italian*) 'as far as', so *fino al segno* means 'as far as the sign'.

fipple flute *see* FLAGEOLET; RECORDER.

Five, The the name given to a group of nationalistic 19th-century Russian composers who were known in Russia as *moguchaya kuchka* (The Mighty Handful). The five were Rimsky-Korsakov (1844–1908), Mily Alexeyevich Balakirev (1837–1910), Aleksandr Borodin (1833–87), César Antonovich Cui (1835–1918) and Modest Mussorgsky (1839–81).

flageolet a small, end-blown FLUTE with six holes, four in front and two at the back, popular in the 17th century.

flamenco a generic term for a type of Spanish song from Andalusia, usually sad and often accompanied by guitar and dancing. Flamenco guitar playing relies heavily on the strumming of powerful, dynamic rhythms.

flat (1) a note which is lowered by one semitone as indicated by the flat sign. (2) a note (or notes) produced at too low a pitch and hence 'out of tune'.

flue pipes all ORGAN pipes that have narrow openings, or flues, into which air passes; the other pipes are REED PIPES.

Flügelhorn (*German*) a soprano brass instrument similar to a bugle in shape, but with three pistons.

flute (1) the tranverse or German flute is a member of the WOODWIND family of instruments, although these days it is normally made of silver or other metal. One end of the instrument is stopped and sound is produced by blowing across the mouthpiece formed around an aperture cut into the side of the instrument at the stopped end. The pitch is controlled by means of a lever system. (2) the English flute is a beaked, end-blown, wind instrument with finger holes, now more usually called the RECORDER.

folk dance any dance, performed by ordinary people, in a pre-industrial society, that has evolved over the years and gained a traditional form. Folk dances differ widely in character and some have symbolic significance, such as war dances, etc.

folk song properly, any song that has been preserved by oral tradition. Many composers and pop musicians have written new compositions that imitate old folk songs.

form the structure of a composition. The basic elements of musical composition which define a given piece's form are repetition, variation and contrast. Examples of recognised forms include FUGUE, RONDO, SONATA FORM, etc.

forte (*Italian*) 'loud' (abbreviation *f*).

fortepiano (*Italian*) an early word for PIANOFORTE. Not to be confused with *forte piano* (loud then soft).

fortissimo (*Italian*) 'very loud' (abbreviation *ff*).

found object *or* **objet trouvé** a form of art that began with DADA and continued with SURREALISM, where an object, either natural or manufactured, is displayed as a piece of art in its own right.

fourth an INTERVAL of four notes (including the first and last) or five semitones, for example C to F.

fp abbreviation for FORTE PIANO (*Italian*) 'loud then soft'.

free reed a type of REED found in such instruments as the ACCORDION and

HARMONICA. It consists of a small metal tongue that vibrates freely in a metal slot when air is blown over it. The pitch of the reed is determined by its thickness and length.

French horn *see* HORN.

fresco a painting directly painted on to a wall that has previously been covered with a damp, freshly laid layer of lime plaster, the paint and plaster reacting chemically to become stable and permanent. Fresco painting worked particularly well in the warm, dry climate of Italy, where it reached its peak in the 16th century.

fret (*French*) one of a series of thin pieces of metal fitted into the wooden fingerboard of a stringed instrument to make the stopping of strings easier and more accurate. Each fret represents the position of a specific note.

fugue a contrapuntal composition for two or more parts (commonly called 'voices') which enter successively in imitation of each other. The first entry is called the 'SUBJECT' and the second entry (a fifth higher or lower than the subject) is called the 'ANSWER'. When all the voices have entered, the EXPOSITION is complete and is usually followed by an EPISODE which connects to the next series of subject entries. A fugue may be written for voices, instruments or both. The form dates back to the 17th century.

full organ a term used in organ music to indicate that all the loud stops are to be used together.

funk a form of heavily syncopated, rhythmic black dance music, originating in the United States. The adjective, often used in JAZZ terminology, is *funky*.

Futurism a movement of writers and artists, originating in early 20th-century Italy, that extolled the virtues of the new, dynamic machine age, which was reckoned to have rendered the aesthetic standards of the past redundant. The founding document of the movement is poet Filipo Marinetti's (1876–1944) *Futurist Manifesto* of 1909, which, in literature, called for the destruction of traditional sentence construction and the establishment of a 'free verse in free words' (*parole in libertà*) owing nothing to the literary standards of the past; the new relationship between words was to be in terms of analogy alone. The English variant of Futurism is *Vorticism*. The Russian variant, *Russian Futurism*, was led by the poet Vladimir Mayakovsky (1893–1930), whose curious love affair with the Soviet dictatorship ended with his suicide,.

Futurism became a spent force by the 1930s, largely because of its close association with Fascism and the establishment of the Futurist hero Mussolini's dictatorship in Italy (Marinetti's vision of war as 'the hygiene of the world' is also Mussolini's).

In art, Futurism attempted to convey a sense of movement and dynamism. It had a resounding influence on subsequent art movements.

G the fifth note (or DOMINANT) of the scale of C major.

galant (*French*) 'polite'; a term applied to certain graceful styles of court music, especially of the 18th century.

gamelan a type of traditional orchestra found principally in Indonesia and South-East Asia. Although such an orchestra includes strings and wood-wind instruments, it is the array of gongs, drums, chimes, xylophones and marimbas that produces the unique and highly complex rhythms of gamelan music.

gamut (1) the note G on the bottom line of the bass clef. (2) an alternative (now obsolete) word for the key of G. (3) the whole range of musical sounds, from the lowest to the highest.

gavotte an old French dance, originally of the upper Alps, in 4/4 time, which usually starts on the third beat of the bar.

genre a distinctive type or category of artistic or literary composition.

genre painting a painting that has as its subject a scene from everyday life, as opposed to a historical event, mythological scene, etc. Genre paintings appear in the backgrounds of medieval paintings, but it was the Dutch painters who were the first to specialise in them and to continue the tradition. The style did not become really popular with painters until the REAL-ISTS painted genre scenes, but gradually the distinction between such scenes and other genres of painting has blurred.

gigue (*French*) a lively dance or jig.

Glasgow Boys *or* **Glasgow School** a group of painters centred in Glasgow in the 1880s and 90s. They represented a move away from academic stric-tures and were inspired by the plein air BARBIZON SCHOOL. They established an outpost of the European vogue for NATURALISM and ROMANTIC lyricism in landscape painting, and their influence extended into the 20th century.

glass harmonica at its simplest, a set of goblets that are played by rubbing a moistened finger around the rims to produce a high pitched humming sound.

glee a simple, unaccompanied composition for male voices in several sections.

glissando (*Italian*) 'sliding'; a rapid sliding movement up or down a scale.

Glockenspiel (*German*), **Campanelli** (*Italian*) literally 'a play of bells', an instrument, produced in a variety of sizes, comprising steel bars of differ-ent lengths that are arranged like a keyboard; each bar sounds a different note. Played with hammers, it produces sounds that have a bell-like qual-ity. It is used in orchestras and military bands (in which it is held vertically).

gong a PERCUSSION INSTRUMENT that originated in the Far East. Gongs are made in many sizes and shapes, but an orchestral gong consists of nothing more than a large sheet of metal with a pronounced rim. Sound is produced by striking it with a hammer.

gospel song a type of popular religious song originated by black American slaves who sang hymns to pulsating BLUES rhythms.

Gothic a style of architecture that lasted from the 12th to the 16th centuries in Northern Europe and Spain. Its effect on art was to produce the INTERNATIONAL GOTHIC style.

Gothic novel a type of NOVEL that was enormously popular in the late 18th century, combining elements of the supernatural, macabre or fantastic, often in wildly ROMANTIC settings, e.g. ruined abbeys or ancient castles. The heroes and/or heroines, whether medieval or modern, for the most part speak in a formal, stilted language curiously at odds (for the modern reader) with the appalling situations they find themselves in.

gouache *also called* **poster paint** *or* **body paint** an opaque mixture of watercolour paint and white pigment.

grace note an ornamental, extra note, usually written in small type, used to embellish a melody.

grandioso (*Italian*) 'in an imposing manner'.

grand opera a term originally used to distinguish serious opera, sung throughout, from opera that contained some spoken dialogue. The term is now also used to describe a lavish production.

grand piano *see* PIANOFORTE.

great stave a STAVE created by pushing the stave with the treble clef and the stave with the bass clef closer together so that both clefs can be located on one exaggerated stave.

Gregorian chant a term that refers to the large collection of ancient solo and chorus PLAINSONG melodies preserved by the Roman Catholic Church. Although named after Pope Gregory I (*c.*540–604), they date from *c.*800.

grisaille a monochrome painting made using only shades of grey, often used as a sketch for oil paintings.

grotesque a term for a style of ornamentation that began in Roman times and reached its height with ROCOCO. It consisted of a series of figurative or floral ornaments in decorative frames that are linked by festoons.

ground bass a BASS line that is constantly repeated throughout a composition, as a foundation for variation in the upper parts.

guitar a plucked STRING instrument, which may have been introduced to Spain from North Africa. Unlike the LUTE, it has a flat back and usually carries six strings suspended over a fretted finger-board (twelve-string guitars were favoured by certain BLUES musicians). The acoustic ('soundbox') guitar has been played by classical, flamenco and folk musicians for generations, but the electric guitar is a comparatively new development. The body may be hollow (or 'semi-acoustic') or solid, with 'pickups' (electrically motivated resonators that respond to the vibration of the strings) mounted under the BRIDGE. The vibrations received by the pickups have to be electrically amplified or else they are virtually featureless. Electric guitars have a huge COMPASS.

gusto (*Italian*) 'taste', so *con gusto* means 'with taste'.

H (*German*) B natural.

habanera (*Spanish*) a dance of Cuban origin with a powerful, SYNCOPATED RHYTHM, most usually associated, however, with Spain.

Hague School a school of Dutch landscape painters, one of whose prominent leaders was Anton Mauve (1838–88).

haiku a 17-syllable sequential verse form devised by the Japanese poet Basho (1644–94).

half note (US) a MINIM.

half step (US) a SEMITONE.

Hallé Orchestra an internationally famous orchestra founded in Manchester in 1848 by the German-born conductor and pianist Sir Charles Hallé (1819–95).

hammer that part of the PIANO mechanism which strikes the strings; a mallet for playing the DULCIMER; the clapper of a BELL.

Hammond organ the brand name of an electric ORGAN first produced by the Hammond Organ Company, Chicago, in 1935. The sound it produces is electronically manufactured and attempts to reproduce the sound of the PIPE ORGAN. It cannot be said to succeed in this, but its unique temperament has been exploited by JAZZ, POP and music-hall musicians the world over.

handbells bells, of various pitch, that are held in the hands of a group of performers and rung in sequence to create a tune.

harmonica a small, FREE-REED instrument commonly called the *mouth organ*. Although it is a small and apparently inconsequential instrument, many BLUES and FOLK musicians have illustrated its potential by exploiting its emotive power.

harmonic minor MINOR SCALE containing the minor sixth with the MAJOR SEVENTH, in which ascent and descent are without alteration.

harmonics the sounds that can be produced on stringed instruments by lightly touching a string at one of its harmonic nodes, i.e. at a half-length of a string, quarter-length and so on.

harmonium a small, portable REED-ORGAN developed in the 19th century. Air is pumped to the REEDS (which are controlled by STOPS and KEYS) by PEDALS worked continuously by the feet.

harmony (1) the simultaneous sounding of two or more NOTES, i.e CHORDS. A harmonious SOUND is an agreeable or pleasant sound (CONCORD); but harmonisation may also produce sounds which, to some ears at least, are unpleasant (*see* DISCORD). (2) the structure and relationship of chords.

harp an instrument, of ancient origin, consisting of strings stretched across an open frame. It is played by plucking the strings, each of which is tuned (*see* TUNING) to a separate NOTE.

harpsichord a keyboard instrument, developed in the 14th and 15th centuries, in which the strings are plucked by quills or tongues (PLECTRA). The tongues are connected to the KEYS by a simple lever mechanism. The harpsichord went out of favour during the late 18th century due to the introduction of the PIANO. However, it has seen a revival in the 20th century, and new compositions exploiting its 'twangy' sound have been written for it.

Hawaiian guitar a style of GUITAR playing in which a steel bar is moved up and down the strings (as opposed to the more usual STOPPING of strings with the fingers) to produce a distinctive slurred sound. The guitar is usually played horizontally.

head voice the upper register of a VOICE, so called because the sound seems to vibrate in the head of the singer. *Compare* CHEST VOICE.

hemisemidemiquaver the sixty-fourth NOTE, i.e. a note with a value of a quarter of a SEMIQUAVER or $^1/_{64}$th of a SEMIBREVE.

heroic tragedy a form of tragedy that became very popular during the RESTORATION. Such tragedies were usually written in bombastic rhymed couplets and featured the adventures in love and war of noble characters in exotic locations, past and present.

heterophony (*Greek*) literally 'difference of sounds', i.e. two or more performers playing different versions of the same MELODY simultaneously.

hexachord a SCALE of six NOTES which was used in medieval times.

hocket (*French*) the breaking-up of a MELODY into very short PHRASES or single NOTES, with RESTS in between them.

homophony a term applied to music in which the PARTS move 'in step' and do not have independent RHYTHMS. *Compare* POLYPHONY.

hook the black line attached to the stem of all NOTES of less value than a CROTCHET.

horn a BRASS INSTRUMENT consisting of a conical tube coiled into a spiral and ending in a bell. The lips are pushed into a funnel-shaped MOUTHPIECE. The modern orchestral horn is called the *French horn* (because that is where it was developed) and is fitted with three (sometimes four, sometimes seven) valves which open and close various lengths of tubing so that the PITCH of the NOTES can be changed. There are two common 'horns', which are in fact WOODWIND instruments, the BASSET HORN (ALTO CLARINET) and the English horn or COR ANGLAIS (alto OBOE).

hornpipe (1) a single-REED WIND INSTRUMENT played in Celtic countries. (2) a 16th-century dance in triple TIME, originally accompanied by the hornpipe and later erroneously associated with sailors.

humoresque (*French*), **Humoreske** (*German*) a word used as the title for a short, lively piece of music.

hurdy-gurdy a medieval stringed instrument, shaped like a VIOL. A wooden wheel, coated in RESIN, is cranked at one end to make all the strings resonate. The strings are stopped by rods operated by KEYS. The hurdy-gurdy was often used to provide dance music.

icon *or* **ikon** a religious image, usually painted on a wooden panel, regarded as sacred in the Byzantine Church and subsequently by the Orthodox Churches of Russia and Greece, where they survive. The word comes from the Greek *eikon*, meaning 'likeness', and strict rules were devised as to the subject, generally a saint, and to the form of the painting and its use, so although icon painting flourished in the 6th century it is extremely difficult to date icons painted then or later. A reaction to what was considered idolatry took place in the 8th century, resulting in *iconoclasm*, the destruction of such images.

iconography, iconology the study and interpretation of representations in FIGURATIVE ART and their symbolic meanings. It is highly important in understanding Christian art, especially of the medieval and RENAISSANCE periods, e.g. the dove signifying the Holy Spirit, or the fish symbolising Christ.

idée fixe (*French*) 'fixed idea', i.e. a recurring theme.

idiophone any instrument in which SOUND is produced by the VIBRATION of the instrument itself, for example, CYMBALS, BELLS, CASTANETS etc.

Imagism a poetry movement of the early 20th century which advocated using everyday language and precise representation of the image of the subject discussed. Imagist poems were short and to the point, anti-ROMANTIC and anti-Victorian in tone.

imitation a device in COUNTERPOINT whereby a PHRASE is sung successively by different VOICES.

impasto an Italian word used to describe the thickness and textures that can be achieved with acrylic or oil paint.

Impressionism an art movement originating in France in the 1860s, centred on a fairly diverse group of artists who held eight exhibitions together between 1874 and 1886. The prominent artists included Paul Cézanne (1839–1906), Edgar Degas (1834–1917) and Claude Monet (1840–1926). The name of the movement was coined by critics from a painting by Monet in the 1874 exhibition entitled *Impression: Soleil Levant*. The advent of photography and scientific theories about colour had their impact on the painters' approach to their work. The Impressionists were concerned with representing day-to-day existence in an objective and realistic manner, and they rejected the ROMANTIC idea that a painting should convey strong emotions. They wanted to record the fleeting effects of light and movement, and so their usual subjects were landscapes or social scenes like streets and cafés. They chose unusual viewpoints and painted 'close-ups', probably influenced by photography, using unusual colours and a lighter palette. Impressionism has had an enormous influence on almost every subsequent major art movement throughout the 20th-century art.

impromptu a type of PIANO music that sounds as if it has been improvised (*see* IMPROVISATION), i.e. written in a free and easy style.

improvisation the art of playing or 'inventing' music that has not already been composed, i.e. spontaneous composition. Some forms of music (especially JAZZ) often rely heavily on the ability of performers to improvise.

incidental music music written to accompany the action in a play, but the term is also commonly applied to OVERTURES and INTERLUDES.

inflected note a NOTE with an ACCIDENTAL placed before it, i.e. it is sharpened or flattened.

inner parts the PARTS of a piece of music excluding the highest and lowest; for example, in a work for SOPRANO, ALTO, TENOR and BASS, the alto and tenor roles are inner parts.

instrument in music, a device on which or with which music can be played. There are five traditional categories of instrument: WOODWIND, BRASS, PERCUSSION, KEYBOARD, and STRING. However, ELECTRONIC and MECHANICAL INSTRUMENTS also exist.

instrumentation *see* ORCHESTRATION.

intaglio the cutting into a stone or other material or the etching or engraving on a metal plate of an image; the opposite of RELIEF. Intaglio printing techniques include ENGRAVING and ETCHING.

interior monologue a form of STREAM OF CONSCIOUSNESS narrative technique employed by the English novelist Dorothy Richardson (1873–1957) which anticipated James Joyce's (1882–1941) use of the technique in *Ulysses*.

interlude a title sometimes used for a short PART of a complete composition, e.g. a piece of music performed between the acts of an opera. *See also* ACT TUNE, ENTR'ACTE, INTERMEZZO.

intermezzo (*Italian*) (1) a short piece of piano music. (2) a short comic opera performed between the acts of a serious opera, especially in the 16th and 17th centuries. *See also* ACT TUNE, ENTR'ACTE, INTERMEZZO.

International Gothic a predominant style in European art covering the period between the end of the Byzantine era and the beginning of the RENAISSANCE, i.e. *c*.1375–*c*.1425. Some variations in styles occurred regionally, but the most influential centres were Italy, France and the Netherlands. International Gothic style was characterised by decorative detail and refined, flowing lines; figures were often elongated or distorted to increase an appearance of elegant charm and the use of gilts and rich colours figured strongly.

interpretation the way in which a performer plays a piece of composed music. No composer can possibly indicate exactly how a piece should be played and, to some degree, it is up to the performer to play it as he or she thinks fit.

interval the gap or 'sound distance', expressed numerically, between any two NOTES, i.e. the difference in PITCH between two notes. For example, the interval between C and G is called a FIFTH because G is the fifth note from C. *Perfect intervals* are intervals that remain the same in MAJOR and MINOR KEYS (i.e. FOURTHS, fifths, OCTAVES.)

intonation a term used to describe the judgement of PITCH by a performer.

intone to sing on one NOTE.

introduction a section, often slow, found at the start of certain pieces of music, notably SYMPHONIES and SUITES.

inversion a term which literally means turning upside-down. It can refer to a CHORD, INTERVAL, THEME, MELODY or COUNTERPOINT. For example, an *inverted interval* is an interval in which one NOTE changes by an OCTAVE to the other side, as it were, of the other note.

Ionian mode a MODE which, on the PIANO, uses the white NOTES from C to C.

isorhythm a term used to describe a short RHYTHM pattern that is repeatedly applied to an existing MELODY which already has an distinct rhythm.

Jacobean tragedy a development of REVENGE TRAGEDY in the Jacobean period. The distinction between Jacobean and revenge tragedy is a disputed one, hinging on the supposed wave of cynicism and pessimism that is alleged by some historians to have accompanied the accession of James VI of Scotland to the English throne, and the end of the Elizabethan era. The debate is a complex one, but it is undoubtedly the case that plays such as Shakespeare's *Hamlet*, and Webster's *The White Devil* and *The Duchess of Malfi*, display an obsession with political and sexual corruption. The language of these plays is highly sophisticated, ironic, and coldly brilliant.

jam session a 20th-century slang expression for an occasion when a group of musicians join forces to improvise (*see* IMPROVISATION) music. It is usually only appropriate to JAZZ, BLUES and ROCK music.

Janissary music the music of Turkish MILITARY BANDS which influenced European composers during the 18th century. It is particularly associated with CYMBALS, DRUMS and TAMBOURINES.

jazz a term used to describe a style of music that evolved in the Southern States of the USA at the turn of the century. It owes a great deal to the RHYTHMS and idioms of BLUES and SPIRITUALS, but many of the favoured instruments (for example, SAXOPHONE, TRUMPET and TROMBONE) were European in origin. Jazz traditionally relies upon a strong rhythm 'section', comprising BASS and DRUMS, which provides a springboard for other instruments. Jazz developed from being a form of music played in the back streets of New Orleans to a sophisticated art form performed by small dedicated groups as well as 'BIG BANDS' or 'jazz orchestras'.

Self-expression, and therefore IMPROVISATION, has always been a crucial aspect of jazz and this has allowed many individuals, such as Louis Armstrong (1900–1971), to blossom and further its cause. See also BEBOP.

Jazz Modern *see* ART DECO.

Jeune France ('Young France') the name adopted by a group of French composers, including Olivier Messiaen (1908–92), who identified their common aims in 1936.

Jew's harp a simple instrument consisting of a small, heart-shaped metal frame to which a thin strip of hardened steel is attached. The open-ended neck of the frame is held against the teeth and the strip is twanged to produce sound, which is modified by using the cavity of the mouth as a soundbox.

jig a generic term for a lively dance. *See also* GIGUE.

jingle a short, catchy piece of music with equally catchy LYRICS, often used to enliven the commentary of radio stations broadcasting popular music.

jingles an instrument consisting of a number of small bells or rattling objects on a strap, which are shaken to produce sound.

Jugendstil the German form of ART NOUVEAU.

kazoo a simple instrument consisting of a short tube with a small hole in the side which is covered with a thin membrane. When a player hums down the tube, the membrane makes a buzzing sound. Although considered a children's instrument, it is frequently used by FOLK and JAZZ musicians.

kettledrum *see* TIMPANI.

key (1) on a piano, harpsichord, organ etc., one of the finger-operated levers by which the instrument is played. (2) On woodwind instruments, one of the metal, finger-operated levers that opens or closes one or more of the soundholes. (3) a note that is considered to be the most important in a piece of music and to which all the other notes relate. Most pieces of Western music are 'written in a key', i.e. all the chords in the piece are built around a particular note, say F minor. The concept of a key is alien to certain types of music, such as Indian and Chinese.

key note *see* TONIC.

key signature the sign (or signs) placed at the beginning of a composition to define its KEY. A key signature indicates all the notes that are to be sharpened or flattened in the piece; should a piece move temporarily into another key, the relevant notes can be identified with ACCIDENTALS.

kinetic art an art form in which light or balance are used to create a work that moves or appears to move.

kit a miniature violin which was particularly popular with dancing masters of the 17th and 18th centuries, who could carry one in the pocket and thereby provide music for lessons.

Klangfarbenmelodie (*German*) literally, 'melody of tone colours'; a term used by Arnold Schoenberg (1874–1951) to describe a form of composition in which the pitch does not change; colour is achieved by adding or taking away instruments.

koto a Japanese zither which has 13 silk strings stretched over a long box. The strings pass over moveable bridges and are played with plectra worn on the fingers. The instrument is placed on the ground and produces a distinctive, somewhat harsh, sound.

Krumhorn or **Krummhorn** (*German*) or **crumhorn** a double-reed instrument, common in the 16th and early 17th centuries. The tube was curved at the lower end and the reed was enclosed in a cap into which the player blew. It was made in several sizes: treble, tenor and bass.

la *or* **lah** (1) the note A. (2) In the TONIC SOL-FA, the sixth note (or SUBMEDIANT) of the major scale.

lacrimoso (*Italian*) 'tearful'.

lambeg drum a large, double-headed bass drum from Northern Ireland.

lament a Scottish or Irish folk tune played at a death or some disaster, usually on the bagpipes.

lamentoso (*Italian*) 'mournfully'.

largamente (*Italian*) 'broadly', meaning slowly and in a dignified manner.

larghetto (*Italian*) 'slow' or 'broad', but not as slow as LARGO.

largo (*Italian*) literally 'broad', meaning slow and in a dignified manner.

lay a song or ballad.

lead (1) the announcement of a subject or theme that later appears in other parts. (2) a sign giving the cue or entry of the various parts.

leader (1) in Britain, the title of the principal first violin of an orchestra or the first violin of a string quartet or similar ensemble. (2) the leader of a section of an orchestra. (3) In the USA, an alternative term for conductor.

leading motif *see* LEITMOTIF.

leading note the seventh note of the scale; it is so called because it 'leads to' the TONIC, a semitone above.

ledger lines *see* LEGER LINES.

legato (*Italian*) 'smooth'.

leger lines *or* **ledger lines** short lines added above or below a STAVE to indicate the pitch of notes that are too high or low to be written on the stave itself.

leggiero (*Italian*) 'light'.

legno (*Italian*) 'wood'; *col legno* is a direction to a violinist to turn the bow over and to tap the strings with the wood.

leise (*German*) 'soft' or 'gentle'.

leitmotif *or* **Leitmotiv** (*German*) literally a 'leading theme', i.e. a recurring theme of music, commonly used in opera, that is associated with a character or idea, thus enabling the composer to tell a story in terms of music.

lentamente (*Italian*) 'slowly'.

lento (*Italian*) 'slow'.

liberamente (*Italian*) 'freely', i.e. as the performer wishes.

libretto (*Italian*) literally 'little book'. It is a term used for the text of an opera or oratorio.

licenza (*Italian*) 'licence' or 'freedom'; *con alcuna licenza* means 'with some freedom'.

Lied, Lieder (*German*) 'song, songs'.

ligature (1) a 12th-century form of notation for a group of notes. (2) a slur indicating that a group of notes must be sung to one syllable. (3) the tie used to link two notes over a bar line. (4) the metal band used to fix the reed to the mouthpiece of a clarinet, etc.

limerick a humorous five-lined piece of light verse, with the first two lines rhyming with each other, the third and fourth lines rhyming with each other, and the fifth line rhyming with the first line.

lira da braccio, lira da gamba Italian stringed instruments of the 15th and 16th centuries. The *lira da braccio* had seven strings and was played like a violin; the *lira da gamba* was a bass instrument played between the knees, and had up to sixteen strings.

literary ballad *see* BALLAD.

liturgy a term for any official, and written down, form of religious service.

loco (*Italian*) 'place'. It is used in music to indicate that a passage is to be played at normal pitch, after a previous, contrary instruction, i.e. the music reverts to its original place on the stave.

lunga pausa (*Italian*) a 'long pause'.

lute a plucked stringed instrument with a body resembling that of a half-pear. It is thought to have a history dating back some three thousand years and was particularly popular during the 16th and 17th centuries; it has since been revived by 20th-century instrument makers. It has a fretted fingerboard with a characteristic 'pegbox' (a string harness) bent back at an angle to the finger-board. A lute can have up to 18 strings.

Lydian mode (1) a scale used in ancient Greek music, the equivalent of the white notes on a piano from C to C. (2) From the Middle Ages onwards, the equivalent of a scale on the white notes on a piano from F to F.

lyre an instrument familiar to the ancient Greeks, Assyrians and Hebrews. It was a small, hollow box from which extended two horns that supported a cross bar and up to 12 strings, which could be plucked or strummed. It is traditionally used to represent a token of love (Orpheus played the lyre).

lyric a short poem, or sequence of words, for a song. The term has a particular application to 20th-century musicals and pop songs. A 'lyricist' is the person who writes the words to a popular tune.

m *abbreviation for* MAIN, MANO, MANUAL.

m (me) in TONIC SOL-FA. the third note (or MEDIANT) of the major scale.

ma (*Italian*) 'but', as *andante ma non troppo*, 'slow, but not too slow'.

machete a small Portuguese GUITAR.

madrigal a musical setting of a secular poem for two or more voices in COUNTERPOINT, usually unaccompanied. The first madrigals date back to the 14th century, and the first publications were made in Italy about 1501. The art of madrigal spread to every part of Europe, with the result that a wealth of polyphonic vocal music was created and reached a high art before the development of instrumental music.

maestro (*Italian*) literally 'master', a term used for a master musician, particularly a conductor.

magic realism a term devised in the 1920s to describe the work of a group of German painters, part of the NEUE SACHLICHKEIT, whose work exhibited a disquieting blend of surreal fantasy with matter-of-fact representationalism. In literature, the term is often applied with particular reference to the work of certain South American novelists, notably the Peruvian novelist Mario Vargas Llosa (1936–) and the Colombian Gabriel Garcia Marquez (1928–), whose work combines deadpan description of the everyday world with (often equally deadpan) excursions into fantasy.

main (*French*) 'hand', so *main droite* means 'right hand' (particularly in piano music).

major (*Latin*) 'greater', as opposed to MINOR or 'lesser'. Major scales are those in which a major third (INTERVAL of four semitones) occurs in ascending from the tonic; while the minor scales involve a minor third (three semitones). A major tone has the ratio 8 : 9; a minor tone has the ratio 9 : 10.

Manchester School the name applied to a group of British composers who studied music at the Royal Manchester College during the 1950s. They include Harrison Birtwhistle (1934–) and Peter Maxwell Davies (1934–), among others.

mandolin, mandoline a stringed instrument, similar to the lute, but smaller, usually played with a plectrum. It has four pairs of strings and is occasionally used as an orchestral instrument.

Mannerism an exaggerated and often artificial sense of style found in Italian art between *c.*1520 and 1600, i.e. between the High RENAISSANCE and BAROQUE periods. It represents a reaction against the balanced forms and perspectives of Renaissance art and is characterised by uncomfortably posed, elongated figures and contorted facial expressions. Harsh colours and unusual modes of perspective were also used to striking effect. The major artists of the period were able to create emotional responses of greater power and sophistication, and they paved the way for the development of Baroque art.

manual a keyboard on an organ or harpsichord; organs may have four manuals, named *solo*, *swell*, *great* and *choir*.

maracas a pair of Latin-American percussion instruments made from gourds filled with seeds, pebbles or shells. Sound is made by shaking the gourds.

march a piece of music with a strict rhythm, usually 4/4 time but sometimes in 2/4, 3/4 or 6/8 time, to which soldiers can march. The pace varies with the purpose of the piece, from the extremely slow *funeral* or *dead march* to the *quickstep* (with about 108 steps a minute) and the *Sturm Marsch* or *pas de charge* with 120 steps a minute.

marcia (*Italian*) 'march', so *alla marcia*, 'in a marching style'.

mariachi (*Spanish*) a Mexican folk group of variable size; it normally includes violins and guitars.

marimba a Latin American instrument which may have originated in Africa. It is similar to a large XYLOPHONE and can be played by up to four people at the same time.

mark a sign or word used in NOTATION to indicate the time, tone, accent or quality of a composition, or the pace at which it should be performed.

martellato (*Italian*) literally 'hammered'; a term used mainly in music for strings to indicate that notes should be played with short, sharp strokes of the bow. The term is also occasionally used in guitar and piano music.

masque a spectacular court entertainment that was especially popular during the 17th century. It combined poetry and dancing with vocal and instrumental music to tell a simple story that invariably flattered its aristocratic audience.

Mass (*Latin* **Missa**, *Italian* **Messa**, *French* and *German* **Messe**) in musical terms, the setting to music of the Latin Ordinary of Mass (those parts of the Mass that do not vary). The five parts are the KYRIE ELEISON, GLORIA, CREDO, SANCTUS with BENEDICTUS, and AGNUS DEI.

Master of the Queen's Musick an honorary position (in Britain) awarded to a prominent musician of the time; it is his (or her) duty to compose ANTHEMS, etc, for royal occasions.

mastersinger *see* MEISTERSINGER.

Matins the name given to the first of the canonical hours of the Roman Catholic Church. The term also refers to morning prayer in the Anglican Church.

mazurka a Polish folk dance of the 17th century for up to 12 people. The music can vary in speed and is often played on bagpipes. Frédéric Chopin (1820–49), amongst other composers, was influenced by the music and wrote some 55 'mazurkas' for piano.

me in the TONIC SOL-FA, the third note (or MEDIANT) of the major scale.

measure (1) a unit of rhythm or notes and rests included between two bars. (2) a stately dance of the minuet or pavanne type. (3) (US) a BAR (of music).

mechanical instruments instruments that can play complex music through the programming of their mechanism (e.g. by punched paper or pins on a spindle) when supplied with power (through foot pedals, clockwork, steam power, electricity, etc).

mediant the third note in a major or minor scale above the TONIC (lowest note), e.g. E in the scale of C major.

medium a material used in art, e.g. OIL in painting, PENCIL in drawing, or BRONZE in sculpture. The term is also used to denote a method, e.g. painting as opposed to sculpture.

Meistersinger (*German*) 'mastersinger', the title of highest rank in the song schools or guilds that flourished in German cities from the 14th until the 19th century. Where the MINNESINGERS drew their members from the aristocracy, mastersingers were usually craftsmen or tradesmen who composed poems and music and who formed themselves into powerful guilds.

melodica (*Italian*) a free-reed instrument which was developed from the harmonica. It is box-shaped and has a small keyboard; the player blows down a tube and plays by pressing the keys.

melodic minor scale *see* SCALE.

melodic sequence *see* SEQUENCE.

melodrama a form of drama (from the Greek for 'song' plus 'drama') that seems to have arisen in 18th-century France and that contained elements of music, spectacle, sensational incidents and sentimentalism (*see* SENTIMENTAL COMEDY). The form reached its peak in the popular theatre of 19th-century England, when quite spectacular stage effects often accompanied the action, and villains became blacker than black in their persecution of pure heroes and heroines. *See also* DOMESTIC TRAGEDY.

melody a succession of notes, of varying pitch, that create a distinct and identifiable musical form. Melody, HARMONY and RHYTHM are the three essential ingredients of music. The criteria of what constitutes a melody change over time.

membranophone the generic term for all instruments in which sound is produced by the vibration of a skin or membrane, for example, DRUM, KAZOO.

meno (*Italian*) 'less', so *meno mosso* means 'slower' (less speed).

menuet (*French*) MINUET.

Messa, Messe *see* MASS.

mesto, mestoso (*Italian*) 'sad'.

metallophone an instrument that is similar to a XYLOPHONE but has metal bars (usually bronze).

metaphysical painting an art movement begun in Italy in 1917 by Carlo Carré (1881–1966) and Giorgio de Chirico (1888–1978). They sought to portray the world of the subconscious by presenting real objects in incongruous juxtaposition, as in their *Metaphysical Interiors* and *Muses* series (1917). Carré soon abandoned the movement, and by the early 1920s both artists had developed other interests. Although short-lived, the movement did have some influence.

metaphysical poetry a poetry movement of the 17th century, noted for intense feeling, extended metaphor and striking, elaborate imagery, often with a mystical element. John Donne (1573–1631) is regarded as the first important metaphysical poet.

meter (1) in verse, the measured arrangement of syllables according to stress in a rhythmic pattern. (2) in music a rhythmic pattern. *See* RHYTHM.

method acting a style of acting, devised by Konstantin Stanislavsky (1863– 1938), which involves an actor immersing himself in the 'inner life' of the character he is playing, and, using the insights gained in this study, conveying to the audience the hidden reality behind the words.

metronome an instrument that produces regular beats and can therefore be used to indicate the pace at which a piece of music should be played. The first clockwork metronome was invented patented in 1816 and had a metal rod that swung backwards and forwards on a stand. The speed of ticking could be altered by sliding a weight up or down the rod. Electronic metronomes are also manufactured today.

mezzo (*Italian*) literally 'half', so *mezzo-soprano* means a voice between soprano and contralto and mezzo forte 'moderately loud'.

microtones INTERVALS that are smaller than a SEMITONE in length, for example, the quarter-tone.

middle C the note C which occupies the first ledger line below the treble staff, the first ledger line above the bass staff, and is indicated by the C clef.

military band a band in the armed forces that plays military music, usually for marching. There are many different types of military band, and the number of players varies. Most bands comprise a mixture of brass, woodwind and percussion instruments.

minim a note, formerly the shortest in time-value, with half the value of a SEMIBREVE; the equivalent of a half-note in US terminology.

Minnesingers the poet-musicians of Germany in the 12th and 13th centuries, who were of noble birth, like the TROUBADOURS of France, and who produced *minnelieder*, or love songs.

minor (*Latin*) 'less' or 'smaller'. Minor intervals contain one semitone less than MAJOR. The minor third is characteristic of scales in the minor mode.

minstrel a professional entertainer or musician of medieval times. Such people were often employed by a royal court or aristocratic family.

minuet a French rural dance in 3/4 time that was popular during the 17th and 18th centuries. It was incorporated into classical sonatas and symphonies as a regular movement.

miracle play *see* MYSTERY PLAY.

mirror music any piece of music that sounds the same when played backwards.

misterioso (*Italian*) 'mysteriously'.

misura (*Italian*) 'measure'; equivalent to a BAR.

Mixolydian mode (1) the set of notes, in ancient Greek music, which are the equivalent of the white notes on a piano from B to B. (2) in church music of the Middle Ages onwards, the equivalent of the white notes on a piano from G to G.

mixture an organ stop that brings into play a number of pipes that produce HARMONICS above the pitch corresponding to the actual key which is played.

moderato (*Italian*) 'moderate' (in terms of speed).

modes the various sets of notes or SCALES, which were used by musicians until the concept of the KEY was accepted (*c*.1650). Modes were originally used by the ancient Greeks and were adapted by medieval composers, especially for church music. Modes were based on what are now the white notes of the piano.

modulation the gradual changing of key during the course of a part of a composition by means of a series of harmonic progressions. Modulation is *diatonic* when it is accomplished by the use of chords from relative keys; *chromatic* when by means of non-relative keys; *enharmonic* when effected by the alteration of notation; *final*, or *complete*, when a new tonality is established; and *partial*, or *passing*, when the change of key is only transient.

molto (*Italian*) 'very', so *allegro molto* means 'very fast'.

monochrome a drawing or painting executed in one colour only. *See also* grisaille.

monodrama a dramatic work for a single performer.

monody a type of accompanied solo song which was developed during the late 16th and early 17th centuries. It contained dramatic and expressive embellishments and devices, and consequently had an influence on OPERA.

monothematic a piece of music that is developed from a single musical idea.

monotone declamation of words on a single tone.

montage an art technique similar to COLLAGE, where the images used are photographic.

mordent a musical ornament whereby one note rapidly alternates with another one degree below it; this is indicated by a sign over the note.

morendo (*Italian*) 'dying', i.e. decreasing in volume.

moresca (*Italian*) a sword dance dating from the 15th and 16th centuries, which represents battles between the Moors and the Christians. It was the origin of the English MORRIS DANCE. It has been included in OPERAS, often to a marching rhythm.

morris dance a style of English dance, the music for which is provided by pipe and tabor. It was orginally a costume dance, the characters often being those from the Robin Hood ballads. Of Moorish or Spanish origin, the dance later became associated with many tunes, some in 4/4, others in 3/4 time.

mosso (*Italian*) 'moved', so *piu mosso* means 'more moved', i.e. quicker, and *meno mosso* 'less speed'.

motet a musical setting of sacred words for solo voices or choir, with or without accompaniment. The first motets were composed in the 13th century.

motif *or* **motive** a small group of notes which create a melody or rhythm, e.g. the first four notes of Beethoven's 5th symphony.

motion the upward or downward progress of a melody. It is said to be *conjunct* when the degrees of the scale succeed each other; *disjunct* where the melody proceeds in skips; *contrary* where two parts move in opposite directions; *oblique* when one part moves while the other remains stationary; and *similar*, or *direct*, when the parts move in the same direction.

moto (*Italian*) 'motion', so *con moto* means 'with motion' or 'quickly'.

motto theme a short theme that recurs during the course of a composition. In this way, it dominates the piece.

mouth organ *see* HARMONICA.

movement a self-contained section of a larger instrumental composition, such as a symphony or sonata.

muffled drum a drum with a piece of cloth or towelling draped over the vibrating surfaces. It produces a sombre tone when struck and is usually associated with funeral music.

musette (*French*) (1) a type of small BAGPIPE popular at the French court in the 17th and 18th centuries. (2) an air in 2/4, 3/4 or 6/8 time that imitates the drone of the bagpipe. (3) a dance tune suitable for a bagpipe. (4) an organ reed stop.

musica (*Italian*) 'music'.

musical a type of play or film in which music plays an important part and the actors occasionally sing, for example, *My Fair Lady*, *West Side Story*.

musical box a clockwork MECHANICAL INSTRUMENT in which a drum studded with small pins plays a tune by plucking the teeth of a metal comb.

musical comedy a term used between 1890 and 1930 to describe a humorous play with light music and singing in it.

music drama a term first used to describe the operas of Richard Wagner (1813–83), where the action and music are completely interlocked, with, for example, no pauses for applause after an ARIA, or repetition within a piece.

musicology the scientific study of music.

musique concrète a term coined by the French composer Pierre Schaffer in 1948 to describe a type of music in which taped sounds are distorted or manipulated by the composer. The term ELECTRONIC MUSIC is now more generally used.

muta (*Italian*) 'change', a musical direction: (1) that the key be changed in horn or drum music; (2) that the MUTE be used.

mutation stops organ stops that produce sound, usually a HARMONIC – which is different from the normal or octave pitch corresponding to the key that is depressed.

mute any device used to soften or reduce the normal volume, or alter the tone, of an instrument. With bowed instruments, a small clamp is slotted onto the bridge; in brass instruments a hand or bung is pushed into the bell; in the piano the soft (left) pedal is pressed; and with drums, cloths are placed over the skins, or sponge-headed drumsticks are used.

mv abbreviation for *mezzo voce*.

mystery play *or* **miracle play** a form of dramatic entertainment based on sacred subjects and given under church auspices which was used before the development of either OPERA or ORATORIO.

Nabis a group of painters working in France in the 1890s. Influenced by the works and ideas of Paul Gauguin (1848–1903) and by oriental art, they worked in flat areas of strong colour, avoiding direct representation in favour of a symbolic approach of mystical revelation.

Nachtmusik (*German*) 'night music', that is, music suitable for performing in the evening or suggestive of night.

naive art works by untrained artists whose style is noted for its innocence and simplicity. Scenes are often depicted literally, with little attention to formal perspective and with an intuitive rather than studied use of pictorial space, composition and colour.

naker the medieval English name for a small KETTLEDRUM (often with snares, *see* SIDE DRUM) of Arabic origin, from which TIMPANI developed. Nakers were always used in pairs.

nationalism a late 19th-century and early 20th-century music movement in which a number of composers set out to write work which would express their national identity, often by reference to FOLK music and by evocation of landscape.

natural a NOTE that is neither sharpened nor flattened.

Naturalism a term deriving from the late-19th French literary movement of the same name, denoting fiction characterised by close observation and documentation of everyday life, with a strong emphasis on the influence of the material world on individual behaviour. Naturalistic NOVELS therefore tended to adopt a very deterministic approach to life and fiction, and most practitioners of the form would have described themselves as socialists or social Darwinists.

natural key KEY of C major.

Nazarenes an art movement based on the Brotherhood of St Luke formed in Vienna in 1809. It involved painters of German and Austrian origin, who worked mainly in Italy. Inspired by the medieval guild system, they worked cooperatively with a common goal of reviving Christian art.

neck the narrow projecting part of a stringed instrument that supports the FINGERBOARD; at the end of the neck lies the PEG-BOX which secures the strings and enables them to be tuned.

Neoclassicism a term denoting any movement in the Arts emphasising the virtues of imitating the style and precepts of the great classical writers and artists (Neoclassicist principles in literature derive mostly from the writings of Aristotle – principally the *Poetics* – and some observations by the Roman poets, Virgil and Horace). The hallmarks of Neoclassicism are traditionally defined as balance, moderation, attention to formal rules – such as the dramatic *Unities*, in which time and space is strictly ordered around a sequential plot with a beginning, middle and end – avoidance of emotional display and distrust of enthusiasm, and the assumption that human nature has changed little since CLASSICAL times.

In literature, Neoclassicism is generally held to have begun with Petrarch (1304–74) in the mid-14th century. The greatest Neoclassical English poets are John Dryden (1631–1700) and Alexander Pope (1688–1744). Neoclassicism had been a powerful influence on French literature of the 17th century, but has never won wide acceptance among writers in English, not even in the 18th century.

In art and architecture, Neoclassicism was the dominant style in Europe in the late 18th and early 19th centuries. It followed on from, and was essentially a reaction against, BAROQUE and ROCOCO styles. Classical forms were employed to express the reasoned enlightenment of the age, and Neoclassical painters adhered to the Classical principles of order, symmetry and calm. At the same time, they felt free to embrace Romantic themes.

In music, Neoclassicism was a 20th-century movement that reacted against the overtly Romantic forms of the late 19th century. Composers who adhered to the philosophy attempted to create new works with the balance and restraint found in the work of 18th-century composers.

Neoimpressionism *see* POINTILLISM.

Neoplatonism a synthesis of Platonic and mystical concepts that originated in the Greek-speaking Mediterranean world of the 3rd century. Plotinus (*c*.205–*c*.270) was the main figure behind the synthesis.

neume a sign used in musical NOTATION from the 7th to 14th centuries before the invention of the STAVE. It indicated PITCH.

Neue Sachlichkeit (*German*) 'new objectivity', the title of an exhibition of postwar figurative art which then came to represent any art concerned with objective representation of real life, such works being the opposition to EXPRESSIONIST subjectivity.

new comedy *see* comedy.

niente (*Italian*) 'nothing'; used in *quasi niente* 'almost nothing', indicating a very soft tone.

Nihilism a philosophical movement originating in mid-19th century Russia that rejected all established authority and values. The revolutionary Bazarov in Ivan Turgenev's *Fathers and Sons* is the first significant fictional portrait of a nihilist. Much of Fyodor Dostoevsky's work is concerned with exposing the essential shallowness and banality of nihilism.

ninth an INTERVAL of nine NOTES, in which both the first and last notes are counted.

No *see* Noh.

nobile, nobilmente (*Italian*) 'noble, nobly'.

nocturne literally a 'night piece', i.e. a piece of music, often meditative in character and suggesting the quietness of night.

Noh *or* **No** a form of highly stylised drama originating in 14th-century Japan. The typical Noh play is short, slow-paced, draws heavily on classical Japanese symbolism, and usually involves song, dance, mime and intricately detailed costume.

noire (*French*) literally 'black', a CROTCHET or quarter note.

nonet a group of nine instruments, or a piece of music for such a group.

normal pitch standard PITCH.

nota (*Latin, Italian*) 'NOTE', so *nota bianca* means 'white note' or half-note; *nota buona* is an accented note; *nota cambita* or *cambiata* is a CHANGING NOTE; *nota caratteristica* is a LEADING NOTE; *nota cattiva* is an unaccented note.

notation *or* **nomenclature** the symbols used in written music to indicate the PITCH and RHYTHM of NOTES, the combination and duration of TONES, as well as the graces and shades of expression without which music can become mechanical.

note (1) a SOUND that has a defined PITCH and duration. (2) a symbol for such a sound. (3) the KEY of a PIANO or other keyboard instrument.

novel a sustained fictional prose narrative. Although most of the essential characteristics of the form can be found in ancient texts, such as the Greek Romances of the 3rd century, and in the works of writers of the Roman world, the novel as the term is generally understood, with complex characterisation and multilayered strands of plot and character development, is essentially a creation of 18th-century writers in English, e.g. Samuel Richardson (1689–1761)

In the early years of the 19th century, the dual tradition of the novel-adventure in the great world outside, and exploration of personality reached striking new levels in the novels of Sir Walter Scott (1771–1832) and Jane Austen (1775–1817) respectively, with the latter setting standards of characterisation that have rarely been matched. In the course of the 19th century, writers throughout Europe and America, e.g. Charles Dickens (1812–1870), Fyodor Dostoyevsky (1821–81), Honoré de Balzac (1799–1860), and Henry James (1843–1916), developed the novel into a highly sophisticated vehicle for exploring human consciousness. The 20th century has seen many adaptations of the traditional form of the novel, from the use of the STREAM OF CONSCIOUSNESS technique, to the MAGIC REALISM of South American writers.

novella a short version of the NOVEL; a tale usually leading up to some point, and often, in early versions of the form, of a satirical or scabrous nature.

nuance a subtle change of speed, TONE, etc.

number (1) an integral portion of a musical composition, particularly in opera where it can mean an ARIA, DUET, etc. (2) one of the works on a programme.

nut (1) the part of the BOW of a stringed instrument that holds the horsehair and that incorporates a screw that tightens the tension of the hairs. (2) the hardwood ridge at the PEG-BOX end of a stringed instrument's FINGERBOARD that raises the strings above the level of the FINGERBOARD.

o when placed over a NOTE in a musical SCORE for strings, indicates that the note must be played on an open string or as a harmonic.

ob abbreviation for OBOE and OBBLIGATO.

obbligato (*Italian*) 'obligatory', a term that refers to a PART that cannot be dispensed with in a performance (some parts can be optional). However, some 19th-century composers used the word to mean the exact opposite, i.e. a part that was optional.

ober (*German*) 'over', 'upper', as OBERWERK.

objet trouvé *see* FOUND OBJECT.

oblique motion two parallel MELODY lines, or PARTS: one moves up or down the SCALE while the other stays on a consistent NOTE.

oboe a WOODWIND instrument with a conical bore and a double REED. The instrument has a history dating back to ancient Egyptian times. SHAWMS evolved from these Egyptian predecessors and became known as *hautbois* instruments in the 17th and 18th centuries. The modern oboe (the word is a corruption of 'hautbois') dates from the 18th century. The established variations of the instrument are: the oboe (TREBLE), the COR ANGLAIS (ALTO), or the BASSOON (tenor), and the double bassoon (BASS).

ocarina a small, egg-shaped WIND INSTRUMENT, often made of clay, which is played in a way similar to a RECORDER.

octave an INTERVAL of eight NOTES, inclusive of the top and bottom notes, e.g. C to C.

octet a group of eight instruments or VOICES, or a piece for such a group.

octobass a huge kind of three-stringed DOUBLE BASS, some four metres in height, which incorporated hand- and pedal-operated levers to STOP the immensely thick strings.

oeuvre (*French*) a 'work' (OPUS).

offertory an ANTIPHON sung (or music played on the ORGAN) while the priest prepares the bread and wine at a communion service.

ohne (*German*) 'without', hence *ohne worte*, 'without words'.

oil paint a paint made by mixing colour pigments with oil (generally linseed oil) to produce a slow-drying, malleable sticky substance. Oil paint has been the dominant medium in European art since the 15th century because of the range of effects that can be produced.

old comedy *see* COMEDY.

Op, op abbreviation for OPUS.

Op Art *or* **Optical Art** an abstract art that uses precise, hard-edged patterns in strong colours that dazzle the viewer and make the image appear to move.

open harmony *see* HARMONY.

open note (1) in stringed instruments, an OPEN STRING. (2) in BRASS or WOODWIND instruments, a NOTE produced without using VALVES, CROOKS, or KEYS.

open string any string on an instrument that is allowed to vibrate along its entire length without being stopped (*see* STOPPING).

Oper (*German*) 'opera'.

opera a dramatic work in which all, or most of, the text is sung to orchestral ACCOMPANIMENT. It is a formidable musical form, and has a history dating back to Italy in the 16th century. This Italian form of opera reached its culmination in the operas of Monteverdi (1567–1743) but thereafter developed into a rigidly prescribed form of art. The growth of the science of HARMONY and the development of the modern ORCHESTRA led to a revolt against Italian opera. Richard Wagner (1813–83) gave a new impetus to operatic composition. His approach assumed that music that detracted from interest in the progress of the drama was bad music, and that the purpose of music was to enforce the dramatic interest of the text.

Opera demands a LIBRETTO, an orchestra, singers, an ample stage and, only too often, considerable funds to produce. It also requires some suspension of disbelief, for opera is the convention of unreality, but in that unreality lies its ability to work magic.

opéra-bouffe (*French*), **opera buffa** (*Italian*) similar to OPÉRA COMIQUE but with the dialogue sung throughout and spoken only occasionally in *opera buffa* modelled on the French style.

opéra comique (*French*) literally 'a comic OPERA', but in fact an opera consisting of dramatic pieces with music and dancing and instrumental ACCOMPANIMENT, often along tragic rather than comic lines. Like the German SPINGSPIEL, all or nearly all the dialogue is spoken.

opera seria (*Italian*) 'serious OPERA', as usually applied to work of the 17th and 18th centuries.

operetta a short OPERA or, more usually, a term taken to mean an opera with some spoken dialogue and a romantic plot with a happy ending.

opus (*Latin*) 'work'; a term used by composers (or their cataloguers) to indicate the chronological order of their works. It is usually abbreviated to Op. and is followed by the catalogued number of the work.

oratorio the musical setting of a religious or epic LIBRETTO for soloists, CHORUS and ORCHESTRA, performed without the theatrical effects of stage and costumes, etc. Oratorio had its beginnings in the MYSTERY PLAYS of the Middle Ages. At first they were performed in MADRIGAL style, and became popular throughout Italy. From Italy, where it was soon overshadowed by OPERA, the oratorio spread to the rest of Europe.

orchestra a group of instruments and their players. The word comes from Greek and means 'dancing place'. This was a space in front of the stage, in which a raised platform was built for the accommodation of the CHORUS. The early composers of OPERA applied the name to the place allotted to their musicians, and it is now used to designate the place, the musicians or the instruments. Orchestras have grown over the centuries in response to larger auditoriums. A standard, modern orchestra contains four families of instruments: STRINGS, WOODWIND, BRASS and PERCUSSION. The exact number of players within each section can vary, and extra instruments can be called for by a particular SCORE.

orchestration the art of writing and arranging music for an ORCHESTRA.

organ a keyboard wind instrument, played with the hands and feet, in which pressurised air is forced through PIPES to sound NOTES. PITCH is determined by the length of the pipe. There are essentially two types of pipe; FLUE PIPES, which are blown like a WHISTLE, and REED PIPES in which air is blown over vibrating strips of metal. Flue pipes can be 'stopped' (blocked off at one end) to produce a sound an OCTAVE lower than when open. There are a number of keyboards on an organ, one of which is operated by the feet (PEDAL board). Those operated by the hands are called MANUALS, and there are four common categories: the solo (used for playing SOLO MELODIES), the swell (on which notes can be made to sound louder or softer, *see also* SWELL ORGAN), the great (the manual that opens up all the most powerful pipes), and the choir (which operates the softer sounding pipes, *see also* CHOIR ORGAN). In addition there are a number of 'STOPS' (buttons or levers) that can alter the pitch or TONE of specific pipes. The organ dates back to before the time of Christ and has gone through many stages of evolution. ELECTRONIC organs (*see* HAMMOND ORGAN) have been invented and these tend to produce sounds rather different from those in which pumped air is actually used.

organum (1) (*Latin*) 'ORGAN'. (2) measured music, as opposed to unmeasured PLAINSONG, an early form of POLYPHONY.

ornaments and graces embellishments to the NOTES of a MELODY, indicated by symbols or small notes. They were used frequently in the 17th and 18th centuries.

Orpheus the legendary poet and musician of Greek mythology whose name has been adopted by numerous musical societies, etc, and has also been used as the title of several collections of vocal music. The story of Orpheus and his search in the underworld for his wife Eurydice has been the subject of many musical forms.

Orphism *or* **Orphic Cubism** a brief but influential art movement developed out of Cubist principles. Their aim was to move away from the objectivity of CUBISM towards a more lyrical and colourful art. The artists were influenced in part by Italian FUTURISM, and typical works use juxtaposed forms and strong colours. The movement had a deep influence on some of the German EXPRESSIONISTS and on SYNCHROMISM.

oscillator an ELECTRONIC INSTRUMENT that converts electrical energy into audible sound.

ossia (*Italian*) 'or', 'otherwise', 'else'; used to indicate an alternative PASSAGE of music.

ostinato (*Italian*) 'obstinate'; a short PHRASE or other pattern that is repeated over and over again during the course of a composition.

ottava (*Italian*) OCTAVE.

overblow to increase the wind pressure in a WOODWIND instrument to force an upper PARTIAL note instead of its fundamental note, thus producing a harmonic.

overtones *see* HARMONICS.

overture a piece of music that introduces an an OPERA, ORATORIO, BALLET or other major work. Overtures may be built out of the principal THEMES of the work that is to follow, or may be quite independent of them. Beethoven composed no fewer than four overtures to his only opera, *Fidelio*, and Verdi's *Otello* and other operas have no overture whatever. Overtures are nearly always in the SONATA FORM, being, in fact, similar to the first MOVEMENT of a SYMPHONY, on a somewhat larger scale. The CONCERT OVERTURE is often an independent piece, written for performance in a concert hall.

p (1) abbreviation for PIANO (*Italian*), meaning 'soft'. (2) abbreviation for 'PEDAL' (ORGAN).

panpipes a set of graduated PIPES, stopped at the lower end, which are bound together by thongs. Each pipe makes a single NOTE, and sound is produced by blowing across the open end. They are popular in South America and parts of Eastern Europe.

pantonality *see* ATONAL.

parameter a 20th-century term used to describe aspects of SOUND that can be varied but which nevertheless impose a limit. It is particularly applied to ELECTRONIC MUSIC with regard to volume, etc.

part a VOICE or instrument in a group of performers, or a piece of music for it.

parte (*Italian*) 'PART', so *colla parte* means 'with the part'.

part-song a composition for unaccompanied VOICES in which the highest part usually sings the MELODY while the lower parts sing accompanying HARMONIES.

passage a FIGURE or PHRASE of music; a RUN.

passage work a piece of music that provides an opportunity for VIRTUOSO playing.

passing note a NOTE that is dissonant with the prevailing HARMONY but that is nevertheless useful in making the TRANSITION from one CHORD or KEY to another.

Passion music the setting to music of the story of Christ's Passion (the story of the Crucifixion taken from the Gospels).

pastoral any piece of literature celebrating the country way of life. The first pastoral poems of any significance are those of Theocritus (*c*.310–*c*.250 BC), a Greek poet whose work established the standard frame of the form: shepherds and shepherdesses singing to one another of their loves in a world of peace and plenty in which the sun always shines. Death, however, is occasionally present in the form of a shepherd lamenting the death of a friend.

pastorale (1) a vocal or instrumental MOVEMENT or composition in COMPOUND triple TIME, which suggests a rural subject; it usually has long BASS notes that imitate the sounds of the BAGPIPE drone. (2) a stage entertainment based on a PASTORAL.

pathos in literature, where the writing elicits feelings of overwhelming sympathy. It is derived from the Greek word to mean suffering. Examples include the denouément of Shakespeare's *Othello*.

patter song a kind of comic SONG that has a string of tongue-twisting syllables and is usually sung quickly to minimal ACCOMPANIMENT. It is often found in opera.

pausa (*Italian*) 'REST'.

pause a symbol over a NOTE or REST to indicate that this should be held for longer than its written value.

pavan, pavane a stately court dance, normally in slow DUPLE TIME, which was occasionally incorporated into instrumental music in the 16th century.

pedal the part of an instrument's mechanism that is operated by the feet, such as on a PIANO, ORGAN or HARP. The *forte*, or loud, pedal on a piano by raising the dampers enriches the TONE. The *piano*, or soft, pedal enables the player to strike only one or two strings or to reduce the volume of tone. Harp pedals sharpen, flatten or neutralise one NOTE throughout the COMPASS.
  Organ pedals produce notes of the lower register independently of the MANUAL or alter the arrangement of the registers.

peg-box the part of a stringed instrument that houses the pegs that anchor and tune the strings.

penny whistle *see* TIN WHISTLE.

pentatonic scale a SCALE composed of five notes in an octave. It is found in various types of folk music from Scottish to Chinese.

percussion (1) the actual striking of a DISCORD after it has been prepared and before its RESOLUTION. (2) the mechanism by which the tongue of a REED is struck with a HAMMER as air is admitted from the wind chest, thus ensuring immediate 'speaking'.

percussion instrument an instrument that produces TONE when struck, such as the PIANO or XYLOPHONE, but more especially one of the family of instruments that produce SOUND when struck or shaken, for example, MARACAS, DRUMS, TRIANGLE.

perfect interval see INTERVAL.

period a complete musical sentence (see PHRASE).

perpetuum mobile (*Latin*) 'perpetually in motion', i.e. a short piece of music with a repetitive NOTE pattern that is played quickly and without any PAUSES.

perspective in art, the representation of a three-dimensional view in a two-dimensional space by establishing a vanishing point in the distance at which parallel lines converge, the objects or figures in the distance being smaller and closer together than objects or figures nearer the viewer. Perspective is demonstrated in the works of Giotto di Bondone (1267–1337), and its rules were formulated by the Italian writer, architect, sculptor and painter Leon Battista Alberti (1404–72) in *De Pictura* (1435), but by the 20th century these were being abandoned by artists.

pesante (*Italian*) 'heavy', 'ponderous' or 'solid'.

philharmonic (*Greek*) literally 'music loving'; an adjective used in the titles of many orchestras, societies, etc.

phrase a short melodic section of a composition, of no fixed length, although it is often four BARS long.

pianissimo (*Italian*) 'very quiet'.

piano (1) (*Italian*) 'soft'. (2) the common abbreviated form of PIANOFORTE.

piano accordion see ACCORDION.

piano à queue. (*French*) a grand PIANO.

piano carré. (*French*) a square PIANO.

pianoforte, piano a keyboard instrument that was invented by Bartolomeo Cristofori in Florence in 1709 and for which important works were being written by the end of the 18th century. Most modern instruments usually have 88 KEYS and a COMPASS of $7^1/_3$ OCTAVES, although it is possible to find larger versions. The keys operate HAMMERS that strike STRINGS at the back of the instrument. These strings can run vertically (*upright piano*) or horizontally (*grand piano*). Most pianos have one string for the very lowest NOTES, two parallel strings for the middle REGISTER notes and three strings for the highest notes. Normally, when a NOTE is played, a damper (*see* DAMP) deadens the strings when the key returns to its normal position, but a sustaining (right) PEDAL suspends the action of the dampers and allows the note to coninue sounding. The soft (left) pedal mutes the sound produced, either by moving the hammers closer to the strings so that their action is diminished, or by moving the hammers sideways so that only one or two strings are struck. On some pianos, a third, SOSTENUTO pedal, allows selected notes to continue sounding while others are dampened.

pibroch (*Gaelic*) a type of Scottish BAGPIPE music with the form of THEME and VARIATIONS.

picaresque novel a type of NOVEL in which the hero (very rarely, the heroine) undergoes an episodic series of adventures. The term derives from the Spanish *picaro*, a rogue or trickster. Many examples appear in 16th-century Spanish literature, when the genre first established itself, but picaresque novels have been appearing since the very earliest days of the novel.

piccolo a small FLUTE with a PITCH an OCTAVE higher than a concert flute. It is used in orchestras and MILITARY BANDS.

pick a common expression for plucking the strings on a GUITAR.

pietà the Italian word for 'pity', used in art to denote a painting or sculpture of the body of the dead Christ being supported by the Virgin.

pipe a hollow cylinder in which vibrating air produces SOUND. On many instruments, the effective length of the pipe can be altered to produce a range of NOTES by means of holes that are opened or closed by the fingers.

pipe organ an American term for a real ORGAN, as opposed to an AMERICAN ORGAN.

pistons the VALVES on BRASS instruments that allow players to sound different NOTES.

pitch the height or depth of a SOUND, which determines its position on a SCALE.

più (*Italian*) 'more', so *più* FORTE 'more loudly'.

pizzicato (*Italian*) 'plucked' (with specific reference to using the fingers to pluck the STRINGS on a bowed instrument).

plainsong the collection of ancient MELODIES to which parts of Roman Catholic services have been sung for centuries. The best-known is GREGORIAN CHANT. Plainsong is usually unaccompanied and sung in UNISON. It is also in free RHYTHM, i.e. it does not have BARS but follows the prose rhythm of the PSALM or prayer.

Platonism the theory of forms devised by the Greek philosophy Plato (*c*.427– *c*.347 BC) in which objects as we perceive them are distinguished from the idea of the objects, a theory that has had a strong influence on many writers (*see also* NEOPLATONISM). Plato's speculations are contained in dialogue form in several works, e.g. the *Symposium* and *Phaedo*, and in *The Republic* (an examination of the principles of good government).

player piano *or* **pianola** a mechanical PIANO operated pneumatically by a perforated roll of paper.

plectrum a small piece of horn, plastic or wood that is used to pluck the STRINGS of a GUITAR, MANDOLIN, ZITHER, etc.

plein air (*French*) 'open air', used of paintings that have been produced out of doors and not in a studio. Plein air painting was particularly popular with the BARBIZON SCHOOL and became a central tenet of IMPRESSIONISM.

poco (*Italian*) 'little' or 'slightly', so *poco* DIMINUENDO means 'getting slightly softer' and *poco a poco* means 'little by little'.

poem an arrangement of words, especially in METER, often rhymed, in a style more imaginative than ordinary speech.

poet laureate a poet appointed to a court or other formal institution. In Britain, the post is held for life and the poet laureate is expected, although not forced, to write a poem to commemorate important events. The first official poet laureate was John Dryden, who was also the first to lose the post before his death, in the upheaval surrounding the 'Glorious Revolution'. The current poet laureate, Ted Hughes (1930–), was appointed in 1984.

poi (*Italian*) 'then', so SCHERZO DA CAPO, *poi la* CODA means 'repeat the scherzo, then play the coda'.

point the tip of a BOW; the opposite end to the part that is held (the heel).

point d'orgue (*French*) 'ORGAN point'. It can indicate a harmonic PEDAL (a NOTE sustained under changing HARMONIES); the sign for a PAUSE; or a CADENZA in a CONCERTO.

pointillism a scientific and logical development of IMPRESSIONISM pioneered by the pointillist painters, notably Georges Seurat (1851–91) and Camille Pissarro (1830–93). The brokenly applied brushwork technique of impressionist was extended and refined to a system of dots of pure colour, applied according to scientific principles, with the intention of creating an image of greater purity and luminosity.

In music, the term was borrowed to describe a style in which NOTES seem to be isolated as 'dots' rather than as sequential parts of a MELODY.

polka a ROUND DANCE in quick 2/4 TIME from Czechoslovakia. It became popular throughout Europe in the mid-19th century.

polyphony (*Greek*) literally 'many sounds', i.e. a type of music in which two or more PARTS have independent melodic lines, arranged in COUNTERPOINT. The blending of several distinct MELODIES is what is aimed for, rather than the construction of a single melody with harmonised ACCOMPANIMENT.

polyptych a painting, usually an ALTARPIECE, consisting of two or more paintings within a decorative frame. *See also* DIPTYCH, TRIPTYCH.

polytonality the use of two or more KEYS at the same time.

ponticello (*Italian*) 'BRIDGE' (of a stringed instrument).

Pop Art a realistic art style that uses techniques and subjects from commercial art, comic strips, posters, etc. The most notable exponents include Roy Lichtenstein (1923–) and Robert Rauschenberg (1925–).

pop music short for 'popular' music, i.e. 20th-century music specifically composed to have instant appeal to young people. There are many types of pop music, with influences ranging from JAZZ and FOLK to ROCK and REGGAE.

portamento (*Italian*) literally 'carrying'; an effect used in singing or on bowed instruments in which sound is smoothly 'carried' or slid from one NOTE to the next without a break.

portraiture the art of painting, drawing or sculpting the likeness of someone, either the face, the figure to the waist, or the whole person. Portraits vary from the idealised or romanticised to the realistic.

position a term used in the playing of stringed instruments for where the left hand should be placed so that the fingers can play different sets of NOTES; e.g. first position has the hand near the end of the strings, second position is slightly further along the FINGERBOARD.

poster paint *see* GOUACHE.

posthorn a simple (valveless) BRASS instrument similar to a BUGLE, but usually coiled in a circular form.

Postimpressionism a blanket term used to describe the works of artists in the late 19th century who rejected IMPRESSIONISM. It was not a movement in itself, and most of the artists it refers to worked in widely divergent and independent styles. They include Paul Cézanne (1839–1906), Paul Gauguin (1848–1903), Vincent Van Gogh (1853– 90) and René Matisse (1869–1954).

postlude the closing section of a composition.

Poststructuralism *see* STRUCTURALISM.

precipitato, precipitoso (*Italian*) 'precipitately', hence also 'impetuously'.

prelude an introductory piece of music or a self-contained PIANO piece in one MOVEMENT.

Pre-Raphaelite Brotherhood a movement that was founded in 1848 by William Holman Hunt (1827–1910), John Everett Millais (1829–96) and Gabriel Dante Rossetti (1828–82), who wanted to raise standards in British art. They drew their imagery from medieval legends and literature in an attempt to provide an escape from industrial materialism. They sought to recreate the innocence of Italian painting before Raphael (1483–1520), and were influenced by the works of the NAZARENES.

presto (Italian) 'lively'; prestissimo indicates the fastest speed of which a performer is capable.

primary colours the colours red, blue and yellow, which in painting cannot be produced by mixing other colours. Primary colours are mixed to make *secondary colours*: orange (red and yellow), purple (red and blue) and green (blue and yellow).

primo (*Italian*) 'first', as the first or top PART of a PIANO DUET (the lower part being termed *secondo*, 'second').

principal (1) the LEADER of a section of an orchestra (e.g. principal HORN). (2) a singer who regularly takes leading parts in an OPERA company, but not the main ones (e.g. a principal TENOR).

principal subject the first SUBJECT in a SONATA FORM or a RONDO.

programme music music that attempts to tell a story or evoke an image. The term was first used by Franz Liszt (1811–86) to describe his SYMPHONIC POEMS.

progression MOTION from NOTE to note, or from CHORD to chord.

Promenade Concerts an annual season of concerts given in London's Royal Albert Hall, popularly known as the 'Proms', which were instituted in 1895. Despite the name, people do not walk about.

pulse see beat.

punta (*Italian*) 'point'; so a punta d'arco means 'at the point of the BOW', indicating that only the tip of the bow should be used to play the strings.

quadrille a French dance that was particularly fashionable in the early 19th century. It comprised five sections in alternating 6/8 and 2/4 time.

quadruplet a group of four NOTES of equal value played in the time of three.

quadruple time *or* **common time** the TIME of four CROTCHETS (quarter notes) in a BAR, indicated by the time signature 4/4 or C.

quarter note (US) *see* CROTCHET.

quarter tone half a SEMITONE, which is the smallest INTERVAL traditionally used in Western music.

quartet a group of four performers; a composition for four SOLO instruments or for four VOICES.

quasi (*Italian*) literally 'as if' or 'nearly'; so *quasi niente* means 'almost nothing', or as softly as possible.

quattrocento an Italian term that refers to 15th-century Italian art, often used descriptively of the early RENAISSANCE period.

quaver a NOTE that is half the length of a CROTCHET and the eighth of a SEMI-BREVE (whole note).

quickstep a MARCH in quick TIME, which also developed into the modern ballroom dance.

quintet a group of five performers; a composition for five SOLO instruments or for five VOICES.

quintuple time five BEATS, usually CROTCHETS, in a BAR, i.e. 5/4 TIME.

racket *or* **rackett** *or* **ranket** a WOODWIND instrument with a double REED used between the late 16th and early 18th centuries. It came in four sizes (SOPRANO, TENOR, BASS, double bass) and created a distinctive buzzing sound.

rag a piece of RAGTIME music.

raga a type of Indian scale or a type of MELODY based on such a scale. Each raga is associated with a mood and particular times of the day and year.

ragtime a style of syncopated (*see* SYNCOPATION) popular dance music, dating from the late 19th century. The combination of ragtime and blues led to the development of JAZZ.

rallentando (*Italian*) 'slowing down'.

ranket *see* RACKET.

rap a term for an influential type of POP MUSIC of the late 20th century, which has a pulsating RHYTHM and in which LYRICS for SONGS are usually spoken to the BEAT and not sung.

rattle a type of PERCUSSION INSTRUMENT that traditionally consists of a hollowed-out gourd filled with seeds that rattle when shaken. An alternative type is a contraption in which a strip of wood held in a frame strikes against a cog-wheel as the frame is twirled round. It is occasionally required as a percussion instrument in orchestras.

re *or* **ray** in the TONIC SOL-FA, the second NOTE of the MAJOR SCALE.

Realism in literature, a true and faithful representation of reality in fiction. Once defined, discussion of the term usually breaks down into personal prejudices of various kinds. The process of distinguishing the term from NATURALISM is particularly fraught; any artist must select from the chaos of life in order to create, and in the process of choosing must impose some personal, even if banal, vision on the world, and in the process either convince the reader that the world portrayed is a real one, or fail.

In art, Realism is taken to be, in general, the objective representation of scenes.

rebec or rebeck a small instrument with a pear-shaped body and, usually, three strings that were played with a BOW.

recapitulation *see* sonata form.

recital a public concert given by just one or two people, e.g. a singer with PIANO ACCOMPANIMENT.

recitando (*Italian*) 'reciting', i.e. speaking rather than singing.

recitative a way of singing (usually on a fixed NOTE) in which the RHYTHM and lilt are taken from the words, and there is no tune as such. It is commonly used in OPERA and ORATORIO.

reciting note in PLAINSONG, the NOTE on which the first few words of each verse of a PSALM are sung.

recorder a straight, end-blown FLUTE, as opposed to a side-blown (concert) flute. Notes can be played by opening or closing eight holes in the instrument with the fingers. Recorders come in CONSORTS (families): DESCANT, TREBLE, TENOR and BASS.

reed the small part found in many blown instruments that vibrates when air is blown across it and creates the sound. It is usually made of cane or metal. In single-reed instruments (e.g. CLARINET, SAXOPHONE), the reed vibrates against the instrument itself; in double-reed instruments (e.g. COR ANGLAIS, BASSOON), two reeds vibrate against each other; in free-reed instruments (e.g. HARMONIUM, CONCERTINA), a metal reed vibrates freely within a slot.

reed organ the generic term for a number of instruments that have no PIPES and use FREE REEDS to produce their NOTES. Examples are the ACCORDION and the HARMONIUM.

reed pipe an ORGAN pipe with a metal reed in the mouthpiece, which vibrates when air is passed over it.

reel a Celtic dance, usually in quick 4/4 TIME and in regular four-BAR PHRASES.

refrain the CHORUS of a BALLAD.

regal a portable REED ORGAN of the 16th and 17th centuries.

reggae a type of Jamaican POP MUSIC with a heavy and pronounced RHYTHM and strongly accented UPBEAT.

register (1) a set of organ pipes that are controlled by a single STOP. (2) a part of a singer's vocal COMPASS, e.g. CHEST register, HEAD register, etc. The term is also applied to certain instruments.

related keys *see* MODULATION.

relative major, relative minor terms used to describe the connection between a MAJOR KEY and a MINOR KEY that share the same KEY SIGNATURE, e.g. A minor is the relative key of C major.

relief a sculptural form that is not freestanding. The three-dimensional shape is either carved, e.g. in stone, wood, ivory, etc, or built up, as in metal, etc. Relief sculpture can be *low relief* (*basso relievo* or *bas-relief*), where the depth of the pattern is less than half; *medium relief* (*mezzo relievo*), where the depth is roughly half; or *high relief* (*alto relievo*), where practically all the medium has been removed.

Renaissance in literature, the revival of the arts that occurred in Europe in the 14th-16th centuries, as a result of the rediscovery of the writing of the great classical writers, notably the works of Plato and Aristotle. The Renaissance period in England is usually given as 1500–1660.

In art, the early Renaissance was established in Italy with the works of Giotto (1267–1337), in a spectacular move away from GOTHIC conventions. The movement reached a peak between 1500 and 1520 with the works of Leonardo da Vinci (1452–1519), Michelangelo (1475–1564) and Raphael. The Northern Renaissance took place as ideas spread to Germany, the Netherlands and the rest of Europe in the early 16th century.

repeat two or four DOTS in the spaces of the STAVE that indicate that the PASSAGE so marked is to be played through twice.

reprise a musical repetition; it is often found in musical comedies when songs heard in one act are repeated in another.

Requiem a MASS for the dead in the Roman Catholic Church, so called because of the opening words at the beginning of the INTROIT, *Requiem aeternam dona eis, Domine* ('Grant them eternal rest, O Lord').

resolution a term for a process in harmony by which a piece moves from DISCORD to CONCORD.

resonance the intensification and prolongation of a sound or a musical note produced by sympathetic vibration.

responses the PLAINSONG replies of a CHOIR or congregation to SOLO CHANTS sung by a priest.

rest a sign employed in NOTATION indicating silence.

Restoration (1) the re-establishment of the British monarchy in 1660, following the return to England of Charles II in that year. (2) the period of Charles II's reign (1660–85). The characteristics of Restoration literature are WIT, salaciousness, and religious and philosophical questioning.

Restoration comedy *see* COMEDY OF MANNERS.

resultant tone *see* COMBINATION TONE.

retable *see* ALTARPIECE.

retardation a SUSPENSION in which a DISCORD is resolved upwards by one step rather than downwards.

retrograde motion a term for music that is played backwards.

revenge tragedy a form of tragedy that appeared in the late Elizabethan period, heavily influenced by the bloodthirsty language and plots of Seneca's plays, in which revenge, often for the death of a son or father, is the prime motive. Thomas Kyd's Th*e Spanish Tragedy* (1588–9) is the earliest example. See also JACOBEAN TRAGEDY.

rhapsody the title commonly given by 19th- and 20th-century composers to an instrumental composition in one continuous movement. Rhapsodies are often based on FOLK tunes, and are nationalistic or heroic in tone.

rhythm the regular recurrence of beat, accent or silence in the flow of sound, especially of words and music. In MUSIC NOTATION, rhythm is determined by the way in which NOTES are grouped together into BARS, the number and type of BEATS in a bar (as governed by the TIME SIGNATURE), and the type of emphasis (ACCENT) that is given to the beats. Along with MELODY and HARMONY, it is one of the essential characteristics of music.

rhythm and blues a type of POP MUSIC that combines elements of BLUES and JAZZ. It developed in the USA and was widely accepted by white audiences and pop musicians. ROCK'N'ROLL evolved from rhythm and blues.

rhythm-names *see* TIME-NAMES.

rhythm section the name given to the PERCUSSION and DOUBLE BASS section of a JAZZ band; it provides the all-important BEAT.

ribs the sides uniting the back and belly of an instrument of the VIOLIN family.

rigoroso (*Italian*) 'rigorously', i.e. in exact TIME.

ritardando (*Italian*) 'becoming gradually slower'.

ritmo, ritmico (*Italian*) 'RHYTHM', 'rhythmic'.

rock a type of POP MUSIC that evolved from ROCK 'N' ROLL in the USA during the 1960s. It mixes COUNTRY AND WESTERN with RHYTHM AND BLUES and is usually played loudly on electric instruments.

rock 'n' roll a type of POP MUSIC, with a strong, catchy RHYTHM, that evolved in the USA during the 1950s and is often associated with 'jiving' (fast dancing that requires nimble footwork).

Rococo a style in art following on from BAROQUE and even more exaggerated in terms of embellishments and mannered flourishes. It became established around the beginning of the 18th century and spread throughout Europe, lasting up until the advent of NEOCLASSICISM in the 1760s. Music from the same period is sometimes similarly termed.

roll a trill on percussion instruments produced by sounding notes so rapidly that they overlap and appear to produce a continuous sound.

romance a love song or composition of a romantic character.

Romanticism a term denoting any movement in the arts which emphasises feeling and content as opposed to form and order. The Romantic movement can be roughly dated from the late 18th century to the early 19th century, although the contrast between the need to express emotion and the desirability of following artistic rules dates back as far as the great Athenian dramatists. Other distinctive features of the Romantic movement are:

the supremacy of individual over collective judgment; a 'progressive' faith in the reformability and essential goodness of humanity; the supremacy of 'natural' and 'organic' virtues over society's artifical construction. *Compare* NEOCLASSICISM.

In art, the movement dates from the late 18th until the mid-19th century. It was a reaction to the balanced harmony and order of Classicism, and identified with the Romantic writers of the age. In response to increasing industrialisation, Romantic painters viewed nature from a nostalgic point of view, imbuing landscapes with powerful emotions, often in a melancholic or melodramatic way.

In music, Romanticism lasted from *c*.1820 to *c*.1920. During this phase music tended to be more poetic, subjective and individualistic than previously. Lyricism, drama and often nationalistic feeling were characteristic of Romantic music.

rondo a form of instrumental music that incorporates a recurring THEME, either in an independent piece or (more usually) as part of a MOVEMENT. It usually starts with a lively tune (the 'SUBJECT'), which is repeated at intervals throughout the movement. Intervening sections are called EPISODES, and these may or may not be in different keys from the subject. Rondo forms often occur in the final movements of SYMPHONIES, SONATAS and CONCERTOS.

root the lowest ('fundamental' or 'generating') NOTE of a CHORD.

round a short CANON in which each PART enters at equal INTERVALS and in UNISON.

round dance a dance in which partners start opposite each other and subsequently form a ring.

roundelay a poem with certain lines repeated at intervals, or the tune to which such a poem was sung.

rumba a sexually suggestive and fast Afro-Cuban dance in syncopated (*see* SYNCOPATION) 2/4 TIME.

run a SCALE or succession of NOTES rapidly played, or, if vocal, sung to one syllable.

S abbreviation for SEGNO, SENZA, SINISTRA, SOLO, SORDINO, SUBITO.

saltando (*Italian*) literally 'leaping', i.e. an instruction to the string player to bounce the BOW lightly off the string.

samba a Brazilian carnival dance in 2/4 TIME but with syncopated (*see* SYNCOPATION) rhythms.

saxhorn a family of BUGLE-like BRASS instruments patented by the Belgian instrument-maker Adolphe Sax (1814–94) in 1845. They were innovative in that they had VALVES, as opposed to the KEYS normally associated with the bugle family.

saxophone a family of instruments patented by Adolphe Sax (*see* SAXHORN) in 1846 which, although made of brass, actually belong to the WOODWIND group because they are REED instruments. Saxophones come in many different sizes (e.g. SOPRANO, TENOR) and are commonly used in JAZZ bands as well as orchestras.

scala (*Italian*) 'staircase', from which the Teatro alla SCALA gets its name, but in music a RUN or SCALE.

Scala, La *or* **Teatro alla Scala** Milan's, and Italy's, premier opera house, which was opened in 1778.

scale an ordered sequence of NOTES that ascend or descend in PITCH. The most frequently used scales in European music are the MAJOR and MINOR scales, which use TONES (whole notes) and SEMITONES (half-notes) as steps of progression.

scat singing a type of singing used in JAZZ in which nonsense SOUNDS rather than words are sung.

scherzando, scherzoso (*Italian*) 'playful', or 'lively', as of a phrase or movement.

scherzo (*Italian*) 'joke', i.e. a cheerful, quick piece of music, either vocal or instrumental. The third MOVEMENT (of four) in many SYMPHONIES, SONATAS, etc, often takes the form of a scherzo.

school in art, a group of artists who hold similar principles and work in a similar style. In art history, it also denotes that a painting has been executed by a pupil or assistant. In music, the characteristics of certain composers, whose style made a school.

Schottische (*German*) 'Scottish'; a ROUND DANCE, similar to the POLKA, popular in the 19th century. It is not in fact Scottish, but is so called because it is what those on the Continent thought a Scottish dance should be like.

Schrammel quartet a Viennese ENSEMBLE usually comprising two VIOLINS, a GUITAR and an ACCORDION, or the music composed for such an ensemble. It takes its name from Joseph Schrammel (1858–93), who wrote WALTZES for such a group.

scordatura (*Italian*) 'mistuning', i.e. the TUNING of stringed instruments to abnormal NOTES, so as to produce special effects.

score music written down in such a way that it indicates all the PARTS for all the performers, i.e. the whole COMPOSITION. A *full* or *orchestral score* is one with separate STAVES for each part. A *piano score* is one in which all the instrumental parts are represented on two staves. A *vocal score* is a piano score with two additional staves for the vocal parts. A *short close* or *compressed score* has more than one part to the stave.

scoring the writing of a SCORE.

Scotch snap the name for a RHYTHM that leaps from a short NOTE to a longer note. It is found in many Scottish FOLK tunes.

scroll the decorative end of the PEG-BOX of a VIOLIN (or other stringed instrument). It may be carved into a curl resembling a scroll, or an animal head.

sec (*French*), **secco** (*Italian*) 'unornamented', 'plain'.

secondary colours *see* PRIMARY COLOURS.

Section d'Or a group of painters in France who associated between 1912 and 1914 and whose aim was to hold group exhibitions and encourage debate of their aesthetic ideals.

segno (*Italian*) 'sign', used in notation to mark a repeat, usually as *al segno*.

segue (*Italian*) 'follows', i.e. a direction to start playing the following MOVEMENT without a break.

seguidilla a Spanish dance in 3/8 or 3/4 TIME in the style of the BOLERO, but much faster.

semibreve a 'half of a BREVE'; the NOTE with the longest time-value normally used in modern Western NOTATION. In US notation, this is called a 'whole note'.

semidemisemiquaver an alternative name for a HEMIDEMISEMIQUAVER or sixty-fourth note.

Semiotics *see* STRUCTURALISM.

semiquaver a NOTE with half the time-value of a QUAVER, and a sixteenth the time-value of a SEMIBREVE. In US NOTATION, it is called a 'sixteenth-note'.

semitone 'half a TONE'; the smallest INTERVAL regularly used in modern Western music.

semplice (*Italian*) 'unornamented', 'in a simple manner'.

sempre (*Italian*) 'throughout', 'continually'; as *sempre* FORTE, 'loud throughout'.

sentimental comedy a form of English COMEDY that arose in the early 18th century, focusing on the problems of middle-class characters. The plays always end happily and feature strongly contrasting good and bad characters and high emotional peaks. The form led on to MELODRAMA (*see also* DOMESTIC TRAGEDY).

senza (*Italian*) 'without', so senza sordino means 'without MUTE' (in music for strings).

septet a group of seven performers or a piece of music written for such a group.

septuplet a group of seven NOTES of equal time-value to be played in the time of four or six.

sequence (1) the repetition of a short PASSAGE of music in a different PITCH. (2) a form of HYMN in Latin used in the Roman Catholic Mass, such as DIES IRAE and STABAT MATER.

serenade (1) a love SONG, traditionally sung in the evening and usually accompanied by a GUITAR or MANDOLIN. (2) a DIVERTIMENTO performed during an evening entertainment.

serenata (*Italian*) an 18th-century form of secular CANTATA or a short OPERA composed for a patron.

serialism a method of composition in which all semitones are treated as equal, i.e. tonal values are eliminated. *See also* TWELVE-NOTE MUSIC.

seventh an INTERVAL in which two NOTES are seven steps apart (including the first and last), for example F to E.

sevillana a Spanish FOLK DANCE originally from the city of Seville. It is similar to the SEGUIDILLA.

sextet a group of six performers or a piece of music written for such a group.

sextolet *or* **sextuplet** a group of six notes to be performed in the time of four notes.

Sezession (*German*) 'secession', adopted as a name in the 1890s by groups of painters in Austria and Germany when they broke away from official academies to work and exhibit in contemporary styles, e.g. IMPRESSIONISM. In Germany, the first German Sezession was in Munich in 1892, followed by the Berlin Sezession of 1899, which in turn in 1910 repudiated Die BRÜCKE, which resulted in the latter forming the *Neue Sezession*.

sforzando (*Italian*) 'forcing', i.e. a strong ACCENT placed on a NOTE or CHORD.

sfumato a subtle modelling of light and shade between figures and background.

shake an alternative term for trill.

shamisen *or* **samisen** a Japanese long-necked LUTE with three strings. It has no FRETS and is plucked with a PLECTRUM.

shanai a double REED instrument from India, similar to a SHAWM.

shanty a SONG, with a pronounced RHYTHM, that was sung by sailors to help them coordinate their actions in the days of sailing ships. Shanties usually follow a format in which SOLO verses are followed by a CHORUS.

sharp the sign that raises the PITCH of the line or space on which it stands on a STAVE by a SEMITONE.

shawm *or* **shawn** a double-REED WOODWIND instrument that dates from the 13th century. It was developed from Middle Eastern instruments and produced a coarse, shrill sound. It was a forerunner of the OBOE.

sheng a sophisticated Chinese mouth organ (*see* HARMONICA), dating back some 3000 years.

shift a change of position of the hands when playing on a string instrument.

shofar *or* **shophar** an ancient Jewish WIND INSTRUMENT made from a ram's horn, which is still used in synagogues.

siciliano a slow dance from Sicily in 6/8 or 12/8 TIME, with a characteristic lilting RHYTHM.

side drum *or* **snare drum** a cylindrically shaped DRUM that is the smallest usually used in an orchestra. Snares, made of gut or sprung metal, are stretched across the bottom parchment and vibrate against it when the upper membrane of parchment is struck; this gives the drum its characteristic rattling sound. The snares can be released to produce a more hollow sound.

signature *see* KEY SIGNATURE; TIME SIGNATURE.

signature tune a few BARS of catchy music that are associated with a performer or broadcast show.

similar motion the simultaneous PROGRESSION of two or more PARTS in the same direction.

simple interval any INTERVAL that is an octave or less. *Compare* COMPOUND INTERVAL.

simple time *see* COMPOUND TIME.

sine tone an electronically produced NOTE that is entirely 'pure'.

sinfonia (*Italian*) 'SYMPHONY', i.e. an instrumental piece. It is also a term used for a small orchestra.

sinfonietta a short SYMPHONY or a symphony for a small orchestra.

Singspiel (*German*) literally 'sing-play', i.e. a comic opera in German with spoken dialogue replacing the sung RECITATIVE.

sinistra, sinistro (*Italian*) 'left', as in MANO *sinistra,* 'left hand'.

sistrum an ancient type of RATTLE in which loose wooden or metal discs are suspended on metal bars strung across a frame.

sitar a type of Indian LUTE, which is believed to have originated in Persia. It has movable metal FRETS and three to seven 'MELODY' strings; below these strings lie twelve or so SYMPATHETIC STRINGS, which create a droning sound. The sitar is plucked with a long wire PLECTRUM. It has a distinctive 'twangy' sound and is usually played in consort with the TABLA.

Six, Les (*French*) 'The Six', the name given in 1920 to six young French composers by the poet and music critic Henri Collet who, with another of their champions, the poet Jean Cocteau (1889–1963), was passionately anti-Wagner. The six were Georges Auric (1899–1983), Louis Durey (1888–1979), Arthur Honegger (1892–1955), Darius Milhaud (1892–1974), François Poulenc (1899–1963) and Germaine Tailleferre (1892–1983).

sixteenth-note (US) *see* SEMIQUAVER.

sketch in art, a preliminary drawing made by an artist to establish points of composition, scale, etc. In music, a short PIANO or instrumental piece.

skiffle a type of POP MUSIC played in England during the 1950s. Skiffle BANDS relied on American idioms (for example BLUES) and attempted to become 'authentic' by incorporating home-made instruments (such as tea-chest 'basses') into their outfits.

slancio, con (*Italian*) 'with impetus'.

sleigh bells small metal bells with steel balls inside which are mounted together in groups to produce a richly textured jingling sound. They are traditionally hung on sleighs, but are occasionally used in orchestras to create special effects.

slide (1) a passing from one to note to another without an INTERVAL. (2) a mechanism on the TRUMPET and TROMBONE that lengthens the tube to allow a new series of harmonics.

slide trombone *see* TROMBONE.

slide trumpet an early form of TRUMPET that had a slide similar to that used in the TROMBONE. It became obsolete when the VALVE trumpet was invented.

slur a curved line that is placed over or under a group of NOTES to indicate that they are to be played, or sung, smoothly, that is, with one stroke of the BOW (VIOLIN music) or in one breath (singing).

smorzando (*Italian*) 'fading' or 'dying away', i.e. the music is to become softer and slower.

snare drum *see* SIDE DRUM.

soave (*Italian*) 'soft' or 'gentle'.

socialist realism the name given to official art in the former Soviet Union, which was intended to glorify the achievements of the Communist Party.

social realism a form of realism, in which an artist's political viewpoint (usually on the left) affects the content of his work.

soft pedal *see* PIANO.

soh in the TONIC SOL-FA, the fifth NOTE (or DOMINANT) of the MAJOR SCALE.

solemnis (*Latin*) 'solemn', as in MISSA *Solemnis,* 'Solemn Mass'.

sol-fa *see* TONIC SOL-FA.

solfeggio (*Italian*) a type of singing exercise in which the names of the NOTES are sung. *See* TONIC SOL-FA.

solo (*Italian*) 'alone', i.e. a piece to be performed by one person, with or without ACCOMPANIMENT.

solo organ a manual on an ORGAN with strong, distinctive STOPS, used for individual effect.

sonata originally a term for any instrumental piece to distinguish it from a sung piece or CANTATA. However, during the 17th century two distinct forms of sonata arose: the *sonata da* CAMERA (chamber sonata), in which dance movements were played by two or three stringed instruments with a keyboard ACCOMPANIMENT, and the *sonata da chiesa* (church sonata), which was similar but more serious. In the 18th century the sonata came to be a piece in several contrasting movements for keyboard only or for keyboard and one SOLO instrument.

sonata form a method of arranging and constructing music that is commonly used (since *c*.1750) for SYMPHONIES, SONATAS, CONCERTOS, etc. There are three sections to sonata form: the EXPOSITION (in which the SUBJECT or subjects are introduced), the DEVELOPMENT (in which the subject(s) are expanded and developed), and the 'recapitulation' (in which the exposition, usually modified in some way, is repeated).

sonata-rondo form a type of RONDO, popular with such composers as BEETHOVEN, which is a combination of rondo and SONATA FORM.

sonatina a short SONATA.

song (1) a musical setting of poetry or prose. (2) a poem that can be sung. (3) a name used to designate the second SUBJECT of a SONATA.

song cycle a set of SONGS that have a common THEME or have words by a single poet.

sopra (Italian) 'above', so come sopra means 'as above'.

soprano the highest PITCH of human VOICE, with a range of about two octaves above approximately middle C. The term is also applied to some instruments, such as soprano SAXOPHONE (the highest pitched saxophone). *See also* MEZZO.

sotto (*Italian*) 'below', as in *sotto voce,* which literally means 'under the VOICE' or whispered.

soul music a type of emotionally charged music developed by black musicians in America. 'Soul', as it is usually called, derives from BLUES and GOSPEL music with the addition of ROCK RHYTHMS.

sound a term in ACOUSTICS for TONES resulting from regular VIBRATIONS, as opposed to noise.

sound hole the opening in the BELLY of a stringed instrument, e.g. the f-shaped holes in a violin or the round hole in a guitar.

soundpost a piece of wood connecting the BELLY of a stringed instrument (such as a VIOLIN) to the back. It helps to distribute VIBRATIONS through the body of the instrument.

sousaphone a giant TUBA that encircles the player's body which was designed for his band by the American bandmaster and composer John Philip Sousa (1854-1932) who formed a successful MILITARY-style BAND that toured the world giving concerts.

Spanish guitar the classic GUITAR with a narrow waist, six strings and a central SOUND HOLE.

special effects a non-specific term used of any extraordinary noises or SOUNDS that may be required of an orchestra, or part of an orchestra, to satisfy the demands of a composer, such as COW BELLS, etc.

species a discipline used in teaching strict COUNTERPOINT, developed by Johann Fux (1660–1741), who listed five rhythmic patterns ('species') in which one VOICE PART could be combined with another.

spinet a type of small HARPSICHORD.

spirito (*Italian*) 'spirit', so *con spirito* means 'with spirit'.

spiritual a type of religious FOLK SONG or HYMN that was developed by black (and white) Americans in the 18th and 19th centuries. Spirituals are characterised by strong SYNCOPATION and simple MELODIES. They were superseded by GOSPEL music.

staccato (*Italian*) 'detached', i.e. NOTES should be shortened and played with brief INTERVALS between them.

staff *see* STAVE.

stave *or* **staff** a set of horizontal lines (usually five) on which music is written. Each line, and the gaps between them, represent a different PITCH.

steel drum a PERCUSSION INSTRUMENT ('pan') made by West Indian musicians (particularly from Trinidad) out of discarded oil drums. Each DRUM can be tuned to play a range of notes by beating and heat-treating different sections of the 'head', i.e. the top of the drum.

Steinway a firm of piano manufacturers founded by Henry Steinway [originally Heinrich Steinweg] (1797–1871) in New York in 1853.

stem the line, or 'tail', attached to the head of all notes smaller than a SEMIBREVE.

stesso (*Italian*) 'same', so *lo stesso* TEMPO means 'the same speed'.

stiacciato *see* RELIEF.

Stijl, De a group of Dutch artists, founded to spread theories on ABSTRACT ART, principally through the *De Stijl* magazine, which was published 1917–28. The group rejected the representational in art, believing that art's object was to convey harmony and order, achieved by the use of straight lines and geometrical shapes in primary colours or black and white.

still life a genre of painting depicting inanimate objects such as fruit, flowers, etc, begun by Dutch artists seeking secular commissions after the Reformation and the loss of Church patronage. Within the genre, the *vanitas* still life contains objects symbolic of the transcience of life, e.g. skulls, hour-glasses. Others contain religious symbols, such as bread and wine.

stop a handle or knob on an organ that admits or prevents air from reaching certain pipes and that can therefore be used to modify the potential output of the MANUALS and PEDALS.

stopping on stringed instruments, the placing of fingers on a string to shorten its effective length and raise its PITCH.

Stradivari *or* **Stradivarius** a violin made by Antonio Stradivari (1644–1737) an Italian violin-maker whose instruments are unsurpassed for the quality of their sound.

strathspey *see* REEL.

stream of consciousness a term adapted by literary critics to denote a fluxive method of narration in which characters voice their feelings with no 'obtrusive' authorial comment and with no orthodox dialogue or decription. The term has particular reference to the work of James Joyce (1882–1941) and Virginia Woolf (1882–1941).

stride (piano) a JAZZ piano technique characterised by the use of single bass notes on the first and third beats and chords on the second and fourth.

string a vibrating cord for the production of tone, in the piano of drawn cast steel wire, in instruments of the violin family of catgut or spun silk, and in the guitar of catgut or wire.

string quartet a group of four performers who use stringed instruments (two VIOLINS, VIOLA and CELLO); or a piece of music written for such a group.

strings a general term for the stringed instruments of the VIOLIN family.

Stroh violin a VIOLIN made of metal (invented by Charles Stroh in 1901) that incorporates a TRUMPET bell and does not have a normal violin body.

Structuralism in literary criticism, a critical approach to literature in which the text being studied is viewed as a 'cultural product' that cannot be 'read' in isolation and in which the text is held to absorb its meaning from the interconnected web of linguistic codes and symbols of which it is but a part.

    Deconstruction a concept developed by the French philosopher Jacques Derrida (1930–), is a term for the process or 'strategy' of examining the elements (signs) of language in isolation from other elements, thus exposing the contradictions inherent within language. It is also called *Poststructuralism*.

study in art, a drawing or painting of a detail for use in a larger finished work. In music, a piece written to demonstrate technique in playing a musical instrument or using the voice.

subdominant the fourth NOTE of the MAJOR or MINOR SCALE.

subito (*Italian*) 'suddenly', as in PIANO *subito,* meaning 'suddenly soft'.

subject a musical THEME on which a composition (or part of a composition) is constructed, e.g. the first and second SUBJECTS in the EXPOSITION in SONATA FORM; the subject in a FUGUE; also the leading VOICE (first PART) of a fugue.

submediant the sixth NOTE of the MAJOR or MINOR SCALE.

subsidiary theme any THEME that is less important than the main theme(s) of a composition.

suite a collection of short pieces that combine to form an effective overall composition; the BAROQUE suite was a set of (stylised) dances.

sul, sull' (*Italian*) 'on' or 'over', so *sul ponticello* means 'over the BRIDGE' (in VIOLIN bowing).

Suprematism a Russian art movement based on principles of non-objectivity, which evolved on a parallel with Constructivism. The influence of Suprematism spread through the BAUHAUS to Europe and the US.

Surrealism an avant-garde art movement of the 1920s and 1930s in France, which grew out of DADA and was inspired by the dream theories of Sigmund Freud (1856–1939) and by the literature and poetry of Arthur Rimbaud (1854–91) and Charles Baudelaire (1821–67). Surrealism took from Dadaism a love for the juxtaposition of incongruous images, the purpose of which in the Surrealist view was to express the workings of the unconscious mind. The movement really got going with the publication by the poet André Breton (1896–1966) of his first Surrealist Manifesto in 1924.

In art there were two main trends: automatism, or free association, whose exponents sought deliberately to avoid conscious control by using techniques of spontaneity to express the subconscious. The world of dreams was the source of inspiration for the incongruously juxtaposed, often bizarre, but precisely painted imagery of Salvador Dali (1904–89) and René Magritte (1898–1967).

suspension a device used in HARMONY, in which a NOTE sounded in one CHORD is sustained while a subsequent chord is played (or sung), producing a DISSONANCE that is then resolved.

sustaining pedal *see* PIANO.

swell organ a MANUAL on an ORGAN. The notes played on this manual can become louder and softer by the opening and closing of the shutters on the swell box, which encloses the PIPES.

swing a type of American POPULAR MUSIC of the 1935–45 era; it was played by BIG BANDS and had an insistent RHYTHM.

Symbolism in literature, a French poetry movement of the late-19th century that rejected the dictates of both REALISM and NATURALISM by seeking to express a state of mind by a process of suggestion rather than by attempting to portray 'objective reality'. Prominent poets associated with Symbolism include Paul Verlaine (1844–96) and Arthur Rimbaud (1854–91). Several important plays of the late 19th century, e.g. Anton Chekhov's *The Seagull* (1895) and Henrik Ibsen's *The Master Builder* (1896), also display the influence of Symbolism.

In art, also in late 19th-century France, it represented a response to the intrinsically visual work of the IMPRESSIONISTS and fell into two distinct trends: some painters were inspired by the images of Symbolist Literature; others explored the symbolic use of colour and line to express emotion.

sympathetic strings strings on certain instruments, such as the SITAR, which are not actually plucked or bowed, but which are set in sympathetic VIBRATION and produce a NOTE without being touched, when the same note is played on a 'melody' string.

symphonic poem *or* **tone poem** an orchestral composition, a form of PROGRAMME MUSIC, usually in one MOVEMENT, which attempts to interpret or describe an emotion, idea, or story.

symphony in essence, a prolonged or extended SONATA for an orchestra. Most symphonies have four MOVEMENTS (sections) that, although interrelated, tend to have recognised forms, for example, a quick first movement, a slow second movement, a MINUET third movement, and a vibrant fourth movement (FINALE).

Synchromism an art movement originating in the US in 1913 the members of which were concerned with the balanced arrangement of pure colour, or 'colours together'. Synchronism influenced a number of American painters.

syncopation an alteration to the normal arrangement of accented BEATS in a BAR. This is usually done by placing ACCENTS on beats or parts of a beat that do not normally carry an accent.

synthesizer an ELECTRONIC instrument, operated by a keyboard and switches, that can generate and modify an extensive range of SOUND.

tabla a pair of Indian DRUMS, beaten with the hands, which are often used to accompany the SITAR in classical Indian music.

table an alternative name for the upper surface, or BELLY, of instruments of the VIOLIN family.

tabor an early type of SIDE DRUM.

tace (*Italian*) 'silent'.

tail the STEM attached to the head of a MINIM (half-note) or a smaller NOTE.

tail piece the piece of wood at the base of a VIOLIN to which the strings are attached.

tail pin the metal rod at the bottom of a CELLO or DOUBLE BASS, which can be pulled out to adjust the height of the instrument above the floor.

tambourin (1) a lively 18th-century piece in the style of FOLK DANCE from Provence, usually in 2/4 TIME. (2) a narrow DRUM, played along with a PIPE, as the ACCOMPANIMENT to dancing.

tambourine a small, shallow DRUM with a single skin fastened over a circular frame. Small metal CYMBALS (jingles) are slotted into the frame and rattle when the instrument is shaken or beaten with the hand.

tampon a drumstick that has a head at each end, held in the middle to produce a DRUM ROLL.

tango a Latin-American dance in moderately slow 2/4 TIME, originating from Argentina. It makes use of syncopated RHYTHMS (*see* SYNCOPATION) and became popular in Europe in the 1920s.

tap dance a dance in which the feet are used to tap out a RHYTHM. Special shoes with steel plates at the toe and heel are usually worn.

tasto (*Italian*) the keyboard of a PIANO or the FINGERBOARD of a stringed instrument.

tattoo originally a night DRUM beat calling soldiers to their quarters, now a military display.

tempera a paint medium made by mixing colour pigments with egg. It was much used until the 15th century and the development of oil paint.

temperament the way in which INTERVALS between NOTES have been 'tempered', or slightly altered, in Western music so that the slight discrepancy in seven OCTAVES is distributed evenly over the range. In EQUAL TEMPERAMENT an octave is divided into twelve SEMITONES, which means that, for example, D SHARP is also E FLAT: this is a compromise, for strictly there is a marginal difference between D sharp and E flat.

tempo (*Italian*) 'TIME'. The time taken by a composition, therefore the speed at which it is performed, hence the pace of the BEAT. *A tempo* means 'in time'. It can also mean a movement of a SONATA or SYMPHONY, e.g. *il secondo tempo*, 'the second MOVEMENT'.

tenor (1) the highest adult male VOICE with a range an OCTAVE to either side of middle C. (2) as a prefix to the name of an instrument, it indicates the size between an ALTO member of the family and a BASS, for example tenor SAXOPHONE. (3) the RECITING NOTE in PSALM singing. (4) an obsolete term for a VIOLA (tenor VIOLIN).

tenor drum a DRUM, frequently used in MILITARY BANDS, between a SIDE DRUM and BASS DRUM in size and PITCH, and without snares.

tenor violin a VIOLONCELLO.

tenuto (*Italian*) 'held'; a term that indicates that a NOTE should be held for its full value, or in some cases, even longer.

ternary form a term applied to a piece of music divided into three self-contained parts, with the first and third sections bearing strong similarities.

ternary time *see* TRIPLE TIME.

tessitura (*Italian*) 'texture'; a term indicating whether the majority of NOTES in a piece are high up or low down in the range of a VOICE (or instrument).

tetrachord a group of four NOTES.

theme the MELODY, or other musical material, that forms the basis of a work or a MOVEMENT and which may be varied or developed. It may return in one form or another throughout a composition.

thirty-second note (US) a DEMISEMIQUAVER.

thorough bass *see* FIGURED BASS.

thunder stick *or* **bull roarer** *or* **whizzer** an instrument consisting of a flat piece of wood fastened to a piece of string. When the piece of wood is whirled around the head, it creates a roaring sound.

tie a curved line that joins two NOTES of the same PITCH together, indicating that they should be played as one long note.

timbre (*French*) the quality of TONE, or the characteristic SOUND of an instrument.

time the rhythmic pattern (number of BEATS in a BAR) of a piece of music, as indicated by the TIME SIGNATURE. DUPLE TIME has two beats in a bar, triple time has three beats in a bar, and so on.

time-names *or* **rhythm-names** a French method of teaching TIME and RHYTHM, in which beats are given names, such as 'ta', 'ta-te', etc.

time signature a sign placed at the beginning of a piece of music that indicates the number and value of BEATS in a BAR. A time signature usually consists of two numbers, one placed above the other. The lower number defines the unit of measurement in relation to the SEMIBREVE (whole note); the top figure indicates the number of those units in a bar, for example, 3/4 indicates that there are three CROTCHETS (quarter notes) in a bar.

timpani *or* **kettledrums** the main orchestral PERCUSSION INSTRUMENTS, consisting of bowl-shaped shells over which the membrane is stretched. The shell is supported on a frame at the base of which, in 'pedal timpani', is the foot PEDAL that can alter the PITCH of the drum as it is played. The drum can also be tuned (*see* TUNING) by screws, which alter the tension of the membrane.

Tin Pan Alley the nickname given to West 28th Street in New York, where the popular-song publishing business used to be situated. It consequently became a slang expression for the POPULAR MUSIC industry.

tin whistle *or* **penny whistle** a metal whistle-FLUTE, similar to a RECORDER but with six finger holes. It produces high-pitched sounds and is commonly used to play FOLK music.

toccata (*Italian*) 'touched'; a type of music for a keyboard instrument that is intended to show off a player's 'touch' or ability.

tonality the use of a KEY in a composition.

tondo (*Italian*) 'round', used in art to denote a circular picture or sculpture.

tone (1) an INTERVAL comprising two SEMITONES, for example the interval between C and D. (2) (US) a musical NOTE. (3) the quality of SOUND, for example good TONE, SHARP tone, etc. (4) in PLAINSONG, a MELODY.

tone poem *see* SYMPHONIC POEM.

tonguing in the playing of a WIND INSTRUMENT, this means interrupting the flow of breath with the tongue so that detached NOTES are played, or the first note of a PHRASE is distinguished.

tonic the first NOTE of a MAJOR or MINOR SCALE.

tonic sol-fa a system of NOTATION and sight-singing used in training, in which NOTES are sung to syllables. The notes of the major scale are: DOH, RE, ME, FAH, SOH, LA, TE, DOH (doh is always the TONIC, whatever the KEY). The system was pioneered in England by John Curwen (1816–80) in the mid-19th century.

tosto (*Italian*) 'rapid', as in PIÙ *tosto*, 'quicker'.

trad jazz literally 'traditional JAZZ'; a term referring to the type of comparatively simple jazz, with a strong MELODY, as played in New Orleans, which preceded the development of BEBOP.

tragedy a form of drama in which a hero or heroine comes to a bad end. The cause of the protagonist's failure can be either a personal flaw or a circumstance beyond his or her control, or both. The earliest tragedies known, those by Aeschylus, Sophocles and Euripides, are still among the greatest.

The great tradition of the Greek tragedians was filtered through the plays of Seneca to the dramatists of the Renaissance, although Renaissance tragedies, such as those of Shakespeare, differ significantly from those of the past. The interplay in Shakespeare's tragedies between the heroic and the ironic or comic commonplace worlds is profoundly foreign to the world of the Poetics, just as the pagan and fate-haunted world of the Greeks was ultimately alien to Renaissance dramatists brought up in the Christian tradition.

Several 20th-century dramatists, e.g. Arthur Miller (1915–) and Eugene O'Neill (1888–1953), have tried, with debatable results, to adapt the form of Athenian tragedy to the modern stage. *See also* DOMESTIC TRAGEDY, HEROIC TRAGEDY, JACOBEAN TRAGEDY, REVENGE TRAGEDY.

tragicomedy *see* COMEDY.

tranquillo (*Italian*) 'calm'.

transcription *see* ARRANGEMENT.

transition (1) the changing from one key to another during the course of a composition. (2) a passage linking two sections of a piece, which often involves a change of key.

transposing instruments instruments that sound NOTES different from those actually written down, e.g. a piece of music in E flat for the B flat CLARINET would actually be written in F.

transposition the changing of the PITCH of a composition. Singers sometimes ask accompanists to transpose a SONG higher or lower so that it is better suited to their voice range.

treble the highest boy's VOICE.

treble clef G CLEF on the second line of the STAVE, used for TREBLE VOICES and instruments of medium or high PITCH, such as VIOLINS, FLUTES, OBOES, CLARINETS, HORNS and TRUMPETS.

trecento the Italian term for the 14th century.

tremolo (*Italian*) the rapid repetition of a single NOTE, or the rapid alternation between two or more notes.

triad a CHORD of three NOTES that includes a third and a FIFTH.

triangle a PERCUSSION INSTRUMENT comprising a thin steel bar bent into a triangle but with one corner left unjoined. It is normally struck with a thin metal bar.

trill *or* **shake** an ORNAMENT in which a NOTE is rapidly alternated with the note above. It is used in both vocal and instrumental pieces.

trio (1) a group of three performers, or a piece of music written for such a group. (2) the middle section of a MINUET, as found in SONATAS, SYMPHONIES, etc. It was originally a section scored for three PARTS.

triplet a group of three NOTES played in the time of two notes.

triptych a painting, usually an altarpiece, consisting of three hinged parts, the outer two folding over the middle section. *See also* diptych, polyptych.

tritone an INTERVAL consisting of three WHOLE TONES.

trombone a BRASS instrument that has changed little for 500 years. The body of the instrument has a cylindrical bore with a bell at one end and a MOUTH-PIECE at the other. A U-shaped SLIDE is used for lengthening or shortening the tubing and therefore for sounding different NOTES. TENOR and BASS trombones are often used in orchestras.

trope (*Latin*) an addition of music or words to traditional PLAINSONG LITURGY.

troppo (*Italian*) 'too much', as in ALLEGRO *non troppo*, meaning 'fast but not too fast'.

troubadour a poet-musician of the early Middle Ages who originally came from the South of France and sang in the Provençal language.

trumpet a BRASS instrument that has a cylindrical bore with a funnel-shaped MOUTHPIECE at one end and a bell (flared opening) at the other. The modern trumpet has three valves (operated by PISTONS) which bring into play extra lengths of tubing and are therefore used to change the pitch of the instrument. Trumpets are used in orchestras, JAZZ BANDS and MILITARY BANDS. 'Trumpet' is also a generic term used to describe any number of very different types of instrument that are found all over the world.

tuba a large BRASS instrument with a wide conical bore, a large cup-shaped MOUTHPIECE, and a large bell that faces upwards. It can have between three and five valves and comes in three common sizes: TENOR (EUPHONIUM), BASS and double bass. Tubas are found in orchestras and military bands.

tubular bells *see* BELLS.

tune a MELODY or AIR.

tuning the adjusting of the PITCH of an instrument so that it corresponds to an agreed note, for example, an orchestra will usually have all its instruments tuned to the note of A.

tuning fork a two-pronged steel device that, when tapped, will sound a single, 'pure' note. It was invented by John Shore in 1711 and is used to tune instruments, etc.

tutti (*Italian*) 'all'; in orchestral music, a *tutti* passage is one to be played by the whole orchestra.

twelve-note music *or* **twelve-tone system** a method of composition formulated and advanced by Alfred Schoenberg (1874–1951). In the system, the twelve CHROMATIC NOTES of an OCTAVE can only be used in specific orders, called 'note rows'; no note can be repeated twice within a note row, and the rows must be used complete. In all, there are forty-eight ways in which a note row can be arranged (using INVERSION, RETROGRADE MOTION and inverted retrograde motion), and it is with note rows that compositions are constructed.

ukelele a small, four-stringed GUITAR that was developed in Hawaii during the 19th century. It was a popular music-hall instrument during the 1920s.

unison the sounding of the same NOTE or its OCTAVE by two or more VOICES or instruments.

Unities *see* NEOCLASSICISM.

up beat the upward movement of a conductor's BATON or hand, indicating the unstressed (usually the last) BEAT in a BAR.

upright *see* PIANO.

Utopian novel a form of NOVEL developed from *Utopia* (1516) a fantasy of a supposedly ideally organised state written by Sir Thomas More (1478–1535). The work spawned a host of imitations over the centuries but the impact of 20th-century totalitarianism has lessened enthusiams for the form.

Utrecht School a movement in Dutch art begun by Gerrit van Honthorst (1590–1656), Hendrick Terbrugghen (1588–1629) and Dirck van Baburen (*c*.1595–1624), who were in Rome between 1610 and 1620 and were strongly influenced by Michelangelo de Caravaggio (1573–1610).

valve a device attached to horns, trumpets and other brass instruments to lengthen or reduce the extend of tubing, hence lowering or raising the pitch respectively, to complete the scale.

vamp to improvise an ACCOMPANIMENT.

variation the modification or DEVELOPMENT of a THEME.

vaudeville (*French*) originally a type of popular, satirical SONG sung by Parisian street musicians. In the 18th century these songs (with new words) were incorporated into plays, and the word came to mean the last song in an opera in which each character sang a verse. In the 19th century stage performances with songs and dances were called 'vaudevilles', and the Americans used the term to describe music-hall shows.

veloce (*Italian*) 'fast'.

verismo (*Italian*) 'realism'; the term is used to describe a type of opera that was concerned with representing contemporary life of ordinary people in an honest and realistic way.

verse (1) a line of poetry or a stanza of a poem. (2) a composition in METER, especially of a light nature. (3) a short section of a chapter in the Bible.

versification (1) the art of making verses. (2) the METER or verses of a poem.

vibraphone *or* **vibes** an American instrument, similar to the GLOCKENSPIEL, which consists of a series of metal bars that are struck with mallets. Underneath the bars hang tubular resonators, containing small discs that can be made to spin by means of an electric motor. When the NOTES are sustained the spinning discs give the sound a pulsating quality.

vibration a term in ACOUSTICS for the wave-like MOTION by which a musical TONE is produced. Sound vibrations are mechanical; radio vibrations are electro-magnetic and inaudible.

vibrato (*Italian*) literally 'shaking', i.e. a small but rapid variation in the PITCH of a NOTE.

villanella (*Italian*) literally a 'rustic SONG', a popular PART-SONG of the 17th century.

viol a family of stringed instruments played with a BOW, which were widely used in the 16th and 17th centuries. The instruments came in several sizes and designs, but they all usually had six strings and FRETS. Although they were similar in appearance to members of the VIOLIN family, they were constructed differently and gave a much softer sound.

viola originally a general term for a bowed stringed instrument. However, it is now the name of the ALTO member of the VIOLIN family. It has four strings.

viola da braccio (*Italian*) literally an 'arm VIOL'; a generic term for any stringed instrument played on the arm. It came to mean a VIOLIN or VIOLA.

viola da gamba (*Italian*) literally a 'leg VIOL', a term originally used of those members of the viol family played vertically between the legs or on the lap, but it came to be used exclusively for the BASS viol.

viola d'amore (*Italian*) literally a 'love VIOL', i.e. a tenor VIOL with seven strings (instead of six) and seven or fourteen SYMPATHETIC STRINGS, so called because it had a particularly sweet TONE.

violin a stringed instrument, played with a BOW, which was introduced in the 16th century. It was developed independently of the VIOL from the medieval FIDDLE. It has no FRETS and just four strings. The violin family includes the violin itself (TREBLE), VIOLA (ALTO) and VIOLONCELLO or 'cello' (TENOR). The DOUBLE BASS developed from the double BASS VIOL, but it is now included in the violin family.

violoncello, cello the tenor of the VIOLIN family, dating from the 16th century. It is held vertically between the legs of the seated player, and the TAIL PIN rests on the ground. It has four strings, which are played with a BOW.

virginal a keyboard instrument dating from the 16th century in which the strings are plucked by quills. It was similar to the HARPSICHORD, but it has an oblong body with strings running parallel to the keyboard. The word has also been used to describe any member of the harpsichord family.

virtuoso (*Italian*) a skilled performer on the VIOLIN or some other instrument. The word was formerly synonymous with 'amateur'.

vivace (*Italian*) 'lively'.

vivamente (*Italian*) 'in a lively way'.

vivo (*Italian*) 'lively'.

vocalisation control of the VOICE and vocal sounds, and the method of producing and phrasing NOTES with the voice.

vocal score *see* SCORE.

voce (*Italian*) 'VOICE', as in *voce di petto*, 'CHEST VOICE'.

voice (1) the SOUND produced by human beings by the rush of air over the vocal chords, which are made to vibrate. There are three categories of adult male voice (BASS, BARITONE and TENOR); three female categories (CONTRALTO, MEZZO-SOPRANO and SOPRANO); and two boy categories (TREBLE and ALTO). (2) Parts in contrapuntal (*see* COUNTERPOINT) compositions are traditionally termed 'voices'.

voluntary (1) an improvised piece of instrumental music (16th century). (2) an ORGAN SOLO (sometimes improvised) played before and after an Anglican service.

waltz a dance in triple TIME. Waltzes evolved in Germany and Austria during the late-18th century and became particularly popular in Vienna.

watercolour a paint medium of colour pigments mixed with water-soluble gum arabic. When moistened, a watercolour paint produces a transparent colour that is applied to paper, usually white, the paper showing through the paint.

whistle (1) a toy FLUTE. (2) the making of a musical sound with the lips and breath without using the vocal cords, the hollow of the mouth forming a RESONANCE BOX. Whistling PITCH is an OCTAVE higher than is generally supposed.

whizzer *see* THUNDER STICK.

whole-tone scale a SCALE in which all the INTERVALS are whole-tones, i.e. two SEMITONES.

wind instrument a musical INSTRUMENT the SOUND of which is produced by the breath of the player or by means of bellows.

wit a term that has had many meanings and shades of meanings through the years, and can denote either the thing itself or a notable practitioner of it. The main shifts of meaning to bear in mind are: (a) Elizabethan usage, meaning intelligence or wisdom; (b) early 17th-century usage, meaning ingenious thought, 'fancy', and original figures of speech; (c) the period, roughly from the mid-17th century to the last half of the 18th, which is discussed below; (d) 19th-century to modern times usage, meaning an amusing, perhaps surprising observation, usually involving paradox.

Wit as defined by Alexander Pope (1688–1744) must be distinguished from what we now regard as humour: Wit can be malicious, humour is benevolent. Wits tended to congregate in groups of like-minded intellectuals sharing similar political, social and religious views.

By the late half of the 18th century, the term largely ceased to be used to describe intellectual groups, implying as it did either heartless frivolity or political faction.

woodwind a term for a group of blown instruments that were traditionally made of wood (some of which are now made of metal, e.g. flutes, oboes, clarinets and bassoons, etc.

xylophone a percussion instrument made up of hardwood bars arranged like a keyboard on a frame. It is played by striking the bars with mallets. Xylophones used in orchestras have steel resonators suspended beneath each bar.

zither the generic term for a range of stringed instruments. The European zither consists of a flat box which is strung with a variety of different kinds of string (up to 40). The player uses a PLECTRUM to play MELODIES on one set of strings while the fingers on the other hand pluck a series of open strings to form a DRONE ACCOMPANIMENT.

World Facts

This section of *The Pocket Encyclopedia* provides a quick, factual reference guide to the countries of the modern world, and to its geographical features – the mountains, lakes, oceans and rivers.

Countries of the World

Country	Continent	Population	Capital
Afghanistan	Asia	18,879,000	Kabul
Albania	Europe	3,415,000	Tirana
Algeria	Africa	27,325,000	Algiers
Andorra	Europe	65,000	Andorra-la-Vella
Angola	Africa	10,675,000	Luanda
Antigua & Barbuda	C. America	66,000	St John's
Argentina	S. America	34,663,000	Buenos Aires
Armenia	Europe	3,550,000	Yerevan
Australia	Oceania	18,424,000	Canberra
Austria	Europe	8,045,000	Vienna
Azerbaijan	Europe	7,553,000	Baku
Bahamas, The	C. America	285,000	Nassau
Bahrain	Asia	550,000	Manama
Bangladesh	Asia	118,000,000	Dacca
Barbados	C. America	260,000	Bridgetown
Belarus	Europe	10,265,000	Minsk
Belgium	Europe	10,100,630	Brussels
Belize	C. America	205,000	Belmopan
Benin	Africa	5,160,000	Porto-Novo
Bermuda	C. America	61,000	Hamilton
Bhutan	Asia	1,615,000	Thimphu
Bolivia	S. America	7,240,000	La Paz
Bosnia & Herzegovina	Europe	3,525,000	Sarajevo
Botswana	Africa	1,441,000	Gaborone

Country	Continent	Population	Capital
Brazil	S. America	154,000,000	Brasília
Brunei	Asia	305,000	Bandar Begawan
Bulgaria	Europe	8,450,000	Sofia
Burkina Faso	Africa	9,900,000	Ouagadougou
Burundi	Africa	6,135,000	Bujumbura
Cambodia	Asia	10,500,000	Phnom-Penh
Cameroon	Africa	12,870,000	Yaoundé
Canada	N. America	29,250,000	Ottawa
Cape Verde	Africa	415,000	Praia
Central African Republic	Africa	3,235,000	Bangui
Chad	Africa	6,215,000	N'Djamena
Chile	S. America	13,995,000	Santiago
China	Asia	1,209,000,000	Beijing
Colombia	S. America	34,520,000	Bogotá
Comoros, The	Africa	600,000	Moroni
Congo	Africa	2,700,000	Brazzaville
Congo, Dem. Rep. of	Africa	42,500,000	Kinshasa
Costa Rica	C. America	3,070,000	San José
Côte d'Ivoire	Africa	13,690,000	Yamoussoukro
Croatia	Europe	4,500,500	Zagreb
Cuba	C. America	10,960,000	Havana
Cyprus	Europe	735,000	Nicosia
Czech Republic	Europe	10,330,700	Prague
Denmark	Europe	5,250,000	Copenhagen
Djibouti	Africa	565,000	Djibouti
Dominica	C. America	871,200	Roseau
Dominican Republic	C. America	7,760,000	Santo Domingo
Ecuador	S. America	11,220,000	Quito
Egypt	Africa	58,980,000	Cairo
El Salvador	C. America	5,743,000	San Salvador
Equatorial Guinea	Africa	390,000	Malabo
Eritrea	Africa	3,440,000	Asmara
Estonia	Europe	1,530,000	Tallinn
Ethiopia	Africa	54,940,000	Addis Ababa
Falkland Islands	S. America	2620	Stanley

Country	Continent	Population	Capital
Fiji	Oceania	784,000	Suva
Finland	Europe	5,100,000	Helsinki
France	Europe	57,750,000	Paris
French Guiana	S. America	140,000	Cayenne
Gabon	Africa	1,283,000	Libreville
Gambia	Africa	1,080,000	Banjul
Georgia	Europe	5,400,000	Tbilisi
Germany	Europe	81,400,000	Berlin
Ghana	Africa	17,435,000	Accra
Greece	Europe	10,425,000	Athens
Greenland	N. America	56,000	Gothåb
Grenada	C. America	92,000	St Georges
Guadeloupe	C. America	421,000	Basse Terre
Guatemala	C. America	10,325,000	Guatemala City
Guinea	Africa	6,500,000	Conakry
Guinea-Bissau	Africa	1,050,000	Bissau
Guyana	S. America	825,000	Georgetown
Haiti	C. America	7,040,000	Port-au-Prince
Honduras	C. America	5,770,000	Tegucigalpa
Hong Kong	Asia	6,310,000	—
Hungary	Europe	10,260,000	Budapest
Iceland	Europe	270,000	Reykjavík
India	Asia	918,500,000	New Delhi
Indonesia	Asia	192,900,000	Jakarta
Iran	Asia	60,000,000	Tehran
Iraq	Asia	19,925,000	Baghdad
Ireland, Republic of	Europe	3,626,000	Dublin
Israel	Asia	5,450,000	Jerusalem
Italy	Europe	57,193,000	Rome
Jamaica	C. America	2,496,000	Kingston
Japan	Asia	124,960,200	Tokyo
Jordan	Asia	5,198,000	Amman
Kazakhstan	Asia	17,025,000	Alma-Ata
Kenya	Africa	29,290,000	Nairobi
Kiribati	Oceania	77,000	Tarawa

Country	Continent	Population	Capital
Korea D.P.R. (North)	Asia	23,480,000	P'yongyang
Korea Rep. of (South)	Asia	44,605,000	Seoul
Kuwait	Asia	1,575,980	Kuwait city
Kyrgyzstan	Asia	4,595,000	Bishkek
Laos	Asia	4,605,000	Vientiane
Latvia	Europe	2,530,000	Riga
Lebanon	Asia	2,915,000	Beirut
Lesotho	Africa	1,995,000	Maseru
Liberia	Africa	2,700,000	Monrovia
Libya	Africa	4,900,000	Tripoli
Liechtenstein	Europe	31,000	Vaduz
Lithuania	Europe	3,707,000	Vilnius
Luxembourg	Europe	413,000	Luxembourg
Macedonia	Europe	2,142,000	Skopje
Madagascar	Africa	14,305,000	Antananarivo
Malawi	Africa	9,460,000	Lilongwe
Malaysia	Asia	20,105,000	Kuala Lumpur
Maldives	Asia	256,100	Malé
Mali	Asia	10,462,000	Bamako
Malta	Europe	367,350	Valletta
Marshall Islands	Oceania	54,000	Dalag-Uliga-Darrit
Mauritania	Africa	2,211,000	Nouakchott
Mauritius	Africa	1,142,500	Port Louis
Mexico	N. America	93,010,000	México City
Micronesia, Fed States of	Oceania	105,000	Palikir
Moldova	Europe	4,335,000	Kishinev
Monaco	Europe	31,000	Monaco-Ville
Mongolia	Asia	2,363,000	Ulan Bator
Morocco	Africa	26,590,000	Rabat
Mozambique	Africa	16,500,000	Maputo
Myanmar (Burma)	Asia	45,550,000	Yangon (Rangoon)
Namibia	Africa	1,500,000	Windhoek
Nauru	Oceania	11,000	Yaren
Nepal	Asia	21,360,000	Kathmandu
Netherlands	Europe	15,500,000	Amsterdam

Country	Continent	Population	Capital
New Zealand	Oceania	3,645,000	Wellington
Nicaragua	C. America	4,405,000	Managua
Niger	Africa	8,850,000	Niamey
Nigeria	Africa	108,465,000	Abuja
Norway	Europe	4,370,000	Oslo
Oman	Asia	2,075,000	Muscat
Pakistan	Asia	127,000,000	Islamabad
Palau	Oceania	15,100	Koror
Panama	C. America	2,630,000	Panama City
Papua New Guinea	Oceania	3,998,000	Port Moresby
Paraguay	S. America	4,750,000	Asunción
Peru	S. America	23,100,000	Lima
Philippines	Asia	67,040,000	Manila
Poland	Europe	38,645,000	Warsaw
Portugal	Europe	9,850,000	Lisbon
Puerto Rico	C. America	3,730,000	San Juan
Qatar	Asia	550,000	Doha
Romania	Europe	22,600,000	Bucharest
Russia	Europe/Asia	148,000,000	Moscow
Rwanda	Africa	7,750,000	Kigali
St Christopher & Nevis	C. America	41,000	Basseterre
St Lucia	C. America	141,000	Castries
St Vincent & Grenadines	C. America	111,000	Kingstown
San Marino	Europe	25,500	San Marino
São Tomé & Príncipe	Africa	125,000	São Tomé
Saudi Arabia	Asia	17,450,000	Riyadh
Senegal	Africa	8,105,000	Dakar
Seychelles	Africa	75,000	Victoria
Sierra Leone	Africa	4,405,000	Freetown
Singapore	Asia	3,400,000	Singapore
Slovakia	Europe	5,350,000	Bratislava
Slovenia	Europe	2,945,000	Ljubljana
Solomon Islands	Oceania	366,000	Honiara
Somalia	Africa	9,077,000	Mogadishu
South Africa	Africa	40,500,000	Pretoria/Cape Town

Country	Continent	Population	Capital
Spain	Europe	39,500,000	Madrid
Sri Lanka	Asia	17,865,000	Sri Jayawardenapura
Sudan	Africa	29,950,000	Khartoum
Suriname	S. America	420,000	Paramaribo
Swaziland	Africa	835,000	Mbabane
Sweden	Europe	8,780,000	Stockholm
Switzerland	Europe	7,000,000	Berne
Syria	Asia	13,845,000	Damascus
Taiwan	Asia	21,450,000	Taipei
Tajikistan	Asia	5,515,000	Dushanbe
Tanzania	Africa	28,845,000	Dodoma
Thailand	Asia	60,700,000	Bangkok
Togo	Africa	3,930,000	Lomé
Tonga	Oceania	98,000	Nuku'alofa
Trinidad & Tobago	C. America	1,257,000	Port-of-Spain
Tunisia	Africa	8,735,000	Tunis
Turkey	Asia/Europe	61,200,000	Ankara
Turkmenistan	Asia	3,809,000	Ashkhabad
Tuvalu	Oceania	9,000	Funafuti
Uganda	Africa	20,620,000	Kampala
Ukraine	Europe	52,100,000	Kiev
United Arab Emirates	Asia	2,378,000	Abu Dhabi
United Kingdom	Europe	58,606,000	London
United States of America	N. America	265,285,000	Washington D.C.
Uruguay	S. America	3,168,000	Montevideo
Uzbekistan	Asia	21,205,000	Tashkent
Vanuatu	Oceania	165,000	Vila
Vatican City State	Europe	1,000	Vatican City
Venezuela	S. America	21,175,000	Caracas
Vietnam	Asia	72,500,000	Hanoi
Western Samoa	Oceania	165,000	Apia
Yemen	Asia	15,800,000	Sana'a
Yugoslavia, Fed. Rep. of	Europe	10,515,000	Belgrade
Zambia	Africa	9,200,000	Lusaka
Zimbabwe	Africa	11,150,000	Harare

Earth's Vital Statistics

Age: Approx 4600 million years

Weight: Approx 5.976×10^{21} tonnes

Diameter: Pole to Pole through the centre of the Earth 12 713 km (7900 miles)
Across the Equator through the centre of the Earth 12 756 km (7926 miles)

Circumference: Around the Poles 40 008 km (24 861 miles)
Around the Equator 40 091 km (24 912 miles)

Area: Land 148 326 000 sq km (57 268 700 sq miles) 29% of surface
Water 361 740 000 sq km (139 667 810 sq miles) 71% of surface

Volume: 1 084 000 million cubic km (260 160 million cubic miles)

Volume of the oceans: 1321 million cubic km (317 million cubic miles)

Average height of land: 840 m (2756 ft) above sea level

Average depth of ocean: 3808 m (12 493 ft) below sea level

Density: 5.52 times water

Mean temperature: 22°C (72°F)

Length of year: 365.25 days

Length of one rotation: 23 hours 56 minutes

Mean distance from Sun: 149 600 000 km (92 960 000 miles)

Mean velocity in orbit: 29.8 km (18.5 miles) per second

Escape velocity: 11.2 km (6.96 miles) per second

Atmosphere: Main constituents:
nitrogen (78.5%),
oxygen (21%)

Crust: Main constituents:
oxygen (47%),
silicon (28%),
aluminium (8%),
iron (5%).

Known satellites: One (The moon)

Oceans

| | Max. Depth | | Area | |
	metres	feet	sq km	sq miles
Pacific	11 033	36 197	165 384 000	63 860 000
Atlantic	8381	27 496	82,217 000	31 744 000
Indian	8047	26 401	73 481 000	28 371 000
Arctic	5450	17 880	14 056 000	5 427 000

Deserts

	sq km	sq miles
Sahara	9 065 000	3 500 000
Australian Desert	1 550 000	598 455
Arabian Desert	1 300 000	501 930
Gobi Desert	1 295 000	500 000
Kalahari	520 000	200 772

Largest Islands

| Island (location) | Population | Area | |
		sq km	sq miles
Greenland (N. Atlantic)	54 600	2 175 600	839 740
New Guinea (S.W. Pacific)	4 528 682	808 510	312 085
Borneo (S.W. Pacific)	11 263 087	751 900	292 220
Madagascar (Indian Ocean)	11 238 000	594 180	229 355
Sumatra (Indian Ocean)	36 881 990	524 100	202 300
Baffin I. (Canadian Arctic)	8298	476 070	183 760
Honshu (N.W. Pacific)	98 352 000	230 455	88 955
Great Britain (N. Atlantic)	54 285 422	229 880	88 730
Victoria I. (Canadian Arctic)	1410	212 200	81 910
Ellesmere (Canadian Arctic)	54	212 690	82 100

Principal Mountains of the World

| Name (location) | Height | |
	m	ft
Everest (Tibet-Nepal)	8848	29 028
Godwin-Austen or K2 (Kashmir-Sinkiang)	8611	28 250
Kangchenjunga (Nepal-India)	8587	28 170

Name (location)	Height	
	m	ft
Makalu (Nepal)	8463	27 766
Dhaulagiri (Nepal)	8167	26 795
Nanga Parbat (India)	8125	26 657
Annapurna (Nepal)	8091	26 545
Gosainthan (Tibet)	8012	26 286
Nanda Devi (India)	7816	25 643
Kamet (India)	7756	25 446
Namcha Barwa (Tibet)	7756	25 446
Gurla Mandhata (Tibet)	7728	25 355
Kongur (China)	7720	25 325
Tirich Mir (Pakistan)	7691	25 230
Minya Kanka (China)	7556	24 790
Kula Kangri (Tibet)	7555	24 784
Muztagh Ata (China)	7546	24 757
Kommunizma (Tajikistan)	7495	24 590
Pobedy (Russian Fed.–China)	7439	24 406
Chomo Lhari (Bhutan–Tibet)	7313	23 992
Api (Nepal)	7132	23 399
Lenina (Kyrgyzstan–Tajikistan)	7134	23 405
Aconagua (volcano) (Argentina)	6960	22 834
Ojos del Salado (Argentina)	6908	22 664
Tupungato (Argentina-Chile)	6801	22 310
Mercedario (Argentina)	6770	22 211
Huascarán (Peru)	6769	22 205
Llullaillaco (Chile)	6723	22 057
Neradas de Cachi (Argentina)	6720	22 047
Kailas (Tibet)	6714	22 027
Incahuasi (Argentina)	6709	22 011
Tengri Khan (Kyrgyzstan)	6695	21 965
Sajama (Bolivia)	6542	21 463
Illampu (Bolivia)	6485	21 276
Antofalla (volcanic) (Argentina)	6441	21 129
Illimani (Bolivia)	6402	21 004
Chimborazo (volcanic) (Ecuador)	6310	20 702
Cumbre de la Mejicana (Argentina)	6249	20 500
McKinley (Alaska)	6194	20 320

Name (location)	Height	
	m	ft
Copiapo or Azifre (Chile)	6080	19 947
Logan (Yukon, Canada)	6051	19 524
Cotopaxi (volcanic) (Ecuador)	5896	19 344
Kilimanjaro (volcanic) (Tanzania)	5895	19 340
Ollagüe (Chile-Bolivia)	5868	19 250
Cerro del Potro (Argentina-Chile)	5830	19 127
Misti (volcanic) (Peru)	5822	19 101
Cayambe (Ecuador)	5797	19 016
Huila (volcanic) (Colombia)	5750	18 865
Citlaltepi (Mexico)	5699	18 697
Demavend (Iran)	5664	18 582
Elbrus (volcanic) (Russian Fed.)	5642	18 510
St. Elias (volcanic) (Alaska, Canada)	5489	18 008
Popocatepetl (volcanic) (Mexico)	5453	17 887
Cerro Lejfa (Chile)	5360	17 585
Foraker (Alaska)	5304	17 400
Maipo (volcanic) (Argentina-Chile)	5290	17 355
Ixtaccihuati (volcanic) (Mexico)	5286	17 342
Lucania (Yukon, Canada)	5228	17 150
Tomila (volcanic) (Colombia)	5215	17 109
Dykh Tau (Russian Fed.)	5203	17 070
Kenya (Kenya)	5200	17 058
Ararat (Turkey)	5165	16 945
Vinson Massif (Antarctica)	5140	16 863
Kazbek (volcanaic) (Georgia)	5047	16 558
Blackburn (Alaska)	5037	16 523
Jaya (Irian Jaya, Indonesia)	5030	16 502
Sanford (Alaska)	4941	16 208
Klyucheveyskava (volcanic) (Russian Fed.)	4750	15 584
Mont Blanc (France-Italy)	4808	15 774
Domuyo (volcanic) (Argentina)	4800	15 748
Vancouver (Alaska-Yukon, Canada)	4786	15 700
Trikora (West Irian, Indonesia)	4750	15 584
Fairweather (Alaska-Br. Colombia, Canada)	4670	15 320
Monte Rosa (Switzerland-Italy)	4634	15 203

Name (location)	Height	
	m	ft
Ras Dashan (Ethiopia)	4620	15 158
Belukha (Kazakhstan)	4506	14 783
Markham (Antarctica)	4350	14 271
Meru (volcanic) (Tanzania)	4566	14 979
Hubbard (Alaska-Yukon)	4557	14 950
Kirkpatrick (Antarctica)	4528	14 855
Karisimbi (volcanic) (Rwanda-Zaire)	4508	14 787
Weisshorn (Switzerland)	4505	14 780
Matterhorn/Mont Cervin (Switzerland-Italy)	4477	14 690
Whitney (California)	4418	14 495
Elbert (Colorado)	4399	14 431
Massive Mount (Colorado)	4397	14 424
Harvard (Colorado)	4396	14 420
Rainier or **Tacoma** (Washington)	4392	14 410
Williamson (California)	4382	14 375
La Plata (Colorado)	4371	14 340
Blanca Peak (Colorado)	4364	14 317
Uncompahgre (Colorado)	4361	14 306
Crestone (Colorado)	4356	14 291
Lincoln (Colorado)	4354	14 284
Grays (Colorado)	4351	14 274
Evans (Colorado)	4347	14 260
Longs (Colorado)	4345	14 255
White (California)	4343	14 246
Colima (volcanic) (Mexico)	4340	14 236
Shavano (Colorado)	4337	14 229
Princeton (Colorado)	4327	14 196
Yale (Colorado)	4327	14 196
Elgon (volcanic) (Uganda-Kenya)	4321	14 176
Shasta (volcanic) (California)	4317	14 162
Grand Combin (Switzerland)	4314	14 153
San Luis (Colorado)	4312	14 146
Batu (Ethiopia)	4307	14 130
Pikes Peak (Colorado)	4301	14 110
Snowmass (Colorado)	4291	14 077

Name (location)	Height	
	m	ft
Culebra (Colorado)	4286	14 070
Sunlight (Colorado)	4284	14 053
Split (California)	4283	14 051
Redcloud (Colorado)	4278	14 034
Finsteraarhorn (Switzerland)	4274	14 022
Wrangell (Alaska)	4269	14 005
Mount of the Holy Cross (Colorado)	4266	13 996
Humphreys (California)	4259	13 972
Ouray (Colorado)	4254	13 955
Guna (Ethiopia)	4231	13 881
Mauna Kea (Hawaii)	4205	13 796
Gannet (Wyoming)	4202	13 785
Hayes (Alaska)	4188	13 740
Fremont (Wyoming)	4185	13 730
Sidley (Antarctica)	4181	13 717
Mauna Loa (volcanic) (Hawaii)	4169	13 677
Jungfrau (Switzerland)	4158	13 642
Kings (Utah)	4124	13 528
Kinabalu (Sabah)	4102	13 455
Cameroon (volcanic) (Cameroon)	4095	13 435
Fridtjof Nansen (Antarctica)	4068	13 346
Tacaná (volcanic) (Mexico-Guatemala)	4064	13 333
Bernina (Switzerland)	4049	13 284
Summit (Colorado)	4046	13 272
Waddington (British Colombia, Canada)	4042	13 262
Lister (Antarctica)	4025	13 205
Cloud Peak (Wyoming)	4016	13 176
Yu Shan (Taiwan)	3997	13 113
Truchas (New Mexico)	3994	13 102
Wheeler (Nevada)	3981	13 058
Robson (British Colmbia, Canada)	3954	12 972
Granite (Montana)	3902	12 799
Borah (Idaho)	3858	12 655
Baldy (New Mexico)	3848	12 623
Monte Viso (Italy)	3847	12 621

Name (location)	Height	
	m	ft
Kerinci (volcanic) (Sumatra)	3805	12 483
Grossglockner (Austria)	3797	12 460
Erebus (volcanic) (Antarctica)	3794	12 447
Excelsior (California)	3790	12 434
Fujiyama (volcanic) (Japan)	3776	12 388
Cook (New Zealand)	3753	12 313
Adams (Washington)	3752	12 307
Lanín (volcanic) (Argentina-Chile)	3740	12 270
Teyde or **Tenerife** (volcanic) (Canary Islands)	3718	12 198
Mahameru (volcanic) (Java)	3676	12 060
Assiniboine (Br.Colombia-Alberta, Canada)	3618	11 870
Hood (vocanic) (Oregon)	3428	11 245
Pico de Aneto (Spain)	3404	11 168
Rheinwaldhorn (Switzerland)	3402	11 161
Perdido (Spain)	3352	10 997
Etna (volcanic) (Sicily)	3323	10 902
Baker (Washington)	3286	10 778
Lassen (volcanic) (California)	3188	10 457
Dempo (volcanic) (Sumatra)	3159	10 364
Siple (Antarctica)	3100	10 170
Montcalm (France)	3080	10 105
Haleakala (volcanic) (Hawaii)	3058	10 032
St. Helens (Washington)	2950	9677
Pulog (Philippines)	2934	9626
Tahat (Algeria)	2918	9573
Shishaldin (volcanic) (Aleutian Islands)	2862	9387
Roraima (Brazil-Venezuela-Guyana)	2810	9219
Ruapehu (volcanic) (New Zealand)	2797	9175
Katherine (Egypt)	2637	8651
Doi Inthanon (Thailand)	2594	8510
Galdhöpiggen (Norway)	2469	8100
Parnassus (Greece)	2457	8061
Olympus (Washington)	2425	7954
Kosciusko (Australia)	2230	7316
Harney (South Dakota)	2208	7242

Name (location)	Height	
	m	ft
Mitchell (North Carolina)	2038	6684
Clingmans Dome (North Carolina-Tennessee)	2025	6642
Washington (New Hampshire)	1917	6288
Rogers (Virginia)	1807	5927
Marcy (New York)	1629	5344
Cirque (Labrador)	1573	5160
Pelée (volcanic) (Martinique)	1463	4800

Principal Rivers of the World

Name (location)	Length	
	km	miles
Nile (Africa)	6695	4160
Amazon (South America)	6516	4050
Yangtze (Chang Jiang) (Asia)	6380	3965
Mississippi-Missouri (North America)	6019	3740
Ob'-Irtysh (Asia)	5570	3460
Yenisey-Angara (Asia)	5553	3450
Hwang Ho (Huang He) (Asia)	5464	3395
Congo (Africa)	4667	2900
Mekong (Asia)	4426	2750
Amur (Asia)	4416	2744
Lena (Asia)	4400	2730
Mackenzie (North America)	4250	2640
Niger (Africa)	4032	2505
Paraná (South America)	4000	2485
Missouri (North America)	3969	2466
Mississippi (North America)	3779	2348
Murray-Darling (Australia)	3750	2330
Volga (Europe)	3686	2290
Madeira (South America)	3203	1990
St Lawrence (North America)	3203	1990
Yukon (North America)	3187	1,980
Indus (Asia)	3180	1975

Name (location)	**Length**	
	km	miles
Syrdar'ya (Asia)	3079	1913
Salween (Asia)	3060	1901
Darling (Australia)	3057	1900
Rio Grande (North America)	3034	1885
São Francisco (South America)	2897	1800
Danube (Europe)	2850	1770
Brahmaputra (Asia)	2840	1765
Euphrates (Asia)	2815	1750
Pará-Tocantins (South America)	2752	1710
Zambezi (Africa)	2650	1650
Amudar'ya (Asia)	2620	1630
Paraguay (South America)	2600	1615
Nelson-Saskatchewan (North America)	2570	1600
Ural (Asia)	2534	1575
Kolyma (Asia)	2513	1562
Ganges (Asia)	2510	1560
Orinoco (South America)	2500	1555
Arkansas (North America)	2350	1460
Colorado (North America)	2330	1450
Xi Jiang (Asia)	2300	1427
Dnepr (Europe)	2285	1420
Negro (South America)	2254	1400
Aldan (Asia)	2242	1393
Irrawaddy (Asia)	2150	1335
Ohio (North America)	2102	1306
Orange (Africa)	2090	1299
Kama (Europe)	2028	1260
Xingú (South America)	2012	1250
Columbia (North America)	1950	1210
Juruá (South America)	1932	1200
Peace (North America)	1923	1195
Tigris (Asia)	1900	1180
Don (Europe)	1870	1165
Pechora (Europe)	1814	1127
Araguaya (South America)	1771	1100

Name (location)	Length	
	km	miles
Snake (North America)	1670	1038
Red (North America)	1639	1018
Churchill (North America)	1610	1000
Marañón (South America)	1610	1000
Pilcomayo (South America)	1610	1000
Ucayali (South America)	1610	1000
Uruguay (South America)	1610	1000
Magdalena (South America)	1529	950
Oka (Europe)	1481	920
Canadian (North America)	1459	906
Godavari (Asia)	1449	900
Parnaíba (South America)	1449	900
Dnestr (Europe)	1411	877
Brazos (North America)	1401	870
Fraser (North America)	1368	850
Salado (South America)	1368	850
Rhine (Europe)	1320	825
Narmada (Asia)	1288	800
Tobol (Asia)	1288	800
Athabaska (North America)	1231	765
Pecos (North America)	1183	735
Green (North America)	1175	730
Elbe (Europe)	1160	720
Ottawa (North America)	1121	696
White (North America)	1111	690
Cumberland (North America)	1106	687
Yellowstone (North America)	1080	671
Donets (Europe)	1079	670
Tennessee (North America)	1050	652
Vistula (Europe)	1014	630
Loire (Europe)	1012	629
Tagus (Europe)	1006	625
Tisza (Europe)	997	619
North Platte (North America)	995	618
Ouachita (North America)	974	605
Sava (Europe)	940	584

Name (location)	Length	
	km	miles
Neman (Europe)	937	582
Oder (Europe)	910	565
Cimarron (North America)	805	500
Gila (North America)	805	500
Gambia (Africa)	483	300

Principal Lakes of the World

Name (location)	Area		Length		Max. Depth	
	sq km	sq mi	km	mi	m	ft
Caspian (Asia-Europe)	371 000	143 205	1172	728	980	3215
Superior (N America)	83 270	32 140	564	350	393	1289
Victoria (Africa)	68 800	26 560	363	225	100	328
Aral (Asia)	65 500	25 285	379	235	68	223
Michigan (N America)	58 020	22 395	495	307	281	922
Tanganyika (Africa)	32 900	12 700	676	420	1435	4708
Great Bear (N America)	31 790	12 270	309	192	319	1047
Baykal (Asia)	30 500	11 775	636	395	1741	5712
Nyasa (Africa)	28 900	11 150	580	360	706	2316
Great Slave (N America)	28 440	10 980	480	298	140	459
Erie (N America)	25 680	9915	388	241	64	210
Winnipeg (N America)	24 510	9460	429	266	21	69
Ontario (N America)	19 230	7425	311	193	237	778
Ladoga (Europe)	18 390	7100	200	124	230	755
Balkhash (Asia)	17 400	6715	605	376	26	85
Chad (Africa)	10–26 000	4–10 000	210	130	4-7	13-23
Onega (Europe)	9600	3705	234	145	124	407
Eyre (Australia)	0-8900	0-3435	145	90	0-21	0-66
Titicaca (S America)	8340	3220	197	122	304	997
Nicaragua (C America)	8270	3190	165	102	71	230
Athabasca (N America)	8080	3120	335	208	92	299
Turkana (Africa)	7105	2743	248	154	73	240
Reindeer (N America)	6390	2470	250	155		
Issyk-Kul (Asia)	6200	2395	186	115	702	2303
Urmia (Asia)	5900	2280	145	90	15	49

Name (location)	Area		Length		Max. Depth	
	sq km	sq mi	km	mi	m	ft
Torrens (Australia)	5780	2230	210	130		
Vänern (Europe)	5580	2155	147	91	98	322
Winnipegosis (N America)	5400	2086	227	141	12	38
Albert (**Mobutu**) (Africa)	5345	2064	161	100	52	168
Mweru (Africa)	4921	1900	73	45	14	46
Nipigon (N America)	4850	1870	116	72	165	540
Manitoba (N America)	4700	1817	226	140		
Qinghai Hu (Asia)	4150	1600	110	68	39	125
Lake of the						
Woods (N America)	3850	1485	116	72	21	69
Van (Asia)	3710	1433	129	80	25	82
Great Salt						
Lake (N America)	2500–5000	1000–2000	121	75	11	35
Dead Sea (Asia)	1020	394	74	46		

The areas of some of these lakes are subject to seasonal variations.

Principal Waterfalls of the World

Name (location)	Height	
	m	ft
Angel (Venezuela)	979	3212
Yosemite (California)	740	2425
Kukenaäm (Guyana)	610	2000
Sutherland (New Zealand)	581	1904
Wolloomombie (Australia)	519	1700
Ribbon (California)	492	1612
Upper Yosemite (California)	436	1430
Gavarnie (France)	422	1384
Tugela (South Africa)	412	1350
Takkakau (British Colombia)	366	1200
Staubbach (Switzerland)	300	984
Trümmelbach (Switzerland)	290	950
Middle Cascade (California)	278	910
Vettisfoss (Norway)	271	889

Name (location)	Height	
	m	**ft**
King Edward VIII (Guyana)	256	840
Gersoppa (India)	253	830
Skykjefos (Norway)	250	820
Kajeteur (Guyana)	226	741
Kalambo (Zambia)	222	726
Maradalsfos (Norway)	199	650
Maletsunyane (South Africa)	192	630
Bridalveil (California)	189	620
Multnomah (Oregon)	189	620
Vöringfoss (Norway)	182	597
Nevada (California)	181	594
Terni (Italy)	180	590
Skjeggedalsfoss (Norway)	160	525
Marina (Guyana)	153	500
Aughrabies (South Africa)	147	480
Tequendama (Colombia)	131	427
Guaíra (Brazil-Paraguay)	114	374
Illilouette (California)	113	370
Victoria (Zambia and Zimbabwe)	108	355
Kegon-no-tali (Japan)	101	330
Lower Yosemite (California)	98	320
Cauvery (India)	98	320
Vernal (California)	97	317
Virginia (North West Territories)	96	315
Lower Yellowstone (Wyoming)	94	308
Churchill (Labrador)	92	302
Reichenbach (Switzerland)	91	300
Sluiskin (Washington)	91	300
Lower Gastein (Austria)	86	280
Paulo Alfonso (Brazil)	84	275
Snoqualmie (Washington)	82	268
Seven (Colorado)	81	266
Montmorency (Quebec)	77	251
Handegg (Switzerland)	76	250
Taughannock (New York)	66	215

Name (location)	Height	
	m	ft
Iguassú (Brazil)	64	210
Shoshone (Idaho)	64	210
Upper Gastein (Austria)	63	207
Comet (Washington)	61	200
Narada (Washington)	52	168
Niagara (New York-Ontario)	51	167
Tower (Wyoming)	41	132
Stora Sjöfallet (Sweden)	40	131
Kabalega (Uganda)	40	130
Upper Yellowstone (Wyoming)	34	109